STUDIES IN CHRISTIAN HISTORY AND THOUGHT

The Supremacy of God in the Theology of Samuel Rutherford

STUDIES IN CHRISTIAN HISTORY AND THOUGHT

A full listing of titles in this series
appears at the end of this book

STUDIES IN CHRISTIAN HISTORY AND THOUGHT

The Supremacy of God in the Theology of Samuel Rutherford

Guy M. Richard

Foreword by David A.S. Fergusson

WIPF & STOCK · Eugene, Oregon

Wipf and Stock Publishers
199 W 8th Ave, Suite 3
Eugene, OR 97401

The Supremacy of God in the Theology of Samuel Rutherford
By Richard, Guy M.
Copyright©2008 Paternoster
ISBN 13: 978-1-60608-479-3
Publication date 2/6/2009
Previously published by Paternoster, 2008

"This Edition Published by Wipf and Stock Publishers
by arrangement with Paternoster"

Series Preface

This series complements the specialist series of *Studies in Evangelical History and Thought* and *Studies in Baptist History and Thought* for which Paternoster is becoming increasingly well known by offering works that cover the wider field of Christian history and thought. It encompasses accounts of Christian witness at various periods, studies of individual Christians and movements, and works which concern the relations of church and society through history, and the history of Christian thought.

The series includes monographs, revised dissertations and theses, and collections of papers by individuals and groups. As well as 'free standing' volumes, works on particular running themes are being commissioned; authors will be engaged for these from around the world and from a variety of Christian traditions.

A high academic standard combined with lively writing will commend the volumes in this series both to scholars and to a wider readership.

STUDIES IN CHRISTIAN HISTORY AND THOUGHT

Series Editors

Alan P.F. Sell — Acadia University Divinity College, Nova Scotia, Canada

David Bebbington — University of Stirling, Stirling, Scotland, UK

Clyde Binfield — University of Sheffield, UK

Gerald Bray — Beeson Divinity School, Samford University, Birmingham, Alabama, USA

Grayson Carter — Fuller Theological Seminary SW, Phoenix, Arizona, USA

For Jennifer, my loving wife and true support, who willingly and regularly sacrificed that I might see this project through to completion

Contents

Foreword by David A.S. Fergusson	xiii
Acknowledgements	xv
Abbreviations	xvii
Chapter 1 Contextualizing Rutherford	1
Introduction	1
Establishing the Context	6
The Socio-Political and Ecclesial Context	6
The Theological Context	10
The Polemical Context	16
The Formal Context	20
A Note on Methodology	22
Chapter 2 Prolegomena to Theology	25
Revelation	26
Theologia archetypa et ectypa	26
Natural and Supernatural Revelation	30
Natural Theology	32
The *duplex cognitio Dei*	33
The Role of Reason and the Necessity of Supernatural Knowledge	37
Scripture as *principium cognoscendi theologiae*	45
The Nature of Scripture	48
The Perfection of Scripture	51
Objections to the Perfection of Scripture	53
The Authority of Scripture	61
The Interpretation of Scripture	71

Chapter 3 The Doctrine of God	**77**
The *natura Dei*	77
The Essence and Attributes of God	78
The Trinity	85
The *scientia Dei*	89
The *voluntas Dei*	94
Voluntas ad intra et ad extra	96
Potentia absoluta et ordinata	97
Theologia archetypa et ectypa	101
Voluntas beneplaciti et signi	103
Voluntas efficiens et permittens	105
Voluntas antecedens et consequens	112
Continuity or Discontinuity with the Reformation?	113
Soteriological Applications of the *voluntas Dei*	116
Predestination	116
Supralapsarianism	117
Election and Reprobation	119
The Order of the Decrees	120
Summary	123
Objections to Supralapsarianism	126
The Atonement of Christ	131
Limited Atonement	131
The Absolute Necessity of the Atonement	133
Chapter 4 Soteriology	**139**
Covenant Theology	139
The Covenant of Redemption	141
The Covenant of Redemption and the Decrees of God	145
The Covenant of Works	147
The Covenant of Works—Continuity or Discontinuity?	151
The Covenant of Grace	156
Conversion	160
God's Work of Regeneration	161
Grace and Free Will	168
Calling and Preparation	177
Our Response of Faith	185
The Nature of Faith	187

The Object of Faith	190
Living by Faith	193
Justification	194
Sanctification	200
Assurance	205
Assurance and Faith	207
The Grounds of Assurance	209
Chapter 5 Rutherford's Theology and the Grounds for his Opposition to Arminianism	**219**
The Grounds for Rutherford's Opposition to Arminianism	221
The Two Strands of Arminianism	221
The Two Ends of Arminianism	229
Concluding Thoughts on the Calvin-Calvinists Debate	234
The Legacy of Rutherford's Theology	239
Appendix	**241**
Bibliography	**247**
Index	**267**

Foreword

Samuel Rutherford (1600–61) is one of Scotland's greatest theologians, yet his life and work resist easy categorisation or simple description. Committed to the covenanting cause, Rutherford published one of the finest works of Scottish political theory, *Lex, Rex*. Had his terminal illness not intervened after the Restoration in 1661, then he would surely have been charged with treason for the views expressed therein. Instead, he could only reply to his accusers, 'I have got summons already before a Superior Judge and Judicatory, and I behove to answer to my first summons, and ere your day come, I will be where few kings and great folks come.'

His political writings aside, Rutherford was also a systematic theologian of considerable force and learning. His defence of Reformed orthodoxy is the outstanding achievement of Scottish theology in the early modern period, and was evident not only in his teaching as Professor of St Mary's College in St Andrews but also at the Westminster Assembly in London. And yet it is probably for his devotional work, especially through the numerous editions of his *Letters*, that Rutherford remains best known. Like much within the Scottish tradition, his piety combines an intellectual rigour with an emotional intensity verging on the erotic.

In this study based on his Edinburgh doctoral thesis, Guy Richard offers the most sustained treatment yet of Rutherford's doctrinal theology. He has achieved this through an articulation of the *Examen Arminianismi*, Rutherford's St Andrews lectures that have remained hitherto untranslated from their Latin original but which provide us with a comprehensive account of his theological position. Through his clear and persuasive exposition, Guy Richard demonstrates the importance both of Rutherford's historical context and also the nuances in his thought as these can be understood within the precarious political context in which he laboured. This measured portrait of Rutherford's theology challenges simple caricatures of his thought as a brash and over confident statement of hyper-Calvinism. By contrast, what emerges is a strenuous effort to defend a theological tradition that may already in Rutherford's lifetime be threatened by irresistible changes in the prevailing intellectual and political climate. The most important study of Rutherford's theology to date, this monograph will become indispensable to any scholar seeking a balanced account of his life and work. It is a landmark in Rutherford scholarship.

David Fergusson
Professor of Divinity, University of Edinburgh
November 2007

Acknowledgements

The story is told of an occasion during the Westminster Assembly in which George Gillespie rose to defend, in the words of Samuel Rutherford, 'the right of the Lord Jesus Christ to govern the Church which He has purchased with His own blood' against the Erastianism of John Selden. As Gillespie returned to his seat, after, in Selden's own words, having 'swept away the learning and labour of ten years of my life', his friends scrambled to examine the scrap of paper on which they assumed were written the notes that formed the basis for his successful oral apology. The only words they found were these, repeated over and over again: 'Da lucem Domine!'[1] The reason I tell this well-known story is this: during the course of the current project (my Ph.D. dissertation at the University of Edinburgh) I have often found myself repeating these very words, or others to the same effect (!), as I worked my way through Rutherford's theology and his *Examen Arminianismi*. Having now completed my work, I can look back with gratitude for the divine light I did receive (some may question this after reading my book!) and for the guidance, support, assistance, encouragement, and constructive criticism that I received from those nearest to me.

First among the individuals to whom I owe so much is my doctoral supervisor at the University of Edinburgh, New College, Prof. David A.S. Fergusson. For his graciousness, even when pointing out the weaknesses in my argument, his promptness in reading everything I wrote and immediately discussing it with me in spite of his own tremendously hectic schedule, his reputation as a scholar, and his concern for the welfare of the worldwide church, I will ever hold him in high regard. In the course of my research, I have also been greatly blessed by the able and friendly help that I received from the staffs of many libraries around the country, chief among which are the New College Library, the University of Edinburgh Library, the National Library of Scotland, and the St. Andrews University Library.

---

[1] 'Give light, O Lord!' Accounts of this story can be found in works like, A. Whyte, *Samuel Rutherford and Some of his Correspondents* (Edinburgh and London: Oliphant Anderson and Ferrier, 1894), pp. 153-4; and M.L. Loane, *Makers of Religious Freedom in the Seventeenth Century* (London: InterVarsity, 1960), p. 77.

Intellectually, I owe a debt of gratitude to Drs. John Coffey and Richard A. Muller, for their tremendous works on Rutherford and the post-Reformation period, respectively. But perhaps my most direct intellectual debt is owed to Drs. J. Ligon Duncan III, Derek W.H. Thomas, and W. Duncan Rankin, for their commitments to scholarship and to the church and for the examples they provided me in word and deed at Reformed Theological Seminary and First Presbyterian Church (PCA) in Jackson, Mississippi. Special thanks go to Ligon Duncan—who first helped me to refine my thinking in regard to the eventual topic for this thesis and who has served as my mentor, boss, teacher, and friend over much of the last ten years.

As is usually the case when giving acknowledgment of thanks, family comes last. I am not altogether certain why that is. Perhaps it is because we have asked from them the greatest sacrifice and, therefore, owe them the greatest debt of gratitude. It would certainly seem to be true in my own case anyway. I would, therefore, be quite remiss if I did not express deep thanks to my parents, the Rev. Gus and Alice Richard, and to my wife's parents, Jack and Jane Buck. Both have been steadfast and overwhelmingly generous in their support and patience while we were, literally, an ocean apart. Most of all, however, I owe the greatest thanks to my wife, Jennifer, mainly because I have asked her to make the greatest sacrifice by far. She has endured my constant ups and downs (I, like Rutherford, am a 'man of extremes'—just ask Jennifer!) and the challenges of living daily with a four-hundred year old house guest for just over three years, of being separated from her family, and of coping with the anxieties associated with finishing this project and beginning the next phase of our lives together on the Hurricane-Katrina-ravaged Mississippi Gulf Coast. I have no trouble in admitting that she is my 'better half', or, more biblically, my 'suitable helper'. I am thankful to the Lord for graciously providing her to be my wife. May he continue to bless her for her faithfulness to me.

Guy Richard
First Presbyterian Church
October 2007

Abbreviations

ACS	P. Van Limborch, *A Compleat System, or Body of Divinity*
Catachisme	S. Rutherford, *Ane Catachisme conteining the Soume of Christian Religion*
CD	K. Barth, *Church Dogmatics*
CH	*Church History*
Christ Dying	S. Rutherford, *Christ Dying and Drawing Sinners to Himselfe*
Communion	S. Rutherford, *Fourteen Communion Sermons*
Confession	S. Episcopius et al., *The Confession or Declaration of the...Remonstrants*
COL	S. Rutherford, *The Covenant of Life Opened*
CTJ	*Calvin Theological Journal*
Disputatio	S. Rutherford, *Disputatio scholastica de divina providentia*
Divine Right	S. Rutherford, *The Divine Right of Church-Government and Excommunication*
DSCH&T	N.M. de S. Cameron, ed., *Dictionary of Scottish Church History and Theology*
Due Right	S. Rutherford, *The Due Right of Presbyteries*
Examen	S. Rutherford, *Examen Arminianismi*
Exercitationes	S. Rutherford, *Exercitationes apologeticae pro divina gratia*
HOC	S. Rutherford, *A Sermon Preached to the Honourable House of Commons*
Influences	S. Rutherford, *Influences of the Life of Grace*
Institutes	J. Calvin, *Institutes of the Christian Religion*
JETS	*Journal of the Evangelical Theological Society*
Letters	S. Rutherford, *The Letters of Samuel Rutherford*
NAvK	*Nederlands Archief voor Kerkgeschiedenis*
PLC	S. Rutherford, *A Free Disputation against Pretended Liberty of Conscience*
PP	S. Rutherford, *A Peaceable and Temperate Plea for*

	Pauls Presbyterie in Scotland
PRRD	R. Muller, *Post-Reformation Reformed Dogmatics*
RD	H. Heppe, *Reformed Dogmatics*
RSCHS	*Records of the Scottish Church History Society*
SCJ	*Sixteenth Century Journal*
SJT	*Scottish Journal of Theology*
SA	S. Rutherford, *A Survey of the Spirituall AntiChrist*
Testimony	S. Rutherford, *Testimony to the Covenanted Work of Reformation*
Tryal	S. Rutherford, *The Tryal & Triumph of Faith*
WA	M. Luther, *Luther's Werke* (Weimar)
WCF	*Westminster Confession of Faith* (Free Presbyterian)
WJA	J. Arminius, *The Works of James Arminius*
WTJ	*Westminster Theological Journal*

CHAPTER 1

Contextualizing Rutherford

Introduction

A study of the theology of Samuel Rutherford (c.1600-1661) is long overdue. As an individual, he is arguably the leading theologian of Scotland's Second Reformation,[1] a man of great importance and influence both in his day and in succeeding generations, extending even to our own. He was perhaps the most influential of the Scottish commissioners to the Westminster Assembly and, as such, is instrumental in interpreting Westminster theology.[2] He was responsible

---

[1] With few exceptions, historians and theologians recognize the importance of Samuel Rutherford to the work of the Reformation in Scotland. K.G. Rendell, in his 'new biography', believes that Rutherford is an 'indispensable link' between the beginning of the Reformation in the late sixteenth century and its conclusion in the late seventeenth century (*Samuel Rutherford: A New Biography of the Man & his Ministry* [Fearn, Ross-shire: Christian Focus, 2003], p. 9). J. Walker calls Rutherford 'the greatest' theologian of Scotland's 'so-called second Reformation' (*The Theology and Theologians of Scotland 1560-1750* [Edinburgh: Knox Press, ²1982], pp. 7-8). R. Gilmour identifies him as 'the most distinctively representative Scotsman in the first half of the seventeenth century' (*Samuel Rutherford: A Study Biographical and Somewhat Critical, in the History of the Scottish Covenants* [Edinburgh: Oliphant Anderson & Ferrier, 1904], p. ix). W.M. Campbell refers to him as 'the greatest and most learned of Scotland's theologians' (*The Triumph of Presbyterianism* [Edinburgh: St. Andrew Press, 1958], p. 90). And M. Lynch, perhaps speaking most objectively, describes him as the 'leading theoretician of the Covenanting Kirk' (*Scotland: A New History* [London: Pimlico, 2001], p. 251). Even Rutherford's contemporaries praised him as a 'great man' and 'learned author' (e.g., J. Owen, *The Works of John Owen*, 24 vols., ed. W. Goold [London: Johnstone & Hunter, 1850-55], X, p. 608).
[2] J. Coffey notes that the Scots commissioners exercised 'an influence out of all proportion to their numbers' at Westminster (*Politics, Religion and the British Revolutions: The Mind of Samuel Rutherford* [Cambridge: Cambridge University, 1997], p. 52). Among the Scots delegates, Rutherford remained in London longer than any other; and he alone received commendation from the Assembly 'for the great assistance he...afforded to [the] Assembly, in his constant attendance upon the debates of it' (A.F. Mitchell and J. Struthers (eds.), *Minutes of the Sessions of the Westminster Assembly of Divines* [Edinburgh and London: Blackwood and Sons, 1874], pp. 151, 487-8). It seems likely, therefore, in light of Rutherford's authoritarian nature, that he

for training ministers and church leaders as a professor of divinity at St. Mary's College in St. Andrews for approximately 21 years. He published thirteen major theological treatises, amounting to just over 7,000 pages of text,[3] not to mention other works, including sermons, letters, an in-depth catechism (totalling 562 questions and answers—over five times the number in the Westminster Shorter Catechism), and a variety of political writings, all of which increase our total by nearly 3,000 pages.[4] When we add Rutherford's unpublished manuscripts and sermons to this collection and a commentary on Isaiah that was tragically lost at the Restoration,[5] we have a literary output that clearly rivals that of John Owen (1616-1683), who is quite possibly England's premier Reformed theologian of the seventeenth century.[6] And, yet, Rutherford's thinking has received comparatively little attention in the scholarship of the period, especially in relation to that of Owen.[7]

---

would have exerted tremendous influence upon the Assembly, probably more so than any other Scotsman and, perhaps, more so than any Englishman as well.

[3] In chronological order these are *Exercitationes apologeticae pro divina gratia* (Amsterdam, 1636); *A Peaceable and Temperate Plea for Pauls Presbyterie in Scotland* (London, 1642); *The Due Right of Presbyteries* (London, 1644); *The Tryal and Triumph of Faith* (London, 1645); *The Divine Right of Church Government and Excommunication* (London, 1646); *Christ Dying and Drawing Sinners to Himselfe* (London, 1647); *A Survey of the Spirituall AntiChrist* (London, 1648); *A Free Disputation against Pretended Liberty of Conscience* (London, 1649); *Disputatio scholastica de divina providentia* (Edinburgh, 1649); *The Covenant of Life Opened* (Edinburgh, 1655); *A Survey of the Survey of that Summe of Church-Discipline Penned by Mr. Thomas Hooker* (London, 1658); *Influences of the Life of Grace* (London, 1659); and *Examen Arminianismi* (Utrecht, 1668). All but the first and last are in 4°.

[4] *A Sermon Preached before the Honourable House of Commons, January 31, 1644* (London, 1644); *Lex, Rex, or The Law and the Prince* (London, 1644); *A Sermon Preached before the Honourable House of Lords, June 25, 1645* (London, 1645); *The Last and Heavenly Speeches and Glorious Departure of John Gordoun, Viscount Kenmuir* (Edinburgh, 1649); *The Power and Prevalency of Prayer* (Edinburgh?, 1713); *A Testimony to the Work of Reformation in Britaine and Ireland* (Glasgow, 1719); *Fourteen Communion Sermons* (Glasgow: Glass, 1877); *Quaint Sermons* (London: Hodder and Stoughton, 1885); *Ane Catachisme conteining the Soume of Christian Religion*, in *Catechisms of the Second Reformation*, ed. A.F. Mitchell (London: James Nisbet, 1886); and *Letters of Samuel Rutherford*, ed. A.A. Bonar (Edinburgh and London: Oliphant Anderson & Ferrier, 1891).

[5] J. Coffey lists 10 unpublished manuscripts containing upwards of 40 sermons, a theological discourse on supralapsarianism, and a political treatise on the power of the civil magistracy (*Politics, Religion and the British Revolutions*, p. 272). F. Cook mentions the Isaiah commentary in her *Samuel Rutherford and his Friends* (Edinburgh: Banner of Truth, 1992), p. 22.

[6] The twenty-four volumes of Owen's *Works* account for approximately 13,700 pages.

[7] Perhaps the most demonstrable and, yet, basic, evidence for this claim lies in the simple fact that Owen's works have been republished, kept in print, and are readily

Of the scholarly attention that Rutherford has received, the majority has been confined either to his political thought, as contained in *Lex, Rex*,[8] or to his spirituality, as reflected in the *Letters*.[9] Only a handful of works have examined his theology. Sometimes, as in the case of David Strickland's discussion of

---

accessible for all to read, whereas the majority of Rutherford's writings have never been republished since the seventeenth century, and his Latin treatises have remained untranslated.

[8] W.M. Campbell, '*Lex, Rex* and its Author', *RSCHS* 7 (1941), pp. 204-28; O.K. Webb, 'The Political Thought of Samuel Rutherford' (unpublished Ph.D. dissertation, Duke University, 1964); J.F. Maclear, 'Samuel Rutherford: The Law and the King', in *Calvinism and the Political Order*, eds. G.L. Hunt and J.T. McNeill (Philadelphia: Westminster, 1965), pp. 65-87; R. Flinn, 'Samuel Rutherford and Puritan Political Theory', *Journal of Christian Reconstruction* 5 (1978-9), pp. 49-74; T.D. Hall, 'Rutherford, Locke, and the Declaration: The Connection' (unpublished Th.M. dissertation, Dallas Theological Seminary, 1984); J.P. Burgess, 'The Problem of Scripture and Political Affairs as Reflected in the Puritan Revolution: Samuel Rutherford, Thomas Goodwin, John Goodwin, and Gerard Winstanley' (unpublished Ph.D. dissertation, University of Chicago, 1986); W.D.J. McKay, 'Samuel Rutherford on Civil Government' (unpublished M.Th. dissertation, Queen's University, Belfast, 1986); C.E. Rae, 'The Political Thought of Samuel Rutherford' (unpublished M.A. dissertation, University of Guelph, 1991); J. Ford, '*Lex, rex iusto posita*: Samuel Rutherford on the origins of government', in *Scots and Britons: Scottish Political Thought and the Union of 1603*, ed. R. Mason (Cambridge: Cambridge University, 1994), pp. 262-90; J.L. Marshall, 'Natural Law and the Covenant: The Place of Natural Law in the Covenantal Framework of Samuel Rutherford's *Lex Rex*' (unpublished Ph.D. dissertation, Westminster Theological Seminary, 1995); and Coffey, *Politics, Religion and the British Revolutions*.

[9] A. Whyte, *Samuel Rutherford and Some of his Correspondents* (Edinburgh: Oliphant Anderson & Ferrier, 1894); A. Philip, *The Devotional Literature of Scotland* (London: James Clarke, 1920), pp. 116-25; C.N. Button, 'Scottish Mysticism in the Seventeenth Century, with Special Reference to Samuel Rutherford' (unpublished Ph.D. dissertation, University of Edinburgh, 1927); H. Martin, *Great Christian Books* (London: SCM Press, 1945), ch. 3; J.M. Ross, 'Samuel Rutherford', *The Month* (July, 1975), pp. 207-11; J.M. Brentnall, *Samuel Rutherford in Aberdeen* (Inverness: John Eccles, c.1981); R.S. Louden, 'Samuel Rutherford', in *The Westminster Dictionary of Christian Spirituality*, ed. G.S. Wakefield (Philadelphia: Westminster, 1983), p. 345; J.K. Cameron, 'The Piety of Samuel Rutherford (c. 1621-1661): A Neglected Feature of Seventeenth Century Scottish Calvinism', *NAvK* 65 (1985), pp. 153-9; H. Meier, 'Love, Law, and Lucre: Images in Rutherfurd's Letters', in *Historical and Editorial Essays in Medieval and Early Modern English for Johan Gerritsen*, eds. M.-J. Arn and H. Wirtjes (Groningen: Wolters-Noordhoff, 1985), pp. 77-96; A.M. Machar, 'A Scottish Mystic', *The Andover Review* 6 (1986), pp. 379-95; F. Cook, *Grace in Winter: Rutherford in Verse* (Edinburgh: Banner of Truth, 1989); idem, *Samuel Rutherford and his Friends*; M. Roberts, 'Samuel Rutherford: The Comings and Goings of the Heavenly Bridegroom', in *The Trials of Puritanism: Papers read at the 1993 Westminster Conference* (privately published, 1994), pp. 119-34.

union with Christ or William Campbell's writings on ecclesiology, only one specific aspect of Rutherford's theology has been studied.[10] At other times, his theology has been considered more broadly but only in the most superficial of terms. Such is the case with the chapter-length surveys provided by James Walker, John Macleod, M. Charles Bell, T.F. Torrance, and John Coffey.[11] Only one book-length study currently exists that presents Rutherford's theology more broadly and, yet, also in sufficient depth. But, as its title suggests, this work concentrates on the scholastic nature of Rutherford's theology rather than on presenting it in a systematic manner.[12] It contains little discussion of his soteriology and no reference at all to what is perhaps his *magnum opus theologiae*, the *Examen Arminianismi* (1668). As a result, it overlooks several key features of Rutherford's theology that are found only in the *Examen*. Furthermore, it devotes only cursory attention to Rutherford's dispute with the Arminians, even though it draws heavily upon his first treatise against them, the *Exercitationes apologeticae pro divina gratia* (1636). Clearly the time is at hand to revisit Rutherford's theology and to produce a comprehensive, systematic, book-length analysis of it. The current study seeks to accomplish just this task by setting forth his theology as it is developed primarily in the *Examen Arminianismi* and anchored within the context of his dispute with the Arminians.

Why the *Examen*? Quite simply, it is the closest thing that Rutherford has to a proper systematic theology text. James Walker, noticing this, has aptly described the *Examen* as 'an excellent theological manual'.[13] In one sense this should come as no surprise, because the *Examen* consists of lectures that Rutherford delivered to his students at the University of St. Andrews for the

---

[10] D. Strickland, 'Union with Christ in the Theology of Samuel Rutherford: An Examination of his Doctrine of the Holy Spirit' (unpublished Ph.D. dissertation, University of Edinburgh, 1972); W.M. Campbell, 'Samuel Rutherford, propagandist and exponent of Scottish Presbyterianism' (unpublished Ph.D. dissertation, University of Edinburgh, 1937); idem, *Triumph of Presbyterianism*, pp. 73-93. For other works interacting with Rutherford's ecclesiology, see Coffey, *Politics, Religion and the British Revolutions*, pp. 188-224; and, in a really broad sense, D.G. Mullan, *Scottish Puritanism, 1590-1638* (Oxford: Oxford University, 2000).

[11] Walker, *Theology and Theologians of Scotland*, pp. 8-13; J. Macleod, *Scottish Theology in Relation to Church History Since the Reformation* (Edinburgh: Publications Committee of the Free Church of Scotland, 1943), pp. 68-78; M.C. Bell, *Calvin and Scottish Theology: The Doctrine of Assurance* (Edinburgh: Handsel Press, 1985), pp. 70-91; T.F. Torrance, *Scottish Theology: From John Knox to John McLeod Campbell* (Edinburgh: T&T Clark, 1996), pp. 93-111; Coffey, *Politics, Religion and the British Revolutions*, pp. 114-45.

[12] S.-D. Kim, 'Time and Eternity: A Study in Samuel Rutherford's theology, with Reference to His Use of Scholastic Method' (unpublished Ph.D. dissertation, University of Aberdeen, 2002).

[13] Walker, *Theology and Theologians of Scotland*, pp. 10.

express purpose of training them in theology. It contains discussion of every major theological locus and provides the most comprehensive presentation of Rutherford's theology that is available in any one treatise,[14] albeit with a decidedly polemical slant. In another sense, however, it may come as a surprise to those who are acquainted with Rutherford's writings and the prolix style and nit-picking nature of his argumentation, influenced as it is by Aristotelian categories of logic. One need not spend long in certain of Rutherford's works to appreciate Tertullian's (160-220) anti-Aristotelian sentiments: 'Unhappy Aristotle! who invented for these men dialectics, the art of building up and pulling down; an art so evasive in its propositions, so far-fetched in its conjectures, so harsh, in its arguments, so productive of contentions—embarrassing even to itself, retracting everything, and really treating of nothing!'[15] The value of such writings in actually teaching theology is rightly to be questioned. But, in point of fact, this is another reason why the *Examen* stands head and shoulders above others of Rutherford's theological works. It represents his thinking at its best and clearest. James Walker claims that it is 'much more interesting than either the *Exercitationes* [1636] or the *De Providentia* [1649]', even though all three are devoted to countering the perceived evils of Arminianism. And William Campbell adds that the *Examen* 'shows no weakness in his power of dialectic and is more lucid and orderly than much of his other polemic'.[16] Although it does employ logical syllogisms and highly contentious argumentation, it contains less of the negative features of Rutherford's other works and, at the same time, is more comprehensive in the topics that it covers. For these very reasons, Thomas Murray has

---

[14] Rutherford's two other Latin treatises, *Exercitationes apologeticae pro divina gratia* (1636) and *Disputatio scholastica de divina providentia* (1649), seek to answer the question of how it is that absolute divine decrees can coexist with real human freedom. They concentrate on the divine will and on metaphysical issues, whereas the *Examen* presents a discussion of every *locus* in systematic theology. The twenty chapters that comprise it are as follows: 'Of the Holy Scriptures' (p. 1), 'Of God' (p. 138), 'Of Election' (p. 238), 'Of Reprobation' (p. 276), 'Of the State of the First Man [*hominis*]' (p. 297), 'Of Original Sin' (p. 310), 'Of the State of Fallen Humankind [*hominis*]' (p. 324), 'Of the State of Grace' (p. 351), 'Of Universal Redemption' (p. 372), 'Of the Covenant of Grace' (p. 426), 'Of the Manner of Conversion' (p. 453), 'Of the Justification of the Sinner' (p. 498), 'Of the Perseverance of the Saints' (p. 549), 'Of the Certainty of Salvation' (p. 625), 'Of the Church and its Notes' (p. 642), 'Of Ministers of the Word' (p. 681), 'Of Synods' (p. 692), 'Of the Sacraments and Ecclesiastical Discipline' (p. 716), 'Of the Magistrate' (p. 728), 'Of the Soul and the Resurrection of the Body' (p. 753).

[15] Tertullian, *The Prescription against Heretics*, section VII, cited in C. Gunton, S. Holmes, and M. Rae (eds.), *The Practice of Theology: A Reader* (London: SCM Press, 2001), p. 157.

[16] Walker, *Theology and Theologians of Scotland*, p. 10; Campbell, *Triumph of Presbyterianism*, p. 85.

appropriately concluded that the *Examen* is Rutherford's 'best production'.[17] It is his *magnum opus* or his *summa theologiae*.

In spite of its importance, the *Examen* has never been translated out of the original Latin and, more significantly, has been completely overlooked in the secondary literature. The works of Bell, Torrance, and Kim do not even mention it at all. Those of Coffey, Walker, and Macleod mention the *Examen*, but do not interact with its contents.[18] The current study seeks to fill both the aforementioned gaps by making Rutherford's theology in the *Examen* available to a wider audience. To accomplish this, citations from it have been made in English rather than in the original Latin, as may be more typical in academic circles, while citations from other Latin treatises—even from those penned by Rutherford—will, as a rule, remain untranslated. Before proceeding to look at Rutherford's theology in the *Examen*, however, we must first introduce the context in which it was developed and articulated. This chapter will, therefore, seek to provide an examination of the socio-political, ecclesial, theological, polemical, and formal contexts of the *Examen* and, then, conclude with a note regarding methodology.

Establishing the Context

THE SOCIO-POLITICAL AND ECCLESIAL CONTEXT

In his work on the cultural background to the Scottish Reformation, John Durkan states: 'In any age there is nothing more difficult to pin down than a climate of thought, and nothing more necessary to reckon with than this particular intangible.'[19] Durkan's statement expresses something that is commonly accepted today among historians of ideas: we are all, to a greater or lesser degree, products of the periods in which we live. That this is the case for Rutherford will become patently obvious throughout the course of this book. Rutherford is a man of his time, or, as Robert Gilmour quips, 'the most distinctively representative Scotsman in the first half of the seventeenth century'.[20] What this means is that, by studying Rutherford, we become better acquainted with the time in which he lived and, by studying the time in which he lived, we become better acquainted with him. Therefore, much of what

---

[17] T. Murray, *The Life of Rev. Samuel Rutherford* (Edinburgh: Oliphant, 1828), pp. 333-4. Apart from Coffey's definitive introduction to Rutherford, Murray's biography offers the best and most well-researched contribution to the field.

[18] Coffey begins his treatment of Rutherford's theology with a note that the 'detailed arguments of Rutherford's Latin works against Arminianism, in particular, require a more extended treatment'. *Politics, Religion and the British Revolutions*, p. 114.

[19] J. Durkan, 'The Cultural Background in Sixteenth-Century Scotland', in *Essays on the Scottish Reformation 1513-1625*, ed. D. McRoberts (Glasgow: Burns, 1962), pp. 292-3.

[20] Gilmour, *Samuel Rutherford*, p. ix.

could be said in this section about the cultural context of the seventeenth century will be revealed only as this thesis unfolds, chapter by chapter. But because the final chapter of the dissertation contains an examination of the grounds for Rutherford's opposition to Arminianism, it, more than any other part of the study, will contribute to a deeper understanding of seventeenth-century thought and Rutherford's relationship to it. For now, however, our goal is simply to introduce—and, then, only in the broadest and most basic of terms—some of the relevant cultural factors that would have influenced Rutherford and the development or expression of his theology.

By all accounts, the sixteenth and seventeenth centuries mark a time of tremendous religious and societal upheaval. Beginning in the early 1500s, the European community as a whole witnessed a large-scale, heretofore unprecedented Reformation within the Roman Catholic Church. This Reformation was essentially a reaction against the elements of corruption and excess that were present within the church at the time.[21] But whereas prior reform movements had allied themselves to papal authority in order to implement their desired changes, the Reformation of the sixteenth century allied itself to the civil authorities instead.[22] And as the work of the Reformation progressed over the course of the century, this link between church and state became further solidified.

In Scotland, the official break with the Roman Church came as a result of an act of Parliament—the so-called 'Reformation Parliament'—in 1560, which was itself a product of the Protestant revolution against France and Rome and against the French regime of Mary of Guise (1554-1560). In response to Mary's actions against early outbreaks of support for the Reformation, many in Scotland appealed to the Protestant Queen Elizabeth I of England (1558-1603) for help. The financial and military assistance they received from her eventually enabled the calling of the aforementioned Reformation Parliament and, thus, ensured the establishment of a Protestant Scotland.[23] After being officially established in this way by a close connection between the ecclesial and political spheres, Scottish Protestantism continued to develop by an even closer connection between church and state, although it was oftentimes more antagonistic than not.

---

[21] A.E. McGrath, *Reformation Thought: An Introduction* (Oxford: Blackwell, ³1999), pp. 2-5. McGrath rightly notes that the Reformation sought more than just doctrinal reforms. It sought to overhaul the church's legal system, bureaucracy, morality, and piety, in addition to its theology.

[22] McGrath explains that the authority of the pope had diminished due in part to the Spanish Inquisition and the Concordat of Bologna. *Reformation Thought*, p. 4.

[23] See J. Kirk, 'Reformation Parliament', and 'Reformation, Scottish', in *DSCH&T*, pp. 693-8; and J.H. Burns, 'The Political Background of the Reformation, 1513-1625', in *Essays on the Scottish Reformation 1513-1625*, ed. D. McRoberts (Glasgow: Burns, 1962), pp. 1-38.

Following the accession of James VI (1567-1625) to the throne in Scotland, the royal policy towards the church—at least initially anyway—'seems to have been to hold a balance between protestant and catholic'.[24] But James' inability actually to pull off this balancing act enabled stronger souls, like Andrew Melville (1545-1622), to have their way. Melvillian Presbyterianism, which had been established in the 1570s during James' minority reign, forced James into a position of weakness and, on at least one occasion, outright capitulation.[25] With the uniting of the kingdoms of Scotland and England in 1603, however, James set about a new work of assimilating the two national churches with a new-found strength. In response to Melvillian Presbyterianism—and its doctrine of the two kingdoms—which was then in control of the Scottish kirk,[26] James claimed *jus divinum regum* and began imposing episcopacy upon the church in Scotland, arguing that Presbyterianism 'as well agreeth with a monarchy as God and the Devil'.[27] Resistance to the king's wishes for the kirk was regarded as treason and punished accordingly. Rutherford's boyhood minister, the staunch advocate of Calvinist and Presbyterian doctrine, David Calderwood (1575-1650),[28] was one casualty of James' policy towards the church, a casualty that would have been indelibly imprinted upon the mind of Rutherford from the earliest of ages.

What started under James was continued under his son, Charles I (1625-1649). But whereas James sought to introduce episcopacy into Scotland progressively, Charles had no such pretence.[29] Again claiming *jus divinum regum*, he insisted that he knew what was best for Scotland and purposed to bring it about immediately. With the help of William Laud (1573-1645)—later Archbishop of Canterbury—Charles set out to conform the church in Scotland to an Anglo-Catholic model. Acts of nonconformity were again met with

---

[24] Burns, 'Background of the Reformation', p. 31.

[25] J.H. Burns recounts a time in 1592 when James was '[s]o weak...that he had to make a concession, if not a surrender, to the presbyterian party' by giving their 'hierarchy of courts...parliamentary authority' to act in a high profile murder case. Burns, 'Background of the Reformation', p. 31.

[26] J.H.S. Burleigh points to an instance of open conflict between Andrew Melville and James in 1596 in which Melville called James '"God's sillie vassal", and forcefully reminded him that "there are two kings and two kingdoms in Scotland. There is Christ Jesus the King and His kingdom the Kirk, whose subject King James the Sixth is, and of whose kingdom not a king, nor a lord, nor a head, but a member."' J.H.S. Burleigh, *A Church History of Scotland* (Edinburgh: Hope Trust, 1988), pp. 204-5.

[27] King James at Hampton Court Conference, 1604, cited in Burleigh, *Church History*, p. 205.

[28] Coffey, *Politics, Religion and the British Revolutions*, p. 31.

[29] Burleigh indicates that James knew '"the stomach" of his people, [and] he walked warily, step by step, and achieved considerable success' (*Church History*, p. 215). Lynch highlights Charles' impatience by calling him 'a king in a hurry' (*Scotland: A New History*, p. 247).

disciplinary action under Charles, as they were under his father. Rutherford himself was subjected to the discipline of the Caroline church by being exiled to Aberdeen in 1636 for his nonconformity and for his attack on the Arminianism espoused by Laud and the 'Canterburian' party.[30] The autocratic methods of Charles in dealing with the church and with the nobles in Scotland led to revolt and culminated in the signing of the National Covenant in 1638. By signing this document, men pledged themselves 'to maintain the freedom of the Church from civil control, to defend the true Reformed religion, and to decline the recent innovations in worship decreed by the King until the General Assembly had ruled on them'. Even though the National Covenant did not explicitly condemn episcopacy, it did directly contradict James' and Charles' policy of *jus divinum regum* by asserting instead the freedom of the kirk from all state control and the sole headship of Christ over all ecclesial affairs.[31]

One year after the signing of the Covenant, at the Glasgow General Assembly of 1639, the church 'adopted a thoroughly Presbyterian programme'.[32] Together with the *jus divinum* Presbyterianism of the 'Covenanting' kirk, the 'impertinent and damnable demands' of the National Covenant—as Charles referred to them—helped to initiate a period of intense conflict between the crown and the church in Scotland. This period, known generally as the period of the Covenanters, was a time marked by extreme intolerance on both sides, which would steadily increase until reaching a climax after the Restoration of 1660.[33]

Having thus sketched out the socio-political and ecclesial context of Rutherford's day, it should be patent that he was in fact a man of his times. His association with David Calderwood ensured that he would be exposed to the controversy between the crown and the church from the earliest of ages, which exposure would then set the course for the remainder of his lifetime. The publication of *Lex, Rex* in 1644 not only confirmed Calderwood's influence upon Rutherford, but also sealed his fate with the Stewart dynasty. As if it was not bad enough to publish a treatise defending biblically the Covenanters' open resistance to Charles I, Rutherford took his diatribe one step further. He repeatedly and uncharitably, in *Lex, Rex*, compared the king and his queen to the wicked Ahab and Jezebel of the Bible.[34] The combination of the treatise and its acerbic tone delivered a knockout punch and would most likely have resulted in Rutherford's martyrdom, were it not for his ill health. In addition to his work in the political realm, Rutherford also staunchly defended *jus divinum*

---

[30] *Letters*, pp. 141-3. Laud's relationship to Arminianism will be discussed in more detail in the section entitled 'The Polemical Context' below and again in chapter five.

[31] J.D. Douglas, 'National Covenant', in *DSCH&T*, p. 620.

[32] K.M. Brown, 'Covenanters', in *DSCH&T*, p. 218.

[33] Brown, 'Covenanters', p. 218; and D. Stevenson, 'Restoration', in *DSCH&T*, pp. 710-11.

[34] Campbell, *Triumph of Presbyterianism*, p. 79.

Presbyterianism in his polemical works against Independency and Erastianism.³⁵ And he did it all with an intolerance that was characteristic of his age. He even devoted a treatise to defending the concept of intolerance itself.³⁶ In all these ways, Rutherford shows himself to be the quintessential Scotsman of the early Covenanting period. His life epitomized the struggle of the church against the tyranny of the Stewart dynasty. His intolerance reflected the best and the worst of the intolerance of his day. Not only does it correspond well to his theology but it also partially explains the reason for his effectiveness.

THE THEOLOGICAL CONTEXT

Of the two basic types of theological writing characteristic of the post-Reformation period, the *Examen* falls into the 'polemical' or 'scholastic' category. Whereas works of 'didactic' or 'positive' theology tend to 'meditate' upon the detailed exegesis of Scripture and to present only basic statements of doctrine—e.g., the *compendia* or *medullae*—those of the 'polemical' or 'scholastic' variety typically contain 'more elaborate systems' of doctrine that are directed 'toward their correct conclusions over against the erroneous conclusions of adversaries in debate'.³⁷ Works of polemical theology are not less scriptural than didactic works. Both types are based wholly upon biblical exegesis. But polemical treatises tend to begin with the basic statements of doctrine provided by didactic works and then to develop them in greater detail within the context of theological dispute. This is precisely what we see in the *Examen*, whose twenty chapters run the gamut of systematic theology and oppose Arminian teaching at each point along the way with tediously intricate detail.

Entering the theological world of the *Examen* is, according to John Coffey, something like 'enter[ing] the world evoked so vividly in Umberto Eco's novel, *The Name of the Rose*'. In short, he says, it is a world of scholastic distinctions and theological argumentation over questions that can be as obscure as the medieval query about 'whether an angel could pass from star to star without traversing the intermediate space'.³⁸ While Coffey's claim should remind us that Rutherford stands within a theological tradition that extends back through the Reformation to the Middle Ages, this should not immediately be taken as conclusive proof that his theology is wholly, or even substantially, the same as

---

³⁵ E.g., *A Peaceable and Temperate Plea for Pauls Presbyterie in Scotland* (London, 1642); *The Due Right of Presbyteries* (London, 1644); *The Divine Right of Church Government and Excommunication* (London, 1646); and *A Survey of the Survey of that Summe of Church-Discipline Penned by Mr. Thomas Hooker* (London, 1658).

³⁶ *A Free Disputation against Pretended Liberty of Conscience* (London, 1649). Rutherford's intolerance will be taken up again in chapter five.

³⁷ *PRRD*, I, p. 202. See, e.g., E. Leigh, *A Systeme or Body of Divinity* (London, 1654), p. a2.

³⁸ Coffey, *Politics, Religion and the British Revolutions*, p. 117.

his medieval scholastic forebears and, thus, discontinuous with the Reformation, as some have assumed. There is, in fact, profound disagreement among modern scholars over the relationship between medieval scholasticism, the Reformation, and the post-Reformation period. On one side of the divide, scholars like Brian Armstrong argue that Rutherford and his post-Reformation peers drifted away from the theology of John Calvin (1509-1564) by rejecting Calvin's more 'balanced', biblical, and humanistic approach to theology in favor of a scholastic worldview exhibiting the following four basic characteristics:

> (1) Primarily it will have reference to that theological approach that asserts religious truth on the basis of deductive ratiocination from given assumptions or principles, thus providing a logically coherent and defensible system or belief. Generally this takes the form of syllogistic reasoning. It is an orientation, it seems, invariably based upon an Aristotelian philosophic commitment and so relates to medieval scholasticism. (2) The term will refer to the employment of reason in religious matters, so that reason assumes at least equal standing with faith in theology, thus jettisoning some of the authority of revelation. (3) It will comprehend the sentiment that the scriptural record contains a unified, rationally comprehensible account and thus may be used as a measuring stick to determine one's orthodoxy. (4) It will comprehend a pronounced interest in metaphysical matters, in abstract speculative thought, particularly with reference to the doctrine of God. The distinctive Protestant position is made to rest on a speculative formulation of the will of God.[39]

By adopting these elements of medieval scholasticism—elements which are perceived to have been definitively eschewed by Calvin and the reformers—theologians of the post-Reformation period allegedly developed a theology that was no longer faithful to the actual thinking of the Genevan reformer.

T.F. Torrance and Charles Bell, whether or not they actually follow Armstrong's definition of scholasticism, have, nevertheless, followed in the

---

[39] B.G. Armstrong, *Calvinism and the Amyraut Heresy: Protestant Scholasticism and Humanism in Seventeenth Century France* (Madison, WI: University of Wisconsin, 1969), pp. 32, and 31n84, 42. Armstrong's viewpoints are held by others with varying degrees of similitude: e.g., E. Bizer, *Frühorthodoxie und Rationalismus* (Zurich: EVZ Verlag, 1963); C.S. McCoy, 'Johannes Cocceius: Federal Theologian', *SJT* 16 (1963), pp. 352-70; O. Gründler, *Die Gotteslehre Girolami Zanchis und ihre Bedeutung für seine Lehre von der Prädestination* (Neukirchen: Neukirchner Verlag, 1965); B. Hall, 'Calvin Against the Calvinists', in *John Calvin*, ed. G.E. Duffield (Appleford, Berkshire: Sutton Courtenay, 1966), pp. 19-37; W. Kickel, *Vernunft und Offenbarung bei Theodor Beza* (Neukirchen: Neukirchner Verlag, 1967); R.T. Kendall, *Calvin and English Calvinism to 1649* (Oxford: Oxford University, 1979); idem, 'The Puritan Modification of Calvin's Theology', in *John Calvin*, ed. W.S. Reid (Grand Rapids, MI: Zondervan, 1982), pp. 199-214; P.C. Holtrop, *The Bolsec Controversy on Predestination, From 1551 to 1555*, 2 vols. (Lewiston, NY: Edwin Mellen, 1993-).

same vein of thinking and suggested that there is substantial theological discontinuity specifically between Rutherford and Calvin. Torrance has even gone so far as to brand Rutherford an 'extreme hyper-Calvinist' for his reliance upon 'strict syllogistic form[s]' and his views on limited atonement and predestination.[40] While agreeing with Torrance's evaluation in the main, Bell adds covenant theology, preparation, and assurance of salvation to his list of Rutherford's 'hyper-Calvinist' doctrines.[41]

On the opposite side of this divide, however, Richard Muller, Heiko Oberman, and David Steinmetz, among others, have more recently initiated a reappraisal of the link between Calvin and the so-called Calvinists and have argued against the existence of substantial theological discontinuity.[42] They have pointed out problems with Armstrong's definition of scholasticism, claiming that it overlooks what Roman Catholic scholars have long understood, viz., 'that to describe a theology as scholastic is to make a statement about its method not its content'.[43] This movement towards reappraisal thus suggests that 'scholasticism' is best understood as a term referring to a method of

---

[40] Torrance, *Scottish Theology*, pp. 109-110. Although Torrance does not define what he means by the slippery term 'hyper-Calvinist', it is likely that he is using it generally to suggest that Rutherford's theology hardened Calvin's own understanding to such a degree that it no longer remained faithful to the thinking of the Genevan reformer.

[41] Bell, *Calvinism and Scottish Theology*, pp. 70-84, especially 83-4.

[42] E.g., R.A. Muller, *Christ and the Decree: Christology and Predestination in Reformed Theology from Calvin to Perkins* (Durham, NC: Labyrinth Press, 1986); idem, 'Calvin and the "Calvinists": Assessing the Continuities and Discontinuities between the Reformation and Orthodoxy', *CTJ* 30 (1995), pp. 345-75, and 31 (1996), pp. 125-60; idem, 'The Problem of Protestant Scholasticism—A Review and Definition', in *Reformation and Scholasticism: An Ecumenical Enterprise*, eds. W.J. Van Asselt and E. Dekker (Grand Rapids, MI: Baker, 2001), pp. 45-64; idem, *PRRD*, 4 vols.; H.A. Oberman, *The Harvest of Medieval Theology: Gabriel Biel and Late Medieval Nominalism* (1963; Durham, NC: Labyrinth Press, ³1983); idem, *Forerunners of the Reformation* (New York: Holt, Rinehart and Winston, 1966); idem, 'The Shape of Late Medieval Thought: The Birthpangs of the Modern Era', in *The Pursuit of Holiness in Late Medieval and Renaissance Religion*, eds., C.E. Trinkaus and Oberman (Leiden: E.J. Brill, 1974), pp. 3-25; idem, *Masters of the Reformation: Emergence of a New Intellectual Climate in Europe*, trans. D. Martin (Cambridge: Cambridge University, 1981); D.C. Steinmetz, *Misericordia Dei: The Theology of Johannes von Staupitz in Its Late Medieval Setting* (Leiden: E.J. Brill, 1968); idem, 'Calvin and the Absolute Power of God', *Journal of Medieval and Renaissance Studies* 18:1 (Spring, 1988), pp. 65-79; idem, 'The Scholastic Calvin', in *Protestant Scholasticism: Essays in Reappraisal*, eds. C.R. Trueman and R.S. Clark (Carlisle, Cumbria: Paternoster, 1999), pp. 16-30; W.J. Van Asselt and E. Dekker, *Reformation and Scholasticism*, pp. 11-43; and C.R. Trueman and R.S. Clark, *Protestant Scholasticism*, pp. xi-xix.

[43] Trueman and Clark, *Protestant Scholasticism*, p. xiv. Cf. J.A. Weisheipl, 'Scholastic Method', in *The New Catholic Encyclopedia* (New York: Catholic University of America, 1967), XII, pp. 1145-6.

approaching or arranging the content of theology rather than of developing or determining the theology itself. Armstrong's definition, they say, overlooks three things in particular: the presence of scholasticism in the Reformation; the presence of humanism in the post-Reformation period; and the existence of vast theological differences between individuals who can, nevertheless, still be classified as scholastic—e.g., between medieval scholastics like Thomas Aquinas (c.1225-1274), Durandus of Saint-Pourcain (1270-1334), John Duns Scotus (c.1270-1308), William of Ockham (c.1280-c.1349), and Gabriel Biel (d. 1495), and also, between seventeenth-century Arminians and Calvinists.[44]

Because a significant percentage of the published work discussing Rutherford's theology approaches it from the perspective of the discontinuity thesis, and because of the prominence both of the authors of those published works and of the Calvin-Calvinist debate itself, it is impossible for the current study to present Rutherford's theology adequately without taking up this issue. In the course of this thesis, then, we will seek to determine which side in this debate is most correct, at least as far as it involves Rutherford. Does Armstrong's definition apply to Rutherford? Is his theology at odds with the teaching of Calvin? Can he, as Torrance believes, legitimately be called a hyper-Calvinist?[45] Or, is the reappraisal school more correct to see substantial continuity between post-Reformation theologians like Rutherford, on the one hand, and Calvin and his Reformation contemporaries, on the other?

Whichever side is most correct, one thing is certain at this point: Rutherford's theology in the *Examen* clearly exhibits characteristics of scholasticism, however it is to be defined. Even the reappraisal school acknowledges this fact. According to Richard Muller, the primary technique that distinguishes the scholastic method in every age is the technique of the *quaestio*, involving the following four components:

> 1. The presentation of a thesis or *quaestio*, a thematic question; 2. The indication of the subjects that stand to be discussed in the *quaestio*, the so-called *status quaestionis*; 3. The treatment of a series of arguments or objections against the adopted positions, the so-called *objectiones*; 4. The formulation of an answer (*responsio*), in which account is taken of all available sources of information, and all rules of rational discourse are upheld, followed by an answer to the objections, which is as comprehensive as possible.[46]

---

[44] Trueman and Clark, *Protestant Scholasticism*, pp. xiv-xv; Van Asselt and Dekker, *Reformation and Scholasticism*, p. 24; and Muller, 'The Problem of Protestant Scholasticism', pp. 45-64. See also, idem, 'Calvin and the "Calvinists"', *CTJ* 30 (1995), pp. 358-75, and 31 (1996), pp. 126-60, where Muller presents no less than ten modifications or qualifications to Armstrong's definition of scholasticism.
[45] A definition for hyper-Calvinism will be offered in chapter five.
[46] R.A. Muller, 'Scholasticism and Orthodoxy in the Reformed Tradition: An Attempt at Definition' (Inaugural Address, Grand Rapids, MI, 1995), pp. 4-5.

This same basic pattern can be found in the *Examen*, each chapter of which is organized around a series of *quaestiones*, readily identifiable from the recurring introductory Latin verb *Quaeritur*, 'It is asked'.[47] The *status quaestionis* then frequently further refines the *quaestio* by offering clarification as to what actually is the point of contention between Rutherford and the Arminians.[48] After this, the adopted positions of each party in the controversy are presented and relevant *objectiones* are offered and rebutted by appropriate *responsiones* from Rutherford.[49] As Muller warns, however, these *responsiones* can be quite comprehensive. At one point, Rutherford offers no less than twenty responses to Arminian claims, and, quite frequently, he amasses sixteen or more.[50] Only rarely is the number of responses from Rutherford less than four. This shows that the *Examen* is unambiguously a work of scholastic theology. Its methodology stands in continuity with medieval scholasticism. What remains to be seen is whether or not it stands in continuity with the Reformation and how, if at all, this affects Rutherford's theology.

Considering the nature of the education he received at Edinburgh's 'Town College',[51] the patent scholasticism in Rutherford should not surprise us. G.D. Henderson has described the curriculum in Edinburgh as one of 'pure scholasticism'.[52] And although Henderson's claim is overstated—insofar as it minimizes the humanistic influences of Andrew Melville and Robert Rollock (c.1555-1599) and their joint emphasis on studying Ramist logic and the classics and the Bible in the original languages—it is a fair general caricature of a curriculum that was overwhelmingly Aristotelian (i.e., almost half the number of texts within the curriculum consisted of works belonging to Aristotle [d. 322 BC]).[53]

What is more, Rutherford's scholasticism should not surprise us in light of

---

[47] See, e.g., *Examen*, 'Index Capitum & Quaestionum', which begins immediately after the main body of the text, for a complete listing of every *quaestio* in each chapter.

[48] See, e.g., *Examen*, pp. 453, 463, 464, 498, 520, 551.

[49] See, e.g., *Examen*, pp. 28-9, 56, 100-103, 108-21.

[50] *Examen*, pp. 171-4 (shows 16 responses), pp. 185-91 (16 responses), pp. 206-10 (18 responses), pp. 241-4 (16 responses), pp. 249-52 (16 responses), pp. 458-65 (19 responses), and pp. 553-63 (20 responses).

[51] According to A. Grant, the medieval term *universitas* was not applied to Edinburgh until the end of the seventeenth century. For the first one hundred years or so it was known simply as the 'Town College'. See A. Grant, *The Story of the University of Edinburgh During its First Three Hundred Years* (London: Longmans, Green, 1884), I, p. 130.

[52] G.D. Henderson, *Religious Life in Seventeenth-Century Scotland* (Cambridge: Cambridge University, 1937), p. 122.

[53] For more on the curriculum in Edinburgh during the early seventeenth century, see T. Crauford, *History of the University of Edinburgh, from 1580 to 1646* (Edinburgh: A. Neill, 1808), pp. 57-62; and Grant, *University of Edinburgh*, I, pp. 148-50. Cf. Coffey, *Politics, Religion and the British Revolutions*, pp. 63-4.

the intellectual climate in which he lived. His thinking is not unusual, nor even distinctively British, for seventeenth-century theology. Though there are, as we will see, distinctive emphases in Rutherford that result, in many cases, from particular doctrinal controversies, his theology and his methodology remain essentially generic to continental Reformed orthodoxy—which is explicitly scholastic in nature. Rutherford's work in Scotland and England in the seventeenth century cannot be isolated from the rest of the European intellectual community. All of Europe, but especially Britain and the Netherlands, were united in the sixteenth and seventeenth centuries. This is partly due to the fact that there was a common academic language in Europe at that time, and partly to the continental migration of those who faced religious persecution at home. The Netherlands, more than anywhere else, became the safe 'hiding place' for British exiles, particularly those with Reformed convictions, largely because it was the economic super-power of the day—with Britain a mere 'junior partner'—and also because it was both accessible and religiously compatible.[54]

According to Keith Sprunger, two key events in the early seventeenth century served to link the religious identities of Britain and the Netherlands. The first was the controversy in 1611-1612 over the appointment of Conrad Vorstius (1569-1622) as successor to James Arminius (1560-1609) in the university at Leiden. So concerned was James VI (and I of England) that Leiden was appointing a suspected Socinian, that he 'gave [them] no peace until Vorstius, "this blasphemous monster", had been banished from the university'.[55] The other key event, according to Sprunger, was the Synod of Dort (1618-1619), to which King James sent a delegation of 'sound, orthodox divines', in order that they might participate in the synod's proceedings.[56] The Canons of Dort that were produced by the synod were received by many in England and Scotland, but particularly in the latter, as an expression of the sum of 'British divinity'. Even to the end of the seventeenth century in Scotland, these canons were acknowledged to be the quintessence of 'Scripture Divinity, the Divinity of the Ancients, and the Divinity that right reason doth countenance'.[57]

For Rutherford, the connection with the Dutch church and with Dutch theology was further strengthened by the fact that his boyhood minister David

---

[54] K.L. Sprunger, *Dutch Puritanism: A History of English and Scottish Churches of the Netherlands in the Sixteenth and Seventeenth Centuries* (Leiden: E.J. Brill, 1982), pp. 7, 9.

[55] Sprunger, *Dutch Puritanism*, p. 355. For more on this controversy and the role played by King James, see F. Shriver, 'Orthodoxy and Diplomacy: James I and the Vorstius Affair', *English Historical Review* 85 (July, 1970), pp. 449-74.

[56] Sprunger, *Dutch Puritanism*, p. 355.

[57] Henderson, *Religious Life*, p. 86, citing a pamphlet published in 1691 in Scotland, entitled *A Vindication of the Church of Scotland*.

Calderwood lived in exile in the Netherlands from 1619-1625. Quite possibly, it was Calderwood's influence that first brought Rutherford to the attention of the church in the Netherlands, resulting in the publication of his first treatise, the *Exercitationes*, in Amsterdam in 1636. Rutherford's theological proclivities—particularly his strict Calvinist view of predestination and his advocacy of *jus divinum* Presbyterian ecclesiology—endeared him to men the likes of Gisbertus Voetius (1589-1676) and Matthias Nethenus (1618-1686) and eventually resulted in offers to teach in the Dutch universities of Utrecht and Harderwyck and in the posthumous publication of his *magnum opus*, the *Examen*. It is this connection with the Netherlands that ensures—but, as we will see, does not fully explain why—Rutherford and his Scottish contemporaries would devote their whole lives to defending the convictions that they shared with mainstream Dutch theology against their common enemy, the Arminians.

THE POLEMICAL CONTEXT

Because the *Examen Arminianismi*, as its title suggests, is a treatise principally devoted to examining and refuting the central tenets of Arminianism, it behoves us, before entering upon the intricacies of its arguments, to make preliminary investigation into Arminian cosmogony. What is Arminianism? Where did it come from? And, what are its roots in Scotland? These are some of the questions to which we hope to formulate answers, in order that we might lay the necessary groundwork for what will follow in the remainder of the study.

The system of thought known as Arminianism derives its name from the Dutch theologian James Arminius. Its main ideas, however, as Carl Bangs has helpfully reminded us, do not originate with its namesake in the Netherlands but have a 'more diffuse source'. Not only do previous Dutch thinkers, like Dirk Volckertz Coornhert (1522-1590), Johannes à Lasco (1499-1560), Johannes Utenhove (1510-1565), and Martin Micronius (1522-1559) aid in the development of Arminian theology,[58] but many of the central themes of Arminianism can be traced back even to the early centuries of the Christian church. Yet, in spite of this prior influence, it is not until Arminius that these themes come together to form a comprehensive system and to initiate profound controversy within the Reformed Church in Holland. After the death of Arminius in 1609, this controversy escalated even further when his disciples published their Remonstrance of 1610, containing five articles directed against what they perceived to be the most noxious of high-Calvinist doctrines: absolute predestinarianism, limited atonement, and the perseverance of the

---

[58] C. Bangs, 'Arminius as a Reformed Theologian', in *The Heritage of John Calvin*, ed. J.H. Bratt (Grand Rapids, MI: Eerdmans, 1973), pp. 212-14. On Arminius and Arminianism, see C. Bangs, *Arminius: A Study in the Dutch Reformation* (Nashville, TN: Abingdon Press, 1971); A.W. Harrison, *Arminianism* (London: Duckworth, 1937); and idem, *The Beginnings of Arminianism to the Synod of Dort* (London: University of London, 1926).

saints. These five articles taught that, (1) God elects unto salvation those fallen men and women who believe in him and persevere in their faith and rejects those who do not; (2) Christ universally obtains the pardon for the sins of all people, the benefit of which only the faithful will enjoy; (3) men and women cannot save themselves but must look instead to grace to accomplish this feat; (4) co-operating grace is necessary for men and women to begin and to persevere in faith; and (5) true believers can ultimately fall away from grace and lose their faith completely and utterly.[59] These articles triggered, among other things, the convening of the Synod of Dort in 1618, which attempted to squelch the rapidly increasing Remonstrant movement and to set forth its own set of assertions—or canons—summarizing its own doctrines, each the obverse of the Arminian articles. Rather than squelching the insurgence, however, Dort and the contra-Remonstrants appear to have had the opposite effect. By the close of this synod, Arminianism had apparently become so commonplace in the Netherlands that 'not onely the Schooles of the Low-countries [were] filled with the noise' of it 'but also the Streetes, Barbers shops, and Tavernes'.[60]

The phenomenon of Arminianism was not confined simply to the 'Low-countries', however. England, too, had its share of controversy involving the Arminian doctrines of conditional predestination and human free will. In fact, many of the views that would later be censured at Dort were first disputed within the church in England in the mid-1590s, some twenty-three years before Dort ever convened. In 1595, William Barrett preached a sermon in Cambridge in which he challenged a list of six principles belligerently introduced by William Whitaker (1548-1595) as 'bastions against the spread of Pelagian heresy'.[61] Barrett, following the lead of his teacher Peter Baro (1534-1599)—the Lady Margaret Professor of Divinity at Cambridge—openly rejected the absolute predestination of Calvin, Theodore Beza (1519-1605), Jerome Zanchi (1516-1590), and Franciscus Junius (1545-1602) and advocated, instead, a semi-Pelagian view, in which predestination was conditional upon human free choice.[62] The Calvinist party, led by William Whitaker and William Perkins (1558-1602), responded and, with the help of John Whitgift (c.1530-1604), Archbishop of Canterbury, formulated the Lambeth Articles and succeeded in imposing them upon all at Cambridge. The eventual result was that both Baro and Barrett were removed from the university—Baro in 1596; Barrett a year later in 1597. The threat to Calvinist hegemony in England was stamped out

---

[59] Harrison, *Arminianism*, pp. 49-50. The fifth article originally indicated an uncertainty as to whether or not true believers could actually fall away from grace. This was later modified to reflect the above reading.

[60] P. Du Moulin, *The Anatomy of Arminianisme* (London, 1620), p. 436.

[61] P.G. Lake, *Moderate Puritans and the Elizabethan Church* (Cambridge: Cambridge University, 1982), pp. 203-4.

[62] Cf. Lake, *Moderate Puritans*, pp. 201-2; with 'Peter Baro's Summary of Three Opinions Concerning Predestination', in *WJA*, I, pp. 92-100.

once and for all after only a relatively minor controversy, or so they thought.[63]

From what we have seen, then, it would appear that the first official early-modern controversy involving Arminian doctrines took place in England rather than in the Netherlands. But this does not mean that what would later be called Arminianism had an English rather than a Dutch provenance. The origin of these proto-Arminian views in England, is quite probably—because of the close relationship between England and the Netherlands, which Keith Sprunger dates to the beginning of Elizabeth's reign in 1558—due to the influence of many of the earliest sixteenth-century Dutch advocates of Arminian theology, men like Coornhert for instance.[64] But even if it is not true that proto-Arminianism entered England from the Netherlands, we do know that there was a close association between the pre-Arminians in both countries in the same decade in which the controversy broke out in Cambridge. Richard 'Dutch' Thomson (d. c.1612), Fellow of Clare College, Cambridge, knew Arminius personally in the 1590s and continued to keep tabs on him and on events in the Netherlands until his death.[65] This in itself would seem to suggest that the development of early forms of Arminianism in both countries was at least integrally related with one another. Nicholas Tyacke's research confirms this close association by pointing to the fact that, in 1613, Hugo Grotius (1583-1645) came before the English Court, 'propagandising in person on behalf of the Dutch Arminian or Remonstrant party'.[66] Obviously, there would be no reason for such a visit unless there was some expectation that he would be favorably received. Notwithstanding the controversy of the 1590s, the seeds of pre-Arminian thinking apparently remained in England, kept alive, no doubt, by colleagues in the Netherlands. And these seeds simply needed encouragement to reach full bloom. According to Keith Sprunger, the requisite encouragement came as a result of English involvement in the Synod of Dort. Though the external manifestation of Arminianism had been dealt with decisively in Cambridge in 1595, the seeds of free will-ism had remained alive in British theology and began growing rapidly in post-Dort England.[67]

Unlike the situations in England and the Netherlands, however, it is difficult to ascertain exactly when Arminianism first appeared in Scotland. G.D. Henderson argues that it was present in Scotland at least a year 'before the

---

[63] See H.C. Porter's account of this controversy in *Reformation and Reaction in Tudor Cambridge* (Cambridge: Cambridge University, 1958), pp. 344-90; and N. Tyacke's in *Anti-Calvinists: The Rise of English Arminianism c.1590-1640* (Oxford: Clarendon Press, 1987), pp. 29ff; and Lake's in *Moderate Puritans*, pp. 201-42.

[64] Sprunger, *Dutch Puritanism*, p. 3.

[65] N. Tyacke, 'Arminianism and English Culture', in *Britain and the Netherlands*, vol. 7, *Church and State since the Reformation*, eds. A.C. Duke and C.A. Tamse (The Hague: Martinus Nijhoff, 1981), p. 95.

[66] Tyacke, 'Arminianism and English Culture', p. 95.

[67] Sprunger, *Dutch Puritanism*, p. 356.

Synod of Dort, as we know from the *Duplyes* of the Aberdeen Doctors'.[68] But the Doctors' statement is vague at best, and the extent of the Arminianism that they allude to would seem to be fairly limited. Shortly after Dort, more accusations of Arminianism appear in Scotland. David Calderwood, for instance, complains of the presence of Arminian sympathies within the Scottish kirk in 1619 and, just one year later, indicates that Arminianism had already made inroads into many Scottish universities.[69] And in 1624 the Scottish Privy Council passed a statute decreeing that Arminians are 'enemyis to religioun, authoritie and peace'.[70] But these claims are equally as vague as those noted by the Aberdeen Doctors. Arminianism may well have existed in Scotland prior to or just after the Synod of Dort, but it is not until many years after Dort that demonstrable accusations become commonplace.

In a letter most likely dated to 1631, Rutherford laments the 'deep furrows' of Arminianism in Scotland, and prior to the signing of the National Covenant in 1638, George Gillespie (1613-1648) bemoans that Arminianism is rampant in all the universities. But, perhaps most significantly, Arminianism becomes a common subject of Scottish theological and polemical writing only in the mid-1630s.[71] Scotland has no equivalent to the controversies that occurred in England during the 1590s. Instead, as Robert Baillie (1599-1662) notes,

---

[68] G.D. Henderson, 'Arminianism in Scotland', *London Quarterly and Holborn Review* (October, 1932), p. 493. The Aberdeen Doctors were a group of professors and ministers in Aberdeen steeped in piety and scholarship who opposed the signing of the National Covenant and held to a mild form of episcopacy. Henderson is here referring to their assertions that the Covenanters 'complained of Arminian corruptions, even before *Pearth* Assembly [in 1618]; branding some of the most learned of our Church, with that Aspersion' (see *The Generall Demands, of the Reverend Doctors of Divinitie, and Ministers of the Gospell in Aberdeene, Concerning the Late Covenant, in Scotland. Together with the Answers, Replyes, and Duplyes that followed thereupon, in the Year, 1638* [Aberdeen, 1663], p. 102). On the Aberdeen Doctors, see D. MacMillan, *The Aberdeen Doctors* (London: Hodder and Stoughton, 1909); G.D. Henderson, *The Burning Bush: Studies in Scottish Church History* (Edinburgh: St. Andrew Press, 1957), ch. 5; and B. McLennan, 'Presbyterianism challenged: A study of Catholicism and Episcopacy in the North-East of Scotland, 1560-1650' (unpublished Ph.D. dissertation, University of Aberdeen, 1977), ch. 5.

[69] D. Calderwood, *A Solution of Dr. Resolutus* (Amsterdam, 1619), p. 49; idem, *The Speach of the Kirk of Scotland to her Beloved Children* (Amsterdam, 1620), pp. 47-8.

[70] Henderson, *Religious Life*, p. 88.

[71] *Letters*, p. 64; G. Gillespie, *A Dispute against the English-Popish Ceremonies* (Leiden[?], 1637), p. A3v. For treatises specifically aimed against the Arminians, see, e.g., S. Rutherford, *Exercitationes apologeticae pro divina gratia* (Amsterdam, 1636); idem, *Christ Dying and Drawing Sinners to Himselfe* (London, 1647); idem, *Disputatio scholastica de divina providentia* (Edinburgh, 1649); idem, *A Free Disputation against Pretended Liberty of Conscience* (London, 1649); idem, *Examen Arminianismi* (Utrecht, 1668); R. Baillie, *Ladensium autokatakrisis, the Canterburians Self Conviction* (London, 1641); and idem, *An Antidote against Arminianism* (London, 1641).

ecclesial issues had been at the forefront of every dispute in Scotland since the beginning of the Reformation in 1560. For these reasons, Baillie, whose work provides the closest thing we have to a contemporary history of Arminianism in Scotland, argues that the movement existed only in seed form amongst the Scots until the early 1630s. It was then that William Laud and the 'Canterburians' in England 'began to blow upon these unhappie seeds of Arminius' by lending protection and even favoritism to those who embraced Arminian tenets and by persecuting those who openly rejected them. Once these 'south-winds' entered Scotland, Baillie says, Arminianism 'began to spring amaine' in all the universities.[72]

Thus, according to Robert Baillie and, more recently, G.D. Henderson,[73] Arminianism entered Scotland via their southern neighbor England rather than by way of the Netherlands. And it did not come alone; it came riding on the backs of Laud and his Canterburian party, yoked together with an ecclesial agenda. Just how pervasive this southern migration was in seventeenth-century Scotland is an issue that will be taken up in chapter five, where we will argue that the English ecclesial influence is the distinguishing feature of the Scottish context and that which helps to establish not only the grounds for but also the intensity of Rutherford's opposition to Arminianism.

THE FORMAL CONTEXT

The *Examen* is comprised of lectures drawn up and composed (*conscriptum et dictatum*) by Rutherford for his divinity students at St. Andrews. They were posthumously edited for publication by the Dutch theologian Matthias Nethenus under the direction of Rutherford's closest friend and most intimate disciple (*intimae admissionis discipulus*) Robert MacWard (d. 1681), with the assistance of Robert Traill (1642-1716).[74] The lectures themselves were most likely originally written and delivered by Rutherford sometime between his appointment as professor of divinity in 1639 and his departure for the Westminster Assembly in 1643. This range of dates is suggested by two facts: (1) none of the works cited by Rutherford in the *Examen* has a publication date later than 1639;[75] and (2) Rutherford makes a passing comment in the *Examen*

---

[72] Baillie, *Ladensium autokatakrisis*, pp. 11-12, 21; idem, *Antidote against Arminianism*, pp. 17-18.

[73] Henderson, 'Arminianism in Scotland', p. 493. Henderson's work is largely founded upon the prior seventeenth-century work of Baillie.

[74] See *Examen*, title page; 'Epistola Dedicatoria', p. *2a; and MacWard's 'Foreward'. MacWard is probably Rutherford's most intimate friend and disciple. He studied under Rutherford at St. Andrews in the early years of Rutherford's teaching career, accompanied him to London as his amanuensis during the time of the Westminster Assembly, edited the first edition of his *Letters* (1664), and authored his first biography.

[75] Among the works cited with the latest publication dates are: Thomas Goodwin's *De aggravatione peccati* (1637); 'Laud's Liturgy' (1637); and William Laud's *A Relation*

about 'Arminians in England' seeking to 'gratify the Anglican Bishops, who are *now* in possession of things' in the church—which would appear to suggest that, at the time of Rutherford's writing, William Laud's control of the church was a contemporaneous event.[76]

In spite of their relatively early development, however, the lectures almost certainly would have remained in use throughout Rutherford's career in St. Andrews. Even though it is true that this period marks a hotbed of activity against Arminianism in Scotland, Rutherford is still writing treatises against the Arminians as late as 1649,[77] and his opponents—who would surely have provoked some kind of response from Rutherford—are active in print well into the 1650s.[78] Others of Rutherford's contemporaries, moreover, continue to speak out against Arminian theology into the late 1640s and, some do so even into the mid-1680s, almost seventy years after the Synod of Dort.[79] The point of all this is simply that Rutherford's lectures, although most likely written during his early years in St. Andrews, would have continued to be used by him within the classroom for as long as he was still lecturing, because Arminianism remained a threat in Scotland until well after he died in 1661. That this is so will become even more apparent when we see the grounds for Rutherford's opposition to Arminianism in chapter five.

Fragments from lectures given by Rutherford in 1648 and 1654 and transcribed by at least two of his students still exist in manuscript form today.[80] Both fragments deal with the doctrine of Scripture and were part of Rutherford's lectures on 'the Common Places of Divinity', which was—ever since Andrew Melville's day—the responsibility of the Principal of St. Mary's

---

of *The Conference betweene William Laud,...and Mr. Fisher the Jesuite* (1639). See, e.g., *Examen*, pp. 50-51, 136, 744.

[76] *Examen*, p. 97, emphasis added.

[77] E.g., Rutherford, *A Free Disputation against Pretended Liberty of Conscience tending to Resolve Doubts moved by Mr. John Goodwin, John Baptist, Dr. Jer. Taylor, the Belgick Arminians, Socinians, and other Authors contending for lawlesse Liberty, or licentious Toleration of Sects and Heresies* (London, 1649); and idem, *Disputatio scholastica de divina providentia. Variis praelectionibus...adversus Jesuitas, Arminianos, Socinianos...* (Edinburgh, 1649).

[78] E.g., J. Taylor, *Unum necessarium: or, The Doctrine and Practice of Repentance* (London, 1655).

[79] J. Goodwin (1593-1665), one of the antagonists of Rutherford's *Pretended Liberty of Conscience*, is publicly branded as an Arminian by T. Edwards (1599-1647) in 1646 and, again, in 1647 (A.P.F. Sell, *The Great Debate: Calvinism, Arminianism, and Salvation* [Grand Rapids, MI: Baker Books, 1983], p. 29). For later treatments of Arminianism, see D. Dickson, *Therapeutica sacra* (London, 1656); and idem, *Truth's Victory over Error* (Edinburgh, 1684).

[80] Unpublished manuscripts, National Library of Scotland, Edinburgh, MSS 16475; and St. Andrews University Library, BS 540.R8.

College.[81] Since neither manuscript bears much resemblance to the *Examen* and since Rutherford was not named Principal of St. Mary's until 1648—after he returned from the Westminster Assembly—this would seem to confirm a date for the *Examen* in the early 1640s. It is possible, given the fact that disputations were a normal part of the classroom experience in the 1630s and 40s and the systematic treatment of theology in the *Examen*, that its lectures were also part of Rutherford's series on 'the Common Places of Divinity'.[82] This would help to explain how Rutherford could have continued using the material in the *Examen* in the classroom even into the early 1660s. But it also raises the question of why he would have failed to update the manuscript of the *Examen* with more recently published material in order to bolster his argument. One possible explanation is that he was prevented from doing so because of time constraints. As Principal of St. Mary's College, Rutherford undoubtedly kept a busy schedule. But if we remember that he also shared at least the preaching responsibilities—if not also the pastoral responsibilities—with Robert Blair in the Town Kirk; that he was at the height of his influence after the Westminster Assembly and, thus, would have been in demand in various denominational matters; that he continued to correspond by letter with friends, fellow-pastors, and many of his former parishioners; and that he published five weighty theological treatises during this time, along with a popular testimonial concerning the death of his patron in Anwoth—we can understand how he might have been prevented from updating what was just one part of his lecture notes.[83]

A Note on Methodology

Because this book presents a study in historical theology rather than in systematic theology, it will tend to be more descriptive than prescriptive of Rutherford's theology and his examination of Arminianism. While opportunity is taken from time to time to offer critique of Rutherford's theology, especially where it is most warranted, the goal of this thesis is not so much to determine whether Rutherford is correct in believing as he does so much as to determine what he actually does believe and to engage with modern scholars who have

---

[81] J.K. Cameron, 'Andrew Melville in St. Andrews', in *In Divers Manners: A St. Mary's Miscellany*, ed. D.W.D. Shaw (St. Andrews: St. Mary's College, 1990), pp. 64, 69.

[82] R.G. Cant, *The University of St. Andrews: A Short History* (Edinburgh and London: Scottish Academic Press, 1970), pp. 70-71.

[83] The five treatises and one testimonial are: *A Free Disputation against Pretended Liberty of Conscience* (1649); *Disputatio scholastica de divina providentia* (1649); *The Covenant of Life Opened* (1655); *A Survey of the Survey of that Summe of Church-Discipline Penned by Mr. Thomas Hooker* (1658); and *Influences of the Life of Grace* (1659); and *The Last and Heavenly Speeches and Glorious Departure of John Viscount Kenmuir* (1649).

misunderstood him. At some points, we have offered critiques of modern evaluations of individual doctrines held by Rutherford in order to help develop the fullness of his thinking on a given topic. Because of this and because of the polemical nature of the *Examen*, the current study may come across in some places as not being critical enough of Rutherford's views. In these cases, it must be remembered that our primary intention is to explain and to clarify his thinking rather than to argue that it is right or wrong. The hope is that, by setting forth Rutherford's theology, this study will advance, albeit ever so slightly, the church's knowledge of Rutherford himself and the times in which he lived and ministered, in order that we might learn from him and be better equipped to address the times in which we live.

What follows, then, is an examination of Rutherford's doctrines of prolegomena (chapter two), God (chapter three), and soteriology (chapter four), all set within the context of his dispute with the Arminians. After looking at these things, we will turn our attention to considering the grounds for Rutherford's systematic opposition to Arminianism and draw our study to a close (chapter five). It would easily have been possible to extend the area of concentration further in this project to include any number of relevant topics in Rutherford's thinking *ad infinitum*. We have confined ourselves to an analysis of those areas that comprise the main *loci* of any systematic theology and that reflect the central issues within the Arminian controversy. As has already been mentioned, we give special attention to Rutherford's *Examen Arminianismi* in this process. But we will augment it at times by referring to other works in his *corpus*, both published treatises and unpublished manuscripts, in order to provide as complete and fully orbed a picture of his theology as is possible. And, yet, it needs to be said that the goal of this book is not simply to present Rutherford's theology *in toto* but to tell a story, a seventeenth-century story involving Rutherford and the condition of Calvinist theology in early modern Scotland. Many Rutherford enthusiasts have considered his lifetime to be the apex of Calvinism's golden age. And, in some ways, it may well be. But this study will consider Rutherford's lifetime from a seventeenth-century perspective and tell a different story, one that uncovers the nature of the threat posed to Scottish Calvinism by Arminian theology. Rather than portraying Scottish Calvinism as flourishing in its vitality, we will show it to be wallowing in the mire of self-preservation. In a real sense, early modern Calvinism is not the vibrant Calvinism that many might think, or wish, it to be. It is a Calvinism that was—at least in its own eyes—backed into a corner and standing at the precipice of defeat.

CHAPTER 2

Prolegomena to Theology

The question of where one should begin in the study of theology—its ontological *principium*, God, or its epistemological *principium*, revelation—poses a dilemma that is anything but new within the church. Without God himself, there could be no revelation of any kind. But without divine self-revelation, no one could know God or anything about him. The question is not an easy one to answer.[1] The tendency among the post-Reformation orthodox is to answer it by beginning with the epistemological *principium*;[2] and so we will launch our study of one such post-Reformation theologian at precisely this point. In this chapter, we will examine Rutherford's understanding of God's self-revelation before moving on to explore the ontological *principium*, God himself, in the next chapter. Under the heading of prolegomena to theology, we will evaluate Rutherford's thinking in regard to revelation, natural theology, the role of reason, the necessity of Scripture, and the nature and interpretation of Scripture, all within the context of his dispute with the Arminians.[3]

The importance of beginning with this discussion should be obvious. In the first place, since all theology is built upon certain principles or presuppositions, uncovering them in Rutherford and in the Arminians is necessary in order to measure accurately the character and integrity of their theological systems. In the second place, accusations of rationalism and of a wholesale acceptance of the speculative philosophical ideals of the medieval scholastics and of Aristotle are, according to Brian Armstrong, part and parcel of the Protestant scholastic

---

[1] K.J. Vanhoozer has recently revisited this question from a modern perspective and concluded that rather than claiming an either-or approach, we should choose a 'both-and approach: we interpret Scripture as divine communicative action in order to know God; [and] we let our knowledge of God affect our approach to Scripture' (*First Theology: God, Scripture & Hermeneutics* [Downers Grove, IL: InterVarsity, 2002], p. 38). This 'both-and approach' is very similar to the way both Rutherford and Arminius handle the *principia* of God and Scripture, as we will see in the course of this thesis.
[2] *PRRD*, II, pp. 151-223.
[3] Although the Reformation's emphasis on *sola Scriptura* resulted in a separate *locus* for the doctrine of Scripture that was distinct from general theological prolegomena, it also resulted in a doctrine of Scripture that was logically prior to theology (Scripture was the *principium cognoscendi theologiae*). In this way, the doctrine of Scripture was a formal prolegomenon to theology, and, for this reason, the current study will subsume it under this larger heading. See *PRRD*, II, pp. 151-5.

tradition to which Rutherford belongs. In order to substantiate or refute Armstrong's claims, and to evaluate the continuity of Rutherford's theology with Reformation thought, his presuppositions must be clarified and examined. In the third place, of all the differences between Rutherford and the Arminians, one of the most basic is their disagreement over prolegomenal issues, and, in particular, over the natural epistemological capacities of individuals.[4] For all these reasons, the current study of Rutherford will seek to begin with a discussion of prolegomena. Much of what we do here will lay the foundation for what will follow in the remainder of the study.

Revelation

Theologia archetypa et ectypa

In continuity with medieval scholastic and Reformation thought, Rutherford believes that divine self-revelation is necessary for all human knowledge of God. To adopt the language of Martin Luther (1483-1546), Rutherford's God is *Deus absconditus*, and the only way he can be known by his creatures is for him to become *Deus revelatus*.[5] According to Rutherford—and Luther as well—this is exactly what God has done. But in so revealing himself to his creatures, God has not, for that reason, ceased to be *Deus absconditus*. The creator-creature distinction, in Rutherford's thinking, necessitates that, while God knows himself perfectly and comprehensively, his creatures—who are ontologically derivative—know him only imperfectly and incompletely. Ultimately, God remains incomprehensible for them.

At the heart of this understanding of revelation is the scholastic distinction between *theologia archetypa* and *ectypa*—a distinction which, according to Willem Van Asselt, can be traced to a similar distinction between *theologia in se* and *theologia nostra* in John Duns Scotus (c.1270-1308).[6] The former term, in each case, denotes the infinite knowledge that God has of himself. As its prior name suggests, it is archetypal knowledge and, thus, forms the pattern for ectypal knowledge—the theology which is available to the finite capacities of

---

[4] J.E. Platt, *Reformed Thought and Scholasticism: The Arguments for the Existence of God in Dutch Theology, 1575-1650* (Leiden: E.J. Brill, 1982), pp. 179-201. Platt suggests that the epistemological differences between Calvinists and Arminians form the foundation for other areas of their dispute. While it is no doubt true that prolegomenal issues are fundamental to the Calvinist-Arminian debate, the doctrine of God, as we will see in the next chapter, is even more fundamental.

[5] B. Lohse, *Martin Luther: An Introduction to his Life and Work*, trans. R. Schultz (Philadelphia: Fortress, 1986), p. 171.

[6] W.J. Van Asselt, 'The Fundamental Meaning of Theology: Archetypal and Ectypal Theology in Seventeenth-Century Reformed Thought', *WTJ* 64:2 (Fall 2002), p. 322.

human creatures through divine revelation.⁷ The object of the distinction between archetype and ectype is to convey the idea that our knowledge of God is limited by and subject to divine self-revelation. The discipline of theology can never portray God as he is really and in himself—*Deus absconditus* or *theologia archetypa*. It is limited to *Deus revelatus* or *theologia ectypa*. But, more than this, the distinction between *theologia archetypa et ectypa* also expresses the fact that, in revealing himself to his creatures, God has accommodated himself to their capacities. Because finite creatures are incapable of comprehending the infinite God as he is in himself, God must, to borrow the expression of John Calvin, lisp to his creatures, much as a parent would to his or her child.

Rutherford's reliance upon this scholastic distinction can be seen implicitly in his embrace of the medieval nominalist distinction between *potentia Dei absoluta et ordinata*—which will be discussed in detail in chapter three—and in the emphasis he gives to the difference between creator and creature throughout his theology, which again will be seen graphically in the next chapter. But this is what we should expect to find in Rutherford. As Willem Van Asselt has written, 'discussion of this topic [i.e., of the distinction between *theologia archetypa et ectypa*] can be found in almost all the important dogmatic systems' of the late sixteenth and seventeenth centuries, both Lutheran and Reformed, both British and continental.⁸ Even though it is not present in Rutherford explicitly, it is there nonetheless. And it is present more explicitly in others of Rutherford's contemporaries, like Francis Turretin (1623-1687). In Turretin we can see plainly how this idea is used to convey revelation by way of divine accommodation.⁹

> When God understands anything he understands it for himself, and as he is infinite [*Deus absconditus*], he understands according to infinity [*theologia archetypa*], but when he speaks [*Deus revelatus*] he is not speaking to himself, but to us, that is, in a manner accommodated to our capacity, which is finite [*theologia ectypa*].¹⁰

Martin Klauber has recently argued that Turretin's use of the distinction between *theologia archetypa et ectypa* is instrumental in linking his view of

---

⁷ R.A. Muller, *Dictionary of Latin and Greek Theological Terms: Drawn Principally from Protestant Scholastic Theology* (Grand Rapids, MI: Baker, 1985), pp. 299-301.
⁸ Van Asselt, 'Archetypal and Ectypal Theology', pp. 323-4.
⁹ On Turretin's views, see F. Turretin, *Institutes of Elenctic Theology*, trans. G.M. Giger, ed. J.T. Dennison Jr., 3 vols. (Philipsburg, NJ: P&R, 1992-7), I, p. 3 (1.1.9); I, p. 151 (2.19.8); and T. Phillips, 'Francis Turretin's Idea of Theology and its Bearing upon his Doctrine of Scripture' (unpublished Ph.D. dissertation, Vanderbilt University, 1986), especially pp. 123-39.
¹⁰ F. Turretin, *The Doctrine of Scripture: Locus 2 of Institutio theologiae elencticae*, ed. and trans. J.W. Beardslee III (Grand Rapids, MI: Baker, 1981), pp. 202-3.

accommodation with that of Calvin. Rather than seeing accommodation—or, actually, the lack of it in the writings of the post-Reformation period—as evidence of discontinuity between Reformation and post-Reformation thought, as Brian Armstrong and others have,[11] Klauber has argued that this distinction plays an important role in demonstrating substantial theological continuity between them.[12] Rutherford's implicit embrace of this distinction confirms that he, like Turretin, stands in substantial continuity with Calvin as well. But it also, as we will see in the next chapter, confirms that he stands in fundamental opposition to the Arminians, who apply this distinction in a wholly different manner than do Rutherford and the Reformed.

John Webster has, perhaps most recently, issued a significant warning that would seem *prima facie* to be aimed against the view of divine revelation advocated by the distinction between *theologia archetypa et ectypa*. Webster advises that '[r]evelation is not to be thought of as the communication of arcane information or hidden truths, as if in revelation God were lifting the veil on something other than his own self and indicating it to us'.[13] Rather, as Colin Gunton has expressed, 'the doctrine of revelation should be understood as a function of the doctrine of salvation'.[14] But, having said this, it is not at all evident, upon deeper reflection, that Rutherford's conception of revelation differs all that much from the aforementioned statements of Webster and Gunton. In the first place, Rutherford in no way denies the express Johannine teaching that Jesus Christ is the Word of God and, as such, divine revelation. In a way typical of the post-Reformation orthodox and also of Calvin, he acknowledges that Christ is the 'essential Word' of God, while Scripture is the written Word. The two are related, for Rutherford, albeit not in the sense that the latter is simply a derivative of and, thus, only a witness to, the former. They are related in that the former, Jesus Christ, is the principal author of all prophecy. Jesus teaches us 'the quhole [whole] will of God, both by himself in the dayes of his flesh, and by sending propheits and apostles for that effect'.[15] Not only is Jesus himself revelation from God in his incarnate state, but he is also chiefly responsible for the same, before, during, and after his incarnation.

But more than this, as Willem Van Asselt has argued, the post-Reformation

---

[11] Armstrong, *Calvinism and the Amyraut Heresy*, p. 173. Cf. J.B. Rogers and D.K. McKim, *The Authority and Interpretation of the Bible: An Historical Approach* (San Francisco: Harper & Row, 1979), p. 177.

[12] M.I. Klauber, 'Francis Turretin on Biblical Accommodation: Loyal Calvinist Or Reformed Scholastic?', *WTJ* 55:1 (Spring, 1993), pp. 73-86, especially 78-80.

[13] J. Webster, *Holy Scripture: A Dogmatic Sketch* (Cambridge: Cambridge University, 2003), p. 14.

[14] C. Gunton, *A Brief Theology of Revelation* (Edinburgh: T&T Clark, 1995), p. 111.

[15] *Catachisme*, pp. 179, 182. Cf. *Institutes* I.xiii.7-9, pp. 129-34. For more on this in the post-Reformation era, see the discussion in R. A. Muller, 'Christ—the Revelation or the Revealer? Brunner and Reformed Orthodoxy on the Doctrine of the Word of God', *JETS* 26:3 (September, 1983), pp. 312-15.

understanding of the concept *theologia ectypa* is cast within clear Christological and soteriological frameworks. Relying upon Franciscus Junius—who is perhaps the first Protestant to use the distinction between *theologia archetypa et ectypa*—as his prototype, Van Asselt demonstrates that post-Reformation theology characteristically distinguished between three forms of *theologia ectypa*: the theology of union in the person of Christ, the theology of vision *coram Deo*, and the theology of revelation to pilgrims *in via*. Because Christ is the God-man, who possesses both archetypal and ectypal knowledge and who, for the salvation of humankind, endured humiliation *in via* followed by exaltation *coram Deo*, he is, therefore, the *principium* or source of both forms of human theology, the theology of vision and the theology of revelation.[16] The person of Christ and his salvific work thus form the context and the basis for revelation.

In the second place, Rutherford, in continuity with the Augustinian tradition, understands theology to be a theoretico-practical discipline but with the ultimate emphasis on the practical. Following English Ramists—like William Ames (1576-1633) and William Perkins—and Dutch Second Reformation theologians—most notably, Gisbertus Voetius, Johannes Maccovius (1588-1644), and Johannes Hoornbeeck (1617-1666)—and continental theologians—like Amandus Polanus von Polansdorf (1561-1610)—Rutherford divides theology into *theoria* or 'faith' and *praxis* or 'obedience', and places the accent on the latter.[17] The goal of theology, for Rutherford, is fundamentally practical—à la Peter Ramus' (1515-1572) well-known definition of theology as 'the doctrine of living well' before God.[18] It is, in the words of the Westminster Shorter Catechism, 'to glorify God, and to enjoy him for ever'.[19] Like the Puritans in general, Rutherford emphasizes the importance of *theoria* in this,

---

[16] Van Asselt, 'Archetypal and Ectypal Theology', pp. 330-31.

[17] See, e.g., W. Ames, *Medulla ss. theologiae* (London, 1630), p. 1; W. Perkins, *A Golden Chaine*, ch. 1, in *The Workes of that Famous and Worthy Minister of Christ in the Universitie of Cambridge, Mr. William Perkins*, 3 vols. (Cambridge, 1616-18), I, p. 11; G. Voetius, *Ta asketika sive Exercitia pietatis in usum juventutis academicae nunc edita. Addita est, ob materiam affinitatem, Oratio de pietate cum scientia conjungenda habita anno 1634* (Gorinchem, 1664); J. Hoornbeeck, *Theologia practica*, 2 vols (Utrecht, 1663-6); J. Maccovius, *Loci communes theologici* (Amsterdam, 1658), I; and A. Polanus, *Partitiones theologicae* (London, 1591), title page, p. 1. Cf. with Rutherford's twofold division of theology into faith and obedience in *Catachisme*, pp. 161, 225. The beginning—as well as the overall structure—of Polanus' *Partitiones* is very similar to Rutherford's catechism.

[18] P. Ramus, *De religione Christiana* (Frankfurt, 1576), p. 6. On the link between Ramus and Puritan theology, see K.L. Sprunger, 'Ames, Ramus, and the Method of Puritan Theology', *Harvard Theological Review* 59:2 (April, 1966), pp. 133-51, especially 145-51.

[19] *WCF*, 287. This emphasis is again reflected in Polanus, *Syntagma theologiae Christianae* (Geneva, 1617), Synopsis Libri I.

but not as an end in itself, only as a means to the practical end of joyful obedience. This ensures that Rutherford will say that revelation is, in Gunton's words, 'a function of the doctrine of salvation', or, perhaps more accurately, that it is *unto* salvation. Revelation is not merely the communication of information in Rutherford's thinking. It is that, to be sure. But it is more than that. If *theologia ectypa* is truly patterned after *theologia archetypa*, then revelation cannot merely be factual information about God. It is God communicating himself *purposively*. Though Rutherford would not, as Webster does, define revelation as reconciliation, he would most certainly agree that the 'knowledge of God in his revelation is no mere cognitive affair: it is to know *God* and therefore to love and fear the God who appoints us to fellowship with himself, and not merely to entertain God as a mental object, however exalted'.[20]

Natural and Supernatural Revelation

God's revelation of himself to his creatures—or, *theologia ectypa in via*—takes two basic forms in Rutherford's thinking: general or 'natural revelation', which is rooted in the created order and is naturally available to all people; and supernatural revelation, which transcends the simple created order itself.[21] Natural revelation is laid open to all people in 'foure bookes': (1) the 'booke of [the] creation of the Heavens and [God's] workes, *Psalme* 19.1'; (2) the 'booke of ordinary providence', which Rutherford calls a 'Chronicle or Diurnall [Journal] of a God-head and a Testimony that there is a God, *Acts* 14.17. *Acts* 17.27'; (3) the 'booke of the extraordinary workes of God, and some report of the true God, upon occasion carried to Nations without the borders of the visible church...*Josh.* 2.10'; and (4) the 'booke of mans conscience, *Rom.* 2.14-15'.[22] Supernatural revelation, on the other hand, is presented to the creature both scripturally and extra-scripturally. Scripturally speaking, supernatural revelation has objective and subjective components. Objectively, it is God's act of giving Scripture. God actively discloses 'his will and Gospell', which was previously hidden, 'to *Prophets* and *Apostles*' as 'the writers of Canonnick scripture'. But it is also the literary product of this divine act—i.e., Scripture itself. Understood in this way, the Bible is merely a passive or 'literal' and '*Grammatical*' revelation.[23] Before it can move beyond a revelation in letter alone, there must be a subjective work of the Holy Spirit, or, what Rutherford

---

[20] Webster, *Holy Scripture*, p. 16.

[21] *Examen*, pp. 83-4, 629. Both forms of revelation are supernatural in the sense that they are from God, but the latter is particularly so, in that it is a form of revelation 'above the natural order'. Cf. Muller, *Dictionary*, pp. 265-6.

[22] *HOC*, 10-11. Rogers and McKim have claimed that Rutherford actually denies nature to be a source of revelation (*Authority and Interpretation of the Bible*, p. 203). From the above, however, it should be obvious that their contention is incorrect.

[23] *Examen*, p. 328; *SA*, p. 39.

and many of his post-Reformation peers—using the so-called 'more "dynamic" or "existential" language of the Reformers'—refer to as subjective supernatural revelation.[24] This entails 'a spiritual opening and declaration of the literal sense' of Scripture to the individual by the Holy Spirit.[25]

Extra-scripturally speaking, supernatural revelation can refer to Jesus Christ, the 'essential Word' of God. But it can also apply to the '*Testimony of the* [Holy] *Spirit*' and to the dreams and predictions of godly men. Since we have already discussed the first of these, we will confine our discussion here to the last two. According to Rutherford, there is a 'special internal revelation', in which the Spirit testifies to the spirit of the elect individual that he or she is indeed a child of God. No person's name is written in Scripture. The Bible does not anywhere say whether 'John' or 'Anne' will be saved. The Holy Spirit alone, by special internal revelation, reveals this to the individual.[26] But, in addition to this, Rutherford—perhaps rather surprisingly to some—acknowledges that the dreams and predictions of godly men that come true are also to be considered supernatural revelation. Here he has in mind such things as this:

> *John Husse, Wickeliefe, Luther,* have foretold things to come, and they certainly fell out, and in our nation of *Scotland, M. George Wishart* foretold that *Cardinall Beaton* should not come out alive at the Gates of the Castle of *St. Andrewes,* but that he should dye a shamefull death, and he was hanged over the window that he did look out at, when he saw the *man of God* burnt.

Now, Rutherford is quick to qualify this. These men did not suggest that their predictions were equally as binding as Scripture; nor did they believe them to be infallibly accurate; nor did they necessarily advocate the ways in which they were brought to fruition (especially so in the case of Wishart and Beaton). Their predictions were by and large in accord with the 'generall rule' of Scripture, which teaches that '*Evill shall hunt the wicked man*'. They were uttered by those who were mature Christians, 'sound in the faith', zealous for the cause of Christ.[27] Thus, although Rutherford calls them revelation, he does not place them on an equal plane with the inspired Scriptures. Before the writing of Scripture, however, godly men like '*Seth, Enoch, Noah,* and *Abraham*...had revelations instead of the Word'.[28] These pre-scriptural revelations, unlike the dreams and predictions of godly men living after the close of the canon, are on an equal plane with the inspired Scriptures.

All this being said, our discussion of revelation is not so much interested in the ways in which God has revealed himself as whether and how his creatures

---

[24] *PRRD*, II, p. 99.
[25] *Examen*, pp. 83-4, 328.
[26] *SA*, pp. 39-41; *Examen*, pp. 22.
[27] *SA*, pp. 42-4.
[28] *Examen*, p. 115.

can receive his revelation. In other words, what we are chiefly concerned with is this: can the creature come to know God by way of his divine self-revelation? And if so, how? Is it possible for an individual to know God or to know things about him by way of natural revelation? Or, is supernatural revelation necessary for all theology? It is to answering these questions that we now turn, in order that we might uncover and evaluate some of the basic epistemological differences that form the backdrop to Rutherford's conflict with the Arminians.

Natural Theology

All one has to do is think about natural theology in contemporary theological dialogue and Karl Barth's rejection of it immediately springs to mind. His resounding 'Nein!' to Emil Brunner's more positive reception is reminiscent of Luther's repeated invective against Ulrich Zwingli (1484-1531) at Marburg, 'Hoc est corpus meum!' Barth states that 'we must learn again to understand revelation as *grace* and grace as *revelation* and therefore turn away all "true" or "false" *theologia naturalis* by ever making new decisions and being ever controverted anew'. He then goes on to say that 'if one occupies oneself with real theology one can pass by so-called natural theology only as one would pass by an abyss into which it is inadvisable to step if one does not want to fall'.[29]

If we are to use the Barth-Brunner debate as a grid through which to read Rutherford's own understanding of natural theology, we will find that Rutherford sides with Brunner in viewing natural theology much more positively than did Barth. For Rutherford, natural theology not only exists, but it serves at least two important functions as well, as we will see—it renders all people without excuse before the divine tribunal; and it acts as an instrument in apologetics. Such a positive view of *theologia naturalis* is not peculiar to Rutherford, however. It is the predominant understanding from at least John Calvin through the time of the Westminster Assembly. In fact, it is Calvin's notion of the *duplex cognitio Dei*—the twofold knowledge of God as creator and redeemer—that can be said, without great exaggeration, to set the paradigm for the thinking of not only his Reformation contemporaries but also his post-Reformation successors on natural theology.[30]

---

[29] E. Brunner and K. Barth, *Natural Theology: Comprising 'Nature and Grace' by Professor Dr. Emil Brunner and the Reply 'No!' by Dr. Karl Barth*, trans. P. Fraenkel (1946; Eugene, OR: Wipf & Stock, 2002), pp. 71, 75. Barth's rejection of natural theology is, as he himself says, a 'hermeneutical rule' that is forced upon him by, among other things, his understanding of the transcendence of God and his definition of revelation as something more akin to reconciliation. Ibid., p. 76. See also Barth, *CD*, I/1, p. 134.

[30] The current author has attempted to demonstrate this by tracing the *duplex cognitio Dei* through the Reformation and post-Reformation periods and into the Westminster Confession of Faith (J.V. Fesko and G.M. Richard, 'Natural Theology and the Westminster Confession', vol. 3, *The Westminster Confession into the 21st Century*, ed.

The duplex cognitio Dei

Rutherford, like Calvin, distinguishes between the knowledge of God as creator and judge and the knowledge of God as redeemer. The former he defines as a natural knowledge of God by which every person 'knoweth ther is a God, and that sinne is forbiddin'.[31] One way this natural knowledge is received by the creature is through the works of creation and providence. The first three 'bookes' of general revelation are 'laid open...to all nations', such that all people without exception know God.[32] But there is also, according to Rutherford, another way in which natural knowledge is received by the creature, and this way is more explicit in his writings—the *imago Dei*. By virtue of creating men and women in his own image, God has placed a knowledge of himself within their minds and consciences. In regard to the former faculty, Rutherford states plainly that 'knowledge in the mind is part of the image of God'.[33] This means that no person is born into the world with a mind as a *tabula rasa*—which is, as we will soon see, a position contrary to that taken up by the Socinians and many later Arminians. Instead, according to Rutherford, speaking in true Calvinian fashion, all people have an internal awareness of God, a *sensus deitatis* or *habitus deitatis*, which manifests itself necessarily in worship of one form or another. All people 'worship some divine power [*numen*] and have some religion, which is a sign that they acknowledge God'.[34] '[T]here is no people so barbarous', Archbishop James Ussher (1581-1656) adds, 'but they will have some forme of Religion', and will acknowledge some form of deity, which is proof that they know God.[35]

J.L. Duncan III (Fearn, Ross-shire: Mentor, forthcoming 2008). On the *duplex cognitio Dei* in Calvin and in the post-Reformation period, see *Institutes* I.ii.1, p. 40; and R.A. Muller, '"*Duplex cognitio dei*" in the Theology of Early Reformed Orthodoxy', *SCJ* 10:2 (1979), pp. 51-61.

[31] *Catachisme*, p. 174.

[32] *HOC*, pp. 10-11.

[33] *Examen*, pp. 139, 452.

[34] *Examen*, pp. 326-7. Calvin speaks of a universal *semen religionis*, *sensus divinitatis*, or *sensus deitatis*, which consists of a divine knowledge placed by God within the mind, and is attested by the universal human tendency toward idol worship. *Institutes* I.iii.1, pp. 43-4; I.iii.3, pp. 45-7; and I.iv.1, pp. 47-8; and idem, *Romans and Thessalonians*, trans. R. Mackenzie, *Calvin's New Testament Commentaries*, eds. D.W. Torrance and T.F. Torrance (Edinburgh and London: Oliver and Boyd, 1960), p. 32.

[35] J. Ussher, *A Body of Divinitie, or the Summe and Substance of Christian Religion* (London, 1645), p. 3. Archbishop Ussher is one of the most important figures in the development of Westminster theology. He was summoned to be a member of the Assembly but never participated in its proceedings. As A. Mitchell has indicated, however, the Assembly 'gave unmistakable proof of its high regard for him' by relying heavily upon the Irish Articles—which are believed to have been prepared by him—and upon his *Body of Divinitie*, in its formulation of the Confession and catechisms (A.F. Mitchell, *The Westminster Assembly: Its History and Standards* [London: James Nisbet,

In regard to the latter faculty, the conscience, Rutherford says that it is an 'Ambassador and deputy Judge from God' to convict individuals of sin and continually to testify to them 'that there is a God'.[36] Within the conscience specifically God has written the same 'naturall Theology, that we had in our first creation':

> in the Cabinet [i.e., the conscience], the naturall habit of Morall principles lodgeth, the Register of the common notions left in us by nature, the Ancient Records and Chronicles which were in Adams time, the Law of Nature of two volumes, one of the first Table, that there is a God, that he createth and governeth all things, that there is but one God, infinitely good, most just rewarding the Evill and the good; and of the second Table, as to love of our Parents, obey Superiours, to hurt no man, the acts of humanity; All these are written in the soule, in deep letters, yet the Inke is dimme and old, and therefore this light is like the Moone swimming through watery clouds, often under a shadow, and yet still in the firmament.[37]

Thus, for Rutherford, the law of nature, which is comprised of both the first and second tables of the Decalogue, was written on Adam's conscience before he fell into sin. And although Adam's fall into sin, as recorded in Genesis 3, affected Adam himself and all who had him as their federal representative (i.e., all people) to such a degree that all by nature became 'dead in sins and inept to a right and good understanding, discerning, probing, believing, and doing in every spiritual thing' apart from the regenerating work of the Holy Spirit, this does not mean that the image of God was wholly effaced. The law of nature remains in the consciences of all people after the fall.[38] Even though 'the Inke is dimme and old' and is 'like the Moone swimming through watery clouds, often under a shadow', it is, nevertheless, written 'in deep letters' and is 'still in the firmament'.

In this way, all people know God naturally both as creator and as judge. They know that 'there is a God, that he createth and governeth all things', and 'that there is but one God, infinitely good, most just rewarding the Evill and the good'.[39] The effects of Adam's sin, however, have corrupted not only their consciences but their minds, wills, and emotions as well. Consistent with the

---

1883], pp. xvi, 98, 117, 372-3, 422-3). Both Ussher and his *Body of Divinitie* are, therefore, quite important in understanding Rutherford.

[36] *Examen*, pp. 131, 326.

[37] *Divine Right*, p. 66; *PLC*, p. 7.

[38] *Examen*, p. 86. Rutherford highlights the federal relationship we have with Adam by speaking of us as 'legally in Adams loins' as well as 'naturally'. He sees three aspects to the corruption passed to us from Adam: 'a partaking' of Adam's first sin, a tarnishing of the image of God, and a 'bent-nesse' of our nature toward sin (*COL*, II, p. 234). But, while the divine image has been tarnished, it has not been completely eclipsed (*Examen*, p. 227).

[39] *PLC*, p. 7.

post-lapsarian voluntarism of Calvin and the Reformation,[40] Rutherford believes that the natural truth contained in the minds of all people by virtue of their being created in the image of God is suppressed by the rebellion inherent in their wills and affections after the fall. All people are thus utterly powerless in and of themselves 'to perform that which pleases God'. Their natural knowledge of God, although it is real, is 'weak and insufficient' for salvation. In and of themselves, people can never come to a saving knowledge of God; they are 'blind' and 'dull' in sin.[41] A natural knowledge of God is not enough. Salvation requires a supernatural knowledge, a knowledge of God as redeemer, which can only be secured by the Holy Spirit working in and through Scripture.[42]

Rutherford is not alone in his understanding of the *duplex cognitio Dei*. Not only is this idea found in Calvin, but it is also found in Calvin's contemporaries Wolfgang Musculus (1497-1563) and Peter Martyr Vermigli (c.1500-1562), albeit with slight nuances. Musculus, for instance, actually advocates a threefold knowledge of God in which he adds the testimony of the Holy Spirit to Calvin's *duplex cognitio*.[43] Vermigli plainly embraces the twofold knowledge of God but reserves natural knowledge for the learned alone. 'Scripture', he says citing Romans 1.19, 'distinguishes wise men and philosophers from the crude and ignorant masses.' Only the former are capable, in his estimation, of attaining to a natural knowledge of God.[44] Despite these nuances in their thinking, both Musculus and Vermigli are in agreement with Calvin and Rutherford that there is a natural knowledge, which is insufficient for salvation. A supernatural knowledge alone can secure this for the individual. After the Reformation, Calvin's *duplex cognitio Dei* continues to be used in succeeding generations of Reformed orthodox discussions of natural theology. Many of Rutherford's predecessors—e.g., William Perkins, Amandus Polanus, Pierre Du Moulin (1568-1658), and James Ussher—and many his contemporaries at the Westminster Assembly—e.g., William Twisse (1578-1646), Anthony Tuckney (1599-1670), and Thomas Goodwin (1600-1680)—explicitly rely on this distinction in their writings.[45]

---

[40] This idea will be discussed in greater detail in the section entitled 'God's Work of Regeneration' below.
[41] *Examen*, pp. 324-5; *HOC*, pp. 11, 16. Cf. *Examen*, p. 139; *COL*, p. 21.
[42] *Catachisme*, pp. 161, 174; *SA*, p. 310.
[43] W. Musculus, *Common Places of Christian Religion*, trans. J. Man (London, 1578), p. 3.
[44] P.M. Vermigli, *In Epistolam S. Pauli Apostoli ad Romanos* (Basel, 1558), pp. 30, and 30-33; idem, *Philosophical Works*, ed. and trans. J.C. McLelland, *The Peter Martyr Library*, vol. 4 (Kirksville, MO: Sixteenth Century Journal, 1996), pp. 19, and 18-27. See also, idem, *The Common Places of the most famous and renowned Divine Doctor Peter Martyr*, ed. and trans. A. Marten (London, 1583), I.ii, pp. 10-17.
[45] Perkins, *Workes*, I, pp. 144, 154, 159, 517; II, pp. 280, 282, 459; Polanus, *Syntagma*, 1.10, p. 12; 9.7, p. 594; P. Du Moulin, *De cognitione Dei tractatus* (Hagae-Comitis,

While Rutherford's Reformation forebears and his post-Reformation peers embrace this understanding of the *duplex cognitio Dei*, the same cannot be said for Arminius and his later disciples. The knowledge distinction, as it is described above, marks a clear point of contention between Rutherford and the Arminians. According to Rutherford, Arminianism collapses the natural knowledge of God into the supernatural by its doctrine of prevenient or universal grace. Because this grace is bestowed by God in creation and sustained by him in providence, even after the fall,[46] it eliminates the possibility of the natural knowledge of God. All knowledge of the divine is supernatural, because it is made possible by the universal grace of God. It is for this reason that Rutherford can say that '*Arminius* calls *supernatural grace* a remnant of the image of God present in us after the fall'; that Simon Episcopius (1583-1643) '*ascribes*' the basic knowledge that God exists '*to grace, not to nature*'; and that other Remonstrants 'teach that the law of nature, a good upbringing [*educatio*], an excellent character, and the remnant of the image of God in people, are *grace*'.[47]

As a result of their collapsing the knowledge distinction through their understanding of universal grace, the Arminians—in Rutherford's view—grant men and women too much power in coming to a knowledge of God apart from the special work of the Holy Spirit and, thus, open themselves up to the charge of Pelagianism. In the *Examen*, Rutherford even goes so far as to offer no less than eleven points at which Arminian theology reflects the perceived errors of Pelagians and Semi-Pelagians.[48] While the accuracy of Rutherford's claims will be examined in more detail in chapter four, especially in connection with our discussion of grace and free will, the important thing to note here is not so much whether Rutherford's claims are warranted as the fact that they are made in the first place. Rutherford perceives profound differences between himself and the Arminians—differences that are at least similar to those between

---

1631), pp. 25-6, 36-7, 126, 128, 161-7; Ussher, *Body of Divinitie*, pp. 5-6, 136, 143-4; W. Twisse, *A Treatise of Mr. Cottons, Clearing certain Doubts Concerning Predestination. Together with an Examination Thereof* (London, 1646); p. 213; idem, *A Discovery of D. Jacksons Vanitie* (n.p., 1631), p. 654; A. Tuckney, *Eight Letters of Dr. Anthony Tuckney, and Dr. Benjamin Whichcote*, in *Moral and Religious Aphorisms, Collected from the Manuscript Papers of the Reverend and Learned Doctor Whichcote*, ed. S. Salter (London: Pater-Noster-Row, 1753), pp. 20, 69; T. Goodwin, *The Works of Thomas Goodwin, D.D.*, 12 vols (Edinburgh: James Nichol, 1861-1866), I, p. 388; VI, p. 375; X, p. 144.

[46] *WJA*, II, pp. 362-4, 366-8; III, pp. 109-19. See also, R.A. Muller, *God, Creation and Providence in the Thought of Jacob Arminius: Sources and Directions of Scholastic Protestantism in the Era of Early Orthodoxy* (Grand Rapids, MI: Baker, 1991), pp. 244-6. Prevenient grace will resurface again in this and in the next two chapters, where it will be discussed in more detail.

[47] *Examen*, pp. 325, 358.

[48] *Examen*, pp. 357-62.

Augustine and Pelagius in the early church—and he reacts against them with vitriol, piling up eleven arguments to sustain his diatribe.

The Role of Reason and the Necessity of Supernatural Knowledge

As previously mentioned, Brian Armstrong has argued that the Protestant scholasticism of which Rutherford is a part placed great emphasis on the role of reason in developing its theology. In general, he says, this emphasis took the form of an increased reliance on logical deduction and syllogistic reasoning. But, more significantly, he claims that reason assumed an 'equal standing with faith in theology, thus jettisoning some of the authority of revelation'.[49] Armstrong's contentions fall within a steady stream of similar sentiment expressed by scholars since at least F.A.G. Tholuck's two works, *Vorgeschichte des Rationalismus* (1861) and *Geschichte des Rationalismus* (1865). This sentiment has placed an important share of the burden for Enlightenment rationalism squarely on the shoulders of post-Reformation protestant scholasticism.[50] In order to evaluate these assertions as they apply specifically to Rutherford, and in order to help us in determining Rutherford's relationship to his Reformation predecessors, we need to examine the role of reason in his thinking. When we do so, particularly in the context of Rutherford's fight against Arminianism, we will see that Armstrong's allegations are more appropriate in describing the Arminians than Rutherford.

The differences between Rutherford and the Arminians over the role of reason in theology develop roughly along the lines of the crisis in Utrecht between Christian Aristotelians Gisbertus Voetius and Martin Schoock (1614-1669) and René Descartes (1596-1650).[51] Following in the Christian-Aristotelian and anti-Cartesian tradition exemplified in Voetius and Schoock, Rutherford believes both in the usefulness of reason and in its limitation. The natural person, as we saw earlier in our discussion of natural theology, is capable of right reason and, thus, of knowing God naturally by virtue of being created in the divine image. But this natural use of reason, like the natural knowledge of God, is limited. It is 'dimme and old' and 'often under a shadow',[52] such that it never leads to salvation but merely serves to render individuals inexcusable (*inexcusatiores*) before the divine tribunal for failing to

---

[49] Armstrong, *Calvinism and the Amyraut Heresy*, p. 32.
[50] See, e.g., P. Althaus, *Die Prinzipien der deutschen reformierten Dogmatik im Zeitalter er aristotelischen Scholastik* (Leipzig: Deichert, 1914); Bizer, *Frühorthodoxie und Rationalismus*; and Barth, *CD*, II/1. Cf. O. Weber, *Foundations of Dogmatics*, trans. D.L. Guder, 2 vols. (Grand Rapids, MI: Eerdmans, 1981), I, p. 118.
[51] On the crisis in Utrecht, see *La querelle d'Utrecht*, textes établis, traduits et annotés par T. Verbeek (Paris: Les impressions nouvelles, 1988); and T. Verbeek, 'Descartes and the Problem of Atheism: The Utrecht Crisis', *NAvK* 71:2 (1991), pp. 211-23.
[52] *PLC*, p. 7. In *Examen*, p. 605, Rutherford states that the 'dictates of natural reason are not clear and plain'.

worship God as they ought.⁵³ The post-lapsarian human will suppresses both the natural use of reason and the natural knowledge of God, with the result that the individual is '*by nature dead in sins*...and incapable [*ne quidem sufficientes*] of knowing any good thing'.⁵⁴ He or she, thus, has a *sic et non* relationship, so to speak, with reason and divine knowledge, as William Perkins classically explains: 'the same man, that by the light of nature thinketh there is a God, may by that corruption and darknes of mind that came by *Adams* fall, thinke there is no God'.⁵⁵ The individual may perceive the divine naturally or by the use of reason, but he or she will never embrace God savingly, nor will he or she want to. Using traditional Augustinian language, as Rutherford himself does, this means that each person is *non posse non peccare* and must look beyond the natural to know God savingly.⁵⁶

The insufficiency of reason and the natural knowledge of God in spiritual things signifies that Scripture is necessary. Contrary to the grandfather of English deism, Lord Herbert of Cherbury (1583-1648), the doctrine of innate ideas does not lead to a denial of the necessity of supernatural revelation, not for Rutherford and the Reformed anyway. 'Had conscience been a faithful register', Rutherford says, 'there should have been no need of a written Bible'. But now the 'Lord [has] lippened [trusted] more to a dead paper than to a living man's soul', because the conscience has not been 'a good Bible'.⁵⁷

More than signifying that Scripture is necessary, however, the insufficiency of reason also signifies that a special work of the Holy Spirit is necessary, because post-lapsarian natural reason is incapable of understanding Scripture on its own. Salvation—or, the knowledge of God as redeemer—requires not only Scripture but also the Holy Spirit giving us a '*spiritual clarity*' (*evidentia*), infusing (*superinfusus*) our understandings with a '*new power*', and anointing us with the 'eye salve of Christ'.⁵⁸ To borrow Calvin's words, the individual must be given 'spectacles' to enable him or her to see and understand true theology in Scripture and to obtain salvation.⁵⁹ Although the natural person can

---

⁵³ *Examen*, pp. 480-81. Cf. *HOC*, p. 11; *SA*, p. 310.

⁵⁴ *Examen*, p. 332.

⁵⁵ *Workes*, II, p. 459.

⁵⁶ *Examen*, p. 349. By *non posse non peccare* Rutherford does not mean that no one can do or know any good thing from a human point of view. What he means is that the natural person is unable to do or to know any spiritual good and that, from God's point of view, every human good deed—of body or mind—falls short of giving him glory and thus is sinful at least in defect. See *Examen*, p. 345; and the section entitled 'Grace and Free Will' below.

⁵⁷ *Communion*, p. 232.

⁵⁸ *Examen*, pp. 85, 328.

⁵⁹ *Institutes* I.vi.1, p. 70. J. McNeill comments that the metaphor of the spectacles 'is probably Calvin's decisive utterance on the role of Scripture as related to the revelation of the Creator in creation' (p. 70n1). Here Rutherford, in a similar way as Calvin, speaks

know right and true things about God from Scripture (and from general revelation as well), he or she can never know God rightly and truly—i.e., in a saving relationship—apart from the work of the Holy Spirit. Natural reason or natural ability can only furnish a vague and 'literal' knowledge of God. It can never lead to an accurate, deep, and true knowledge of God in relationship.[60] As Rutherford himself says: 'Wee teach no such thing, as that Reasonings, Syllogismes, or the *Scriptures*, without the *Spirit* can produce Faith.'[61] Scripture is soteriologically necessary, for Rutherford. But it is soteriologically insufficient, because of the post-lapsarian limits on natural reason. A special and subjective work of the Holy Spirit is, therefore, also necessary.

This special work of the Spirit is not a creation *ex nihilo* within the individual, nor is it in opposition to his or her own natural faculties. In traditional Thomistic language, Rutherford explains that grace restores and perfects the divine *imago*, which has been tarnished as a result of the fall.[62] The metaphor of the eye-salve or, in Calvin's case, the spectacles, proves that restoration and perfection is what grace provides. New eyes are not needed, only the correction of the vision problem. Thus, there is no contradiction in Rutherford's thinking—or in Calvin's either, for that matter—between faith and reason, only between faith and *natural* reason. Whereas, on the one hand, a sinner can never become a Christian by logic or by natural reason, the believer, on the other hand, is 'the most reasonable man in the world'; and the one 'who doth all by faith, doth all by the light of sound reason'.[63] The Spirit restores and perfects the created reason of men and women and enables them, in a distinctively Ramist fashion, to apply the rules of logic rightly and discern the truth. Scripture itself demonstrates that '[w]hen the rules of logic [are] followed, the truth [comes] immediately to view, even though it may have been obscure before'.[64] In Matthew 21.31-2, for example, Jesus, the perfect God-man, argues 'from an Antecedent to a consequent by naturall logick' and reproves the Sadducees for 'their unbeliefe and dulnesse' in not doing the same and, thus, for their not seeing the doctrine of resurrection in the Old Testament.[65]

In referring to the importance of 'naturall logick', here, Rutherford is not talking about the use of logic by the natural person—i.e., one without the Holy Spirit—but about the use of human logic, insofar as it, like all other arts and

---

of the Holy Spirit working in and through Scripture as an 'eye salve' to enable one to see.

[60] *Examen*, pp. 82-7.

[61] *Christ Dying*, pp. 278-9.

[62] *Examen*, p. 299. Rutherford's use of Thomistic language in arguing that grace does not destroy, but rather perfects, nature occurs specifically in, e.g., *Lex, Rex*, pp. 122, 324, 327; and *Christ Dying*, p. 62.

[63] *HOC*, p. 22. Cf., *RD*, pp. 9-10.

[64] Sprunger, 'Ames, Ramus, and Puritan Theology', p. 142.

[65] *SA*, pp. 49-50.

sciences, is common to humans created in the image of God. He is not advocating natural logic and reason *per se* but the spiritual, or perhaps better, Spiritual, use of them. His justification for doing so is rooted in the *imago Dei* and in Jesus' own example in passages like Matthew 21. Rutherford's statements about the importance of human reason also should not be taken to indicate that he emphasizes rationality to the exclusion of other faculties within the human psychology. As we will see in chapter four, Rutherford, in typical Puritan fashion, places great weight on the role of the affections in knowing God. They are 'like the needle, the rest of the soul like the thread; and as the needle makes way and draws the thread, so holy affections pull [the soul] forward and draw all to Jesus'.[66] Humans are reasonable creatures by virtue of their creation *imagine Dei*. But they are also affective and volitional creatures by virtue of this same fact as well. Rutherford, like the Puritans as a whole—reflecting the emphasis on *praxis* in theology—never advocates an exclusively rational religion but a whole-soul relationship with Jesus Christ. This is not to suggest, as John Coffey unfortunately does, that Rutherford believes this relationship is fostered more by 'special and private raptures' with Christ than by the Holy Spirit's work in and through Scripture.[67] Although the Spirit is not tied to Scripture and is free to work or not-work through it or apart from it—a feature of Rutherford's doctrine of God that will become much more apparent in the next two chapters—he, nevertheless, ordinarily uses it as his '*officina*' or 'workhouse'. The Spirit goes along 'with the word [and] makes it effectual'. His work is 'to enlighten, to teach, to rebuke, to convince, [and] to persuade'.[68]

It is precisely the Spirit's work in and through Scripture and human argumentation—rather than an exalted view of the natural epistemological capabilities of fallen creatures—that allows Rutherford to ascribe positive uses to natural theology in the work of apologetics. Even though the fall has affected every faculty within the human psychology, 'some remanents of the Image of God' do remain in all of us after the fall.[69] Natural theology is, thus, not always or altogether idolatrous. In continuity with Calvin and Reformation and post-Reformation thinking in general, Rutherford believes that it is possible to speak rightly and truthfully about God apart from Scripture, and even to know right and true things about him, although it is never possible to know him savingly or in the way he means for us to know him.[70] Instead of utterly rejecting natural

---

[66] *Communion*, p. 316. See the section on justification below.
[67] Coffey, *Politics, Religion and the British Revolutions*, p. 94. The current author has examined Coffey's claim in greater detail in a forthcoming essay entitled, '"And the Two shall become One Flesh": An "Affectionate" Theology of Union with Christ in the Song of Songs', which is scheduled to appear in 2008 in a collection of essays on Rutherford.
[68] *Influences*, pp. 60, 172.
[69] *COL*, p. 14.
[70] Rutherford, thus, affirms E.A. Dowey's understanding of Calvin's doctrine of the knowledge of God over T.H.L. Parker's. Cf. Dowey, *The Knowledge of God in Calvin's*

theology and working *de novo* in apologetics, Rutherford clearly sees a use for it. It serves as a common point of contact between the Christian and the non-Christian world, which must be corrected where it is deviant by the teaching of Scripture.[71] In this process, reason and rhetoric are not to be relegated to the back seat. Even though these human enterprises can never 'convert soules, and lead high thoughts captive, to the obedience of *Christ*' in and of themselves, we should, nevertheless, use them and look for them to be 'sanctified' and 'fitly made use of, by the Spirit' unto salvation.[72] As his colleague at the Westminster Assembly, William Twisse, once said: not to use reason and rhetoric in this way is to 'derogate from the wisdom and sufficiency of God', who gave us such things as 'means and helps of seeking after the Lord, and finding mercy from him'.[73]

The Arminians, on the other hand, reflect a Cartesian approach to reason by removing the limitations to its usefulness in matters of faith. Their notion of universal grace effectively does away with the sanctions imposed on created human reason by the fall and ensures that Arminius and his later successors will assign greater significance to the post-lapsarian use of reason. Although it is true that Arminius' understanding of the effects of the fall would appease even staunch Calvinists like Rutherford,[74] it is also true that his understanding of prevenient grace, which is established in creation and then re-established and sustained in providence, renders this view of the fall virtually meaningless—a point that is not overlooked by Arminius' opponents in the seventeenth century.[75] What is more, Arminius' later disciples seem not to have shared his

---

Theology (Grand Rapids, MI: Eerdmans, 1994); with Parker, *Calvin's Doctrine of the Knowledge of God* (Edinburgh: Oliver & Boyd, 1969).

[71] *Examen*, pp. 38-40. B. Gerrish, in commenting on the *Institutes* (I.vi.1), says: '[I]t seems clear that the saving knowledge, when it comes, attaches itself to a remnant of the natural knowledge; otherwise, Calvin's famous comparison of the Word to a pair of spectacles, which bring to clear focus a confusa alioqui Dei notitia, would make no sense.' B.A. Gerrish, 'From Calvin to Schleiermacher: The Theme and the Shape of Christian Dogmatics', in *Schleiermacher-Archiv*, International Schleiermacher-Kongress, 1984, 2 vols., eds., H. Fischer, H.-J. Birkner, G. Ebeling, H. Kimmerle, and K.-V. Selge (Berlin: Walter de Gruyter, 1985), II, p. 1043n40.

[72] *SA*, p. 55.

[73] Twisse, *A Treatise of Mr. Cottons*, pp. 207-8.

[74] Arminius plainly states that all people are dead in sins and trespasses after the fall in *WJA*, II, pp. 192-4.

[75] E.g., Du Moulin states: 'There meete us in the writings of these innovators [i.e., the Arminians], some places, in which they say, that man in his corrupted state was altogether dead, and that of himselfe, he can neither thinke, nor will, nor doe, any thing that is good. But these things are said but for a colour, and that they might deceive the unwary reader: For they say, that a man is able to doe no good without grace; but by this grace, they understand universall grace, which is common to all men, and sufficient grace, which is given, even to them to whom Christ was made knowne, and which doth extend it selfe as farre as nature.' *Anatomy of Arminianisme*, p. 298.

views in regard to the fall. Some of these disciples explicitly embrace the more Aristotelian, and Socinian, view that sees every newborn human mind as a *tabula rasa*.[76] In the place of a universal, irresistible, and internal natural knowledge of God endorsed by Calvinists like Rutherford—and in contrast with Arminius' own convictions as well—these disciples substitute the idea that all people, if they simply apply themselves to the right use of human reason with the help of prevenient grace, can discover principles in nature and, thereby, come to know God 'naturally'.[77]

Leaving aside for now the question of prevenient grace, there are at least three factors that ensure the Arminians will place greater emphasis on human reasoning and rationality than will Rutherford and the Calvinists. First, one would expect to find a greater openness to rationalism in a theological system whose focus is more anthropocentric. And from what we have seen thus far, it would appear that Arminianism is at least more inclined to anthropocentrism than is Rutherford's Calvinism—a fact that will be demonstrated conclusively in the next two chapters. Second, Arminius redefines the scholastic distinction between *theologia archetypa et ectypa* and his later disciples reject it outright, thereby revealing a different understanding of the epistemological relationship between creator and creature in their theology than what we have seen in post-Reformation theologians like Rutherford.[78] Though this will be explored in more depth in chapter three after the introduction of *potentia Dei absoluta et ordinata*, for now suffice it to say that the effect of redefining or rejecting this distinction is that the Arminians collapse *Deus absconditus* into *Deus revelatus*, thus removing much of the element of divine incomprehensibility from their theology.[79] After we see how the Arminians regard the medieval nominalist power distinction, this feature of their theology will become much more apparent.

---

[76] C. Vorstius, *Tractatus theologicus de Deo* (Steinfurt, 1606), p. 128; S. Episcopius, *Opera theologica* (Hagae-Comitis, ²1678), p. 6; P. Van Limborch, *Theologia Christiana ad praxin pietatis ac promotionem pacis Christiana unice directa* (Amsterdam, 1735; originally published as *Institutiones theologiae Christianae*, 1686), 1.2.16. On this, see J.E. Platt, 'The Denial of the Innate Idea of God in Dutch Remonstrant Theology: From Episcopius to Van Limborch', in *Protestant Scholasticism: Essays in Reassessment*, eds. C.R. Trueman and R.S. Clark (Carlisle, Cumbria: Paternoster, 1999), pp. 216-20; and idem, *Reformed Thought*, pp. 202-38.

[77] 'Quare alia responsione opus est: videlicet cognitionem Dei, non esse sic naturalem, ut necessario omnino homini insit, eique non possit non inesse, tanquam ex naturae principiis fluens, sed sic tantum naturalem, ut si homo velit ratione tantum uti, principia quaedam reperire possit in nature, auxilio rationis istius rectae, per quae deveniat in Dei cognitionem.' Episcopius, *Opera theologica* (1678), p. 16.

[78] For Arminius' use of the distinction, see Muller, *God, Creation, and Providence*, pp. 60-62. For its rejection in later Remonstrant thought, see Episcopius, *Opera theologica* (1678), pp. 12-13; and Van Limborch, *Theologia Christiana*, 1.1.1.

[79] See the section on *theologia archetypa et ectypa* below.

The third, and most conclusive, factor ensuring that the Arminians will place greater stress on human reason is their embrace of Thomistic anthropological intellectualism. It is in this philosophy, with its emphasis on the priority of the intellect over the other faculties of the human psychology, that Arminius finds a resolution to the epistemological problem existing between the creature and his or her creator. Against the more voluntaristic tendency, which is found in Rutherford and in the Reformed in general, Arminius argues that the intellect possesses the ability to know good and spiritual things and to direct the will accordingly, even after the fall. It is the 'understanding [which] extends itself to acts of volition', and in 'this act of the mind...the salvation of man and his perfect happiness consist'.[80] Arminius' receptivity to rationalism and his divergence from the general trend among the Reformed come into sharper focus when we discover, as Richard Muller has shown, that Arminius weds this intellectualism, rather surprisingly, to a Scotistic and Ramistic orientation towards *praxis* in theology instead of the Thomistic orientation toward *contemplatio*.[81] Of this union, Muller states:

> [It] points, in turn, to the profound soteriological disagreement between Arminius and the Reformed and, consequently, toward the greater receptivity of the Arminian system to philosophical rationalism: Arminius, in contrast to his Reformed contemporaries and, indeed, in contrast to Aquinas, assumes that a practical theology can also be intellectualistic because, even in the problem of salvation, the intellect leads the will. Reason, therefore, can play a greater role in the construction of theological system than it could on the assumption of a soteriological priority of will [as is found in Rutherford].[82]

In keeping with this intellectualist approach, Arminius' later disciples elevate human reason and, correspondingly, minimize the effects of sin upon the understanding to such a degree that they deny the necessity of both Scripture and special grace in salvation. Van Limborch explicitly states that sin, while influencing other human faculties, leaves the reason wholly unaffected. Thus, when the Bible speaks of the '*Carnal Mind*', he says, 'we are not to understand that Reason with which God has endow'd Man'.[83] Episcopius acknowledges that Scripture is not necessary but only 'useful' (*utilis*) as an aid and argues that all people are capable of knowing God without it, 'si ullo modo ratione recta duci velint'. Others of the Remonstrants, like Vorstius, even go so far as to

---

[80] *WJA*, I, p. 363; II, pp. 189-94. Arminius' intellectualism and the implications of it are discussed more fully in the sections on regeneration, the nature of faith, and justification below.

[81] For more on the object and goal of theology in Arminius' thinking, see *WJA*, I, pp. 321-73; and II, pp. 335-7. For the same in Arminius' later disciples, see, e.g., Van Limborch, *Theologia Christiana*, 1.1.5.

[82] Muller, *God, Creation, and Providence*, p. 79.

[83] Van Limborch, *Theologia Christiana*, 5.1.4-5; *ACS*, I, p. 43.

deny the need for a special work of grace in salvation.[84]

Thus it would seem that while Brian Armstrong is correct in seeing an increased emphasis in the post-Reformation period on the use of reason and logic when compared with the reformers—a fact that even the reappraisal school acknowledges—he is incorrect in claiming that reason and logic assumed an 'equal standing with faith in theology' and, thus, diminished the authority of revelation. Rutherford, true to his Ramist roots—which can themselves be traced back through the Reformation to such late medieval humanists as Rudolf Agricola (c.1443-1485)—does plainly assign a significant role to reason in theology, but not to natural reason.[85] Rather than assigning reason a place of 'equal standing with faith', Rutherford unambiguously subordinates the former to the latter. Reason and logic are wholly impotent in spiritual matters until they are restored and perfected in faith. Reason never achieves principial status in Rutherford's thinking, not even after conversion. Scripture and God remain the only two *principia* of his theology. Rutherford emphasizes the usefulness of reason to the degree that he does because he believes that Scripture teaches it to be part of the *imago Dei* and, most especially, because Jesus himself relied upon reason and the rules of logic in interpreting the Old Testament Scriptures. But he limits the usefulness of reason by his use of Calvin's *duplex cognitio Dei* and his belief in the necessity of both Scripture and a special subjective work of grace by the Holy Spirit.

The Arminians, on the other hand, attach more significance to the role of reason in their theology and, as a result, most closely reflect Armstrong's criteria. Even though Arminius' own theology does contain distinct features that tend towards rationalism—features that will be explored in greater depth in chapter four, in the sections on faith and justification—it is primarily in the thinking of his later followers that the rationalistic trend becomes more readily apparent. By denying the necessity of Scripture and the need for special grace, these later Arminians do just as Armstrong claims about Protestant scholastics like Rutherford: they exalt reason to an 'equal standing with faith in theology', and, 'thus jettison...some of the authority of revelation'. G.J. Hoenderdaal, while not taking up the issue of Arminius' own tendencies towards rationalism, identifies the 'stronger rationalist bent' of his disciple Episcopius. He also argues, contra the stream of sentiment engendered by Tholuck, that it was 'Episcopius' successors at the Remonstrant seminary...in Amsterdam', rather than post-Reformation Reformed scholastics like Rutherford, who helped to bring about the European Enlightenment by their emphasis upon reason in

---

[84] Episcopius, *Opera theologica* (1678), p. 6; Du Moulin, *Anatomy of Arminianisme*, pp. 299-300.

[85] W.J. Ong has linked many of Ramus' ideas with those of Rudolf Agricola in his *Ramus, Method, and the Decay of Diaglogue* (Cambridge, MA: Harvard University, 1958), pp. 146, 199-200, 214-20, 258-9.

matters of faith.[86] Although some later Arminians, as we have seen, denied any concept of innate ideas and, so, cannot be considered rationalists in a Cartesian sense, there were some, like Stephanus Curcellaeus (1586-1659), who demonstrated clear affinities for the Cartesian New Philosophy. According to Hoenderdaal, Curcellaeus so imbibed this Philosophy that he 'translate[d]...Descartes' *Discours de la Méthode* from French into Latin'.[87] Even though Episcopius and Van Limborch may have believed that the newborn human mind was a *tabula rasa*, they, like the latter's close friend John Locke (1632-1704), still regarded human reason as the 'arbiter of revelation'.[88] While not completely discarding the value of Scripture, these later Arminians, by their rationalist bent, did, nonetheless, encourage an 'anti-supernaturalism', in which 'reason, instead of being regarded as revelation's handmaid became its master, and in some cases, its replacement'.[89]

This same Arminian emphasis on reason in matters of faith—eschewed by Rutherford as Pelagianism—can also be found in England, quite significantly, in the writings of William Laud. The issue of whether Laud himself can actually be considered an Arminian will be discussed in chapter five. But, for now, it is enough to point out the similarities in the teachings of Laud and the Arminians. Sounding much like the later Arminians and John Locke too, Laud declared that 'reason by her own light can discover how firmly the principles of religion are true'.[90] Because of the Laudian imposition into Scotland, this feature of Arminian theology would not merely have been a continental phenomenon, for Rutherford, but an ever-present reality near at hand.

Scripture as principium cognoscendi theologiae

Perhaps the most striking feature of Rutherford's natural theology and his understanding of the role of reason is that they do not derive from nature or

---

[86] G.J. Hoenderdaal, 'The Debate about Arminius outside the Netherlands', in *Leiden University in the Seventeenth Century: An Exchange of Learning*, eds. Th. H. Lunsingh Scheurleer and G.H.M. Posthumus Meyjes (Leiden: E.J. Brill, 1975), p. 142.

[87] Hoenderdaal, 'Debate about Arminius', p. 142. Descartes' rationalistic approach can be seen in the full title of this work: E.g., *A Discourse of a Method for the Well Guiding of Reason, and the Discovery of Truth in the Sciences* (London, 1649).

[88] A.P.F. Sell, 'Arminians, Deists, and Reason', *Faith and Freedom* 33 (Autumn, 1979), pp. 19, 24. Not only did Van Limborch and Locke frequently correspond by letter, but Locke dedicated his *A Letter on Toleration* (1689) to Van Limborch as well, both of which indicate a fairly close association existed between the two men. See J. Locke, *Some Familiar Letters between Mr. Locke, and Several of his Friends* (London, 1708); Sell, 'Arminians, Deists, and Reason', pp. 20, 22; and Hoenderdaal, 'Debate about Arminius', p. 144.

[89] Sell, 'Arminians, Deists, and Reason', p. 24.

[90] W. Laud, *A Relation of the Conference between William Laud...and Mr. Fisher the Jesuit* (London, ^{3}1673), p. 49.

philosophy but from Scripture. It is not because reason, creation, or any other part of general revelation tells him there is a natural theology that he believes it, but because Scripture teaches it. And it is not because of an inherent rationalism that Rutherford believes in the usefulness of human reason, but because he sees it on the pages of Scripture. In order to prove the existence of a *theologia naturalis vera*, Rutherford appeals to the same biblical texts as his Reformation predecessors and post-Reformation colleagues—Psalm 19; Acts 14 and 17; Romans 1 and 2.[91] And, as we have seen, in order to prove the usefulness of reason, Rutherford points to Jesus' own use of it in Matthew 21.31-2.

What is true of his natural theology and his understanding of the role of reason, however, is also true for all his theology: Scripture functions as his *principium cognoscendi theologiae verae*.[92] This means, in the words of James Ussher, that every true doctrine will not only be 'consonant unto [the Scriptures]' but will find 'the ground thereof in them', such that 'unto them onely is the Church directed for the saving knowledge of God'.[93] To label Scripture the cognitive foundation of theology is not to deny that natural revelation, philosophy, or tradition have a place in theological discourse. It is to suggest that natural revelation, philosophy, and tradition—along with every other human enterprise—must be held up to and examined by the light of Scripture.[94]

Even *prima facie*, the *Examen* substantiates the idea that Scripture is the *principium cognoscendi theologiae* in Rutherford's thinking. Each of its twenty chapters is organized around the exposition of key Bible passages that relate to the topic under examination. The first chapter on Scripture, for example, is structured around seven main biblical texts: John 5.39; 1 Corinthians 2.14; 2 Corinthians 4.3; Colossians 2.6-7; Hebrews 13.9; 2 Timothy 3.16; and Romans 14.14. And the same architectonic principle can be seen throughout the *Examen*.[95] Each chapter is not only organized around scriptural headings,

---

[91] *Examen*, pp. 325-6; *HOC*, pp. 10-11, 16. Cf. Calvin, *Romans and Thessalonians*, p. 32; idem, *Acts 14-28*, trans. J.W. Fraser, *Calvin's New Testament Commentaries*, eds. D.W. Torrance and T.F. Torrance (Grand Rapids, MI: Eerdmans, 1960), p. 112; Musculus, *Common Places*, pp. 2-5; Vermigli, *Ad Romanos*, pp. 30ff; Du Moulin, *De cognitione Dei*, passim; Ussher, *Body of Divinitie*, p. 5; *WCF*, § 1.1, pp. 19-20; § 1.6, pp. 22-3.

[92] On Scripture as *principium cognoscendi theologiae*, see *PRRD*, II, pp. 151ff.

[93] Ussher, *Body of Divinitie*, p. 18.

[94] This is what *sola Scriptura* means, as A.N.S. Lane makes clear in his article, '*Sola Scriptura*? Making Sense of a Post-Reformation Slogan', in *A Pathway into the Holy Scripture*, eds. P.E. Satterthwaite and D.F. Wright (Grand Rapids, MI: Eerdmans, 1994), pp. 297-327.

[95] If we group the twenty chapters of the *Examen* according to the seven major *loci* of systematic theology, then Theology proper, which begins with chapter two, is structured around twenty-four texts of Scripture: Colossians 1.10; 1 Corinthians 8.6; Acts 13.48;

however, it is also replete with scriptural proof-texts. Rutherford repeatedly develops and defends his doctrinal positions by way of appeal to the Bible.[96] While he certainly draws on theological and philosophical arguments and methodological distinctions gleaned from the medieval scholastics (and others) in order to disprove the Arminians, his primary concern throughout the *Examen* is to show that Scripture contradicts their theology.[97] Quite often Rutherford simply makes a bare appeal to a certain text of Scripture in order to do this. From the beginning of the Reformation through the end of the sixteenth century, this was all that was required in order for theologians to validate their positions and to protect themselves from the naturalistic claims of rationalism. The dawn of the seventeenth century, however, brought an end to that, as heterodox groups—such as the Arminians and Socinians—claimed to adhere to the same Protestant Scripture principle as the Reformed orthodox and, yet, embraced a theology that was, in some cases, radically different.[98] This new seventeenth-century challenge did at times lead post-Reformation theologians to draw out the 'philosophical absurdities or ancient heresies implicit in the[ir] opponent's teaching', as J.P. Donnelly asserts.[99] But more frequently and more importantly, it led Rutherford and others like him to place greater stress on the nature of Scripture and, in particular, on the interpretation of Scripture and the significance of the church in the hermeneutical process. For this reason, the remainder of the chapter will focus on the nature and interpretation of Scripture in the theology of both Rutherford and the Arminians.

15.18; 17.27; Romans 8.32; 9.5; 9.11; 9.18; 9.19; 11.23; Philippians 2.6; Hebrews 1.6; 4.13; Matthew 6.10; 28.19; James 1.17; Ephesians 1.3; 1.4; 1.11; Luke 21.18; 1 Thessalonians 2.16; 4.3; 2 Thessalonians 2.11; Anthropology, beginning at chapter five, around four texts: Ephesians 4.24; Romans 5.12; 8.7; and 1 Timothy 2.3, 4; Christology, in chapter nine, around nine texts: John 10.11; Ephesians 1.7; John 3.19; 15.13; Romans 5.10; 8.34; 2 Corinthians 5.19; 1 Peter 2.24; and 1 Corinthians 1.4; Soteriology, beginning in chapter ten, around twenty-four: Hebrews 6.4; 8.8; Romans 3.28; 4.3; 7.14; 7.17; 7.18; 8.35; 9.8; Matthew 3.10; 10.5; 13.20; 16.18; Ephesians 1.18, 19; 1 John 1.7, 8; Galatians 5.17; Acts 2.21; 13.43; 1 Timothy 1.15; 1.19; John 10.28; 2 Peter 2.20; and Philippians 2.21; Ecclesiology, which begins in chapter fifteen, around seven: Matthew 18.17; 28.19; 1 Timothy 5.22; John 10.28; Romans 10.15; 13.4; and Acts 15.6; and Eschatology, in the final chapter, around two: Acts 7.59; and Matthew 25.41.

[96] Nowhere is this more apparent than chapters three (election) and four (reprobation): *Examen*, pp. 238-96.

[97] E.g., *Examen*, pp. 161, 167, 178, 189.

[98] C.R. Trueman, 'Faith Seeking Understanding: Some Neglected Aspects of John Owen's Understanding of Scriptural Interpretation', in *Interpreting the Bible: Historical and Theological Studies in Honour of David F. Wright*, ed. A.N.S. Lane (Leicester: Apollos, 1997), pp. 150-51; J.P. Donnelly, 'Italian Influences on the Development of Calvinist Scholasticism', *SCJ* 7:1 (1976), p. 85. On Arminian and Socinian views of Scripture, see *WJA*, II, pp. 80-92; and *The Racovian Catechisme* (Amsterdam, 1652), pp. 1-8.

[99] Donnelly, 'Italian Influences on the Development of Calvinist Scholasticism', p. 85.

The Nature of Scripture

What is Scripture like? What attributes rightly characterize it? Why is it, rather than something else, the cognitive foundation of Rutherford's theology? Before we can answer such questions, we need to examine the underlying issue of the divinity of Scripture in Rutherford's thinking. The reason being, the divinity of Scripture fundamentally addresses the problem of the origin or cause of Scripture. Before we can look at what Scripture is like, we need to establish where it comes from. The post-Reformation era, of which Rutherford is a part, tends to deal with the problem of the origin of Scripture by adopting language from the medieval scholastics and from Aristotle to describe God as the primary author of Scripture and the prophets and apostles as secondary authors and instruments. In order to further systematize this position, post-Reformation theologians appeal to four Aristotelian causal categories, all of which can be explicitly found in the writings of Rutherford and in the *Examen*,[100] and all of which foreshadow doctrines that will be presented more fully in the following two sections of the current chapter.

The *efficient cause* of Scripture, for Rutherford, is God himself—Father, Son, and Holy Spirit. The Father is said to be the author of Scripture, insofar as he immediately writes 'the Ten Commandments...on Tables of stone', and mediately leads the 'hand [of the apostles and prophets] at the pen'.[101] The Son, too, is the author of Scripture, insofar as he is the essential and living Word of God and the principal author of all prophecy. But, in a way that is typical of the Reformed orthodox in general, and of Calvin as well, Rutherford places the greatest emphasis on the work of the Holy Spirit in the causality of Scripture. Following the lead of Calvin's *Institutes*, Rutherford specifically refers to the Spirit as the 'Author' and 'efficient cause' of Scripture.[102]

Two things are worth noting at this point in connection with efficient causality. First, the divine authorship of Scripture, more than any other single factor, forms the basis for Rutherford's view of the Bible as the *principium cognoscendi theologiae*. Second, it is important that we call attention to the explicitly trinitarian nature of Rutherford's understanding of efficient causality. Authoring Scripture, in Rutherford's estimation, is not a segregated act of one divine person set over against the others. It is an integrated act involving the triune God as a unified whole. As a consequence, it cannot be argued that Scripture contains merely the will of the Father—or of any one of the divine persons, for that matter—as opposed to the united will of the triune God. This will be especially significant when considered in light of the remaining three causes, but, most particularly, the purpose of Scripture.

---

[100] Cf., e.g., *Examen*, p. 521; with *PRRD*, II, pp. 224-8.
[101] *SA*, II, p. 211; *Divine Right*, p. 66.
[102] *Influences*, p. 172; *Christ Dying*, p. 536; *Examen*, pp. 3, 9, 60; *SA*, p. 316; II, pp. 164, 211. Cf. *Institutes* I.ix.1-2, pp. 93-5; and J.T. McNeill, 'The Significance of the Word of God for Calvin', *CH* 28 (1959), pp. 134, 139.

Scripture's *formal cause*, according to Rutherford, is divine truth, and for that reason, there are certain requisite divine characteristics that can be seen in it. There is, Rutherford says, 'some character, some sound of Heaven...and a stampe of Divine Majesty' in the Bible that is not found in any human literary work, such that 'the style, liveliness, majesty and divinity that may be seen in the letter of the Scripture are eminently above the like in other Writers'.[103] As Calvin writes, the Bible does not contain a 'dead and killing letter', because God 'has stamped upon the Scriptures' his 'own image'.[104] For Rutherford, formal causality means that Scripture must be received on its own, at face value, according to its literal sense. This may or may not coincide with the way the church 'expoundeth it'.[105] What is more, the formal cause of Scripture—as it is *theologia ectypa*—also means that a wedge is not to be driven between God and his words. God's words must reflect who he is (*theologia archetypa*), and who he is must be revealed in the words that he speaks. Again, to cite the words of Calvin:

> [The Spirit] is the Author of the Scriptures: he cannot vary and differ from himself. Hence he must ever remain just as he once revealed himself there. This is no affront to him, unless perchance we consider it honorable for him to decline or degenerate from himself.[106]

The *final cause* of Scripture, in Rutherford's thinking, is to 'teach us quhat [what] God is in himself, and his holie nature, and quhat he is in his workis towards us'.[107] Considering Rutherford's primary emphasis on *praxis* in theology, this means that Scripture is not merely intellectual information about God but purposive divine self-revelation. Scripture is given to us *unto* salvation. Indeed, as we have seen, salvation is ordinarily impossible without it. Thus, Rutherford can speak of the Bible as the 'formal means of Faith' and, in characteristic Ramist language, as that which contains everything necessary both for faith—because 'Scripture is a precise rule...of Religion towards God' and the only fountain of 'all things to mak us wise to salvation'—and for obedience—because 'Scripture is [also] a precise rule...of Justice and Mercy towards one's neighbor.'[108] Since all three persons of the Godhead—but particularly the Spirit—wrote the Bible and intended it for salvation, it is, therefore, in Rutherford's thinking, a primary means that God uses to convey his grace to people. Ordinarily, there will be no salvation apart from the Spirit

---

[103] *Tryal*, p. 98; *Influences*, p. 172. Cf. *WCF*, § 1.5, pp. 21-2.
[104] *Institutes* I.ix.1-2, pp. 93-4.
[105] *Christ Dying*, p. 536.
[106] *Institutes* I.ix.2, pp. 94-5.
[107] *Catachisme*, p. 162.
[108] *Examen*, pp. 112, 114; *Catachisme*, p. 161. Calvin refers to the teleological nature of Scripture by citing 2 Timothy 3.16 and by arguing that Scripture 'leads the children of God even to the[ir] final goal'. *Institutes* I.ix.1, p. 93.

working in and through Scripture.

But if the purpose of Scripture is to teach us who God is and what he is towards us, then obviously its *material cause*, or subject matter, will be such as will enable that purpose to be fulfilled. Therefore, according to Rutherford, it is God himself who is presented to us in the text of Scripture, not so much as he is in his essence but as he is in his attributes—which is, as we will see in the next chapter, a key distinction in Rutherford's theology especially over against Arminian teaching—not comprehensively but sufficiently for faith and obedience, and then always accommodated to the capacities of human creatures. Because the material cause of Scripture is God himself 'lisping' to us, and because its efficient cause is also God, Rutherford is willing to ascribe to Scripture a corresponding '*material*' power, 'even as contradistinguished from the [Holy S]pirit acting with it'. In this way, the Bible functions like 'a Sword or an Axe of steel', which from 'the matter and artificer that made them hath *actu primo* sharpness and aptness to cut'.[109]

Significantly and, perhaps, rather surprisingly, Arminius also adopts these Aristotelian causal categories in order to explain the divinity of Scripture.[110] The mere fact that he does so demonstrates the influences of medieval scholasticism upon his thinking, which, in itself, has implications for our evaluation of Brian Armstrong's definition. But, it also demonstrates the need for an urgent and decisive response on the part of Rutherford to the threat posed by the Arminians. By adopting the same language and the same basic approach to Scripture—notwithstanding the presuppositional differences between Arminius and his later followers, who are, nonetheless, still classified as Arminians—and, yet, holding to radically different theological positions, the Arminians posed a threat to Calvinist orthodoxy unlike that posed by the Roman Church in the sixteenth century, which developed its theology from fundamentally different presuppositions. If, following Heiko Oberman, we say that the Reformation was, in the main, a clash between two different approaches to theology—on the one hand, 'Tradition I', or 'the single-source or exegetical tradition', which derived its theology *sola Scriptura*, and, on the other, 'Tradition II', or 'the two-sources theory', which allowed 'for an extra-biblical oral tradition' in developing its doctrine—then the Arminian-Calvinist struggle clearly falls within the bounds of 'Tradition I'.[111] Arminianism claimed the same presuppositional starting point for their theology as did Calvinists like Rutherford and, yet, reached sometimes far different conclusions. As we will see in the next chapter, this is because of a different understanding of the doctrine of God. But, regardless, Arminianism represented, in the eyes of

---

[109] *Influences*, pp. 172. This too seems to be in continuity with Calvin's doctrine of accommodation. See McNeill's treatment in 'The Significance of the Word of God for Calvin', pp. 137-8.

[110] *WJA*, II, pp. 80-109.

[111] Oberman, *Harvest of Medieval Theology*, p. 371.

Prolegomena to Theology 51

Rutherford, a system of thought whose basic presuppositions jeopardized theological certainty, and, for that reason, it could not be tolerated.

The Perfection of Scripture

In the *Examen*, Rutherford gives almost no explanation of his doctrine of the perfection of Scripture. But this is not unusual. None of his published writings contains an organized—much less a comprehensive—discussion of the perfection of Scripture. This doctrine is almost universally accepted in the sixteenth and seventeenth centuries. Even the Arminians, as Rutherford himself admits, embrace this doctrine wholeheartedly.[112] In spite of the fact that there is little here to distinguish Rutherford from the Arminians, we will offer an examination of Rutherford's views of inspiration and infallibility because they form an important backdrop to understanding the rest of his theology. What is more, Rutherford's views and their relationship to the views of Calvin have often been misrepresented in the secondary literature. In order to present as full a picture of Rutherford's theology as possible and to get as accurate an account of the condition of seventeenth-century Calvinism as we can, we will examine Rutherford's doctrine of the perfection of Scripture. In doing so, we will rely mainly upon sources outside of the *Examen*—chief among which will be the lectures that he gave on the *locus* of Scripture in his series on the 'Common Places of Divinity'.[113] Though Rutherford did not publish a treatise on the doctrine of Scripture, he did lecture on it to his students at St. Andrews.

Following in the tradition of the Reformation, Rutherford holds to a strict view of the inspiration of Scripture. His doctrine is in fact closer to a dictation theory of inspiration than not:

> in writing every jot, tittle, or word of Scripture, they [the human authors] were immediately inspired, as touching the matter, words, phrases, expression, order, method, majesty, stile and all: So I think they were but Organs, the mouth, pen and *Amanuenses*; God as it were, immediately dyting, and leading their hand at the pen.[114]

And commenting on 2 Peter 1.20-21, Rutherford says:

> So the Prophets were inspired φερόμενος carried, rolled, moved, acted immediately by the *Holy Ghost*, for *God* used not reason, or humane discoursing as an intervening organ or acting instrument to the devising and inventing of

---

[112] *Examen*, p. 5. For Arminian doctrines of Scripture, see *WJA*, II, pp. 80-92, 322-31; and *Confession*, pp. 59-77.

[113] Unpublished manuscripts, National Library of Scotland, Edinburgh, MSS 16475, pp. 2, 3-6; and St. Andrews University Library, BS 540.R8, pp. 17-41.

[114] *Divine Right*, p. 66.

spirituall or Gospell truths...but yet this immediately inspiring Spirit spake written Scripture.[115]

In light of these two citations, one might be tempted to argue that Rutherford favors the divinity of Scripture even to the exclusion of its humanity. But such a distinction between the two cannot be made. Unlike many modern theologians operating under the influence of men like Barth and Berkouwer, Rutherford sees no contradiction between a high view of inspiration and the humanity of Scripture.[116] This is because of the close relationship that exists between inspiration and providence in his thinking. The writing of Scripture, like every other event in the created order, falls under the umbrella of God's providential dealings with his creatures, albeit to an extraordinary degree. Both divine sovereignty and human agency are preserved together by seeing God as the first and efficient cause and his free creatures as contingent second causes. The end product is thus both divine and human. And the two are not to be separated but taken together. The very words written by the human authors are, themselves, the very words of the Holy Spirit, and everything that the 'Prophets spake, God spake'.[117] Thus, Rutherford would criticize the above-mentioned modern theologians in much the same way that he criticizes the Antinomians and Familists in his own day, viz., for their drawing too sharp a divide between the divinity and humanity of Scripture and, as a result, coming up with two words: one that is human and, thus, subject to all the shortcomings of other human productions; and another that is divine or spiritual and, thus, free from those very shortcomings.[118]

Yet even though the relationship between the divine and the human in Scripture is analogous to the relationship between the divine and the human in every day events, it is not identical. Rutherford believes that the authors of Scripture are kept from error in a way that humans are not in the course of ordinary providence. The result is an infallible Bible.[119] Scripture is infallible

---

[115] *SA*, p. 314.

[116] Cf. K. Barth, *CD*, II/2, pp. 532ff; and G.C. Berkouwer, *Holy Scripture*, trans. J.B. Rogers (Grand Rapids, MI: Eerdmans, 1975), pp. 18ff.

[117] *SA*, pp. 39ff; II, pp. 164, 211.

[118] This is not in any way to suggest that theologians operating under the influence of Barth and Berkouwer are simply modern-day Antinomians or Familists, but only that Rutherford would level the same critique against them as he does against the Antinomians and Familists. (n.b., The Familists were members of the sect 'Family of Love', which was founded in the sixteenth century by the German Roman Catholic Henry Nicholas. For more see C. Marsh, *The Family of Love in English Society, 1550-1630* [Cambridge: Cambridge University, 1994].)

[119] Rutherford exemplifies the tendency among post-Reformation theologians to speak of the infallibility of Scripture instead of its inerrancy. The Bible does not err, because it is infallible. There does not appear to have been any attempt to 'construct a noun out of the verb *errare*' and apply it to Scripture as an attribute. See *PRRD*, II, p. 300n26.

because God, who is incapable of error, inspired its human authors in such a way that they were preserved from all error: 'The immediately inspiring Spirit, rendred the Prophets and Apostles in that they spake and wrot by such inspiration, the immediate organs of the *Holy Ghost*, and such as could not erre.'[120] For this reason, to ascribe error to any of the human author's words is to ascribe error to God's words, and thus to God himself. God's perfect nature stands behind the words of the Bible. This applies not simply to the original Greek and Hebrew manuscripts. It also applies to copies and, in some way, to English translations as well. Although 'the meanes of conveying' Scripture, such as 'writing, printing, translating, speaking, are all fallible meanes of conveying the truth of old and new Testament to us', nevertheless, 'the Word of God in that which is delivered to us is infallible'. Here again there is a link between the perfection of Scripture and divine providence. The God who inspired Scripture infallibly has also preserved it down through the ages by 'an unerring and undeclinable providence'. This does not mean, however, that there is no possibility of error in any one copy or in translations of the original manuscripts. Rutherford, in fact, admits that there are 'errours of number, genealogies, &c.' in the copies of Scripture as we have it.[121] But it does mean that God has kept pure the original—among all the copies—and the translations—insofar as they are faithful to the original. And this is true to such a degree that 'in the body of articles of faith, and necessary truths, we are certaine with the certainty of faith, [that] it is that same very word of God' that was originally given to the prophets and apostles.[122] Scripture, therefore, is perfect, because it is divinely given through human instruments, and remains perfect, because it is divinely preserved.

Objections to the Perfection of Scripture

Jack Rogers and Donald McKim have claimed that Rutherford, like the Puritans in general, did not hold to a strict view of scriptural perfection. They insist that such an understanding did not even develop within the church historically until the nineteenth century, when Princeton theologians B.B. Warfield and A.A. Hodge fostered a more stringent theory of inspiration and inerrancy that was then 'read back into' history. Rogers and McKim do admit that 'Rutherford was, on occasion, driven to a theory of dictation', but they allege that he took up this position merely in polemic against Richard Hooker's (1554-1600) views on worship and that he was 'much more circumspect' in his other writings. Thus, they say that while Rutherford may have 'on occasion' been pushed to a strict view of inspiration and inerrancy, his overarching concern was to extend the perfection of Scripture only to matters of salvation.

---

[120] *SA*, II, p. 211.
[121] *PLC*, pp. 362-3, 366.
[122] *PLC*, p. 366. Cf. *WCF*, § 1.8, pp. 23-4.

Rogers and McKim argue that Rutherford understood the Bible to speak perfectly in moral actions and in the fundamentals of the faith but not in other matters. Scripture was not to be used as an infallible 'encyclopedia' on such subjects as the arts and sciences; its purpose was to 'mediate salvation' not to provide 'interesting information'.[123]

In responding to the claims of Rogers and McKim in regard to Rutherford's doctrine of Scripture, at least two things can be said. First, although they are correct to point out that Rutherford's dictation comments are made in polemical contexts, they trivialize his comments by calling them 'occasional' and by alleging that he was 'driven' to embrace them only because the demands of those polemical situations forced him into an extreme position that he ordinarily would not have endorsed. This, however, ignores the fact that Rutherford makes these comments on at least three different occasions and overlooks the fact that the specific polemical question he is seeking to answer in at least two out of the three concerns the *manner* in which the Apostles and Prophets were 'inspired' in the writing of Scripture. In response to the allegation of the '*Papists* and *Formalists*', who would argue that the reason we can add traditions to the written Word of God is because the Prophets and Apostles made canonical additions to the writings of Moses, Rutherford says that the Apostles and Prophets were inspired by the Holy Spirit in a different way than we are today. They were inspired in such a way that their 'every syllable and word' was God's syllable and word. God did not give them the 'power to devise a Gospel' and then write it. Nor did he merely give them his 'rude thoughts', as 'Princes and Nobles do' to 'their Secretary' in writing to a 'Forraign Prince', and then 'go to bed and sleep', leaving the rest of the letter to the 'wit and eloquence of the Secretary'. Rather, God gave his '*Amanuenses*' the 'matter, words, phrases, expression, order, method, majesty, stile and all'.[124] Likewise, in response to the Antinomians, Rutherford says that the Apostles and Prophets were immediately inspired 'above the reach' of their 'free will, humane doubtings, discourses, [and] ratiocinations' in such a way that they 'could not erre'. This 'priviledge' is not given even to the 'most sanctified' believer today.[125] Thus, it would seem that although these comments are made in polemical contexts, Rutherford is responding to specific questions in regard to inspiration with specific answers. There is no reason to disregard them simply because he is engaging in debate.

Second, and more significantly, Rogers and McKim overlook the explicit,

---

[123] Rogers and McKim, *Authority and Interpretation of the Bible*, pp. xvii-xxiii, 205-7, 250n23. J.D. Woodbridge has offered a devastating critique of the Rogers and McKim thesis generally (*Biblical Authority: A Critique of the Rogers/McKim Proposal* [Grand Rapids, MI: Zondervan, 1982]). We will offer a critique of their thesis only as it applies directly to Rutherford and his theology.
[124] *Divine Right*, pp. 65-6.
[125] *SA*, II, p. 211.

systematic, and non-polemical statements that Rutherford makes in his lectures on the doctrine of Scripture. In lecture notes from the year 1654, for example, Rutherford clearly states his strict view of inspiration: 'God himself, without any secondary counselors, organs, or authors, either among angels or men, devised [*excogitavit*] the word as its common [*vulgus*] and primary author; and the matters [*res*], words [*verba*], and series of words [*verborum series*] are immediately by the Holy Spirit [*a spiritu sancto*].'[126] And in lecture notes from 1648, Rutherford just as clearly says that the whole of Scripture is 'divinely inspired' to the extent that the Holy Spirit did not merely 'assist and approve of' what the human authors wrote, but 'dictated' (*dictaverit*) the 'individual words [*singula verba*], the order [*ordo*], and the series of words [*series verborum*]' in Scripture. The human authors are, in this way, 'amanuenses' who wrote the very words of the Holy Spirit as he spoke them.[127] Furthermore, in the lecture notes from both years, Rutherford mentions the Greek word θεοπνευστος, from 2 Timothy 3.16, and then cites texts like Matthew 22.32, 2 Samuel 23.1-3, and Luke 1.70, among others, as proof that 'inspiration' extends to the very words of the text.[128]

When we couple these explicit statements with Rutherford's doctrine of the divinity of Scripture, and specifically, with his view of God as its efficient cause, we can at least say that the assertions made by Rogers and McKim are a bit premature. Rutherford's dictation comments are not 'occasional', nor are they merely confined to polemical contexts. They are patent and recurring, even though many of them are found only in Rutherford's most obscure writings.

But not only are Rutherford's dictation comments not 'occasional', they are also not atypical among the Puritans of the post-Reformation period. So, William Ames, using many of the same words as Rutherford, says: 'In all those things which were made known by supernaturall inspiration, (whether they were matters of right, or fact) he did inspire not onely the things themselves, but did dictate [*dictavit*] and suggest all the words [*singula verba*] in which they should be written.'[129] James Ussher similarly writes that the 'tongue, phrase, matter, and all other circumstances' of Scripture are the products of divine authorship.[130] And William Whitaker—whose doctrine of Scripture, according to at least one scholar, is the formative influence behind the first chapter of the Westminster Confession of Faith[131]—explains that the human

---

[126] Unpublished manuscript, National Library of Scotland, Edinburgh, MSS 16475, p. 2.

[127] Unpublished manuscript, St. Andrews University Library, BS 540.R8, pp. 32-4.

[128] Unpublished manuscripts, St. Andrews, BS 540.R8, pp. 34-5; and National Library, MSS 16475, p. 2.

[129] Ames, *The Marrow of Sacred Divinity* (London, 1642), p. 168, as compared with idem, *Medulla*, p. 179.

[130] Ussher, *Body of Divinitie*, p. 8.

[131] W.R. Spear has written a series of articles in which he seeks to demonstrate this point: 'William Whitaker and the Westminster Doctrine of Scripture', *Reformed Theological Journal* 7 (November, 1991), pp. 38-48; 'The Westminster Confession of

authors of Scripture 'were induced and moved to write by the special authority of Christ and the Holy Spirit: for the scripture is called θεόπνευστος, that is, delivered by the impulse and suggestion of the Holy Ghost....The men were merely the instruments; it was the Holy Ghost who dictated to them'. And lest we be unsure as to the extent of the Spirit's dictation, Whitaker, citing Augustine's (354-430) analogy of Christ as the head and the apostles as his hands, further explains what he means: 'Christ wrote all those things which the apostles and evangelists wrote; because the apostles were only the hands, but Christ the head. Now the hands write nothing but as the head thinks and dictates.'[132]

A second objection—this time from the opposite perspective—has been raised by Wilhelm Niesel, John McNeill, and J.K.S. Reid, among others, who have argued that such an emphasis on verbal inspiration is not found in the teachings of Calvin and thus represents a warping of his theology.[133] According to this point of view, Calvin does not regard the individual words themselves as being divinely dictated but only the doctrines, and he subordinates even this concern to the importance of the Holy Spirit in illumining the individual to understand those doctrines. While these claims do helpfully remind us of valuable emphases in the writings of Calvin, it is not clear that they accurately reflect his view of Scripture. What is more, it is not clear that they accurately appraise the relationship between Calvin and his successors. Although it would take us well beyond the scope of this thesis to enter into a comprehensive examination of this complex debate, we will seek to discern whether the above-mentioned assertions are fair, at least insofar as Rutherford is concerned. There are at least five links between Calvin's and Rutherford's understandings of Scripture that have been underdeveloped in assertions similar to those mentioned above. These links show that a closer relationship exists between Calvin and Rutherford than some have previously assumed.

First, Calvin's use of language to describe the perfection of Scripture is strikingly similar to Rutherford's own. He calls Scripture the Word of God 'set down and sealed in writing...under the Holy Spirit's dictation' and refers to the human authors in this process as 'amanuenses of the Holy Spirit'. Even the

---

Faith and Holy Scripture', in *To Glorify and Enjoy God: A Commemoration of the 350th Anniversary of the Westminster Assembly*, eds. J.L. Carson and D.W. Hall (Edinburgh: Banner of Truth, 1994), pp. 85-100; and 'Word and Spirit in the Westminster Confession', in *The Westminster Confession into the 21st Century: Essays in Remembrance of the 350th Anniversary of the Westminster Assembly*, ed. J.L. Duncan III, vol. 1 (Fearn, Ross-shire: Mentor, 2003), pp. 39-56.

[132] W. Whitaker, *A Disputation on Holy Scripture*, trans. and ed. W. Fitzgerald (Cambridge: Cambridge University, 1849), pp. 526-7.

[133] W. Niesel, *The Theology of Calvin*, trans. H. Knight (London: Lutterworth, 1956), pp. 26-30, 35-7; McNeill, 'The Significance of the Word of God for Calvin', pp. 140-45; and J.K.S. Reid, *The Authority of Scripture: A Study of Reformation and Post-Reformation Understanding of the Bible* (London: Methuen, 1962), pp. 36-45.

historical narratives of the Bible were so 'composed [*compositae*]' by divine dictation.[134] It is true, as McNeill rightly points out, that this dictation applies to the doctrines of Scripture. But it also applies, 'in a certain way' at least, to the very words themselves. Thus, Calvin writes: '*Verba quodammodo dictante Christi Spiritu.*'[135] While we need to be careful not to read too much into the dictation theory of Calvin—as his qualifier, *quodammodo*, would indicate—it, nonetheless, remains true that Calvin did believe, according to his own words, in some form of verbal inspiration. When we add to these statements other comments taken from his commentary on 2 Timothy 3.16, the potential for substantial discontinuity between Calvin and his successors is lessened even further. Expressing himself in language which is reflective of Rutherford, Ames, Ussher, and Whitaker, Calvin says: 'the prophets did not speak at their own suggestion, but...being organs of the Holy Spirit, they only uttered what they had been commissioned from heaven to declare'. And, shortly thereafter, he boldly asserts that 'it [Scripture] has proceeded from him [God] alone, and has nothing belonging to man mixed with it'.[136] Although these statements may not be definitive in and of themselves, they do make it highly unlikely that there would be substantial theological discontinuity between Calvin and Rutherford.

Second, Rutherford's dictation comments should not be interpreted as negating the importance of the human author. He, like Calvin, 'habitually keeps in view the human writer of each book, his purpose and intent in each passage; he often features what experts in our time have called the *Sitz im Leben*; and he manifestly feels that such matters are important if the full meaning and message of Scripture are to be conveyed'.[137] This link will become more evident in Rutherford once we have examined his understanding of the interpretation of Scripture. Others of his post-Reformation peers, however, demonstrate their continuity with Calvin more explicitly. William Ames, for instance, writes:

> But Divine inspiration was present with [the human] writers with some variety, for some things to be written were before altogether unknowne to the writer, as doth sufficiently appear in the History of the Creation past, and in foretellings of things to come: but some things were before knowne unto the writer, as appeares in the History of Christ, written by the Apostles: and some of these they knew by a naturall knowledge, and some by a supernaturall: In those things that were hidden and unknowne, Divine inspiration did performe all by it selfe: in those things which were knowen, or the knowledge where of might be obtained by ordinary meanes, there was also added a religious study (God so assisting them) that in writing they might not erre.

---

[134] *Institutes* IV.viii.6, pp. 1153-4; IV.viii.9, p. 1157.

[135] *Institutes* IV.viii.8, p. 1155 and note 7.

[136] Calvin, *Commentaries on the Epistles to Timothy, Titus, and Philemon*, trans. W. Pringle (Edinburgh: CTS, 1856), pp. 248-9.

[137] McNeill, 'The Significance of the Word of God for Calvin', p. 139.

In all those things which were made known by supernaturall inspiration, (whether they were matters of right, or fact) he did inspire not onely the things themselves, but did dictate and suggest all the words in which they should be written: which notwithstanding was done with that sweete attempering, that every writer, might use those manners of speaking which did most agree to his person and condition.[138]

Third, Rutherford and his post-Reformation contemporaries also believe, like Calvin, that the doctrines of Scripture are divinely dictated. This is the basis upon which they regard Scripture to be the *principium cognoscendi theologiae*. Amandus Polanus even uses the same words as Calvin to describe this idea, saying: 'Verbum Dei, est doctrina dictante Spiritu Sancto per Prophetas & Apostolos conscripta, perfecte tradens rationem consequendi vitam aeternam.'[139] William Whitaker adds that though there were 'various men who wrote' the Scriptures, there was 'one Spirit under whose direction and dictation they wrote', with the result being, 'one continuous body of doctrine'.[140]

Fourth, Rutherford and Calvin express their dictation comments in virtually identical contexts and come to virtually identical conclusions. Both men are attempting to distinguish between the apostles and prophets and their 'successors' and to answer the question as to the difference between the two. And both men reply by stating that the former group was inspired by the Holy Spirit in a different way than we are today. The apostles and prophets were, in Calvin's words—which Rutherford would echo—'*certi et authentici Spiritus sancti amanuenses*'.[141] This means, for Rutherford and for Calvin, that the apostles and prophets did not 'devise a Gospel' and then write it down. They wrote 'only' what they received from the Holy Spirit, so much so that Calvin and Rutherford both adopt absolutist language in ascribing Scripture to God 'alone' with 'nothing belonging to man mixed with it'.[142]

Fifth, as we have seen above, Rutherford attaches the same significance to the work of the Holy Spirit in enabling the individual to understand Scripture as Calvin does. The Holy Spirit illumines and persuades each person not only in regard to what Scripture says but in regard to Scripture's own divinity as well. The Spirit gives us eyes to see the Word of God and then testifies to us that what we see is, in fact, the Word of God. In a way that is typical for post-Reformation theologians, William Perkins, following Calvin, cites this testimony of the Holy Spirit as 'the argument of all arguments, to settle and

---

[138] Ames, *Marrow*, pp. 167-8.
[139] Polanus, *Partitiones*, p. 1.
[140] Whitaker, *Disputation*, p. 661.
[141] *Institutes* IV.viii.9, p. 1157.
[142] Cf. *Divine Right*, pp. 65-6; with Calvin, *Commentaries on the Epistles to Timothy, Titus, and Philemon*, pp. 248-9.

resolve the Conscience, and to seale up the certaintie of the word of God'.[143]

For these reasons, there does not appear to be substantial theological discontinuity between Rutherford and Calvin in regard to the perfection of Scripture. Though there may be some difference in the extent of the inspiration of Scripture in their thinking—in light of Calvin's *quodammodo* qualifier— there is, nonetheless, significant continuity between both men. Rutherford, in this way, confirms the conclusions reached by Geoffrey Bromiley regarding the elements of continuity and discontinuity between the Reformation and post-Reformation periods:

> In these writers the doctrine of scripture is no doubt entering on a new phase. Tendencies may be discerned in the presentation which give evidence of some movement away from the Reformation emphases. The movement, however, has not yet proceeded very far. The tendencies are only tendencies. What change there has been is more in style, or, materially, in elaboration. The substance of the Reformation doctrine of scripture has not yet been altered, let alone abandoned.[144]

A third objection—one that also carries a well-founded warning—has been raised recently to the language of dictation that occurs in Rutherford, in others of the post-Reformation period, and in Calvin as well. According to John Webster, 'What is problematic about the language of dictation, or of the biblical writers as amanuenses of the Spirit, is not only that such notions make the text unrecognisable as a human historical product, but that they trade upon a confusion of God's omnicausality with God's sole causality.'[145] Webster has helpfully put his finger on a linguistic problem common to Reformation and post-Reformation theologians alike. Rutherford's propensity to emphasize the divinity of Scripture by speaking of it as being dictated to amanuenses in the same manner that 'Princes and Nobles' would to 'their Secretary', does tend to minimize the humanity of Scripture and, potentially, to encourage wrong ideas about the way God works to bring actions and events to pass in the world. To be fair to Rutherford, however, we must point out that there was no controversy over the doctrines of inspiration and infallibility either prior to or during his own lifetime. These doctrines were accepted largely without question. We should not fault him for a less than clear expression of them. Furthermore, he did explicitly warn against seeing the text of Scripture as anything other than a document in which the human and the divine come together inextricably; and he also spoke out in favor of human free will and the necessity of second causes in bringing actions and events to pass, as we will see in the next two chapters. And if B.B. Warfield's claim in regard to Calvin is correct—viz., that dictation corresponds not so much to the mode of inspiration as to its result—then this

---

[143] Perkins, *Workes*, II, p. 56.
[144] G.W. Bromiley, *Historical Theology: An Introduction* (Grand Rapids, MI: Eerdmans, 1978), p. 328.
[145] Webster, *Holy Scripture*, p. 39.

would indicate that, though Rutherford's (and Calvin's) language may need to be refined, he does not understand the divinity of Scripture in a way that excludes its humanity.[146] Nonetheless, Webster's warning is important, and it must be said that many of the abuses of Scripture in seventeenth-century Scotland might have been avoided had a warning like his been given at that time and heeded.

G.D. Henderson cites two such abuses of Scripture that appear to stem from an overemphasis on its divinity. The first involves the practice of 'making lottery of the Holy Scriptures' or 'of opening the Bible at random and seeking guidance in the first words observed'. And the second involves the paranormal use of the Bible to disclose the identity of a thief in a room full of people.[147] Rutherford was apparently aware of such cases of abuse, because he explicitly denounced this kind of bibliolatry in his own day:

> We professe we hate with our soules that Christians should adore and fall downe before an inke-Divinity, and mere paper-godlinesse, as if the Spirit were frozen into inke, and dead figures, writings, letters, or as if naked languages of Hebrew, Greeke, and Latine, could save us. The Kingdome of God is not in letters, nor in externals, but in life and power.[148]

The weakness of the Rogers and McKim thesis is further seen when we broach the subject of the authority of Scripture in Rutherford's thinking. Biblical authority is intimately connected with the perfection of Scripture. In the *Examen*, the perfection of the Bible—itself grounded on the divinity of Scripture—provides the foundation for its authority.[149] When Rutherford cites 2 Timothy 3.16, for example, rather than explaining the doctrine of inspiration from it, he draws the following conclusion: 'Hence it is evident that the Scriptures are complete [*plenas*] and perfect to the point that not only the traditions of the *Papists*, but also all human ceremonies, and whatever is devised by the Anti-Christ or by False-Prophets for the positive observance in divine worship, would fight against the completeness [*plenitudine*] of the Scriptures.'[150] This conclusion confirms that Rutherford embraces biblical authority at least to some degree. In order to answer Rogers and McKim, however, we need to see the extent to which he does so. Does he view Scripture as authoritative only in matters of faith and morality, as they assert, or in every subject to which it speaks?

---

[146] See B.B. Warfield, *Calvin and Calvinism* (New York: Oxford University, 1931), pp. 62-4.

[147] Henderson, *Religious Life*, pp. 12-13.

[148] *SA*, p. 304. See also p. 236, where Rutherford states: 'If any idolize the preached or written Word, it is not our doctrine.'

[149] This is not, however, to deny the testimony of the Holy Spirit, as we will see.

[150] *Examen*, p. 97.

The Authority of Scripture

Rutherford devotes a great deal of space in the opening chapter of the *Examen* to discussing the issue of the authority of Scripture. Whereas the perfection of Scripture is not a matter of contention between him and the Arminians, its authority clearly is.[151] According to Rutherford, the Arminians in England 'sin shamefully', because they subvert the authority of Scripture in order to 'gratify the Anglican Bishops, who are now in possession of things' in the church. In currying the favor of these bishops, Rutherford believes the Arminians are 'deliberately' contradicting themselves. On the one hand, they state that they embrace the perfection and authority of Scripture, and yet, on the other hand, they undermine both by teaching—among other things—that both the Presbyterian and Episcopal forms of church government are acceptable.[152] This is unthinkable for Rutherford, because, as he alleges, the Bible plainly commands the Presbyterian form of church government. To advocate any other form besides what is commanded is to subvert the authority of Scripture. Contrary to Arminius' claim that some things in the Bible are more authoritative than others,[153] Rutherford regards everything in Scripture as equally authoritative. Christians are obligated to receive 'Occasional, Chronological, and Historical things'—like the fact that '*Paul* left his cloak, books, and parchments in Troas' and the fact that '*Abraham* begot *Isaac*'—'*Astronomical* things about *Orion* and the *Pleiades, Arcturus* and the Northern signs', and numerical things—like the fact that 'eight people were in Noah's Ark'—as no less true and, thus, no less authoritative, than this statement: 'Christ came into the world to save sinners.'[154]

While Rutherford does distinguish between things that are fundamental to the faith and things that are not, he adopts a fairly intricate hierarchy in order to differentiate between the two categories, the end result of which is to make the former category unusually comprehensive. 'The Fundamentals', he says, 'are those things that pertain to the vital parts, to the soul and the life of faith.' Following Theodore Beza, Rutherford defines them as the doctrines that are found 'either expressly or by consequence in the *Apostles' Creed*'.[155] Historically, they have been received 'by the consent of all', according to Calvin, as containing the foundation of the Christian faith. All who subvert this foundation are not a part of the '*true Church*' but prove, instead, that they are members of a 'false Synagogue'. Following after the fundamentals, and built

---

[151] Rutherford deals with the Arminians on issues relating to biblical authority throughout the first chapter, but he concentrates his diatribe in a thirty-one page section near the end of it (*Examen*, pp. 97-127).

[152] *Examen*, pp. 97-8. Cf. S. Episcopius, *Opera theologica* (Rotterdam, 1665), II, pp. 223-7.

[153] See, e.g., *WJA*, II, p. 106.

[154] *Examen*, pp. 12, 14.

[155] *Examen*, pp. 11, 32.

upon them, are the *Supra-Fundamentalia*. These things proceed 'from the foundations by plain and necessary consequence' and are, thus, 'Fundamentals secondarily and materially'. All who 'deny such *supra-Fundamentalia*, subvert the Foundation, just as the one who denies a clear and plain consequence, denies its antecedents'. Next in line are the *Circa-Fundamentalia*. In this category, Rutherford places everything mentioned in Scripture, even the 'Occasional, Chronological, and Historical things', the '*Astronomical* things', and the numerical things we mentioned above. These are necessary by necessity of precept but not by necessity of means. In other words, they are not so fundamental to salvation that a person cannot be saved without adhering to them, but they are, nonetheless, fundamental to salvation insofar as no one who is genuinely saved will deny them.[156] The one who denies anything that 'God clearly and plainly reveals in his Word' is guilty of a 'Fundamental' sin. Although Rutherford does allow for '*Praeter-Fundamentalia*' or '*adiophora*'—indifferent things—he limits this category to what is specifically 'neither forbidden nor commanded' in Scripture. Everything in the Bible is fundamental, for Rutherford, 'because to resist the light of the Word clearly displayed, even in matters of the greatest indifference, is to deny the Authority of God in the Word'.[157]

The confusing part in all this is that although he defines the fundamentals as the sum of the doctrines contained in the Apostles' Creed, he adds to this an undefined number of supra-fundamentals and circa-fundamentals, some of which—borrowing the language of 1 Corinthians 3.12—are 'gold' and thus 'necessary to be believed', while others are 'hay and stubble' and 'such as extinguish not saving faith'. Because the *supra-fundamentalia* and *circa-fundamentalia* are largely undefined, one is left wondering how far the category 'fundamental' extends in actual practice. On at least one occasion, when speaking of the Roman Catholic Church, Rutherford takes a broader stance with regard to the fundamentals both explicitly—by including several doctrines that are not mentioned in the Apostle's Creed—and implicitly—by blurring the lines of distinction between the fundamentals, on the one hand, and the *supra-fundamentalia* and *circa-fundamentalia*, on the other:

> [T]he *Church* of *Rome* erres in the fundamentals, in the doctrine of our Saviour and his offices, in the doctrine of merit, humane satisfactions, indulgences, the Scriptures, the Church....[T]hey [also] erre about baptisme, the Lords supper, confirmation, unction, pennance, though of themselves the[se doctrines] happily deprive not of life eternall, yet because the subject about which the matter is versed is most necessary, they are pernicious errors....[Then also, they err] touching creation, providence, mortification, though of themselves the[se beliefs]

---

[156] This is, as we will see, Rutherford's and the reformers' basic argument in regard to the necessity of works. They are necessary by necessity of precept but not by necessity of means. See the section on justification below.

[157] *Examen*, pp. 4, 11-13.

might be called errours, simple ignorance, yet for the dangerous consequences, they are pernicious heresies.[158]

By referring to the circa-fundamentals and the supra-fundamentals as 'most necessary' and as 'dangerous consequences' that flow from fundamental errors, Rutherford reveals the comprehensive and intricate nature of his view of the fundamentals of the faith. And Rutherford's statements with regard to the *circa-fundamentalia* elsewhere would appear to support this assertion. Even historical and numerical things are necessary to the Christian life, by necessity of means. To deny such things is a fundamental sin. To deny them publicly and obstinately, however, is a 'pernicious heresy'. Either way, all errors in *circa-fundamentalia* are not to be tolerated by the church or by the civil magistrate.[159] The genuine and practicing Christian will embrace everything in God's Word, outwardly at least, because everything carries the stamp of divine authority.

Thus, when Rogers and McKim insist that Rutherford does not view the Bible as an authoritative 'rule' in areas beyond faith and morality, they show that they are misinformed. Just the opposite is true, in fact; Rutherford views the Bible as an authoritative rule in *every* area to which it speaks. Granted, Rutherford does not believe that Scripture addresses every conceivable issue. It does not teach us how to plow a field (*arandi*), or how to sing (*canendi*), or how to speak in Latin (*Latine loquendi*). These things are learned from the principles of agriculture, music, and Latin grammar. The Bible does not address them in the same way it does matters of faith, because the final cause of Scripture is not to convey factual information about everything in life but to reveal the triune God purposively. But when the Bible does speak to the arts and sciences, it speaks authoritatively and perfectly, as we saw in regard to historical and astronomical things in Scripture. Even when it does not directly address a certain area—like 'plowing' or 'speaking in Latin'—it still has something to say. It addresses these areas as they are 'moralized' or 'Theologized'. It may not teach us how to plow, speak in Latin, or even make 'mathematical demonstrations'. But it does teach us that we are to glorify God through the arts and sciences and that we are not to lie while speaking Latin or defend false conclusions while completing a mathematical problem.[160]

Rogers and McKim are correct to see a difference between matters of faith and morality and other areas of life in Rutherford's thinking. But the difference is not that he believes the Bible to be perfect and authoritative only in the first case. The difference is that the Bible is *sufficient* in matters of faith but is not so in other areas of life. The divine causality of Scripture guarantees that the Bible must be sufficient to fulfill the divine purposes. Matters pertaining to the arts and sciences fall outside these parameters. But this does not mean that Scripture

---

[158] *PLC*, pp. 60-61.
[159] *PLC*, p. 61.
[160] *Examen*, pp. 108, 109-10, 114. Cf. *Divine Right*, p. 108.

should be regarded as less perfect or authoritative in dealing with those issues. As John Woodbridge has demonstrated, the authority and infallibility of the Bible in speaking to the arts and sciences is widely assumed at this juncture in history. Even Galileo (1564-1642) and other fellow-Copernicans of his day contend that their revolutionary discoveries are in accord with a strict view of the Bible. Many in the church at this time, like Blaise Pascal (1623-1662) and Archbishop Ussher among others, go to great lengths in attempting to reconcile the teachings of the Bible with the findings of science. The idea that the Bible is anything short of completely infallible and authoritative does not really appear on the radar screen of the church until biblical critics like Baruch Spinoza (1632-1677), Richard Simon (1638-1712), and Isaac La Peyrère (1596-1676), writing near the end of Rutherford's lifetime, begin to challenge this prevailing notion.[161] Rogers and McKim unfortunately overlook this and reveal instead a tendency to read Rutherford's doctrine of Scripture through Enlightenment goggles.

Rutherford's view of the equal infallibility and authority of every part of Scripture is even more blatant when it is seen in contrast to his perception of Arminian theology. According to Rutherford, by acknowledging that some things in the Bible are more authoritative than others and by ignoring the clear teaching of Scripture—clear, that is, to Rutherford—concerning the requisite form of church government, the Arminians minimize the authority of Scripture and open the door to the possibility of a second authoritative source. To Rutherford this is tantamount to a rejection of 'Tradition I'—to borrow Heiko Oberman's categories once again—and a move towards Roman Catholicism and 'Tradition II'. That such a move is endemic to Arminian theology is confirmed, to Rutherford's way of thinking, by their refusal to ascribe ultimate authority in controversies to Scripture. Using forensic language analogously, the Arminians assert that *'the Scriptures cannot be the Judge when the debate is over the sense of the Law, because Law and Judge are separate and distinct'*.[162] But, then, instead of going the full distance and assigning ultimate authority to the church, as in Roman Catholicism, the Arminians locate it in the interpreting individual. Each person, without coercion—but with direction perhaps—from the civil magistrate, the church, or even the Bible itself, is to 'search the Scriptures' and 'try the Spirits', and then to examine 'Controversies of Faith' by what they have gleaned.[163]

David Mullan has recently pointed to this feature of Arminian theology and concluded that the Arminians 'empowered the individual as a theologically significant centre of interpretation and criticism', with the result being that they 'recognized [the individual's judgment] as an essential locus of theological

---

[161] See Woodbridge, *Biblical Authority*, ch. 5.
[162] *Examen*, pp. 1-3. Cf. Episcopius, *Opera theologica* (1665), II, p. 124; *Confession*, pp. 68-9; *ACS*, I, pp. 32ff.
[163] *Confession*, p. 69.

authority'.[164] Because each person is led to a private apprehension of Scripture by 'his or her very own spirit of prophesying', the Arminian empowerment of the individual, in Rutherford's opinion, had the effect of rejecting the Bible as the ultimate authority and the church as a secondary authority. And, as a result, it undercut the Reformation principle *sola Scriptura*. Although the Arminians still assigned Scripture a *modicum quid* of positive authority, they did so only subjectively, insofar as the individual understood it by 'his or her dreaming spirit'.[165]

It is important to point out here that Rutherford is not being entirely fair with the Arminian doctrine of the 'liberty of prophesying'. Arminians, like Van Limborch, embrace the liberty of prophesying in order to preserve the unity of the church and to prevent the consciences of individuals from being bound by anything but Scripture, not in order to encourage hermeneutical licentiousness. Furthermore, it is not a 'dreaming spirit' that leads an individual to comprehend Scripture, according to Van Limborch, but his or her use of 'Right Reason'. Even keeping this in mind, however, it remains true that because Van Limborch and the Arminians relegate the interpretive decisions of the church to a 'Discretionary...not Authoritative' status, and because they refuse to allow anything or anyone other than God himself to have any form of coercive power over the individual's conscience,[166] they subjectivize and individualize the interpretation of the Bible and, in so doing, pave the way for 'millions of faiths with millions of senses [of Scripture], and so no faith at all'.[167] For Rutherford and the covenanters in general, such ideas helped to introduce a Pyrrhonian crisis within the church, the immediate threat of which was to endanger theological certainty.

Rutherford's theological response to this latitudinarian threat is to defend the Reformation understanding of *sola Scriptura*, in continuity with the medieval understanding of 'Tradition I'. This means, in the first place, that Scripture is the ultimate authority in all controversies. Of the seven reasons Rutherford gives as to why this is so, three are of particular interest. First, the Bible itself teaches that it is a binding arbiter. Therefore, to deny that the Bible functions as the ultimate authority in controversies is to reject what it says about itself. Second, in response to the forensic analogy of the Arminians, he says that Scripture is not 'pure law, and nothing else'. If it were, 'Judge and Law by necessity would be separate. But because Scripture is the standard of that which is to be judged, and at the same time has the *Holy Spirit* joined to it...it is not necessary that this Law and Judge be separated as a human law and earthly

---

[164] D.G. Mullan, 'Masked Popery and Pyrrhonian Uncertainty: The Early Scottish Covenanters on Arminianism', *The Journal of Religious History* 21:2 (June, 1997), pp. 174-5.
[165] *Examen*, pp. 89, 91-2.
[166] *ACS*, I, p. 39; II, p. 1015.
[167] *PLC*, p. 28.

judge are separated.' Third, he states that if the Arminians are correct and Scripture merely directs and does not compel the individual 'to receive the true sense, intended by the Holy Spirit', and if there is no objective meaning to Scripture, then no one 'would sin *by perverting the Scriptures*'. But this 'is said to be done by many, *2 Pet.* 3.16'.[168]

This understanding of Scripture as the ultimate authority in controversies raises the question of whether biblical authority is objective or subjective for Rutherford and, thus, of whether Rutherford faithfully reflects Reformation teaching on this matter. Whereas other post-Reformation theologians—like William Perkins and James Ussher, for example—devote considerable time and effort to developing objective proofs for the authority of Scripture, Rutherford does not do so.[169] Instead, he more modestly suggests one objective and one subjective proof:

> [H]ow [do] we know Scripture to be the Word of *God*; there is two things here considerable; one within, and another without. How knoweth the Lambe its mother amongst a thousand of the Flock? *Naturall instinct* teacheth it. From what Teacher or Art is it, that the Swallow buildeth its clay house and Nest, and every Bee knoweth its owne cell and waxen House; so the instinct of Grace knoweth the voyce of the Beloved amongst many voyces...and this discerning power is in the *Subject* [i.e., it is discerned by the individual according to the testimony of the Holy Spirit]. There is another power in the *Object*, of many thousand Millions of men, since the Creation, not one, in figure and shape, is altogether like another, some visible difference there is; amongst many voyces, no voyce like mans tongue; amongst Millions of divers Tongues of men, every voyce hath an audable difference printed on it, by which its discerned from all other. To the new Creature, there is in *Christs* Word some character, some sound of Heaven, that is in no voyce in the world, but in his only, in *Christ* represented to a beleevers eye of Faith; there is a shape, and a stampe of Divine Majesty, no man knoweth it, but the beleever; and in Heaven and Earth, *Christ* hath not a Marrow like himselfe.[170]

Quite significantly, these comments reveal that the Holy Spirit is the connective link between the objective and subjective proofs of biblical authority in Rutherford's thinking. Though the divine causality of Scripture does provide grounds for its objective authority, this objective authority cannot be perceived apart from the work of the Spirit granting the eyes and the mind of faith. Not only does the Spirit enable us to see the objective authority of Scripture, but it also subjectively and definitively testifies to us about it.[171]

It is this same emphasis on the work of the Spirit as providing the link between the objective and subjective proofs for biblical authority that can be seen in Calvin. Thus, while putting great stress upon the subjective testimony

---

[168] *Examen*, pp. 2-4.
[169] E.g., Perkins, *Workes*, II, pp. 54-6; Ussher, *Body of Divinitie*, pp. 8-11.
[170] *Tryal*, p. 98.
[171] *Examen*, pp. 21-3.

of the Holy Spirit in the *Institutes*, Calvin also offers objective proofs that stem from the divinity of Scripture.[172] When commenting on the Apostle Paul's words in 2 Timothy 3.16, Calvin remarks: 'In order to uphold the authority of the Scripture, he [Paul] declares that it is *divinely inspired*; for, if it be so, it is beyond all controversy that men ought to receive it with reverence.' But, lest we be tempted to understand this in isolation from the Spirit's work, he adds: 'If it be objected, "How can this be known?" I answer, *both to disciples and to teachers*, God is made known to be the author of it [Scripture] by the revelation of the same Spirit [that dictated it].'[173] Then, in order to put the matter beyond all dispute by explicitly combining both the objective and subjective in the Spirit's work, he writes: 'Accordingly, we need not wonder if there are many who doubt as to the Author of the Scripture; for, although the majesty of God is displayed in it, yet none but those who have been enlightened by the Holy Spirit have eyes to perceive what ought, indeed, to have been visible to all, and yet is visible to the elect alone.'[174]

Wilhelm Niesel has incorrectly concluded that these objective proofs 'are not of great value' for Calvin, whereas, for his later successors, they became of primary importance.[175] Such comments not only overlook Rutherford's position, which is virtually identical to Calvin's, but they also ignore the statements in others, like Perkins, that assert the testimony of the Holy Spirit to be the 'argument of all arguments, to settle and resolve the Conscience, and to seale up the certaintie of the word of God'.[176] Thus, Reinhold Seeburg would seem to be justified when he states that 'Calvin establishes the authority of the Scriptures partly upon their divine dictation, and partly upon the testimony of the Holy Spirit working through them', so long as we remember that the Spirit is as necessary in the first as in the second. Seeburg's conclusion would then also seem to be justified: 'Historically considered, [Calvin] thereby combines the later medieval conception of inspiration with the theory of Luther....[and] is therefore the author of the so-called inspiration theory of the older dogmaticians' of the post-Reformation era.[177] Rutherford's understanding of the role of the Holy Spirit in establishing the authority of Scripture helps to demonstrate substantial continuity between Calvin and the post-Reformation period. He, like Calvin, rightly deserves John Hesselink's ascription, 'The theologian of the Holy Spirit.'[178] That this is so will be more evident after our

---

[172] *Institutes* I.vii-viii, pp. 74-92.

[173] Calvin, *Commentaries on the Epistles to Timothy, Titus, and Philemon*, pp. 248-9, emphasis added in latter citation.

[174] Calvin, *Commentaries on the Epistles to Timothy, Titus, and Philemon*, p. 249.

[175] Niesel, *The Theology of Calvin*, p. 37n1.

[176] Perkins, *Workes*, II, p. 56.

[177] R. Seeburg, *Text-book of the History of Doctrines*, trans. C.E. Hay, 2 vols. (Grand Rapids, MI: Baker, 1977), II, pp. 395-6.

[178] I.J. Hesselink, 'The Charismatic Movement and the Reformed Tradition', *Reformed Review* 28 (1975), pp. 149-51, cited in Sell, *The Great Debate*, pp. 3, 103n10.

discussion of the role of the Spirit in interpreting Scripture in the next section and in effecting salvation in chapter four.

In the second place, *sola Scriptura*, according to Rutherford, means that the church has binding authority. The church is the 'minister' (*ministra*) of Scripture, and, as such, it fulfills an interpreting role and 'determines' (*proponit*) what Scripture says. Its decisions are not merely beneficial to individuals but are binding upon them, albeit only insofar as they are in accordance with the plain teaching of the Bible. The church's authority is thus 'instrumental' only. Contra Roman Catholicism, it is secondary to and derivative from the authority of the Bible itself.[179] What this means is that scriptural interpretation is not merely a matter of an encounter between the individual and the Holy Spirit, because the church, rather than the individual, is the 'minister' of Scripture. Although it is true that the Holy Spirit opens the eyes of individuals so that they can see the meaning and authority of Scripture, it is also true that the individual's ensuing interpretation is subject, first of all, to the overall teaching of the Bible and, second of all, to the interpretation of the church. The idea here is that the collective wisdom and knowledge of the church as a whole is ordinarily greater than that of any one individual, as our examination of the church's role in interpreting Scripture in the next section will show.

In an issue closely related to the authority of the church, viz., the legitimacy and role of a confession of faith, the Arminians once again frame their opinions in order to ensure maximal latitude in their approach to Scripture. Arminius states that confessions, and all other public interpretations of Scripture, ought to be confined to the express words of the Bible and ought not, 'as far as [the church] is capable', to utilize 'foreign words or phrases'.[180] Van Limborch adds that 'no Man' should ever be 'tied up' or forced to embrace 'such Words and Expressions as are not contain'd in the Holy Scripture, but are only of Human Invention'.[181] While this position may have much to commend it—especially when it is viewed in comparison with a position of extreme intolerance— nonetheless, from Rutherford's perspective, it overlooks the God-given responsibility that the church has in the propagation of the truth. The church, as the 'minister' of Scripture, is entrusted with—to again use the words of Heiko Oberman—the '*fides* or *veritas* contained in Holy Scripture'.[182] The church is responsible to teach the people what it perceives to be the right interpretation of the Bible and to protect the people from what it perceives to be harmful and false interpretations. Ever since the fourth century and the Arian controversy, the church had seen the need for confessions and creeds 'to preserve its commitment to the New Testament proclamation' by distinguishing the

---

[179] *Examen*, pp. 3, 16; *PLC*, pp. 23ff.
[180] *WJA*, II, p. 422.
[181] *ACS*, I, p. 22.
[182] Oberman, *Harvest of Medieval Theology*, p. 372.

accepted interpretation of Scripture from heretical alternatives.[183] Such an emphasis on the use of confessions, however, should not suggest that they would carry an equal status with the Word of God. Rutherford regards them as only secondary standards, subordinate to the teaching of Scripture. Individuals are not to subscribe to a confession, 'formally and to the extent that it was written by the Church, but materially, to the extent that it is the word of God'. Scripture alone is 'the object of our faith', says Rutherford, not the 'set of words' of a confession. Subscription, therefore, is not 'absolute' but 'conditional' upon a confession's faithfulness to the teaching of Scripture.[184]

The latitudinarian emphasis in Arminian theology provokes more than just a theological response from Rutherford. It provokes a move to censure the Arminians for their subversion of the authority of Scripture. As a result of extending a liberty of prophesying to all persons, the Arminians effectively eliminate the objective line of demarcation between fundamental and non-fundamental articles. This leads them to offer religious toleration to a wide variety of sects and to expand the bounds of the church to include even heretical groups like '*Socinians, Anabaptists, Anti-trinitarians, Arians, Tritheists, Sabellians,* and *Papists*'.[185] For Rutherford, the toleration of such groups is itself a sinful disregard of the Bible's authority to speak clearly to matters pertaining to faith. Tolerance can never be extended to groups who err in the fundamentals.

But more problematic than this, for Rutherford, is the fact that the Arminians place themselves in league with the above heretical groups not merely by tolerating those views but by publicly holding and obstinately defending their own views as well. There is a difference, in Rutherford's opinion, between privately held beliefs and those that are publicly promulgated and stubbornly defended. Individuals who hold Arminian convictions may still 'retain the Foundation' and, if private in their profession, are worthy of true toleration. But those who publicly inculcate Arminian ideals are not due this same indulgence.[186] Even though they err in non-fundamentals—which fact is not certain according to Rutherford's comprehensive conception of the fundamentals—they promulgate and defend these non-fundamental errors vigorously. And, because the authority of God 'is as great in non-fundamentals, and our obligation to beleeve no lesse, then in the most necessary [of] fundamentals', as we saw before, true toleration is not to be shown to public and hardened Arminians either.[187] Instead, the church and the civil magistrate

---

[183] A.E. McGrath, *The Genesis of Doctrine: A Study in the Foundations of Doctrinal Criticism* (Oxford: Basil Blackwell, 1990), p. 7.

[184] *Examen*, pp. 8-9. In *PLC*, p. 25, Rutherford speaks of a confession as a 'secondarie rule of faith'.

[185] *Examen*, p. 6.

[186] *Examen*, p. 46; *PLC*, ch. 6.

[187] *PLC*, p. 124.

are to use all the power at their disposal to ensure that every external manifestation of their error is eliminated. Rutherford does not shrink from extending the magistrate's power in this process to include even 'the sword', in order that it might 'restrain the externall act[s]' of religion and ensure that all people outwardly adhere to the fundamentals of the faith and the Word of God.[188] As we will see in chapter five, there is more at stake in Rutherford's censure of the Arminians than the mere fact that they hold to non-fundamental errors publicly and obstinately and embrace the liberty of prophesying. These things form part of a bigger picture that will help us to see why Rutherford reacts with such intolerance towards Arminian theology.

More than anything else, Rutherford's understanding of the authority of Scripture and his view of the fundamentals of the Christian faith beg the question of the interpretation of Scripture. This question was one that had not previously required much in the way of an answer before the middle of the sixteenth century. But now, with the emergence of Arminianism and Socinianism in the late sixteenth and early seventeenth centuries—both of which professed to hold high views of Scripture and, yet, developed theologies that were at odds with Reformed orthodoxy—Rome's accusation that the Reformation's emphasis on *sola Scriptura* had empowered hermeneutical abuses of Scripture without any ultimate means of differentiating between varying interpretations was beginning to appear prophetic.[189] The changing context of the period in which Rutherford lived required a shift in polemical methodology. The issues of the perspicuity and interpretation of Scripture now came to the fore.[190] The demand for this shift was further exacerbated by the sharp increase in the number of religious sects in England during the early decades of the seventeenth century that tended to treat the Bible as a 'nose of wax' to be formed and fashioned according to fancy.[191] Rome's solution to this issue was to locate ultimate authority in the church. Although they too interpreted Scripture subjectively, 'with equall propension to contradictory senses',[192] the ballast of church authority kept them from sinking into the depths of utter subjectivity. Rutherford's hermeneutics, to which we now turn, are developed in such a way as to avoid the Scylla of Rome's accusations of subjectivity and of Arminian uncertainty, while, at the same time, steering clear of the Charybdis of Rome's ecclesiology.

---

[188] *PLC*, pp. 46-7.

[189] C. Hill, *The English Bible and the Seventeenth-Century Revolution* (London: Penguin, 1993), p. 428.

[190] Trueman, 'Faith Seeking Understanding', p. 157n28.

[191] *Christ Dying*, p. 536. See also H.C. Porter, 'The Nose of Wax: Scripture and the Spirit from Erasmus to Milton', *Transactions of the Royal Historical Society* 14 (1964), pp. 155-74; and other post-Reformation theologians: e.g., Ussher, *Body of Divinitie*, p. 21. In *PLC*, p. 254, Rutherford says that 'above twenty sundry Religions in England came to the streets' during the 1640s.

[192] *Christ Dying*, p. 536.

The Interpretation of Scripture

In his attempt to defend a *via media* between the extremes of subjectivity and uncertainty, on the one hand, and of ascribing final authority to the church, on the other, Rutherford articulates his belief that Scripture is perspicuous (*perspicua*). God, he says—sounding very much like William Ames—has not revealed the 'deep and high Mysteries, [which are] necessary for salvation' in 'dark and enigmaticall prophecies, but plainly'.[193] Although 'the things themselves are for the most part hard to be conceived, yet the manner of delivering and explaining them, especially in those things which are necessary, is cleere [*clarus*] and perspicuous [*perspicuus*]'.[194] In continuity with the Reformation understanding of *sola Scriptura*, Rutherford and his post-Reformation contemporaries believe that the Bible, at least in the fundamental articles of the faith, is clear and can be understood by all people, even the most unlearned.

As may be anticipated, vast differences arise between Rutherford and the Arminians with respect to the ways in which they perceive the perspicuity of Scripture. These differences foreshadow many of the issues that will surface in the following chapters and demonstrate the immense significance that Rutherford, like Calvin, attaches to the role of the Holy Spirit in his theology. Adopting similar language to the Reformed orthodox, albeit with a strongly rationalist bent, the Arminians state that Scripture is perspicuous, 'especially in Meanings necessary to be understood unto salvation, [so] that all that read them, not only the Learned, but the Ignorant also (*that are endued but with common Sense and Judgment*) may, as far as it is sufficient, attain to the understanding of them'.[195] Van Limborch and Episcopius, in their own writings, make this link between perspicuity and the 'right use of Reason' more explicit. Episcopius even claims that '*the light of the Holy Spirit is not required to understand the sense of Scripture*'.[196] Although they attribute this use of reason in comprehending Scripture to the realm of grace, the effect of their emphasis on reason is that they teach that all people are able to interpret Scripture rightly if only they apply themselves and their natural capacities. Rutherford, however, argues instead that the 'Gospel is hidden [*tectum*] to the blind and to those who are perishing'.[197]

But how can he assert that Scripture is both perspicuous (*perspicua*) and hidden (*tectum*) at the same time? In order to answer this question and to differentiate his position from Arminianism and Roman Catholicism, Rutherford—very much in line with other post-Reformation theologians like John Owen—speaks of a *duplex evidentia Scripturae*, and, correspondingly, of

---

[193] *Christ Dying*, p. 536. Cf. *Catachisme*, p. 162.
[194] Ames, *Marrow*, p. 170; idem, *Medulla*, pp. 181-2.
[195] *Confession*, p. 72, emphasis added.
[196] *ACS*, I, p. 18; *Examen*, p. 83; Episcopius, *Opera theologica* (1665), II, pp. 126-7.
[197] *Examen*, p. 87.

a *duplex cognitio Scripturae*.[198] On the one hand, there is a 'literal and grammatical clearness' to Scripture, by which all people can 'grasp' the 'literal and grammatical sense' of the Bible by their natural understandings and thus come to a 'literal [and grammatical] knowledge' of it. This literal knowledge is insufficient for Christian salvation. Even 'Devils, Heretics, and *those...whom* Satan, *the god of this age, has blinded*' can achieve that. Salvation, as we have seen, requires a supernatural knowledge of God, which is gained by a 'spiritual [or, better, a Spiritual] opening and declaration of the literal sense' of the Bible. Thus, there is, on the other hand, a 'supernatural clearness' to Scripture, which is productive of this supernatural knowledge. It is 'obscured [*obscuras*] to Devils and to the blind reprobate in the same way that the sun is obscured to the [physically] blind, though in itself it is exceedingly clear [*clarus*] and visible'. So it is that, although Scripture itself is perspicuous (*perspicua*), the effects of sin have rendered all people incapable of grasping anything other than the literal and grammatical meaning of it. The 'Gospel' or the spiritual meaning of the Bible is 'hidden and obscured' (*tectum et obscurum*) and can only be seen when the Holy Spirit removes our spiritual blindness, giving us eyes to see and illumining our minds to understand.[199] Apart from this work of the Spirit, the 'word of God by itself is [simply] a dead letter'.[200]

This is not to say, as the Arminians 'falsely' accuse, that there are two senses to Scripture, a '*literal and grammatical* sense', which is understood by all people, and a '*supernatural* sense added over and above it', which is only seen by those who are supernaturally enlightened. For Rutherford, this is 'most false'. Just because 'the nearly blind' and the 'sharp-sighted see the same sun in different ways', does not mean that there are 'two Suns'. And, so, just because Scripture is understood differently by two opposing groups of people, does not mean that it has two senses. Instead, there is only one sense to Scripture and that is the literal sense. But there are 'two ways of seeing' this literal sense: one, literally or naturally and, the other, spiritually or supernaturally. For the believer, the Word of God is perspicuous (*perspicuum*) 'in each way, in both its *natural* and *its supernatural clearness*' (*evidentia*). But for the unbeliever, it is perspicuous 'in its *natural clearness*'—contra Roman Catholicism—and is 'hidden and obscured in its *supernatural clearness*'—contra Arminianism. Both read the same literal sense, but while the unbeliever has eyes to see only the literal and grammatical meaning of that sense, the believer has eyes to see its spiritual meaning. It is the Holy Spirit, or the lack thereof, that is the chief difference between the two.[201]

The literal sense of Scripture is, therefore, the key to its interpretation in Rutherford's theology. Anyone who has eyes to see and who applies himself or

---

[198] Cf. *Works of John Owen*, IV, p. 156.
[199] *Examen*, pp. 83-4, 87-8, 328.
[200] *Examen*, p. 590.
[201] *Examen*, p. 88.

herself to the 'literall exposition' of the Bible, can clearly understand at least those things that are necessary for salvation. But what is this literal sense? And what does literal exposition look like? For Rutherford, the literal sense is the 'native sense that the words offer, without violence or straining'. It is not the same thing as the 'radical Scripture principal of the Socinians' and later Arminians,[202] i.e., some sort of literalistic interpretation that reads the Bible only 'according to the letter'. Scripture is full of metaphorical, as well as 'figurative and typicall', language that must be taken into account. Jesus' words in Matthew 18.8-9, for example, cannot be interpreted to mean that we are actually to pluck out our eyes or to cut off our hands and feet. Figurative passages like this should rather be understood as if 'they were turned into modified and simple expressions'. These modifications of 'figurative speeches' into 'simple expressions' are to be done in a way that is faithful to the text itself and the 'analogie of faith'.[203] The *literal* sense of Scripture is, therefore, something more akin to its *literary* sense. It is the sense that the human author intended to convey to his original audience through a particular literary genre.

Thus, if we were to borrow John McNeill's comparison, Rutherford would side with Calvin, rather than with Gregory the Great, in his high regard for the human authors of Scripture. Though Rutherford can consciously call these authors amanuenses—as Calvin does as well—they are 'far more than a pen' to him.[204] This is because the literal or literary sense that was intended by the human author is the 'very meaning and kindly sense of the Holy Ghost'.[205] Rutherford follows the humanistic historical-grammatical method of exegesis typical of the reformers and arrives at the divine meaning of a given text by discerning what the human author originally meant to say in writing it. What is more, this identification of the divine intent with the human intent in Scripture also ensures that there will be no contradiction in Rutherford's thinking between a reliance upon the Holy Spirit in interpreting Scripture and the need for real human effort in discerning the author's original meaning.

One obvious consequence of this emphasis on the historical-grammatical method of exegesis is the necessity of knowing the original languages. William Ames expresses this need succinctly: '[B]ecause the Scriptures...were written in those tongues, which were most commonly vulgar in the Church at that time when they were written [i.e., Hebrew and Greek]....there is some knowledge at least of these tongues [that is] necessary to the exact understanding of the Scriptures.' Another obvious consequence of this method is that 'the Scriptures are to be understood by the same meanes that other humane writings are'. It is precisely because the human authors are of central importance in grasping the

---

[202] C.R. Trueman, *The Claims of Truth: John Owen's Trinitarian Theology* (Carlisle, Cumbria: Paternoster, 1998), p. 85.
[203] *SA*, pp. 311-12.
[204] McNeill, 'The Significance of the Word of God for Calvin', pp. 139-40.
[205] *SA*, II, pp. 164, 211.

message of the divine author that post-Reformation theologians, like Rutherford, attach such significance to '*Logick, Rethorick, Grammar*', and history in the hermeneutical process, not because they have some sort of an overriding rationalistic bent.[206]

In keeping with the Reformation's method of exegesis, Rutherford not only draws upon his knowledge of the original languages but also refers to the original context and the analogy of faith in order to establish the best interpretation of a passage of Scripture, when its plain sense is not immediately explicit. His overarching hermeneutical principle is that Scripture is always the 'rule of exponing scripture'.[207] Because of this, he refers to clearer passages of the Bible for help in interpreting those that are less clear. For particularly challenging texts, Rutherford also turns to a whole host of biblical commentators and, in many such cases, shows a profound erudition and breadth of knowledge. For example, in both the *Examen* and *A Peaceable Plea for Paul's Presbyterie*, Rutherford argues that when Scripture says 'Tell the Church' in Matthew 18, it actually means the elders or the 'Ministeriall Church' rather than all the members of the church, by offering, in each treatise, over thirteen pages of textual evidence from both Old and New Testaments to prove his contention. In *Paul's Presbyterie*, three of the pages are devoted to disproving those who would argue against him from Scripture based upon the use of the word 'church'. On these occasions, Rutherford reveals a thoroughgoing familiarity with the original Greek and Hebrew, the Septuagint, and Jewish culture, as well as with a myriad of theologians, among whom he cites such 'Fathers' as Augustine, Ambrose (c.340-397), Cyprian (d. 258), Jerome (c.340-420), and Chrysostom (347-407); such 'Scholastics' as Aquinas, Ockham, Nicholas of Lyra (1270-1340), Dominico Bañez (1528-1604), Franciscus Suárez (1548-1617), Gabriel Vasquez (1549-1604), and Gregory de Valentia (c.1550-1603); and such reformers and post-reformers as Musculus, Calvin, Beza, Polanus, David Pareus (1548-1622), and Robert Parker (d. c.1650).[208] On other occasions in the *Examen*, Rutherford enters into detailed word studies in order to discern the meaning of the human author and, in doing so, even shows an awareness of different biblical codices and their renderings of particular words and phrases.[209]

Interpretive situations like these, in which the plain meaning of the text is difficult to ascertain, serve to establish further the necessity of the church in the hermeneutical process. But even in these situations, Rutherford sees the church as necessary *ad bene esse* not *ad esse*. Many people can be and are saved, who never have the help of the church to 'cleare their faith'. This is because those things that are necessary for salvation are plain for all who have eyes to see.

---

[206] Ames, *Marrow*, p. 171.
[207] *SA*, p. 67.
[208] *Examen*, pp. 650-63; *PP*, pp. 85-98.
[209] *Examen*, pp. 545-6, 571-4, 575.

Other things in Scripture, however, are not so plain. But this is not because of any defect in Scripture. The Bible is clear and leaves nothing 'in it selfe controversall'. Some of the things it teaches, though, are 'controverted' by us, because of our 'dulnesse and sinfull blindnesse'. In these cases, it is the domain of the church to 'determine from the light of the word' the best interpretations.[210] Their determinations are by no means always infallible, although they can be. Rutherford certainly believes that it is possible for the fallible church to speak infallibly, but this is so only insofar as what they say is according to Scripture.[211] The church pronouncing on controverted doctrines is likened, by Rutherford, to ministers preaching the word. In both cases what they say is the word of God and, thus, infallible, but only secondarily so, to the extent that it is in accord with Scripture.

Quite obviously, this stance with regard to the church necessitates a trained ministry. And so Rutherford decries as 'intruders' to the ministry those 'sectaries' who 'goe from weaving, sowing, Carpentarie, Shoo-making to the pulpit to the representing of God, and being his mouth to his people, being voyd of all learning, tongues, logick, arts, sciences, and the literall knowledge of the scripture'.[212] Ministers must be schooled in 'human arts and tongues', because these things are tools to help interpret the Bible rightly. The example of Christ and the Apostles in making use of languages and logic in interpreting the Old Testament—by translating Hebrew passages into Greek and drawing logical conclusions from scriptural texts—confirms that such 'human learning is lawfull for, and necessary to the opening and understanding of the Scripture' for us as well.[213] This takes on added significance in light of Rutherford's belief that '[w]hat is in Scripture by consequence is Scripture'.[214] Ministers, whose work it is to interpret and expound the Bible, ought, therefore, above all others, to be trained in languages, logic, and rhetoric, as well as other arts and sciences, in order that they might rightly understand and apply Scripture for the benefit of the church.

It is important that Rutherford's convictions regarding the necessity of the church in interpreting Scripture not be understood in contradiction to the work of the Holy Spirit. His definition of the church as 'Godis people chosen to lif everlasting, and called by his Word and Spirit from sinne to grace and glorie', helps to demonstrate this fact.[215] As Rutherford sees it, the church is the community of the Holy Spirit. It is organized by the Spirit's calling and comprised of individuals who have been given Spiritual eyes to see the 'supernatural sense' of Scripture. Furthermore, its ministers have been trained

---

[210] *PLC*, pp. 24, 33.
[211] *PLC*, pp. 24-5; *SA*, II, p. 211.
[212] *SA*, p. 49.
[213] *SA*, pp. 49-51; *Examen*, p. 29.
[214] *PLC*, p. 60.
[215] *Catachisme*, p. 191.

in the original languages and in the use of other such arts and sciences as would aid in the interpretation of Scripture. And because, as we saw previously, the use of certain human skills in employing the historical-grammatical method of exegesis is perfectly compatible with the Holy Spirit's work in interpretation—which is itself a product of the identification of the intent of the human authors with the intent of the divine author—the church and, most particularly, church synods, are most qualified to interpret biblical teaching. It makes sense, therefore, that Rutherford would refer to the church as the minister or steward of Scripture.

In short, what all this shows is that in attempting to walk a hermeneutical *via media* between the Arminians and the Roman Church, Rutherford emphasizes three basic interpretive categories—the spiritual, the historical-grammatical, and the ecclesial—each of which is inextricably tied to the work of the Holy Spirit.[216] The Arminians, like the Papists, deny this threefold approach to biblical interpretation. By doing so, they reduce the work of the Holy Spirit in the hermeneutical process to, at best, an individual event. While their motivation for this move towards individualization is a laudable desire to preserve the unity of the church by allowing for theological latitude in non-fundamentals, they elicit Rutherford's censure for it in at least three important ways. First, in denying the Reformation's threefold approach to biblical interpretation, the Arminians, to Rutherford's way of thinking, identify themselves *principially* with the Roman Catholic Church. Second, by allowing for theological latitude in non-fundamentals, the Arminians function as a living apology for the work of the counter-Reformation. The Arminian latitude, according to Rutherford, effectively opens the door for theological subjectivity and thus embodies the Papists' accusation that the Reformation doctrine of *sola Scriptura* was productive of such subjectivity. The objectivity that Rome provided by their belief in the ultimate authority of the church, Rutherford and the Reformation attempted to provide through the above mentioned threefold approach to biblical interpretation. The Arminians represented a threat to the work of the Reformation—a point we will argue more vigorously in chapter five—by their rejection of *sola Scriptura* and their openness to theological subjectivity. Third, by undermining theological certainty, the Arminians endangered not only the work of the Reformation but the Christian faith itself. Because, as we will see in chapter four, Rutherford believes assurance to be of the essence of saving faith, the Arminian Pryhonnian crisis threatened to undermine the foundations of Christianity itself. And, for all these reasons, it could not be tolerated.

---

[216] Rutherford's understanding at this point is virtually identical to John Owen's, as can be seen in Trueman, *Claims of Truth*, p. 85.

CHAPTER 3

The Doctrine of God

The most important aspect of Rutherford's theology is his doctrine of God. No other doctrine is more fundamental. It controls and affects Rutherford's whole approach to theology and influences his understanding of revelation, creation, election, Christology, and soteriology. In the *Examen*, it stands at the heart of his dispute with the Arminians, because the Arminian doctrine of God is equally as fundamental in determining their theology as it is in Rutherford. This is not to suggest that every doctrine is simply a derivative of the doctrine of God. In Rutherford and the Arminians, as in other Reformed writers of the sixteenth and seventeenth centuries, there is, as Richard Muller has stated, 'significant interrelation, even interplay, between the doctrine of God and the other topics of…theology'. By identifying God as the *'principium essendi* of theology', Reformation and post-Reformation theologians—including both Rutherford and the Arminians—'actually produced a theological system in consistent dialogue with the doctrine of God'.[1] In Rutherford's quarrel with the Arminians, it is the specific interrelation or dialogue between the doctrine of God and soteriology that takes center stage. The current chapter will demonstrate this by presenting Rutherford's doctrine of God and the main areas of contention between him and the Arminians. We will follow the same basic outline that is offered in the *Examen*, concentrating first on the nature of God, then on the will of God, and finally on two particular applications of the divine will to salvation, predestination and the atonement of Christ.

The *natura Dei*

There is nothing particularly novel about Rutherford's view of the nature of God. His thinking is not only characteristic of the seventeenth century, but can be traced back through the Reformation to medieval scholastics like Aquinas, Duns Scotus, and Anselm (d. 1109) and, before that, to the Patristic tradition of the Latin West.[2] Nevertheless, before considering the more controversial doctrine of the divine will in Rutherford's thinking, we will briefly survey his

---

[1] *PRRD*, III, p. 33. For post-Reformation use of the phrase, *principium essendi*, see, e.g., Leigh, *Body of Divinity*, p. 121.
[2] For cogent surveys of the nature of God from the medieval era through to the post-Reformation period, see *PRRD*, vols. 3 and 4; and *RD*, pp. 47-190.

view of the nature of God and highlight several areas in which it can be distinguished from the Arminians. We will look at the essence and attributes of God—specifically, divine perfection, simplicity, and omnipresence—and then at the Trinity, before concluding with a treatment of Rutherford's view of divine knowledge and what he regards to be a pernicious error amongst the Arminians, namely, *scientia media*.

The Essence and Attributes of God

Rutherford begins his examination of the doctrine of God in the *Examen* not by answering the questions *an sit Deus?* or *quid sit Deus?*, as do other post-Reformation treatments of the doctrine of God,[3] but, like Calvin, by answering the question *qualis sit Deus?*[4] In other words, Rutherford, like Calvin, is most concerned with uncovering what God is like towards his creatures rather than with proving the divine existence or with examining what God is essentially, in and of himself. To be sure, Rutherford and his contemporaries do discuss the divine essence (*quid sit Deus*)—some more than others—but only insofar as *Deus revelatus* and *theologia ectypa* enables them. Contrary to Brian Armstrong, they have no 'pronounced interest in metaphysical matters, [or] in abstract speculative thought' in their understandings of God.[5] Instead, in keeping with their emphasis on *praxis* in theology, Rutherford and the Reformed orthodox are chiefly concerned with what God is like in relation to his creatures. Even the attempts that they make to answer *quid sit Deus* are made only as a means to this end. And although it is true that Calvin questions the helpfulness of asking *quid sit*,[6] this does not prevent him from devoting a chapter of his *Institutes* to answering it. As with Rutherford and his peers, however, Calvin insists that this knowledge of the divine essence is not speculative but practical, because 'it invites us first to fear God, then to trust in

---

[3] Rutherford actually begins this part of the *Examen* with a two-page discussion of our knowledge of God. But unlike other post-Reformation treatments of the doctrine of God, this short discussion only seeks to answer one question, namely, whether or not 'a true and right knowledge of God' can properly be commanded of all people without exception. Rutherford does not enter into speculative questions about whether God's existence can be proved (*Examen*, pp. 138-41). Other post-Reformation theologians, however, place more emphasis on the proofs for God's existence before proceeding to an examination of the divine essence and attributes. See, e.g., Leigh, *Body of Divinity*, pp. 122-35; and, to a lesser extent, Perkins, *Workes*, I, p. 11; and Ussher, *Body of Divinitie*, pp. 28-9.

[4] On these questions and their priority in the Reformation and post-Reformation eras, see *PRRD*, III, pp. 153-9.

[5] Armstrong, *Calvinism and the Amyraut Heresy*, p. 32.

[6] Calvin says: 'What is God [*quid sit*]? Men who pose this question are merely toying with idle speculations. It is more important for us to know of what sort he is [*qualis sit*] and what is consistent with his nature.' *Institutes* I.ii.2, p. 41.

him'.⁷ All of the questions asked by reformers and post-reformers alike are designed not to answer *quid sit*, at least not insofar as it invites speculation, but *quis sit* or *qualis sit* instead.⁸ As T.F. Torrance has remarked in regard to Calvin—which would apply equally to Rutherford as well—these latter questions are not ones 'in which the essence and the existence of God are held apart from one another, but [those] in which God is allowed to disclose who he is in actual relation toward us'.⁹

That being said, how does Rutherford answer the question, *quid sit Deus*? or, perhaps better, *qualis sit Deus*? In a way reflective of the influence of Duns Scotus, in particular, and before that, of Anselm, Rutherford believes that God is, by definition, 'absolutely perfect'. He is the being than which nothing greater can be conceived.¹⁰ Although Rutherford does not attempt to prove this from Scripture, the Westminster Confession of Faith, which he helped to write, does.¹¹ Even so, it should be noted that there was little, if any, reason for him to prove this assumption. Divine perfection was not questioned at this juncture in the church. Nor was it necessarily linked with the influence of Greek philosophy. Were Rutherford challenged on this idea, he would no doubt have made reference to biblical passages similar to the ones cited in the Confession. Be that as it may, divine perfection is only mentioned in the *Examen* as a means to an end. Following in the tradition of Anselm, Rutherford develops several key divine attributes by way of deduction from God's essential perfection. But, at the same time, he consciously borrows from Peter Lombard's (c.1100-1160) tendency to present and defend these attributes with biblical and ecclesiastical justification.

First among these deductions, for Rutherford, is divine simplicity. Although simplicity is one attribute that was normatively acknowledged within the church from the time of the early fathers through the end of Rutherford's lifetime, it received renewed attention during high and late medieval scholasticism in the face of Islamic and Jewish philosophical attacks on the

---

⁷ See *Institutes* I.x.1-3, pp. 96-9, and especially, I.x.2, pp. 97-8.

⁸ Thus, William Ames could use the phrases *quid sit*, *quis sit*, and *quails sit* virtually interchangeably in *Marrow*, pp. 13-15; and *Medulla*, pp. 13-15.

⁹ T.F. Torrance, 'The Distinctive Character of the Reformed Tradition', *Reformed Review* 54:1 (Autumn, 2000), p. 6.

¹⁰ *Examen*, p. 141. For Duns Scotus, God is a 'maximally excellent' being, which means, in the first place, that God is 'maximally *perfect*'. This in turn seems to be the foundation from which Duns Scotus constructs his doctrine of God, inferring a whole host of divine attributes (R. Cross, *Duns Scotus* [New York: Oxford University, 1999], pp. 23-4, 31). For Anselm, God is 'aliquid quo nihil maius cogitari posit'. See the helpful discussion of this phrase in K. Barth, *Anselm: Fides Quaerens Intellectum, Anselm's Proof of the Existence of God in the Context of his Theological Scheme* (London: SCM, 1960), pp. 73ff.

¹¹ The Confession cites Job 11.7-9 and 26.14 as proof-texts of divine perfection in *WCF*, § 2.1, pp. 24-5.

doctrine of the Trinity. The question these medieval scholastics faced was this: how could there be distinctions made between persons in God and, yet, still be only one God? In order to answer such questions, theologians wrangled over what was meant by the term distinction and what they perceived to be the relationship of the persons and attributes of God to the divine essence. The way one responded in this debate was largely a matter of what one believed about universals and their relationship to God. Rutherford, true to Reformed theology in general, was faithful to one of the Nominalist schools—the anti-Pelagian *schola Augustiniana moderna*, of which more will be said later—and embraced a Thomistic conception of divine simplicity.[12] According to this way of thinking, 'Attributes, Relations, and Modes of Subsisting' are not different parts or aspects of God. That would make God a composition and deny his simplicity. Neither are they merely divine qualities, actions, or ways of speaking about him, as we say that '*white* is in *milk*' and '*justice* in *humankind*. But they are God himself, considered and presented to our Understanding in different ways.'[13]

Alvin Plantinga and Nicholas Wolterstorff have recently claimed that this Thomistic understanding of divine simplicity actually eliminates the reality of distinctions within the Godhead, even those among the persons of the Trinity.[14] If every distinction in the Godhead is God himself, then, as Plantinga explains, God becomes 'identical with his nature and [with] each of his properties'. Such a notion, he says, is subject to at least 'two difficulties':

> In the first place if God is identical with each of his properties, then each of his properties is identical with each of his properties, so that God has but one property. This seems flatly incompatible with the obvious fact that God has several properties; he has both power and mercifulness, say, neither of which is identical with the other. In the second place, if God is identical with each of his

---

[12] On Aquinas' understanding of divine simplicity, see B. Davies, *The Thought of Thomas Aquinas* (Oxford: Clarendon, 1992), pp. 44-57. On the different schools within Nominalism, see H.A. Oberman, 'Some Notes on the Theology of Nominalism: With Attention to its Relation to the Renaissance', *Harvard Theological Review* 53 (1960), pp. 47-76. Here Oberman differentiates between four such 'schools' or 'threads of tradition' within Nominalism, the third of which includes men like Gregory of Rimini (d.1358) and Thomas Bradwardine (c.1290-1349) and drew upon an Augustinian view of the compatibility of human free will and divine sovereignty. Cf. A.E. McGrath, 'John Calvin and Late Mediaeval Thought: A Study in Late Mediaeval Influences upon Calvin's Theological Development', *Archiv für Reformationsgeschichte* 77 (1986), pp. 64-6, 70-73, where McGrath links the *schola Augustiniana moderna* specifically to Gregory of Rimini and Hugolino of Orvieto and outlines its features from their writings.

[13] *Examen*, p. 142. Cf. Aquinas, *Summa theologiae* Ia.3.1-8.

[14] A. Plantinga, *Does God have a Nature?* (Milwaukee, WI: Marquette University, 1980), pp. 46-7; N. Wolterstorff, 'Divine Simplicity', in *Philosophical Perspectives*, vol. 5, *Philosophy of Religion*, ed. J. Tomberlin (Atascadero, CA: Ridgeview, 1991), pp. 531-52.

properties, then, since each of his properties is a property, he is a property—a self-exemplifying property. Accordingly God has just one property: himself. This view is subject to a difficulty both obvious and overwhelming. No property could have created the world; no property could be omniscient, or, indeed, know anything at all. If God is a property, then he isn't a person but a mere abstract object; he has no knowledge, awareness, power, love or life. So taken, the simplicity doctrine seems an utter mistake.[15]

But claims such as these made by Plantinga and Wolterstorff fail to take into account the variety of ways in which terms like *identitas* and *distinctio* have been used within scholasticism historically.[16] *Identitas* cannot, in this case, mean identical in every way, because few, if any, scholastic theologians who embrace the traditional doctrine of divine simplicity would deny that there are also distinctions within the Godhead. Simplicity is designed not to mean that there are no distinctions whatsoever in God but to protect the unity of the divine essence by providing an environment in which discussions of those distinctions can rightly take place. The distinction between the justice of God and the mercy of God, for example, or between the persons of the Trinity, cannot refer to different parts or components, because the divine essence is one numerically. But this does not mean that there is no distinction at all between divine justice and mercy, on the one hand, or between the Father, the Son, and the Holy Spirit, on the other. Finding a solution to the problem presented by Plantinga and Wolterstorff does not necessitate a denial of divine simplicity. The scholastic solution—a perfectly legitimate one—is simply to qualify what is meant by the term 'distinction'. Following the pattern established by Henry of Ghent (c.1217-1293) and Aquinas, Rutherford explains that the distinctions between the attributes of God, or the persons of the Godhead, are not *real* distinctions—i.e., they do not refer to different things (*res*) in God; nor are they *formal* distinctions, as Duns Scotus believes; but they are 'distinction[s] of *Reason*' and of the way in which God is considered (*ratiocinatae*) not only by us but also by the divine essence itself.[17] In reference to the persons of the

---

[15] Plantinga, *Does God have a Nature?*, pp. 46-7. Plantinga's conclusions are repeated in Wolterstorff, 'Divine Simplicity', pp. 535-6.

[16] See G. Bridges, *Identity and Distinction in Petrus Thomae, O.F.M.* (St. Bonaventure, NY: Franciscan Institute, 1959), pp. 31-42; and R. Deferrari, M.I. Barry, and I. McGuiness (eds.), *A Lexicon of St. Thomas Aquinas based on 'The Summa Theologica' and selected passages of his other works* (Washington: Catholic University of America, 1948), pp. 326-7 and 497. Cf. *PRRD*, III, p. 40n63.

[17] *Examen*, p. 142; *PRRD*, III, pp. 40-44; IV, p. 191; and Cross, *Duns Scotus*, pp. 29, 39, 43-5, and, especially, 149. Duns Scotus' idea of formal distinctions is, as Cross explains, basically a *via media* between real distinctions and Aquinas' rational distinctions. In order for something to be formally distinct it has to be both really identical and really inseparable. But, for Duns Scotus, the merely rational distinctions of Aquinas do not go far enough. As a result of his belief that God is formally distinct from his attributes and that each attribute is formally distinct from every other attribute, Duns Scotus rejects

Trinity, as we will see, Rutherford also allows for a *relational* distinction between the Father as unbegotten, the Son as begotten, and the Spirit as proceeding.

A second deduction from divine perfection is that God is not perfectible. He is, by definition as the most perfect being, incapable of becoming more perfect. Such an idea is significant because it lies at the center of a dispute between Rutherford and the Arminians, which, although relatively minor, reveals at least one important lesson for our discussion here. Rutherford and the Arminians both assert divine omnipresence. But, for Rutherford, perfection requires that the omnipresence of God is an omnipresence of his essence not simply of his '*Power*, and *Providence*, and *Knowledge*', as some Arminians admit.[18] Episcopius and others of the Remonstrants argue that Scripture does not teach 'Deum *secundum essentiam* suam ubique esse, nedum Deum secundum essentiam suam esse extra caelum & terram in spatiis omnibus, etiam imaginariis.'[19] Perhaps demonstrating his reliance upon Anselm's deductive approach to the divine attributes, Rutherford responds to the Remonstrants by arguing that their claim makes the divine essence perfectible, because the 'essence which is [present] in all things and everywhere is more perfect than the essence which is merely *here*, such that it cannot be *elsewhere*'.[20]

This relatively minor disagreement between Rutherford and the Arminians reveals his profound attitude of intolerance and his overriding concern for the glory of God. The Arminians explicitly acknowledge that God is omnipresent, but they assert that Scripture is ambiguous as to the manner of that omnipresence. Rutherford responds by bringing no less than ten arguments to bear upon the Arminian position. Quite possibly, he perceives an implicit rejection of divine simplicity by their locating omnipresence in the attributes rather than in the essence of God. Such a view would only have been exacerbated by the Arminian doctrine of the Trinity, which will be examined in the next section. In any case, it does not appear as though there is anything of any consequence that would justify Rutherford's response other than his overwhelming intolerance for Arminian theology and its tendency to stress the glory of human free will over the glory and freedom of God. Other seventeenth-century polemical treatises aimed specifically against Arminianism do not make an issue of omnipresence.[21] There appears to be no reason for Rutherford's tirade except his intolerance and his zeal for divine glory.

Aquinas' (and Rutherford's and Augustine's) view that God is 'identical with his attributes, and...that his attributes are identical with each other'. Cross, *Duns Scotus*, p. 29.

[18] *ACS*, I, p. 59. Van Limborch is actually agnostic on the question of whether omnipresence refers to the divine essence or to certain divine attributes only.

[19] Episcopius, *Opera theologica* (1665), II, p. 130.

[20] *Examen*, p. 145.

[21] E.g., Du Moulin, *Anatomy of Arminianisme*.

The Doctrine of God

Besides being perfect, simple, and omnipresent, however, God is also, according to Rutherford, first (i.e., prior to everything else), absolute, and independent. These attributes should not be understood primarily as inferences from Greek philosophy in general or from Aristotle in particular but from Moses. Like the medieval scholastics, Rutherford believed that the Tetragrammaton, the name of God given to Moses in Exodus 3.14-15, functions as the primary source for discussions about the essence and existence of God.[22] In this passage of Scripture, he perceives God's proper name to be linked with the 'to be' verb, היה. And this link, together with the testimony of other texts of Scripture—like Amos 9.6, Genesis 15.7, Isaiah 42.8, and Acts 17.28—yields at least two metaphysical deductions: God is the one who has 'being from himself' and the 'one who is Jehovah in his essence'.[23] In other words, Rutherford understands Exodus 3—not in and of itself but when it is read in light of the analogy of faith—to teach that God is the source and sustainer of all creaturely being, while he himself has no such source or sustainer. God is independent of his creation and absolute over it. He wills and acts according to his own good pleasure and is not in any way dependent upon anything outside of himself.[24]

Today there is a great deal of uncertainty among contemporary theologians as to the correct interpretation of Exodus 3 and the divine name. Karl Barth argues that Exodus 3 does not reveal the divine name at all. It is, he says, 'in content, a refusal of any name—"I am that I am" can scarcely mean anything else than just, I am He whose name proper no one can repeat'.[25] Wolfhart Pannenberg states that Exodus 3 demonstrates merely that God 'will show himself in his historical acts'. The only 'clearcut saying[s] about God's essential nature', Pannenberg says, come from 1 John 4.8, 16, and John 4.24.[26] Other scholars believe that Exodus 3 does present the name of God and that it conveys the idea of 'divine faithfulness to self', an interpretation that implies a metaphysical truth about God as the basis for his actions with Israel.[27] In spite of this uncertainty today, however, two things bear mentioning here. First, Rutherford's understanding of Exodus 3 is the consensus view among medieval, Reformation, and post-Reformation theologians. Moses Maimonides (1135-1204), could thus say:

---

[22] E. Gilson, *The Spirit of Medieval Philosophy*, trans. A.H.C. Downes (New York: Scribner, 1936), p. 51.
[23] *Examen*, pp. 141-2.
[24] *Examen*, pp. 183-4.
[25] *CD*, I/1, p. 365. E. Brunner expresses a similar sentiment in *The Christian Doctrine of God*, trans. O. Wyon (London: Lutterworth, 1949), pp. 120, 128-9.
[26] W. Pannenberg, *Systematic Theology*, trans. G.W. Bromiley (Grand Rapids, MI: Eerdmans, 1991), I, pp. 205, 395-6.
[27] T. Fretheim, 'Yahweh', in *The New International Dictionary of Old Testament Theology and Exegesis*, ed. W. VanGemeren (Carlisle, Cumbria: Paternoster, 1996), IV, pp. 1295-6.

God taught Moses…how to establish amongst them [the Israelites] the belief in the existence of Himself, namely, by saying *Ehyeh asher Ehyeh*, a name derived from the verb *hayah* in the sense of 'existing', for the verb *hayah* denotes 'to be', and in Hebrew no difference is made between the verbs 'to be' and 'to exist'. The principle point in this phrase is that the same word which denotes 'existence', is repeated as an attribute.…This is, therefore, the expression of the idea that God exists, but not in the ordinary sense of the term; or, in other words, He is 'the existing Being which is the existing Being', that is to say, the Being whose existence is absolute.[28]

Reformers like Calvin, Zwingli, Bullinger (1504-1575), and Vermigli could all point to Exodus 3 and draw a similar conclusion from it, namely, that God is, in the words of Calvin, 'self-existent and therefore eternal; and thus [he] gives being and existence to every creature. Nor does he predicate of himself anything common, or shared by others; but he claims for himself eternity as peculiar to God alone.'[29] Among men of the post-Reformation era, Perkins, Ames, Ussher, and Leigh could all state that the '*Essence* of God' is, to cite Ames, 'declared in his Name, *Jehova*', and several conclusions flow from this: 'First, that God is one, and only one'; 'Secondly, that God is of himselfe, that is, neither from another, nor of another, nor by another, nor for another'; and 'Thirdly,…that he is voyd of that power which is called passive, hence he is unchangeable.'[30]

Second, Rutherford's essentialist understanding of God, which is derived from Exodus 3, should not be relegated to the realm of metaphysical speculation. It should rather be seen as a doctrine that is laden with soteriological import and especially so in the context of Rutherford's debate with the Arminians. Since no one but God can make the claims of Exodus 3, this text lies at the foundation of the creator-creature distinction. God is not a mere creature; he is absolute and independent, while his creatures are derived and dependent upon him for everything in their lives.[31] What is more, Exodus 3 also teaches that God alone is absolutely trustworthy. Vermigli highlights both the creature's dependence and the trustworthiness of God when he says, 'there is no creature that may saie; *I will be*. For if God drawe backe his power, all

---

[28] M. Maimonides, *The Guide for the Perplexed*, trans. M. Friedländer (London: George Routledge & Sons, ²1919), pp. 94-5.

[29] J. Calvin, *Commentaries on the Four Last Books of Moses*, trans. C.W. Bingham, 4 vols. (Edinburgh: CTS, 1852-5), I, p. 73; *Institutes* I.x.2, p. 97; H. Bullinger, *The Decades of Henry Bullinger*, ed. T. Harding, vol. 4 (Cambridge: Cambridge University, 1849-52), sermon 3; U. Zwingli, *Commentary on True and False Religion*, eds. S.M. Jackson and C.N. Heller (1929; Durham, NC: Labyrinth Press, 1981), pp. 62-4; and Vermigli, *Common Places*, I.xii, p. 100.

[30] Ames, *Marrow*, p. 11. Cf. Perkins, *Workes*, I, p. 11; Ussher, *Body of Divinitie*, p. 29; Leigh, *Body of Divinity*, pp. 132-3.

[31] *Examen*, pp. 141-2.

things do straitwaie perish. God [alone] doubtlesse may trulie saie so, bicause he cannot faile nor forsake himselfe.'[32] Exodus 3, the centrality of the creator-creature distinction, and the importance of divine trustworthiness are interpreted differently by Rutherford and the Arminians and will result in profound soteriological differences in their respective systems, as we will see both later in this chapter and in the next.

The Trinity

Following a pattern characteristic of Reformed confessions from the sixteenth and seventeenth centuries, including the Westminster Confession, the *Examen* moves from a statement of the unity of the essence and attributes of God to an account of the doctrine of the Trinity.[33] And it is in regard to the doctrine of the Trinity that we begin to see greater areas of disagreement emerge between Rutherford and the Arminians. These areas of disagreement, as we will see, extend beyond the limits of the doctrine of God into the realm of soteriology. But before we can show this, we must first survey the doctrine of the Trinity in both Rutherford and the Arminians.

In typical polemical fashion, Rutherford and the Arminians accuse one other of tritheism and Sabellianism or Arianism for the ways in which they see the relationship between the persons and the essence of God. Arminius, aligning himself more with the Greek East—at least insofar as that tradition is reflected in Basil (c.330-379) and Gregory of Nyssa (c.335-c.395),[34] but, as we will see, without the protective measures that they employ—than with the Latin West, argues that the Father is 'the source [*principium*] of the whole Deity'. The Son and the Holy Spirit receive not just their persons but also their 'essence[s] by being born of the Father' and by proceeding from the Father, respectively.[35] Because of this, the Father alone is said to have 'Deity from no one', while the Son and the Spirit have their 'origin' and 'Deity from the Father'.[36] The Father alone is *autotheos*, in the sense that he is '*God from himself*'. The Son and the Spirit are *autotheos* in a subordinate way, only insofar as it refers to '*one who is truly and in himself God*'.[37] To speak of the three persons of the Godhead as each being *autotheos* in the former sense, is, according to Arminius, to suggest

---

[32] Vermigli, *Common Places*, I.xii, p. 100.
[33] See *PRRD*, III, p. 93; and *WCF*, §§ 2.1-3, pp. 24-7. Also, cf. *Examen*, pp. 141-6 with pp. 147-62.
[34] T.F. Torrance, *Trinitarian Perspectives: Toward Doctrinal Agreement* (Edinburgh: T&T Clark, 1994), pp. 29-30.
[35] *WJA*, II, pp. 693, 696. Arminius is actually agnostic on whether the Spirit proceeds from the Father alone or from the Father and the Son. Such an issue, he says, 'far surpasses [his] capacity' to determine (*WJA*, II, p. 691). Later Remonstrants, however, do plainly favor a double procession (*Confession*, p. 94).
[36] *WJA*, II, pp. 693, 696. Cf. *Confession*, p. 30.
[37] *WJA*, II, pp. 30-31. Cf. *Examen*, pp. 149-50.

either 'that there are three Gods, who have together and collaterally the Divine Essence' or that the Son and Spirit 'differ from the Father in nothing but...name,—which was the opinion of Sabellius'.[38]

Rutherford, on the other hand, claims that it is Arminius' understanding of the Trinity that is inherently tritheistic. Because Arminius states that *'the Son, both as the Son and as God, has his Deity from the Father'*, Rutherford accuses him of ascribing to the Son a derived essence and, thus, of having 'another distinct Essence and Deity' from the Father. And since the 'same thing can be said of the *Holy Spirit'*, this means that there are in fact three essences and three Gods in Arminian theology. Such an idea, for Rutherford, is contrary to the plain sense of Scripture. Passages like Deuteronomy 6.4, 32.39, and 1 Corinthians 8.6, teach that the three persons of the Godhead have one essence numerically.[39] In Rutherford's view—also reflected in his Reformed contemporaries—it is not enough to posit only a generic identity among the three persons, as the Greek fathers and some later Arminians do.[40] God is not one in the same way that three human beings are one.[41] Even though 'three humans are sharers in the class [*genus*] of *living being*' in the same way that the '*three Persons* [of the Godhead] *are sharers in the divine nature'*, nevertheless, they are 'not one and the same living being in number'.[42] Whereas, as Edward Leigh states, 'men' or 'Angels...may be without the other', God cannot exist without Father, Son, and Holy Spirit.[43] To remove one person from the Trinity is not merely to remove part of God—as it would be in removing one human being from a group of three; it is to remove God in his entirety. Therefore, rather than saying '*the Son, both as the Son and as God*', has '*his Deity from the Father*', Rutherford differentiates between the Son *qua* Son and the Son *qua* God. He, like Calvin and Augustine before him, is quite willing to allow

---

[38] *WJA*, I, p. 692; II, pp. 137-44, 690-96.

[39] *Examen*, pp. 147-9.

[40] See the discussion of generic identity in the Cappadocian fathers in J.N.D. Kelly, *Early Christian Doctrines* (London: A&C Black, [5]1977), pp. 267-9; and in J.D. Zizioulas, 'The Doctrine of the Holy Trinity: The Significance of the Cappadocian Contribution', in *Trinitarian Theology Today: Essays on Divine Being and Act*, ed. C. Schwöbel (Edinburgh: T&T Clark, 1995), pp. 45-9. For an Arminian view of generic identity, see C. Vorstius, *Apologetica responsio ad ea omnia* (n.p., 1618), pp. 1-17. It is not certain whether other Arminians held to generic identity or to numerical identity. In their *Confession*, these Arminians state that God is 'one' but do not explain the way in which he is one. But because they move from this statement of God's oneness immediately to a discussion of the attributes of God shared by each person, they lead the reader to believe that they support generic identity. This is not readily apparent, however. See *Confession*, pp. 81ff.

[41] Rutherford is not criticizing the Greek fathers' views on generic identity so much as the less careful views of the Arminians, as we will see.

[42] *Examen*, pp. 147-8.

[43] Leigh, *Body of Divinity*, p. 205.

that the Father is the cause or *principium* of the persons (*hypostases*) of the Son and the Spirit but not of their essences (*ousias*). In regard to their essences, the Son and the Spirit are, as Calvin says, 'absque principio', and, thus, each has *aseitas* and is *autotheos* in the same way as the Father.[44] This is not tritheism, however, because, as Calvin again says, 'the whole divine nature is understood' to be 'in each hypostasis' or person. It is not Sabellianism, because each of the three persons has 'his own peculiar [relational] quality'.[45] The Father 'is begetting'; the Son 'is begotten'; and the Spirit proceeds. But this is true only 'in reference to Personality' not essence.[46]

Rutherford, furthermore, has a problem with the inherent subordinationism in Arminius' view of the Trinity. He believes that to say '*the Son, both as the Son and as God, has his Deity from the Father*', is to say not only that the Son's essence is distinct numerically but also that it is unequal with the Father. When this is coupled with Arminius' ascription of *autotheos* to the Father alone, the result, for Rutherford, is disastrous: 'There will be one supreme God and two little Gods, the *Son* and the *Holy Spirit*.'[47] It is this perceived element of subordinationism in the Arminian doctrine that leads Rutherford to accuse them of Arianism. Though, he admits, there are some among them who profess with their words that the Son is *homoousios* and consubstantial with the Father, they deny 'the thing itself' by their practice of establishing different levels of worship for the Son and the Father. Because the Arminians 'establish that [the Son] is an inferior God to the Father...[and] is to be adored with an inferior adoration', Rutherford says he has 'really suspected them of *Arianism*'.[48]

Having thus traced the arguments of Rutherford and the Arminians in regard to the Trinity, it must be said that each side is exaggerating in their appraisal of the other. Both sides stand squarely within the Niceno-Constantinopolitan tradition. The accusations they level at each other are excessive. Rutherford clearly avoids Sabellianism by delineating relational and personal distinctions within the Godhead. And the Arminians steer clear of Arianism by plainly stating that the Son is just as much God as is the Father; though he is not '*God from himself*', he is '*truly and in himself God*'.[49] What is more, Rutherford appears to have misread the distinctions that the Arminians make with respect to worship. His claim that the Arminians ascribe 'inferior adoration' to the Son is too simplistic, because it presents only half the story. Arminians like Van

---

[44] This language of Calvin is also found in Beza and became typical of post-Reformation orthodoxy. See *Expositio impietatis Valen. Gentilis* (1561), *Ioannis Calvini opera*, eds., G. Baum, E. Cunitz, and E. Reuss (Brunswick: Schwetschke, 1863-1900), IX, p. 368; *Institutes* I.xiii.17-20, pp. 141-5; and T. Beza, *Quaestionum et responsionum Christianarum libellus* (Geneva, 1570).
[45] *Institutes* I.xiii.19, p. 143.
[46] *Examen*, pp. 147-8, 160-62.
[47] *Examen*, p. 150.
[48] *Examen*, pp. 150-52.
[49] *WJA*, II, pp. 30-31.

Limborch, for example, explicitly state that the Son 'as he is the Son of God' and 'Partaker of the same Nature with God' is to be worshiped with 'the same Worship which is paid to God himself'.[50]

But, having said this, it must also be said that the Arminian position is the least careful of the two linguistically in its presentation of the doctrine of the Trinity. This can be seen in the following two ways. First, although the Arminians seem to favor Eastern causal language in order to keep themselves from tritheism, they are not as careful in protecting themselves from subordinationism as are the Greek fathers. The Cappadocians expressly locate the source (ἀρχή) or cause (αἰτία) of deity in the Father but avoid subordinationism by consistently arguing that deity (θεότης) cannot be derived and, thus, belongs equally to each person of the Godhead.[51] The Arminians, however, do not employ such protective measures. In point of fact, they run in the opposite direction and openly adopt the language of derivation. Arminius himself says that the Son 'is from the Father with respect to his essence'. Van Limborch states that the Father has 'the Divine Nature from himself, whilst the Son and the Holy Ghost *derive* it from the Father'. And Episcopius, going a step further and sounding more like the Socinians than the Greek fathers, claims that although all three persons of the Trinity are 'divine in nature', there is some 'difference in being' between them.[52]

Secondly, when pushed by charges of tritheism in polemical situations, the Greek fathers exercise great care in differentiating between human existence, in which human 'nature precedes the [individual] person', and the divine existence, in which the persons perfectly 'coincide with' the divine nature.[53]

---

[50] *ACS*, II, p. 539.

[51] Gregory of Nyssa, *Contra Eunomium*, I.33, in *Patrologia Graeca Cursus Completus*, ed. J.P. Migne, 161 vols. (Paris: Vives, 1857-66), XLV, pp. 393-6; Basil of Caesarea, *Epistolae*, 8.3, in *Patrologia Graeca*, XXXVI, pp. 1073-6; Gregory of Nazianzus, *Orationes*, 30.18-20, *Orationes theologica*, IV, in *Patrologia Graeca*, XXXVI, pp. 125-32. Cf. T.F. Torrance, *The Trinitarian Faith: The Evangelical Theology of the Ancient Catholic Church* (Edinburgh: T&T Clark, 1995), pp. 239-41, 317-18.

[52] *WJA*, II, p. 696; *ACS*, I, p. 110, emphasis added; Episcopius, *Opera theologica* (1665), I, p. 69; Hoenderdaal, 'The Debate about Arminius', pp. 149-50. Episcopius' later position, as he expresses it in the 1665 *Opera*, appears to be at odds with his earlier view in the *Confession*, in which he and his peers do adopt some of the protective measures of the Greek fathers and speak more prudently of the Son and the Spirit as being 'truly partakers of *the same Deity, or Divine Essence and Nature* absolutely and in common considered with the Father' (*Confession*, p. 94, emphasis added)—which position, if genuinely believed, would clearly be different than what the Socinians are willing to say (see, e.g., *Racovian Catechisme*, pp. 18-19, 33, 59). Either Episcopius later changed his mind on this issue, or the earlier expression of his thinking in the *Confession* is vague and imprecise or, perhaps, even intentionally deceptive.

[53] Zizioulas, 'The Cappadocian Contribution', p. 48. This shows how it is that Rutherford's criticisms regarding generic identity apply not to the Greek fathers' so

The Doctrine of God

Sometimes, the Cappadocians even go so far as to speak of the identity of the Godhead in terms that are perhaps more characteristic of the West. Gregory of Nyssa, '[i]n his anxiety to evade the tritheistic implications of likening the Triad to three men sharing the same *ousia* of manhood...is forced to conclude that...we should not speak of a multiplicity of men but of one man.' Gregory of Nazianzus (c.325-c.389), likewise, 'emphasizes that the unity of the divine Persons is real as opposed to the purely "notional" (μόνον επινοία θεωρητόν) unity of several men'.[54] The Arminians, on the other hand, are again less careful in their use of language. Arminius opts to rely on the causal language of the Eastern tradition without any of their protective measures. And some later Arminians refuse to qualify their teaching to insure it against the charge of tritheism and even plunge headfirst towards it by speaking of the three persons as 'tres divinas essentias'.[55]

Rutherford's critique of the Arminian view of the Trinity, however, should be seen as more than just a petty reaction to this lack of linguistic caution. It should be seen as a reaction to the Christological and soteriological errors that he and his Reformed contemporaries perceive to be reflected in Arminius' subordinationist tendencies. Because this feature of Rutherford's dispute with the Arminians involves their respective views of the divine decrees and of the covenantal relationships between the persons of the Trinity, we will reserve our discussion of it until these issues have been introduced later in this chapter and in the next.[56]

The scientia Dei

After developing and refuting those things that he perceives to be erroneous in the Arminian understanding of the Trinity, Rutherford broaches the subject of the knowledge of God in the *Examen*. In accord with traditional scholastic approaches to divine knowledge, Rutherford believes that the objects of God's knowledge are himself and all things outside himself.[57] The former he calls a '*reflex* Knowledge', which is 'plainly natural' to God. The latter he subdivides into two categories: a 'knowledge of *Simple Intelligence*' and a '*Visionary*, or *intuitive*, or *definite*' knowledge.[58] Whereas the scholastic tendency is to

---

much as to the Arminians. The Cappadocians went to great lengths to protect themselves from such criticisms, as Zizioulas has shown.

[54] Kelly, *Early Christian Doctrines*, pp. 267-8. Gregory of Nazianzus continues by stating that 'the analogy between the Trinity and Adam, Eve (made out of his rib) and Seth (the product of both) breaks down because the divine essence is indivisible'.

[55] Vorstius, *Apologetica responsio*, p. 1.

[56] See 'Objections to Supralapsarianism' in this chapter and 'The Covenant of Redemption and the Decrees of God' and 'The Object of Faith' in the next.

[57] E.g., Leigh, *Body of Divinity*, p. 160.

[58] *Examen*, p. 163. This is characteristically scholastic language. See, e.g., Aquinas, *Summa theologiae*, Ia.14.9.

discuss God's knowledge of himself under the category of simple intelligence,[59] Rutherford does not do so in the *Examen*. He dedicates the abovementioned two categories to describing the divine knowledge of all things outside of God, without respect to God's knowledge of himself. Simple intelligence, then, for Rutherford, is the '*natural, indefinite,* [and] *abstract*' knowledge of God, by which he 'knows all possibilities.' It is necessary in God insofar as he is God and omniscient. It is '*natural*', because he possesses it by nature; it is '*indefinite*' and '*abstract*', because it only pertains to 'possibilities', not to actualities. Visionary knowledge, the *scientia Dei visionis*, is that 'by which God knows all the things outside of himself that [actually] are, have been, or will be, or are not'. This knowledge is free in God, because it is a product of his free will or decree. As such, it is '*definite*' or determined and refers to all actualities.[60] To put it more simply, the *scientia visionis* is comprised of those things, and only those things, that the divine will has chosen to bring into actuality from among the possibilities contained in the *scientia simplicis intelligentiae*. What this means for Rutherford is that God knows every future actuality not because he sees it in the future as having existence of its own, but because he wills that it, rather than something else, should come to pass.[61]

In addition to these two categories of divine knowledge, the Arminians, introduce a third, *scientia media*, which falls in between the two just previously outlined. The idea of a 'middle' knowledge, however, did not originate with Arminius. According to Gisbertus Voetius, it was first developed in 1566 by Pedro de Fonseca (1528-1599).[62] Fonseca's better-known disciple, Luis de Molina (1535-1600), then perfected and popularized it in his *Concordia liberi arbitrii cum gratiae donis, divina praescientia, providentia, praedestinatione et reprobatione*, which was originally published in 1588. Although there does not appear to be an explicit connection between Arminius and the Jesuit Molina, the latter's influence, according to Richard Muller, 'is quite apparent in several places in Arminius' system', chief among them being in regard to divine *scientia media*.[63] Following Molina, Arminius defines *scientia media* as that

---

[59] See *RD*, pp. 73-4; Muller, *Dictionary*, pp. 274-6. Cf. Turretin, *Institutes*, 3.12-13, I, pp. 206-18.

[60] *Examen*, p. 163.

[61] Cf. *WCF*, § 3.1, p. 28.

[62] Voetius states that Fonseca 'gloriatur se primum hujus scientiae authorem & inventorem fuisse, cujus cogitatio sibi primum inciderit an. 1566.' Voetius, *Selectarum disputationum pars prima* (Utrecht, 1648), p. 265. Cf. R.M. Adams, *The Virtue of Faith and Other Essays in Philosophical Theology* (New York: Oxford University, 1987), p. 91n2; with E. Vansteenberghe, 'Molinisme', *Dictionnaire de théologie catholique*, eds. A. Vacant, E. Mangenot, and É. Amann (Paris: Librairie Letouzey et Ané, 1928), X, p. 2096.

[63] Muller, *God, Creation, and Providence*, pp. 43 and 154-66. Other recent studies also link *scientia media* in Arminius with the teaching of Molina. See especially, E. Dekker, 'Was Arminius a Molinist?', *SCJ* 27:2 (1996), pp. 337-52; and idem, *Rijker dan Midas:*

knowledge by which God foresees what free creatures will do given a certain, or infinite, set of possibilities. In the words of Arminius himself, it is 'that by which [God] knows, that "if this thing happens, that will take place"'.[64] Not only does God know all possibilities (*scientia simplicis intelligentiae*), but he also knows all things that will come to pass by the acts of free creatures. The divine will draws from one or the other of these two 'knowledges' in choosing what events to bring to pass. Middle knowledge only 'intervene[s] in things which depend on the liberty of created [*arbitrii*] choice or pleasure'. Those things that do not depend on human free will are brought to pass directly by God from his knowledge of simple intelligence. But when human free will is involved, God is either 'moved by those deeds of [his] creatures' or he 'at least...receive[s]' them by way of his *scientia media* and then decrees or permits them accordingly or does not.[65]

The central issue in this seventeenth-century debate between Rutherford and the Arminians is much the same as it was in the sixteenth-century contest between the Jesuits Luis de Molina and Franciscus Suarez and the Dominicans Franciscus Zumel (1540-1607) and Dominico Bañez, namely, God's knowledge of future contingents. How should God's foreknowledge of future contingents be reconciled with human free will?[66] Rutherford and the Reformed in general were concerned to defend a Thomistic harmonization of human free will with divine sovereignty. The Boethian conception of time as an eternal present for God enabled Aquinas and the Reformed in general to assert that

---

Vrijheid, Genade en predestinatie in de theologie van Jacobus Arminius (1559-1609) (Zoetermeer: Boekencentrum, 1993).

[64] *WJA*, II, p. 123. Molina defines *scientia media* as that knowledge 'qua ex altissima et inscrutabili comprehensione cuiusque liberi arbitrii in sua essentia intuitus est, quid pro sua innata libertate, si in hoc vel illo vel etiam infinitis rerum ordinibus collocaretur, acturum esset' (*Concordia liberi arbitrii cum gratiae donis, divina praescientia, providentia, praedestinatione et reprobatione* [Antwerp, 1595], 4.52.9). For a lucid account of Molina's theory of divine knowledge, see W.L. Craig, *The Problem of Divine Foreknowledge and Future Contingents from Aristotle to Suarez* (Leiden: E.J. Brill, 1988), pp. 167-206.

[65] *WJA*, II, p. 342; III, pp. 65-6. The Arminians and Jesuits were by no means alone in breaking from the traditional twofold view of the *scientia Dei* and replacing it with a threefold understanding. Richard Baxter—under the influence of Tommaso Campanella's threefold metaphysical distinction between omnipotence, knowledge, and will—also embraced a threefold view of divine knowledge, which included, first, a knowledge of all possibilities; second, a knowledge of all appropriate or fitting things; and third, a knowledge of all things actually willed. See R. Baxter, *Catholick Theologie* (London, 1675), 1.4.45-52; and C.R. Trueman, 'A Small Step Towards Rationalism: The Impact of the Metaphysics of Tommaso Campanella on the Theology of Richard Baxter', in *Protestant Scholasticism: Essays in Reassessment*, eds. Trueman and R.S. Clark (Carlisle, Cumbria: Paternoster, 1999), pp. 189-92.

[66] See A.J. Freddoso's introduction to L. de Molina, *On Divine Foreknowledge*, trans. A.J. Freddoso (Ithaca, NY: Cornell University, 1988).

God's knowledge of contingent things is necessary, because God is their 'first cause', while the things themselves remain contingent upon the 'proximate causes', which occur in time.[67] Even though Arminius fully embraced the idea that God's knowledge of contingent things was necessary—as a corollary of divine infinity—he denied the Thomistic assumption that this knowledge involved causality in God. He pointed instead to human causality—foreseen by God's *scientia media* and then actively willed or not willed or passively permitted—in bringing all things to pass.[68]

Rutherford reacts harshly to this way of thinking, labelling it 'blasphemous' for compromising God's sovereignty and making the divine decree contingent upon either the free wills of creatures, who do not yet exist, or upon the whims of chance (*fortuna*). The problem that Rutherford has with *scientia media* is that it makes either the will of the creature or fate the first cause of all things and the divine will the second cause, because God looks out of himself to see what free creatures will do before making his decree. Thus, the creature, or fate, is put in the place of God and God in the place of the creature, because the creature's will takes precedence over the divine will in determining those things that come to pass.[69] But Rutherford also believes that *scientia media* is itself based upon wrong notions of divine foreknowledge, especially as it is held by the Arminians. It wrongly attributes to God a kind of paranormal ability or clairvoyance, by which he can see every future contingent before it exists. But future contingents have no existence outside of the will or decree of God and, thus, cannot be known apart from it.[70] Because God knows the future only by declaring it to be, divine foreknowledge is, therefore, limited to those things that God actually brings to pass. Foreknowledge, for Rutherford, is not a bare foresight, as it is for the Arminians, but is inextricably tied to the divine will.

Since the Arminians deny that God knows the future by way of his decree and substitute instead the 'fictitious' idea of middle knowledge, Rutherford accuses them of the Socinian error of denying God's knowledge of future contingents.[71] But this is somewhat disingenuous on Rutherford's part. The very reason that Arminius employs the concept of *sceintia media* is in order to explain how it is that God knows future contingents. And Arminius' later

---

[67] Aquinas, *Summa theologiae*, Ia.14.13. Boethius (c.480-c.524) said: 'But if it is appropriate to compare the divine present with the human, then just as you men see certain things in this temporal present of yours, so God sees all things in his eternal present. Hence this divine foreknowledge does not change the nature and character of things; God sees them as present before his eyes as they will emerge at some time in the future.' Boethius, *The Consolation of Philosophy*, trans. P.G. Walsh (Oxford: Oxford University, 1999), p. 112.
[68] Muller, *God, Creation, and Providence*, p. 158.
[69] *Examen*, pp. 163-4, 191-3.
[70] *Examen*, pp. 163-9.
[71] See *Examen*, pp. 166-7.

disciples explicitly retain this same view.[72] Rutherford, furthermore, misquotes from the *Apologia* of Episcopius and applies words meant for 'Censorem hunc, aliosque' to Episcopius himself.[73] By doing so, he makes it appear as though the Remonstrants are overtly rejecting God's knowledge of future contingents, which is not at all what Episcopius intends. The point the Remonstrant leader is trying to make is that the Reformed orthodox, and, specifically, the authors of *Censura in confessionem sive declarationem sententiae eorum qui in foederato Belgio Remonstrantes vocantur* (1626), are themselves denying God's knowledge of future contingents by claiming that they have no existence apart from the divine decree. But things that are caused by the decree of God cease to be contingent and become, instead, quite necessary. So, in the opinion of Episcopius, it is actually the Contra-Remonstrants who are guilty of the Socinian error. They not only renounce God's knowledge of future contingents; they reject the existence of them as well.

It must also be said in defense of the Arminian, and Jesuit, notion of *scientia media*, that Rutherford's vehemence against it is somewhat extreme. It is, to be sure, a new idea, but, as William Lane Craig remarks, it is a new idea that attempts to 'resolve a number of the most profound theological conundrums' and does so in a way that is 'almost breathtaking'.[74] Furthermore, it is an idea that is developed and defended from the pages of Scripture. Both Molina and Arminius are keen to show biblical justification for their theory of divine *scientia media*. They point to passages like 1 Samuel 23.10-12 and Matthew 11.21, to show that God has a foreknowledge of what people will do given certain circumstances that are different from the current situation or from that which could soon come to pass.[75] It must also be admitted that Rutherford's response to these scriptural texts is rather unsatisfactory: he simply emphasizes the fact that these foreseen things must have been a part of the decree of God, otherwise, 'God would know certainly that which is not knowable.'[76] But this

---

[72] Vorstius, *Tractatus theologicus*, pp. 42-7; Episcopius, *Opera theologica* (1665), I, p. 394; idem, *Opera theologica* (1678), pp. 299-304.

[73] Cf. Episcopius, *Opera theologica* (1665), II, p. 130; with *Examen*, pp. 166-7. The 'Censores' were those Contra-Remonstrant professors in Leiden—including among them Johannes Polyander, Andreas Rivetus, Antonius Walaeus, and Antonius Thysius— who together wrote *Censura in confessionem sive declarationem sententiae eorum qui in foederato Belgio Remonstrantes vocantur* (Leiden, 1626), in order to censure Arminian doctrines.

[74] Craig, *The Problem of Divine Foreknowledge*, p. 206.

[75] *WJA*, III, p. 65; Craig, *The Problem of Divine Foreknowledge*, p. 183.

[76] *Examen*, p. 166. Other attempts by the Reformed orthodox to explain these biblical passages are more convincing. See J.A. Van Ruler, 'New Philosophy to Old Standards: Voetius' Vindication of Divine Concurrence and Secondary Causality', *NAvK* 71:1 (1991), pp. 73-6, where he states: 'Catholic [i.e., Dominican] and Calvinist adversaries of Molinism...said that in the first example [1 Samuel 23], God does not contemplate a future conditional, but something already present, viz. the actual mental disposition of

does not restrain his invective in the least. While we, in the twenty-first century, may be able to appreciate the philosophical value of and biblical rationale for divine *scientia media*, Rutherford is clearly in no position to do so. For him, this theory represents a 'blasphemous fabrication' that essentially removes God from his sovereign's throne and places human beings there in his place. Consequently, it is not to be tolerated.

But there is something more behind Rutherford's intolerant reaction to *scientia media* than simple narrow-mindedness. Karl Barth explains that '[i]t was the express intention of the Jesuits' in developing the doctrine of *scientia media* 'to aid a new semi-Pelagianism to gain its necessary place and right…in opposition to the Augustinian-Thomist teaching of the Dominicans, which they accused of being dangerously near to Luther and Calvin'.[77] If Barth is right, then, by embracing the Jesuit doctrine of *scientia media*, the Arminians would have been consciously adopting a position that was itself intended from its inception to be in opposition to the thinking of the Reformation. And by reacting against *scientia media*, Rutherford would have been consciously defending the Reformation viewpoint from such opposition. As we will see in chapter five, this, more than anything else explains the fervor of Rutherford's response to Arminian teaching.

The debate over the *scientia Dei* is closely linked with the issue of the divine will. Many of the ideas we have presented here will resurface and be further developed in connection with the will of God. For this reason, we will bring our discussion of divine knowledge to a close at this point and revisit it and the related issues of divine omnipotence and immutability as we work through the *voluntas Dei*. After doing so, we will be able to evaluate such soteriological applications of the will as predestination and the atonement of Christ.

The *voluntas Dei*

In keeping with a large part of the scholastic tradition, the most distinctive and perhaps most complex feature of Rutherford's theology is his understanding of the *voluntas Dei*. It has a profound affect upon his thinking in many other areas, as we will see, especially his views in regard to the decrees and salvation, the

---

Saul and of the Kehilite citizens. In other words, their decision was already made. As for the second example [Matthew 11], Christ there only makes an exaggerated comparison, in order to point out the haughtiness of the Galileans.' Van Ruler further notes that Voetius' preferred explanation of 1 Samuel 23 is found in William Ames, who distinguishes between formal decrees and implicit decrees in God: 'The latter have a bearing on those future conditionals which will never actually pertain. For instance, God from all eternity decided, or "formally decreed", to liberate David from the hands of the Kahileans. From this, it is legitimate to infer the following implicit condition: "if David would not flee, he would be handed over".' Van Ruler, 'New Philosophy to Old Standards', pp. 74, 75n52.

[77] *CD*, II/1, p. 569.

preaching of the gospel, and the atonement of Christ. That being said, it is worth noting that Rutherford does not regard this doctrine in isolation from the doctrine of God or a discussion of his attributes. The divine will, for Rutherford and for scholastic thinkers in general, is itself an attribute of God.[78] And as we have already mentioned, divine simplicity means that each of God's attributes, including his will, is identical with God himself.[79] Even though Rutherford operates from a voluntarist understanding of God, emphasizing the primacy of the divine will over the intellect,[80] we should be wary of drawing too sharp a contrast between the intellect, which is also a divine attribute, and the will. For Rutherford, as for Duns Scotus, the will does not function in isolation from the intellect, nor does it function in an unwise, irrational, or contradictory manner, because 'a will destitute of knowledge [*cognitio*] is a brute appetite, blind, reckless, and inferior in sensitivity'.[81] The divine intellect precedes the will and exercises some restraint upon it. The intellect limits the set of possibilities that can be brought into actuality by the will, since God can only will what is contained within his *scientia simplicis intelligentiae*. But the intellect does not direct or compel the divine will in its choosing. The will is free and 'does not need direction as though it could err or choose something unsuitable, and *in this sense* the divine will is its own rule', a point which post-Reformation theologians the likes of Rutherford and Theodore Beza were wont to make.[82] It is the will—the *potentia Dei appetitiva*—that freely moves everything from the 'state of possibility to the state of future actuality' and from *scientia simplicis intelligentiae* to *scientia visionis*.[83] As we will see, however, there are

---

[78] Ussher, *Body of Divinitie*, p. 39; Muller, *Dictionary*, p. 331.

[79] *Examen*, pp. 169-70. Rutherford discusses the divine will not as a separate chapter in the *Examen* but as part of his study of the essence and attributes of God in chapter two.

[80] On voluntarism vs. intellectualism in medieval scholastic thought, see F. Copleston, *A History of Philosophy*, 9 vols. (London: Burns, Oates & Washbourne, 1946-75), II, pp. 382-3, 538-41.

[81] *Examen*, p. 173. On Duns Scotus and voluntarism, see B.M. Bonansea, 'Duns Scotus' Voluntarism', *John Duns Scotus, 1265-1965*, eds. Bonansea and J. Ryan (Washington: Catholic University of America, 1965), pp. 83-121; and Cross, *Duns Scotus*, pp. 91-5. Recently, Alexander Broadie has argued that Duns Scotus is 'no Scotist', or, in other words, that he is not the extreme voluntarist that many scholars have thought him to be. Broadie highlights a phrase in Duns Scotus, 'pondus et inclinatio', to show that he believes that the intellect provides not only the raw material from which the will selects but that it actually 'car[ries] weight with will and incline[s] it'. Dun Scotus' position, he asserts, is, therefore, something of a *via media* between intellectualism and voluntarism. See A. Broadie, *The Shadow of Scotus: Philosophy and Faith in Pre-Reformation Scotland* (Edinburgh: T&T Clark, 1995), lecture 3.

[82] Copleston, *History of Philosophy*, II, p. 531; T. Beza et al., *An Evident Display of Popish Practices* (London, 1578), p. 256.

[83] *Examen*, p. 163. See the discussion on 'voluntas' and 'voluntas Dei' in Muller, *Dictionary*, pp. 330-31.

influencing factors that incline the will of God to certain courses of action over others and to bringing certain things to pass instead of others.

Explaining Rutherford's understanding of the divine will is not a simple task. It requires presenting and exploring a series of scholastic distinctions, distinctions which men like Rutherford were driven to embrace by their desire to be faithful to the teaching of Scripture. As Peter Lombard had previously pointed out in his massively important *Sententiae*, the Bible's picture of God's will is complex and multifaceted and, this, more than anything else, demands some kind of a series of distinctions in order to come to terms with it.[84] Contrary to Brian Armstrong's assertions, Rutherford and scholasticism in general—whether of the Protestant or medieval variety—are not so concerned with 'speculative formulation[s] of the will of God', much less with building their theology upon such a foundation.[85] As we will see, both in this chapter and in the next, Protestant scholastics like Rutherford are driven to embrace these distinctions by their understanding of the biblical portrait of the divine will, and they build their theology, not upon formulations of the divine will *per se*, but—once again in keeping with their emphasis on *praxis* in theology— upon formulations of divine covenantal relationships.

Voluntas ad intra et ad extra

The first distinction that must be made in regard to the divine will is that between the *voluntas Dei ad intra et ad extra*. This distinction is designed to express the difference between the divine will as it is within God himself and as it is directed towards us and known by us. It allows Rutherford to explain the relationship between the nature and will of God. But it should not be understood as introducing a sharp divide between the divine will and nature, and then engendering speculative metaphysical questions as to whether or not will precedes nature in God. As our discussion of divine simplicity indicates, Rutherford—true to the Nominalist thinking of William of Ockham and Gabriel Biel—believes that 'God's intellect and will coincide with His essence in such a way that His decisions cannot be separated from His being'.[86]

The distinction between *ad intra* and *ad extra* serves a more practical end in Rutherford's theology. It allows him to establish the ultimate incomprehensibility of God and to preserve absolute divine freedom by differentiating between those things that are necessary for God to will and those that are not. The will of God, as it is within God himself—i.e., *ad intra*—is bound by his nature. God must will his own existence by necessity of nature.

---

[84] P. Lombard, *Sententiae in IV libros distinctae*, 2 vols. (Rome: Collegii S. Bonaventurae ad Claras Aquas, 1971-81), I.xlv.5, I, p. 309.
[85] Armstrong, *Calvinism and the Amyraut Heresy*, p. 32.
[86] Oberman, 'Notes on Nominalism', p. 61.

The Doctrine of God

He must also love himself and beget and love the Son by necessity of nature.[87] Other things, outside of himself—i.e., *ad extra*—God wills freely and without any compulsion whatsoever, even from his own nature. Therefore, although God is good, merciful, and just in and of himself, and must will accordingly with respect to himself (*ad intra*), he is under no obligation to be good, merciful, and just towards his creatures (*ad extra*). As Rutherford says: 'God is good in creating the world, in giving faith to *Peter*, and in communicating being and goodness with his creatures,...[but] he could have been not-good, in this way, if he would not have created the world and not have given Faith to *Peter*, and if he would have annihilated the creatures.'[88]

POTENTIA ABSOLUTA ET ORDINATA

Lurking behind this idea of the *voluntas Dei ad intra et ad extra* is the dominant medieval Nominalist distinction between the *potentia Dei absoluta et ordinata*. Both Heiko Oberman and Francis Oakley see this 'power distinction' as the defining characteristic of Nominalist thought.[89] While it obviously reflects the traditional Aristotelian approach to being (comprised of potency and act), it appears not to have been used explicitly until Aquinas used it to differentiate between God's hypothetical power *per se* and the power by which he works out his decrees.[90] It is then further developed and given prominence in the voluntaristic systems of Duns Scotus and Ockham.[91] William Twisse,

---

[87] *COL*, pp. 29-31. Rutherford reflects his view of the Trinity when he states that the Son—because he is self-existent in his essence—also cannot will his non-existence. *COL*, p. 29.

[88] *Examen*, p. 146. Cf. *Examen*, pp. 405-6; *COL*, pp. 27-34; *Disputatio*, pp. 342, 345.

[89] Oberman, *Harvest of Medieval Theology*, pp. 37ff; and F. Oakley, *Omnipotence, Covenant, and Order: An Excursion in the History of Ideas from Abelard to Leibniz* (Ithaca, NY: Cornell University, 1984), pp. 77-84. The centrality of this distinction within Nominalism has also received support from P.O. Kristeller. See, e.g., Kristeller's article, 'The Validity of the Term: "Nominalism"', in *The Pursuit of Holiness in Late Medieval and Renaissance Religion*, eds. C.E. Trinkaus and H.A. Oberman (Leiden: E.J. Brill, 1974), p. 66.

[90] M.A. Pernoud, 'The Theory of the *Potentia Dei* According to Aquinas, Scotus, and Ockham', *Antonianum* 47 (1972), pp. 73-80. Though the terminology first appears in Aquinas, the basic ideas, according to L. Moonan, originated with the theology faculty of the University of Paris in the thirteenth century (*Divine Power: The Medieval Power Distinction up to its Adoption by Albert, Bonaventure, and Aquinas* [Oxford: Clarendon, 1994], p. 6). Oberman traces the basic ideas behind the power distinction to the twelfth century and Hugh of St. Victor (1096-1141) in 'Notes on Nominalism', p. 56.

[91] Pernoud notes that the so-called 'power distinction' is just one of the ways in which similarities between Aquinas and Duns Scotus can be seen. Many 'historians of philosophy and theology first mention the use of God's omnipotence as a matter of importance and as an indication of the new direction scholastic thought took, in their studies of the Subtle Doctor [Duns Scotus]'. But this is actually not so, because the

whose thinking is very similar to Rutherford's on this and other fronts, provides us with a good post-Reformation definition of these two terms:

> For Gods absolute power is one thing, his ordinate power is another thing, for this includs his will. God coulde have refused to make the world, when he did make it, & he made it freely; but supposing Gods decree to make it, & to make it at that time it was impossible it should be otherwise, as it is impossible that Gods will shoulde be changed.[92]

Although Rutherford uses the terminology of this distinction only sparingly, his affinities for Nominalist thought—again as reflected in the *schola Augustiniana moderna*—and his strong voluntarism clearly evidence its influence. One of the ways in which this influence manifests itself in Rutherford is in the differentiation he makes between omnipotency and sovereignty. Whereas omnipotency is 'what the Lord *can doe*', sovereignty is more than that; it includes the divine will: 'Soveraignty is not only his holy Nature what he can doe and so supposeth his Omnipotency, but also what he doth freely, or doth not freely, and doth by no natural necessity, and so it includes his holy supreme Liberty.'[93] According to Heiko Oberman, the difference between omnipotency and sovereignty parallels exactly the Nominalist power distinction. Omnipotency, or, 'what God is able to do', corresponds to *potentia absoluta*, whereas sovereignty, or, 'what God actually decides to do', includes the will and, thus, corresponds to *potentia ordinata*.[94] God is not only *able* to do as he pleases (omnipotency), though that is certainly true, but God actually *does* as he pleases (sovereignty), and, in doing so, his 'holy Will [is] essentially wise and just, [and] is a Law and Rule to himself'.[95]

In *Christ Dying and Drawing Sinners to Himselfe*, Rutherford speaks more explicitly—albeit in English—and with greater detail of the divine *potentia absoluta et ordinata*. He refers to God's '*absolute power* without respect to his *free decree*', and, by doing so, establishes the parameters of divine *potentia*.[96] The power of God, in and of itself, without respect to his free decree *ad extra*, is an absolute power—an omnipotency—in a classical or Thomistic sense, whereby God can do whatsoever he pleases. But his decree, even though it is made freely by his own will, necessarily limits his consequent power. Although God, by his *potentia absoluta*, can freely choose to create or not-create and then

---

'basic tenets' which come to the foreground in Duns Scotus and Ockham were first found in Aquinas. See Pernoud, 'The Theory of the *Potentia Dei*', pp. 80, 83.

[92] Twisse, *D. Jacksons Vanitie*, p. 5.

[93] *Influences*, pp. 33-5.

[94] Oberman, 'Notes on Nominalism', p. 58. This is the same way that Rutherford's contemporaries—even such New England Puritans like Samuel Willard—speak of this distinction. See S. Willard, *A Compleat Body of Divinity* (Boston, 1726), p. 70.

[95] *Influences*, pp. 33-5.

[96] *Christ Dying*, pp. 7-8, emphasis added.

The Doctrine of God

to be good or not-good, merciful or not-merciful, and just or not-just to his creatures, once he decides to act in a given way *ad extra*, his subsequent power is bound by his free decree.[97] He cannot act against his *ad extra* decree. For him to do so would require mutability, which, according to Rutherford, is impossible for God: 'Scripture argues from the Immutability of God to the immutability of the willed thing: And for this reason if he [God] would will that and afterwards will not for that; then there would be a *final* [*terminativa*] change in him.'[98] Therefore, the omnipotency of God refers to his absolute and unbounded power (*potentia absoluta*), and the sovereignty of God refers to his power as it has been constrained by his own free decree (*potentia ordinata*).

Significantly, this relationship between the *potentia ordinata* and the *potentia absoluta* suggests that the nature of God does in fact restrain the will of God *ad extra* in Rutherford's thinking. This presents a twofold problem, however. If, on the one hand, it is only immutability that restrains the divine *potentia absoluta* (given God's free decree), then why should we not go the whole way and deny that any attribute can control the divine will *ad extra*? Why keep immutability as the only limiting factor? The logical law of non-contradiction does not require this, if, according to Rutherford and his fellow Nominalists, the divine will is indeed a rule or a law unto itself. Why not say that God's *potentia* and freedom transcend his decree, such that he is free to change his mind as he so pleases and to go against his decree if he so wishes? It would seem correct to suggest that Rutherford's answer to these questions is to point to the teaching of Scripture. Immutability restrains God's *potentia*, because Scripture teaches that it does. But this raises a second difficulty. If immutability limits the sovereignty of God *ad extra*, then why would other attributes of the divine nature not also? This appears to be a capitulation, at least in theory, to the intellectualist position.

But this is not the only inconsistency that one finds in regard to Rutherford's voluntarism. Rutherford's own interpretation of Exodus 3.14-15, as discussed above, would also appear to contradict his understanding of the priority of the divine will. In Exodus 3, God gives Israel his own name, which, according to Rutherford, is descriptive of who he is in his very being. If we understand this passage to present a metaphysical fact about God, as Rutherford does, then the context of the passage would seem to suggest that God's actions on behalf of Israel will be tied to the metaphysical truth just presented. God is giving his name to Israel not as an end in itself but in order to comfort the Israelites and to assure them of his trustworthiness in the future. In other words, by giving them his name, a name which is grounded in his nature, God is telling them that they can rest assured, because he *will* act in the future in accord with who he is in his very being. Such a reading of Exodus 3, however, runs contrary to Rutherford's voluntaristic system, which is keen to sever ties between God's being *ad intra*

---

[97] *Examen*, pp. 146, 284. Cf. *COL*, pp. 27-34; *Communion*, p. 28.
[98] *Examen*, p. 177.

and his actions towards his creatures.

In connection with the *potentia Dei absoluta et ordinata* and the *voluntas Dei ad extra*, a fundamental difference between Rutherford and the Arminians emerges. Whereas Rutherford believes that God has *potentia absoluta* in and of himself and, so, is not bound to act in any way *ad extra* by anything other than his decree, Arminius rejects the concept of the *potentia absoluta* and seeks to redefine God's power strictly in terms of the *potentia ordinata*. The rationale behind this move in Arminian theology is the doctrine of creation, a doctrine which Richard Muller suggests 'occupies a pivotal and virtually principial position in [Arminius'] thought'. Because Arminius understands creation in a Thomistic sense, as 'an emanation of the divine potency for being and of the existence of the created order by participation in the goodness of divine being', God's power and will are necessarily bound *ad extra* by his act of creation.[99] But this act stems more from the nature of God than from his will: the 'impelling cause' (*causa impellens*) of creation, says Arminius, 'is the Goodness of God, according to which he is [*affectus*] inclined to communicate his good'. God is the highest good (*summum bonum*) and creation is a communication of that good, and, because of this, all things have their 'existence' (*quod sint*) and 'goodness' (*quod bona sint*) by their 'participation' in divine goodness.[100]

Such a view of creation necessitates that the purpose of God towards those he creates will be 'the good of the creatures themselves, and especially of man'.[101] Otherwise, as Muller states, the nature of the act of creation is violated:

> God freely wills to create the world, but—granting that the world is the result of God's goodness and exists by participation in that goodness—once the world as such belongs to his willing, [he] is bound by his own goodness and by its reflection in the world to exercise his dominion in a manner 'proportioned to the powers of the creature on whom it is imposed'. 'Any other mode' of divine intervention, whether to assist or to hinder human activity, 'will be directly contrary to the good of the universe, inasmuch as the good of the universe consists just in this, that any creature be endowed with a free will, and that the use of its own proper free judgment or choice be allowed to it without any divine interference'.[102]

---

[99] R.A. Muller, 'God, Predestination, and the Integrity of the Created Order: A Note on Patterns in Arminius' Theology', in *Later Calvinism: International Perspectives*, ed. W.F. Graham (Kirksville, MO: Sixteenth Century Journal, 1994), pp. 440, 445. The extent to which Arminius is faithful to Thomist thinking is not clear. Brian Davies argues, for instance, that Thomas believed human free will after creation to be limited by divine providence. See his *Thought of Thomas Aquinas*, pp. 177-8, 248-9.

[100] *WJA*, II, pp. 339, 355. Cf. Muller, 'Patterns in Arminius' Theology', p. 440.

[101] *WJA*, II, p. 356.

[102] Muller, 'Patterns in Arminius' Theology', p. 441, where he is citing from *WJA*, III, pp. 284-5.

Although Arminius does apparently allow for something like the *potentia absoluta* in God before the decree to create, he, nonetheless, assigns so central a place to creation that it transcends God's decrees and forms the basis from which they flow.[103] All of God's decrees *ad extra* fall within the category of *potentia ordinata*, because they are limited by God's overarching act of creation, and, therefore, cannot contradict the nature of creation as a communication of and participation in divine goodness. This means that even God, as the later Remonstrants say, has no right to 'require, that a Man should wholly devest himself of the exercise of his Liberty, which he received by Creation'.[104]

In short, then, we see a basic difference in the theological systems of Rutherford and the Arminians. While Rutherford is driven by an overriding concern to protect divine freedom and the good, or glory, of God in the development of his doctrine of the divine will, Arminius consciously develops a system in which human freedom and the creature's good take center stage. It is important to note, however, that, despite this difference, both believe zealously in the sovereignty of God. But, whereas Arminius has constructed a world order wholly under the rubric of *potentia ordinata*, in which God's every act is limited by his decree of creation, Rutherford has instituted one in which *potentia absoluta* and *potentia ordinata* co-exist. The result, for Rutherford, is that God is both omnipotent and sovereign in the current world order, even over the free wills of his creatures. In addition to this, by advocating a world order in which *potentia absoluta* and *potentia ordinata* exist together, Rutherford is allowing room for the immediacy of God. God is free to work above, beyond, and apart from his given means. But, in Arminius' world order, because God has subjected his sovereignty to the free wills of creatures by creating them with liberty, he now works only mediately, adopting a hands-off approach, so to speak, to divine providence. This difference between Rutherford and Arminius has profound soteriological implications, as we will see later in this chapter and in the next, and will result in theological systems that are diametrically opposed to one another in their entireties.

THEOLOGIA ARCHETYPA ET ECTYPA

Because the *potentia Dei ordinata* represents the sphere in which God has revealed himself to his creatures through his decrees, while the *potentia Dei absoluta* represents a larger sphere, transcending our comprehension, the scholastic emphasis on the power distinction points towards another distinction that is important for our discussion of Rutherford and the Arminians, viz., that between *theologia archetypa* and *theologia ectypa*, which was introduced in chapter two.[105] By bringing the whole world order under the sphere of God's

---

[103] Muller, 'Patterns in Arminius' Theology', pp. 434-5. See also *WJA*, I, pp. 653-4.
[104] *Confession*, p. 103.
[105] See the discussion on pp. 25-29 above.

potentia ordinata, Arminius emphasizes *theologia ectypa* over *theologia archetypa*, and, thereby, justifies and accentuates the rationality of religion.[106] By removing the sphere of the *potentia absoluta* from consideration in the present world order, he is removing the element of God's incomprehensibility from his theology, while Rutherford, who maintains a world in which God has both *potentia absoluta* and *potentia ordinata*, retains a balance between God's comprehensibility and his ultimate incomprehensibility. What is more, the dynamic relationship that exists between the *potentia absoluta* and the *potentia ordinata* and between *theologia ectypa* and *theologia archetypa* helps to explain the element of mystery that exists in Rutherford's theology. Things like the sovereignty of God and human free will can both be subscribed to by Rutherford at the same time without any necessity of resolving the relationship between them philosophically. But the same cannot be said of Arminius' theology. Since everything is confined to the sphere of the *potentia ordinata*, no such mystery is justified.[107] Arminius must, to be consistent, attempt to resolve the relationship between such things as God's sovereignty and human free will. More significant than this, however, is the fact that by denying God's ability after creation to work immediately, the Arminians make *theologia ectypa* knowable by all people without exception, whereas, for Rutherford, the noetic effects of sin cloud the minds of all people after the fall and prevent them from knowing *theologia ectypa* savingly apart from the immediate work of God upon their minds and wills.[108]

This feature of Rutherford's theology further confirms Brian Armstrong's error in asserting that reason assumed an 'equal standing with faith' in post-Reformation thinking and further demonstrates how his claims apply best to Arminian theology instead. But it also reveals how the doctrine of God lies at the foundation of the theological differences that exist between Rutherford and the Arminians. No matter how central prolegomenal differences are, the doctrine of God—and the *potentia Dei absoluta et ordinata*, in particular—is more fundamental. Whereas Rutherford's God reigns on high within the current world order, the Arminians' God has willingly subjected himself to his free creatures. Most, if not all, of the key differences between their respective theologies can be explained in light of these *ad intra/ad extra* distinctions.

---

[106] Although Arminius embraces the scholastic distinction between *theologia archetypa et ectypa*, later Arminians, like Episcopius and Van Limborch, reject it outright. By doing so, they reveal this penchant for relegating all theology to *theologia ectypa*. See Muller, *God, Creation, and Providence*, pp. 60-62; Episcopius, *Opera theologica* (1678), pp. 12-13; Van Limborch, *Theologia Christiana*, 1.1.1.

[107] See Oberman's helpful discussion of the effects of the *potentia absoluta et ordinata* on medieval Nominalism in 'Notes on Nominalism', pp. 57ff.

[108] By 'immediate', we do not intend to suggest that Rutherford understands God to work apart from his appointed means (e.g., Scripture) but to work specially upon one individual at a time, opening his or her eyes to see the truth in Scripture and enabling him or her to believe, rather than generally instituting a sphere of grace in which all people are able to be saved.

Voluntas beneplaciti et signi

The second and most common distinction that Rutherford makes in regard to the divine will is one that involves the relationship between the will *ad intra* and *ad extra*, namely, the *voluntas Dei beneplaciti et signi*. Even though Rutherford remarks that the 'Scholastics unanimously acknowledge this', he is quick to point out that they differ amongst themselves and is equally as quick to explain the way in which he is using the terms himself.[109] Rutherford defines the *voluntas beneplaciti* as 'the decree of God', by which he determines all things, both good and bad, that will come to pass 'in his own time'. It is the hidden or decretive (*decretiva*) will of God, that which God 'cannot not satisfy'.[110] It differs from the *voluntas signi*, which is the 'revealed' (*revelata*), 'approving' (*approbans*), or 'commanding' (*praecipiens*) will of God, whereby he makes known to his creatures all that he approves of, as being 'morally lawful and noble, even if the future actuality of...[those] good thing[s] may never be decreed by God'.[111] In this way, God desires, approves, and commands many things to be done, which he decrees not to be done in actuality, and he forbids many things from being done, which he decrees to be done in actuality. Although it may sound like it, these two wills are not contradictory. God does not decree by his *voluntas beneplaciti* or command by his *voluntas signi* that something be both done and not done.[112] But he does approve of certain things being done by his *voluntas signi* that he does not actually decree to be done by his *voluntas beneplaciti*. And the reverse is true as well: God decrees (permits) certain things to be done by his *voluntas beneplaciti* that he does not approve of nor command to be done by his *voluntas signi*. For example, Rutherford says that God 'desires the obedience of *Judas* and *Herod* and *Pilate*', by his approving, commanding, and revealed will, and 'yet he decreed [by his hidden or decretive will] that they should crucify the *Lord of glory*'. And he approves and commands 'by his *Voluntas Signi* the perfect obedience of his own Law: But he decreed by his *Voluntas Beneplaciti* from eternity that there would be no one besides *Christ*, who would

---

[109] *Exercitationes*, p. 213. Heinrich Heppe has claimed that post-Reformation theologians in general 'disapproved of the distinction between *voluntas signi et beneplaciti*' (*RD*, pp. 87-8). But this claim does not bear up against the evidence both in regard to Rutherford and the Arminians, as we will see, and, as Richard Muller has shown, in regard to many others of the post-Reformation period as well, including Wendelin, Poole, Leigh, Maccovius, Cocceius, Twisse, and Baxter (*PRRD*, III, pp. 457-9). Interestingly, Heppe himself points to several others who employ this distinction favorably and in the same way that Rutherford does: e.g., Polanus, Walaeus, Hottinger, Braun, Alting, and Heidan (*RD*, pp. 85-7). There were different opinions about this distinction among scholastics (see, e.g., Leigh, *Body of Divinity*, p. 165) but rather than wholly disregard and disapprove of it, men like Rutherford, Arminius, and many of the later Remonstrants, embrace it and define what they mean by it.

[110] *Examen*, pp. 181-2, 285.

[111] *Examen*, p. 182; *Exercitationes*, p. 214.

[112] *Examen*, p. 204.

perfectly satisfy the Law.'[113]

In Rutherford's opinion, the Arminians virtually equate these two wills, the only difference being that the *voluntas beneplaciti* is hidden while the *voluntas signi* is revealed.[114] By making this charge, however, he is again exploiting the Arminian position and ignoring the explicit statements that they make in order to distinguish between them. Both Arminius and his later disciples identify the *voluntas beneplaciti* as that 'by which [God] wills to do or to prevent something' by using 'his absolute and irresistible Omnipotency' to dispose 'of all outward actions, and events of all things *according to his alone pleasure*'. They differentiate it from the *voluntas signi*, 'by which [God] wills something to be done, or to be omitted, by creatures endued with understanding'.[115] But, having acknowledged this, it must be said that Rutherford is putting his finger on an inherent contradiction in Arminian thinking. Following this almost-Calvinistic definition of the *voluntas beneplaciti*, the Remonstrants make the following remark:

> yet the natural contingency of things, and the innate liberty of Mans will, once long since given it in Creation, [God] doth never take away thereby: but leaveth ordinarily the natures of things safe and entire: and in such sort concurreth with the will of Man in acting, that he suffers it also to act according to its own nature, and freely perform its part: and *therefore doth not at any time lay upon it a necessity of doing well, much less of doing ill.*[116]

Rutherford recognizes that the Arminians are speaking of God's decree in absolute terms—he disposes all things 'according to his alone pleasure'—and then qualifying it out of existence by adding that God does not 'at any time' place any kind of necessity upon the free wills of his creatures. By making this qualification, they do appear to empty the contents of the *voluntas beneplaciti* and to transubstantiate it into the *voluntas signi*. God no longer wills according to his good pleasure alone but merely approves of what his creatures will according to their own good pleasure.

That such a transubstantiation of wills occurs is more apparent when sin is taken into account. The Arminians say that God does not will sin in any way whatsoever but only permits it by 'suffer[ing] our Actions to proceed', according to our own freedom of choice. God's permission is not an active willing on his part but a mere 'Remission' of his will. Were he actively to will sin or even sinful events, he would 'overthrow the order [of creation] once setled by himself, and destroy and void that liberty, which he gave his Creature'.[117] As a result, the Arminians collapse the *voluntas beneplaciti* into the *voluntas signi*. God can only forbid sin to happen by legislating against it in

---

[113] *Examen*, p. 182.
[114] *Examen*, p. 181.
[115] *WJA*, II, p. 128; *Confession*, p. 113, emphasis added.
[116] *Confession*, p. 114, emphasis added.
[117] *Confession*, pp. 84-5; *WJA*, II, p. 128.

his external commands; he has no real power to prevent its actuality once establishing the order of things in creation. Positively, this way of thinking seems to clear God of the charge that he is the author of sin by laying it at the feet of the creature instead. Negatively, it renders God powerless—albeit by divine choice—in preventing or overturning sinful actions or evil people. And, as we will see, it does not completely clear God of the charge of being the author of sin. Before we can explore how this is so, however, we need to look at yet another distinction within the divine will.

Voluntas efficiens et permittens

The third distinction that Rutherford makes in regard to the divine will is the *ad extra* distinction between the *voluntas efficiens et permittens*. Both terms fall under the umbrella of the *voluntas beneplaciti* and help to explain how it is that the will of God determines all future things and functions in concurrence with the free wills of creatures. In continuity with much of Thomistic philosophy, Rutherford operates in strict premotionist terms,[118] attributing to God—the first cause of all things—not only a simultaneous concurrence with every secondary cause but also a physical or material predetermination of it.[119] The *voluntas efficiens* is the '*first and highest cause of all positive existents*'. It is the will by which God directly accomplishes all things, either by himself or by his divine predetermination of and concurrence with secondary agents. In regard to morally good things, the *voluntas efficiens* determines not only the physical

---

[118] Whether or not Aquinas is a premotionist is a subject of debate. William Lane Craig has recently argued that 'Aquinas interpreted the notion of divine concurrence to mean that God not only supplies and conserves the power of operation in every secondary cause, but that He acts on the secondary causes to produce their actual operations, a view that came to be known as the doctrine of premotion' (*The Problem of Divine Foreknowledge*, p. 201). For those who take an opposite view to Craig, see Van Ruler, 'New Philosophy to Old Standards', p. 67n27. For our purposes here it does not really matter where Aquinas comes down on this question, because, as Van Ruler points out, 'later Thomistic thinkers…were generally held to be premotionists' (Van Ruler, 'New Philosophy to Old Standards', p. 65).

[119] 'Premotionism' derives its name from the predetermination, or pre-moving, of God in bringing secondary causes into motion in the first place (see Van Ruler, 'New Philosophy to Old Standards', pp. 64ff). Van Ruler gives the following helpful diagram in order to explain this theory:

$$\begin{array}{c} \text{Prime Cause} \\ {}^{a}\diagup \quad \diagdown^{c} \\ \text{Secondary Cause} \;\; \text{---} \;\; \text{Effect} \\ b \end{array}$$

where, a = God's 'physical predetermination of the secondary cause'; b = the 'natural operation of the secondary cause', i.e., human beings acting according to their own free wills; and c = the 'simultaneous concurrence of the Prime Cause' with the free operation of the second cause.

acts themselves but the morality of those acts as well.[120] Evil or sinful acts, however, fall under the *voluntas permittens*, God's permitting will, whereby he allows evil to be done by his creatures but does not directly accomplish it. This will, for Rutherford as well as for Calvin, is not a 'bare' permission, as the Arminians say. It is not a 'bare denial of the will' or a 'non-willing' on the part of God but a 'positive act of the *voluntas Beneplaciti*', in which the predetermination and concurrence of God together with the secondary agent produces the physical act of the sin. But the morality of the sinful act is only and completely caused by the secondary agent. Thus, although the *voluntas permittens* affirms a positive act of God's will, it denies two important things: '1. It denies *moral efficiency*: for God is not the cause of those things, which he permits. 2. It denies *voluntas approbans* [or, *signi*]. For that which God permits, he does not approve or prescribe for the creature to do.'[121]

The Arminians, following later scholastics and, in particular, the thinking of Molina, reject this theory of premotionism in favor of a cooperationism, whereby God simply works together with secondary causes to bring about certain effects, but he does not predetermine or 'pre-move' those secondary causes into action.[122] Were God to do so, he would violate the free wills of his creatures, something he cannot do after creating them. From the Arminian point of view, the premotionist position, as developed by Rutherford, is subject to at least two significant criticisms. First, if God is the predetermining cause of sin, or even of the sinful act, such that his predetermination is the sufficient condition for its existence, then God is necessarily the author of sin. Rutherford denies the accusation by arguing that God cannot be considered the author of sin if he is not the direct or efficient cause of it. He distinguishes between the physical and moral natures of sinful acts and asserts that the one who is responsible for the moral character of a sinful act is the rightful author of sin. Even Arminius, he says, 'admits that *eating* is in itself a natural act, *having no disorder in itself*'. But the 'prohibition of the Legislator' against wrongful eating—i.e., overeating—does not remove the distinction between the physical

---

[120] *Examen*, pp. 184-5, 223-4, 226-7.

[121] *Examen*, pp. 185, 205. Cf. *Institutes* I.xviii.1, pp. 228-31.

[122] Craig, *The Problem of Divine Foreknowledge*, pp. 200-202. See also Van Ruler, 'New Philosophy to Old Standards', pp. 64-7. Once again, Van Ruler gives the following helpful diagram in order to illustrate how the cooperationist view differs from the premotionist. As should be obvious from the diagram, 'a', God's 'physical predetermination of the secondary cause', is absent from the cooperationist scheme. But, 'b' is still the 'natural operation of the secondary cause', as before, and 'c' is the 'simultaneous concurrence of the Prime Cause' with the second cause.

```
Prime Cause  — c
              \
              Effect
              /
Secondary Cause — b
```

See Van Ruler, 'New Philosophy to Old Standards', p. 64n21.

and the moral natures of the act, nor does it equate the physical act with the sinful use of that act. It is not the act of eating that is sinful but the act of overeating (i.e., eating sinfully). In the same way, according to Rutherford, even though God is the material first cause of the sinful act, he cannot rightly be considered the author of the sin itself.[123] Only the one who acts sinfully can be so considered.

While this distinction between the physical and moral natures of an act does show that it is inappropriate to allege that Rutherford makes God the author of sin, it still leaves a nagging problem unresolved. How can God be the first and sufficient cause of a sinful act, such that a given sin would not occur without him, and, yet, not have some amount of moral culpability? Whether or not God is actually the author of sin in Rutherford's theology, then, is really beside the point, because God still appears to be culpable, as an accomplice at least, for his role in predetermining the physical act.

Secondly, the Arminians criticize Rutherford by suggesting that if God is the predetermining cause of everything, even of evil and affliction, then there is nothing separating his understanding of God from the fate of the Stoics or the Manichees.[124] But rather than deny this accusation, Rutherford acknowledges it, saying that 'if *fate* is the will of God, we do not hesitate to assert that *all things happen by fate*'. In order to clarify this and to avoid at least two problems that would result from such a potentially controversial statement, he offers the following two points of dissimilarity between his version of 'fate' and Stoicism: first, 'Divine Fate' is not the cause of wickedness, whereas the 'Fate of the Heathens' is; and, second, divine fate 'works sweetly in harmony with' the free acts of creatures—or, as the Westminster Confession says, God determines 'whatsoever comes to pass' but in such a way that 'the liberty or contingency of second causes is [not] taken way, but rather established'— whereas this emphasis is missing from the fate of the Stoics.[125] Since we have already dealt with the former point, we will now explore the latter in more detail.

Rather than precluding human freedom, as one might be tempted to guess, divine fate, in Rutherford's thinking, actually assumes it. Divine sovereignty and human freedom are completely compatible, as he sees it. Scripture, the *principium cognoscendi theologiae*, teaches both that God is sovereign and that humans are free. Commenting upon Nehemiah 1.10—a text which attributes the redemption of the people of Israel primarily to God—Rutherford says: 'But this power manifested itself by *free* acts in *Pharaoh*, who *freely* sent out the people; by *Moses* and *Aaron*, who *freely* proclaimed and performed miracles; [and] by the people, who *freely* went out.'[126]

Rutherford believes that the relationship between the sovereignty of God and human freedom in Scripture extends even to sinful acts. He offers fours ways in

---

[123] *Examen*, pp. 220, 224, 230.

[124] *Examen*, p. 227; *Confession*, p. 115.

[125] *Examen*, pp. 228-9; *WCF*, § 3.1, p. 28.

[126] *Examen*, p. 198.

which this can be seen. First, Scripture teaches that God decrees sin and is the predetermining cause of its existence: in Genesis 45.7, God, and not Joseph's brothers, is said to be the one who sends Joseph into Egypt; in Acts 2.23, 4.27, and 13.29, we are informed that '*those who crucified Christ did nothing other than what God decreed to be done*'; in 2 Samuel 24.1, we are directed that '*God incited David to number the people of God*', which was a sinful act; and in 1 Chronicles 5.26, we read that the '*God of Israel stirred up the spirit of Pul &c. so that he would take the people captive.*'[127] Second, Scripture teaches that 'God uses Devils and individuals in the act of sinning, as his own instruments', in order to accomplish his purposes: so, in Isaiah 10.5, '*Assyria is* [said to be] *the rod of* [God's] *wrath*'; in Isaiah 7.20, the king of Assyria is called a '*hired razor*'; and in Jeremiah 51.7, '*Babylon is a gold chalice in the hand of God.*'[128] Third, Scripture establishes the fact that God works together with sinful actions by permitting them materially but not morally: thus, in Job 1.12, 15, and 21, we are told that in one and the same act 'the *Sabeans* took away good things from *Job*, and God, through the *Sabeans*, took away those same good things'; and in 2 Samuel 12.11 and 16.21-2, we see that in one and the same '*material* action', 'God castigates *David* by *Absalom* polluting his...bed'. In each of these cases, Rutherford says, the action of the 'instruments is morally unjust and vitiated'.[129] Fourth, Scripture demonstrates that God decrees some things (by his *voluntas beneplaciti*) that he has expressly forbidden (by his *voluntas signi*). So, in 1 Kings 22.20, 23, God sent a 'lying spirit in the mouth of the Prophets' to allure Ahab to a battle that had been forbidden by God, 'in order that he might be killed there'. And, in 2 Samuel 12.11, God 'appointed *Absalom* to pollute wickedly his own Father's bed,' in order to discipline David for his sin with Bathsheba.[130]

Whether or not such ideas are in fact true to the biblical text is an issue that will not be entered into here. Biblical interpretation is an enterprise that, even in Rutherford's day, could be highly subjective. As we saw in the previous chapter, many of the Christian sects which surfaced in England and Scotland in the 1640s treated Scripture as a nose of wax to be molded and shaped according to their every whim. In setting this question aside, however, it should be noted that Rutherford's ideas are at least philosophically unsatisfying. The Arminians argue, as many others have over the last almost four hundred years, that such an emphasis on God's sovereign predetermination of every event precludes any possibility of true or 'significant' human freedom.[131] Although Rutherford

---

[127] *Examen*, p. 206. Rutherford lists other biblical passages: 2 Chronicles 21.16-17; Isaiah 45.7; Job 1.21; Ezekiel 14.9; 1 Corinthians 1.19-20; 2 Thessalonians 2.11; and 1 Peter 3.17.

[128] *Examen*, p. 207. Rutherford adds Jeremiah 25.9; 27.6; 50.23; and Revelation 17.17.

[129] *Examen*, pp. 230-31. Rutherford adds Isaiah 10.12.

[130] *Examen*, p. 206.

[131] Most recently Open Theists like John Sanders and Gregory Boyd have taken this stance. Sanders says that libertarian freedom, which is genuine or 'significant' freedom, is 'necessary for a truly personal relationship of love to develop' between God and

denies this accusation, his compatibilism leaves us with an unresolved tension that the Arminian position seems to address: How can God be sovereign and humans still retain any semblance of true freedom? While the tension between God's sovereignty and human free will is anticipated in Rutherford's understanding of the *potentia absoluta et ordinata*, it is still somewhat unsatisfying philosophically for him to leave the issue unresolved. The Arminians do attempt to resolve it, an attempt which is also anticipated in their reaction to the medieval power distinction, by stating that God foresees human free actions and then decrees to work together with them in divine concurrence.

It should be noted that Rutherford's emphasis on the sovereignty of God in predetermining everything that comes to pass, is at times so stark that it leaves one wondering if there actually is anything that separates his understanding from fatalism. A good example of this extreme emphasis on divine sovereignty is Rutherford's defense of the practice of casting lots.[132] Historian Robert Wodrow records an incident in Rutherford's lifetime in which he took up the casting of lots in order to determine God's choice for a vacant regency at St. Andrews. Even though he insisted it be done twice—because the first time the prayer that had been offered was 'not right gone about' and so the 'determination' was 'not to be sisted in'—he did, nonetheless, finally acknowledge and submit to God's decision in the outcome, but only after he himself had prayed and the result had turned out the same.[133]

Despite the difficulties inherent in Rutherford's system, however, it must be said that the Arminian alternative is subject to several problems that are at least as troubling. First, Arminian theology does not fully clear God of moral culpability either. As William Wainwright argues:

> A person is responsible or accountable for events of which she is not the author if she was able to prevent their occurrence and knew that they would occur if she did not interfere. It follows that since God knew that Judas would betray Christ if he

---

ourselves (J. Sanders, *The God Who Risks: A Theology of Providence* [Downers Grove, IL: InterVarsity, 1998], pp. 214, 251). Boyd echoes Sanders' sentiments and adds that 'agents are genuinely free only if the agents themselves are the *ultimate explanations* of their own free activity' (G. Boyd, *Satan and the Problem of Evil: Constructing a Trinitarian Warfare Theodicy* [Downers Grove, IL: InterVarsity, 2001], p. 19). For a response to these claims of Open Theists and Arminians and a cogent comparison of libertarian and compatibilist freedom written from a compatibilist perspective, see M.R. Talbot, 'True Freedom: The Liberty that Scripture Portrays as Worth Having', in *Beyond the Bounds: Open Theism and the Undermining of Biblical Christianity*, eds., J. Piper, J. Taylor, and P.K. Helseth (Wheaton, IL: Crossway, 2003), pp. 77-109; and P.K. Helseth, 'The Trustworthiness of God and the Foundation of Hope', also in *Beyond the Bounds*, pp. 275-307.

[132] *Examen*, pp. 194-5.

[133] R. Wodrow, *Analecta: or, Materials for a History of Remarkable Providences; Mostly Relating to Scotch Ministers and Christians*, 4 vols. (Edinburgh: Maitland Club, 1842-3), I, pp. 140-1.

and Jesus were created, and created them, He is responsible or accountable for Judas's betrayal even if he [sic] isn't the author of that betrayal. That God isn't the *author* of sin doesn't absolve Him of *moral responsibility* for it.[134]

But Wainwright proves more than this. Sin, he claims, for both the Calvinist and the Arminian, is ordained by God as a means to the end of achieving divine purposes. Even Arminians would agree that 'God's ultimate aim includes the redemption of the world through Christ's atonement'. But if this is so, then 'sin is a means to that end, and not just an unfortunate by-product of something else God aims at'. And if this is the case, then 'in creating free agents whom He knows will freely sin if they are created, God knowingly "initiates a harmful causal sequence"' in order to fulfill his ultimate aims. Wainwright's conclusion: 'The Arminian isn't much better off than the Calvinist with respect to God's alleged authorship of human sin.'[135] Both systems are unable wholly to clear God of moral culpability and both teach that God ordains sin as a means to accomplishing his purposes.

Secondly, Arminians face similar difficulties as do Calvinists in regard to the inherent determinism of their respective theological systems. For the Arminians, the difficulties stem from their reliance upon *scientia media*, a notion that had been traditionally challenged by Thomistic theologians on the basis that it leads ineluctably to a 'determinism of circumstances'.[136] By bringing one particular world into actuality instead of another—say, a world in which 'Jane' will be surrounded by good influences and so freely choose to believe and to persevere in her faith, whereas 'John' will be surrounded by bad influences and so freely choose not to believe or not to persevere in faith; or, a world in which Judas will freely betray Jesus so that Jesus might die to redeem humankind—God has effectively determined the fate of not only Jane and John, or Judas and Jesus, but of all individuals in that particular world. God could have chosen not to create John and Judas. But by choosing to create them, knowing that they would not believe, he has predetermined a certain course of events. Why create John or Judas in the first place? Would that not be more 'good' for them than creating them unto destruction? Regardless of how much the Arminians protest against the determinism of Calvinists like

---

[134] W.J. Wainwright, 'Theological determinism and the problem of evil: Are Arminians any better off?', *International Journal for Philosophy of Religion* 50 (2001), p. 87.

[135] Wainwright, 'Theological determinism', p. 90.

[136] See, e.g., R. Garrigou-Lagrange, 'Prémotion Physique', in *Dictionnaire de théologie catholique* (Paris: Librairie Letouzey et Ané, 1936), XIII, p. 68: 'Enfin, les thomistes rétorquent l'objection [that premotionism is incompatible with human freedom] en disant: c'est la théorie de la science moyenne qui détruit la liberté, car elle suppose que Dieu, antérieurement à tout décret divin, *voit infailliblement* ce que *choisirait* le libre arbitre de tel homme, s'il était placé en telles circonstances. Comment, en effet, éviter alors le déterminisme des circonstances? *Où* Dieu peut-il *voir infailliblement* la détermination à laquelle le libre arbitre créé s'arrêterait, sinon dans l'examen des circonstances, qui deviennent dès lors infailliblement déterminantes?'

The Doctrine of God

Rutherford, their alternative does not wholly free them from its blight.

In Rutherford's opinion, however, there is a greater problem with the determinism of the Arminians; it is grounded ultimately not in the will of God but in the will of the creature or in some sort of fate. The Arminians reject the absolute decree of God and opt instead for a conditional one that 'envelops God in fate, and forces his Omnipotency', which by definition should work 'freely *ad extra*', to cooperate 'in contributing to acts which have future actuality prior to his every decree'.[137] In other words, Rutherford says, by denying that the divine will determines everything absolutely, and teaching instead that God decrees, in light of his *scientia media*, what he foresees will necessarily happen in and of itself, apart from his divine will, the Arminians place a far greater emphasis on the fate of the Stoics than he could ever be accused of doing. Their fatalism is not a 'divine fate' but one that removes God from the throne of the universe and places humans there in his place as those who are ultimately responsible for determining all things.

Thirdly, the Arminians open the door to certain pastoral issues that are, again, at least as troubling as those raised by Calvinism. The most noteworthy of these is the issue of prayer within the church. There can be no doubt that Rutherford's perception of God and the *voluntas beneplaciti* leaves many of the problems with respect to prayer unresolved. The question arises for Rutherford: if God is sovereign, why is prayer necessary? And although this is not a question that he answers, it is clear that, as far as he is concerned, the problem raised by Arminianism is much more serious pastorally: why pray, if God is unable to answer that prayer? The God of the Arminians 'could only respond [to our prayers] like this: *I am unable to help, it is not my will that the wicked should have a hatred for you*'.[138] For God to intervene in the world order in answer to prayer would mean he would have to overturn the free wills of at least some of his creatures, which is impossible for him to do after creating them. The pastoral implications of this are grave, according to Rutherford, not only in regard to prayer, but also in regard to 'our faith,...hope, gratitude, fear, desire', and patient endurance in suffering. All these things would not 'rest and repose in God' but would be a source of great anxiety for the church were God not the one who has decreed all things 'from eternity'.[139]

In short, after examining Rutherford's understanding of the distinction between the *voluntas efficiens* and the *voluntas permittens* and comparing it with similar notions in the Arminians, it can be said that neither Rutherford nor the Arminians resolve all the problems regarding the relationship between divine sovereignty and human free will. Each side in the debate presents a theology with some elements that commend it and others that would seem to undermine it. What should be evident, however, is that both sides are diametrically opposed to one another. Rutherford exalts God's sovereignty and free will by establishing a world order in which God can reign and rule from on

---

[137] *Examen*, pp. 192-3; cf. *Examen*, pp. 164-5, 185, 190.

[138] *Examen*, pp. 202, 207.

[139] *Examen*, pp. 207, 228-9.

high, while the Arminians place their emphasis on human autonomy instead.

Voluntas antecedens et consequens

The final distinction that Rutherford makes in regard to the divine will is the distinction between the *voluntas antecedens et consequens*. Although Rutherford believes that the Arminians wrongly employ this distinction, he feels that the terms themselves could be useful to differentiate between the end and the means to the end or between the *voluntas signi et beneplaciti*.[140] In his *Exercitationes*, Rutherford also adds a third way in which these terms could rightly be utilized. This third option is similar to the relation between the *voluntas signi* and *beneplaciti* and is found in such medieval scholastics as Duns Scotus and Durandus. According to it, 'Deum id velle antecedenter...quod vult in antecedente causa, ex qua...effectus sequitur, quamvis non necessario; ut Deus antecedenter vult omnes salvari, quatenus dedit omnibus naturam salutis capacem, & media sufficientia non negavit, & Deus id vult consequenter quod non in causa sua, sed in se vult, ut credentes salvari.'[141] Here we have Rutherford's explanation of how it is that God can will the salvation of the whole world and yet not have the whole world be saved. God wills antecedently that all natural barriers to salvation be removed, even though spiritual barriers may remain. While this does provide a universal warrant for faith,[142] it does not guarantee that faith will inevitably follow. The consequent will of God removes the spiritual barriers and guarantees that faith will follow in the elect.

But this is not how the Arminians employ this distinction. Picking up on and perhaps modifying the examples of Chrysostom and John of Damascus (c.675-c.749), the Arminians speak of God antecedently willing the salvation of all people but consequently punishing some of them and withholding salvation from them for their sins.[143] This way of thinking renders the *voluntas antecedens* wholly inefficacious and the *voluntas consequens* conditional upon the performance or non-performance of the creature.[144] Rutherford's problem with the Arminians, however, is not so much that the *voluntas antecedens* is

---

[140] *Examen*, pp. 170-71. Rutherford is not alone in his belief that these terms could be rightly used when properly defined. Maccovius, Cocceius, Heidanus, Owen, Turretin, and Rijssen—among post-Reformation theologians—and Vermigli and Musculus—among the reformers—all voiced similar opinions. See *PRRD*, III, pp. 442-3, 465; *RD*, pp. 90-92.

[141] *Exercitationes*, p. 323.

[142] The soteriological concern over the warrant of faith is a problem that was later to plague men like James Fraser of Brea (see his *Memoirs of the Life of the Very Rev. Mr. J.F. of Brea* [Edinburgh, 1738]). It is possible that had Fraser understood Rutherford properly at this point, he might have been spared some of the spiritual agony he endured for the better part of his life.

[143] Muller, 'Patterns in Arminius's Theology', p. 434.

[144] *Examen*, p. 171; *Exercitationes*, p. 323. Cf. *PRRD*, III, p. 465.

inefficacious, because in the second and third ways that he himself gives for properly using this scholastic distinction, it is equally so. His problem is that there is no place in the Arminian system for an efficacious and absolute divine will. By not affording a place for an efficacious and absolute will, the Arminians are once again—in Rutherford's opinion—exalting human autonomy over divine free will and, in the process, undermining the sovereignty and glory of God.

Continuity or Discontinuity with the Reformation?

Before moving on to look at two key soteriological applications of the divine will in Rutherford's thinking, we need briefly to address the question of whether or not the preceding view of the *voluntas Dei* is continuous with Reformation theology. Doing so will enable us to demonstrate further the tenuous nature of Armstrong's claims in regard to the characteristic Protestant scholastic understanding of the divine will. Rather than being a source of discontinuity between the Reformation and post-Reformation periods, as Armstrong would have us to believe, the intricate doctrine of the *voluntas Dei* represents substantial continuity instead. This can be seen in at least the following three ways. First, although many of the reformers consistently express their disregard for doctrinal speculation, they, nonetheless, recognize the methodological necessity of adopting a series of distinctions to describe the divine will. Thus, Calvin and Musculus agree with Vermigli in saying that 'the will of God is of one sort, but...the objects [are] diverse'.[145] And because the objects of the divine will are diverse, 'our perception [of] God's will is manifold'.[146] Some sort of system of distinctions is, therefore, necessary in order to explain the divine will as it is perceived by us.

Secondly, in order to meet this need of explaining the will of God as it is understood by human beings, Calvin, Musculus, and Vermigli all adopt scholastic distinctions. Thus, Calvin differentiates between God's 'hidden will' (*voluntas arcana*) and his 'revealed will' (*voluntas revelata*) and uses these terms in the same way that Rutherford uses *voluntas beneplaciti et signi*, viz., to distinguish between God's hidden decree, on the one hand, and the commands that meet divine approval as revealed in Scripture, on the other.[147] Vermigli and Musculus not only embrace the medieval distinction between *voluntas beneplaciti et signi*, but, as we have previously indicated, they also accept the terms *voluntas antecedens* and *voluntas consequens*, although they use these latter terms interchangeably with the former pair. According to Vermigli, the 'will signified is that, which sheweth what we ought to do, or

---

[145] Vermigli, *Common Places*, I.xvii, p. 200. Cf. J. Calvin, *Commentary on a Harmony of the Evangelists, Matthew, Mark, and Luke*, trans. W. Pringle (Edinburgh: CTS, 1846), I, pp. 320-21; *Institutes* I.xviii.3, pp. 232-5; Musculus, *Common Places*, pp. 920ff.
[146] *Institutes* III.xxiv.17, p. 986.
[147] *Institutes* III.ii.14, p. 560; III.xx.43, p. 906; III.xxiii.4, p. 951; idem, *Commentary on a Harmony of the Evangelists*, III, p. 109.

what we ought to avoid; for thereby we gather the judgment and ordinance of God, and that consisteth in the lawe, in the commandements, promises, thretnings and counsels'. The 'other will of God', the *voluntas beneplaciti*, 'is that, which is called mightie, effectuall, and according to his good pleasure, which by no power can be vanquished and overcome'.[148] Calvin, like Rutherford, also distinguishes between the 'effecting' will of God and the 'permitting' will of God by referring favorably to medieval scholastics like Peter Lombard. For Calvin, as for Rutherford, God's permissive will is that by which 'he directs the…malice [of Satan and all the wicked] to whatever end seems good to him, and uses their wicked deeds to carry out his judgments'. This is done in such a way that 'the figment of bare permission vanishes' and, yet, not so as to establish God as the author of sin.[149]

Calvin's use of scholastic distinctions notwithstanding, his rejection of the particular distinction between the *potentia absoluta et ordinata* would seem to be at odds with post-Reformation thought, which, as we have previously seen, adopted the two powers of God in its 'classical' expression.[150] As David Steinmetz has argued, Calvin's unwillingness 'to entertain even a hypothetical separation of God's power from his justice', would seem to be 'not only opposed to the abuse' of the power distinction, as Turretin was later to suppose, but 'to the distinction as such'.[151] In spite of this fact, however, there is good reason 'to acknowledge', with Francis Oakley, that Calvin embraces the theology laying behind this distinction—as it is understood in its classical expression—even though he denounces the distinction itself. According to Oakley, there is an implicit embrace of the two powers of God in Calvin's view of 'God's preordination of things' as 'divine action reaching beyond the fixed order of nature and grace',[152] a view which, in the words of another twentieth-century scholar, is 'on a par with the distinction between *providentia ordinaria* and *extraordinaria*' as it is found in such early English Puritans as Perkins and Ames and, later, in the Westminster Confession.[153]

Thirdly, although it is true that reformers like Calvin, Musculus, and Vermigli refuse to pronounce definitively on the *ad intra* priority of the will or intellect in God, this does not necessarily mean that Rutherford's explicit voluntarism is, therefore, at odds with Reformation teaching. There appears to be good reason for seeing Rutherford's voluntarism as, at the very least, not contradictory to Reformation thought. For one thing, the theology of Calvin,

---

[148] Vermigli, *Common Places*, I.xvii, p. 201. Cf. Musculus, *Common Places*, p. 932.

[149] *Institutes* I.xviii.1, pp. 228-31.

[150] F. Oakley, 'The Absolute and Ordained Power of God in Sixteenth- and Seventeenth-Century Theology', *Journal of the History of Ideas* 59:3 (July 1998), pp. 444-9.

[151] D.C. Steinmetz, *Calvin in Context* (New York: Oxford University, 1995), pp. 49-50. Cf. Turretin, *Institutes* 3.21.5, I, p. 245.

[152] Oakley, 'Absolute and Ordained Power of God', p. 458.

[153] G. Van den Brink, *Almighty God: A Study of the Doctrine of Divine Omnipotence* (Kempen: J. Kok, 1993), p. 90. Cf. the discussions of providence in Perkins, *Workes*, I, p. 159; III, pp. 609, 657; Ames, *Marrow*, pp. 45-50; and *WCF*, §§ 5.1-7, pp. 33-8.

Musculus, and Vermigli is concerned to protect the freedom of the divine will from every constraint and to locate the causal basis for all things in the will of God. But whereas Musculus and Vermigli write that Augustine—when he says 'that there is nothing prior to or greater than the will of God'—is correct only insofar as it applies to 'those things that are not in God',[154] Calvin is at least more open to voluntaristic interpretation. Thus, in the *Institutes*, he says the following about the divine will without clarifying whether he is speaking *ad intra* or *ad extra*:

> [God's] will is, and rightly ought to be, the cause of all things that are. For if it has any cause, something must precede it, to which it is, as it were, bound; this is unlawful to imagine. For God's will is so much the highest rule of righteousness that whatever he wills, by the very fact that he wills it, must be considered righteous. When therefore, one asks why God has so done, we must reply: because he has willed it. But if you proceed further to ask why he so willed, you are seeking something greater and higher than God's will, which cannot be found.[155]

Prominent scholars have picked up on statements like this in Calvin and have used them to argue that Calvin is a voluntarist, influenced more by Duns Scotus than by Aquinas.[156] And Hans Emil Weber has described both Calvin and Luther in voluntaristic terms, referring to them as the heirs of the 'medieval tradition of the divine will and its sovereign freedom'.[157] There is, moreover, a striking similarity between Rutherford and Calvin in regard to the soteriological applications of the divine will, as should be evident after the succeeding discussion. All this is to say that, although we may not be able to pronounce definitively that Rutherford's voluntarism is identical with Calvin's, there does appear to be reliable evidence for seeing their theologies as continuous, nonetheless. The use of scholastic distinctions in speaking of the divine will and the implicit (at least) reliance upon the power distinction are both areas that represent significant continuity between Reformation and post-Reformation periods.

---

[154] Musculus, *Common Places*, p. 931. Cf. Vermigli, *Common Places*, I.xvi, p. 170.
[155] *Institutes* III.xxiii.2, p. 949.
[156] See, e.g., F. Wendel, *Calvin: The Origins and Development of his Religious Thought*, trans. P. Mairet (London: Collins, Fontana Library, 1965), pp. 127ff; and T.F. Torrance, *The Hermeneutics of John Calvin* (Edinburgh: Scottish Academic Press, 1988). Wendel cites Albrecht Ritschl, Henri Bois, Williston Walker, and Reinhold Seeberg as linking Calvin's conception of the will of God to Duns Scotus. Although, as we have indicated previously, Alexander Broadie has argued that Duns Scotus actually took up a position between the voluntarism of his later followers and the intellectualism of Aquinas, the sixteenth century viewed Duns Scotus as a voluntarist whose system was opposed to Aquinas' intellectualism. That this is the case can be seen in Vermigli, *Common Places*, I.xvi, p. 170.
[157] Muller, *Christ and the Decree*, pp. 5-6.

Soteriological Applications of the *voluntas Dei*

The centrality of the divine will in Rutherford's theology can be seen more clearly when we examine the effect that it has upon his views of the planning and purchasing of salvation. The most important of these soteriological applications of the divine will, as far as our discussion in this chapter is concerned, are predestination and the atonement of Christ. Not only are these two issues counted among the main areas of contention between him and the Arminians, they are also the primary bases of both contemporary and modern-day criticisms of his theology.

Predestination[158]

Perhaps the most notorious aspect of Rutherford's theology is his penchant for a strict predestinarianism. It is the quintessential hallmark of the rigid Calvinism for which he is known. As a supralapsarian, he is thought to be in continuity with such high Calvinists as Theodore Beza, Petrus Plancius (1552-1622), Franciscus Gomarus (1563-1641), William Perkins, William Twisse, and Gisbertus Voetius—men whose teaching formed the theological context in which Arminius was to develop his doctrine of predestination and whose opinions represented the radical extremes against which Arminius and his later disciples were to react.[159] Rutherford's continuity with such men and his taking up of their mantle against Arminius gained him an international reputation and helped to secure invitations from the divinity departments of two leading Dutch universities, Utrecht and Harderwyck.

That being said, recent evaluations of Rutherford's doctrine of predestination have exaggerated its rigidity, labelling it 'breathtakingly stark' and 'stern and extreme' because of its supralapsarian scheme.[160] But it is not at all certain that such critiques are fair to Rutherford. He has no dogmatic preoccupation with supralapsarianism or with the decrees in general. Supralapsarianism is set forth only implicitly in the majority of his writings and, when it is set forth explicitly, it is surprisingly moderate. Rather than presenting a harsh supralapsarian scheme, as many like Kingsley Rendell have assumed,[161] Rutherford seems, instead, to frame his supralapsarianism in

---

[158] A large portion of this section has been reproduced for publication in G.M. Richard, 'Samuel Rutherford's Supralapsarianism Revealed: A Key to the Lapsarian Position of the Westminster Confession of Faith?', *SJT* 59:1 (2006), pp. 27-44.

[159] Arminius' reaction against supralapsarianism is not unanticipated. James Orr has argued that such a doctrine 'is bound to provoke revolt against the whole system with which it is associated.' *The Progress of Dogma* (London: James Clarke, n.d.), p. 296.

[160] D.A.S. Fergusson, 'Predestination: A Scottish Perspective', *SJT* 46 (1993), p. 465; Bell, *Calvin and Scottish Theology*, p. 83; Rendell, *Samuel Rutherford*, p. 82.

[161] Rendell says: 'Rutherford's doctrine of election may seem stern and extreme to all but ultra Calvinists, but it appears even sterner when we examine his view of reprobation.' *Samuel Rutherford*, p. 82.

consistently infralapsarian terms. In order to demonstrate this, we need to explore further Rutherford's supralapsarianism, his doctrines of election and reprobation, and the order of the decrees in his thinking.

SUPRALAPSARIANISM

Supralapsarianism—which derives from *supra lapsum*, meaning 'above or prior to the fall'—is the designation for the system of thought that understands the decree of God to elect and reprobate as occurring before his decrees to create and permit the fall. It sees '*electio* and *reprobatio* as positive, coordinate decrees of God by which God chooses those who will be saved and those who will be damned, in other words, [it is] a fully double predestination, or *praedestinatio gemina*'. It should be distinguished from infralapsarianism—a word taken from *infra lapsum*, meaning 'below or subsequent to the fall'—which speaks of election and reprobation as occurring after the divine decrees to create and permit the fall. Infralapsarians see election alone as a positive decree of God and reprobation as 'a negative act or passing over of the rest of mankind, leaving them in their sins to their ultimate *damnatio*'.[162] At the heart of the seventeenth-century dispute between these two ways of ordering the divine decrees *sub specie aeternitatis* is the issue of the *objectum praedestinationis*. Karl Barth explains:

> The question is put in this way: What do we mean when we say that from all eternity man was elected by God, or, as we should have to say with equal emphasis according to the presuppositions of their theology, rejected by God? Is it that in His eternal election God was thinking simply of man, man as not yet created but still to be created, man as not yet fallen but still to fall by divine permission and human action [the supralapsarian position]? Or is it that He was thinking of man as already created and already fallen in virtue of this divine permission and human action [the infralapsarian position]? In other words, is the one elected or rejected *homo creabilis et labilis*, or is he *homo creatus et lapsus*? The whole difference of opinion [between infralapsarians and supralapsarians] narrows down ultimately to this formula.[163]

The resulting order of the decrees for a supralapsarian would be along these lines: (1) the decree to elect some and reject others; (2) the decree to create both elect and reprobate; (3) the decree to permit the fall of both into sin; and (4) the decree to provide salvation for the elect alone. For an infralapsarian, however,

---

[162] Muller, *Dictionary*, pp. 155, 234-5, 292.
[163] *CD*, II/2, p. 127. Barth offers a helpful survey of the seventeenth-century supralapsarian-infralapsarian debate. For other works with similar discussions of this subject, see G.C. Berkouwer, *Divine Election*, trans. H. Bekker (Grand Rapids, MI: Eerdmans, 1960), pp. 254-77; W. Cunningham, *Reformers and the Theology of the Reformation* (1862; Edinburgh: Banner of Truth, 1989), pp. 358-71; *RD*, pp. 148ff, 157-62; and H. Bavinck, *The Doctrine of God*, trans. W. Hendriksen (Edinburgh: Banner of Truth, 1977), pp. 382-94.

it would look like this instead: (1) the decree to create human individuals; (2) the decree to permit them to fall into sin; (3) the decree to elect some and pass by the rest; and (4) the decree to provide salvation for the elect alone.[164]

The most explicit statement of Rutherford's supralapsarianism is found in an unpublished manuscript discourse on Ephesians 1.4, written in his own hand. In this discourse, Rutherford reveals his belief that election stands logically prior to every decree: 'Some' believe 'our election to be both after the decrees of creating us and permitting us to fall into sin. [But] we prove that God's electing of us cannot be after the consideration of our creation and fall.'[165] What is most striking about this statement, and the whole of the discourse for that matter, is not what it says but what it leaves unsaid. It clearly mentions that election is prior to every other divine decree, an explicitly supralapsarian attitude, but it says nothing about reprobation.[166]

In the *Examen*, Rutherford again reveals his supralapsarianism by stating that 'the object of predestination is *homo creandus & nondum creatus*'. But, after doing so, he goes on to speak of this predestination only in terms of establishing individuals 'for glory'. Once again, reprobation is not mentioned at all.[167] And while there is a double decree in Rutherford, whereby the 'potter' makes 'from the same clay, vessels for honor and vessels for dishonor [*ignominia*]',[168] this is not necessarily indicative of supralapsarianism. As John Fesko points out, many infralapsarians also believe in a *praedestinatio gemina*.[169] When speaking of predestination, moreover, Rutherford consistently uses nomenclature which is at least equally as characteristic of infralapsarianism as it is of supralapsarianism. He refers to *praedestinatio ad gratiam*, *ad adoptionem*, *ad obtinendam salutem*, and, perhaps most significantly, *ad vitam*, in addition to the more distinctive *praedestinatio ad gloriam* which one would expect from a supralapsarian.[170] Thus, although Rutherford clearly supports the supralapsarian position, he states his views only in the most moderate of terms. He places election first among the divine

---

[164] *CD*, II/2, pp. 128-30. Cf. J.V. Fesko, *Diversity Within the Reformed Tradition: Supra- and Infralapsarianism in Calvin, Dort, and Westminster* (Greenville, SC: Reformed Academic Press, 2001), pp. xxiii-xxv.

[165] Unpublished manuscript, University of Edinburgh Library, La.II.394, p. 5.

[166] Rutherford's manuscript does mention reprobation on a couple of occasions. When it does so, however, it speaks only in the most vague of terms and with infralapsarian language.

[167] *Examen*, p. 272.

[168] *Examen*, p. 257. For more on the double decree in Rutherford, see *Examen*, chs. 3 and 4; and *Catachisme*, p. 163; *Christ Dying*, pp. 311, 382, 410.

[169] Fesko, *Diversity Within the Reformed Tradition*, p. xxv.

[170] See, e.g., *Examen*, pp. 260, 264-5. John Fesko remarks that 'Infralapsarianism is often called *praedestinatio ad vitam*' in his 'The Westminster Confession and Lapsarianism: Calvin and the Divines', in *The Westminster Confession into the 21st Century: Essays in Remembrance of the 350th Anniversary of the Westminster Assembly*, vol. 2, ed. J.L. Duncan III (Fearn, Ross-shire: Mentor, 2004), p. 481.

decrees but ignores the issue of reprobation, and he frequently employs bipartisan terminology in describing his understanding.

ELECTION AND REPROBATION

When we look at Rutherford's doctrines of election and reprobation, we see this same tendency toward a moderate supralapsarianism together with a use of terminology that is characteristically infralapsarian. 'Election', for Rutherford, 'is a singular, indivisible act concerning the ordaining of a determined number of people to glory.' It is an 'act of divine love' that eternally, absolutely, immutably, and irrevocably 'separates' a certain people unto God to be his own.[171] By definition, it is particular or limited in its scope, because 'if election is an election of all, it is not election'.[172] Rather than it being less loving for God only to choose some, it is actually more loving for him to do so. Even though the extent of election is limited, its nature is not. Its nature is absolute, immutable, and irrevocable. This means that those who are elect will never be otherwise. The doctrine of election, thus, provides one important part of the grounds for the believer's assurance of salvation, as we will see in the next chapter. Ultimately, salvation depends not on the will of the creature but on the absolute and unchangeable decree of God. Such an idea is in direct contrast with the Arminian understanding of election, which believes that the divine decree is conditional upon the free will of the creature, foreseen by *scientia media*.[173]

By saying that God's election is absolute, Rutherford does not mean that it does away with human free will, but that,

> the good pleasure [*beneplacitum*] of God, ordaining *Peter* to glory rather than *Judas*, is not moved to predestine him, neither *causatively* moved, nor *occasionally* inclined, nor determined by some order of the *Justice* or *Veracity* of God, nor by some *meritorious* cause, either a cause *proceeding from congruity*, or *decency*, or some *quality*, *disposition*, or *condition* in *Peter*.

Because election is not based on anything outside of God but solely on his sovereign *beneplacitum*, it must logically take place before all other divine decrees. Placing it after the decree of the fall, the infralapsarian view, would make 'God look out of himself for determining his will' and thus make election conditional upon a foreseen fall, an error that would concede far too much to Arminianism and destroy the 'all sufficiencie' of God by making him 'go forth of himself, seeking knowledge from things without him, as we [who are mere

---

[171] *Examen*, pp. 238-42.

[172] *Examen*, p. 279.

[173] *WJA*, II, p. 719. Cf. *Exercitationes*, p. 25, where Rutherford claims that the Arminians conceive predestination in an entirely different manner than he does: 'credunt electionem & destinationem ad gloriam esse temporarium, & ex hominum arbitrio, qui credere vel non credere possunt, adeoque mutabilem esse'.

creatures] doe'.[174]

When speaking of reprobation, on the other hand, Rutherford delineates a twofold process by distinguishing reprobation, obviously taken in a more broad sense, from *praeteritio*. He acknowledges that,

> it should be distinguished between *preterition* [*praeteritio*] or *non-election* (by which God is able to deny his favor to an individual who is guilty of nothing evil, with his own Justice preserved) and *reprobation*, by which God has decreed from his own absolute good pleasure [*beneplacitum*] to create some and to deny efficacious grace to them in order to declare the glory of his Justice.[175]

In other words, for Rutherford as for William Perkins, reprobation consists in two acts.[176] There is, in the first place, an absolute act, which Rutherford calls preterition or 'non-election'. It refers to God's mere 'passing by' (*praeterit*) of some who are 'guilty of nothing evil'. It is the necessary antithesis to and coordinate of election, because election, by definition, cannot be universal: if 'God absolutely elects some unto eternal glory by his own free will, he necessarily (for if election is an election of all, it is not election) passes by all others and non-elects them unto glory'.[177] This preterition is just as much an absolute, definite, immutable, and irrevocable decree as is election.[178] But it is a decree that is at least phrased negatively.

The second act of reprobation that Rutherford alludes to is one that we will call 'preterition$_2$', because it too is a passing by or a withholding. In this case, however, God withholds 'efficacious grace' from a people he has decreed to create, which implies the need for such grace and, thus, assumes not just the decree of the fall, but also the decree of God's justice *ad extra*.[179] Here too this act of reprobation is phrased negatively. God passes by some and leaves them in their sins 'in order to declare the glory of his justice'. Together these two acts make up reprobation, in the broadest sense of the word.

THE ORDER OF THE DECREES

Before going any further, it would be helpful to pause and work through the order of the decrees in Rutherford's thinking. Doing so will help us to evaluate more accurately the place he affords to election, preterition, and reprobation, as

---

[174] *Examen*, pp. 246-7; Unpublished manuscript, La.II.394, p. 8.

[175] *Examen*, pp. 278-9. Rutherford is speaking against the Arminians, who collapse these two terms and allow for no difference between them.

[176] W. Perkins, *A Christian and Plaine Treatise of the Manner and Order of Predestination, and of the Largeness of Gods Grace* (London, 1606), p. 25. Perkins says that reprobation has 'two actes. The first is the purpose to forsake some men, and to make knowen his justice in them.' And the second 'is the ordaining of them to punishment or due destruction' for their sin.

[177] *Examen*, pp. 278-9.

[178] *Examen*, pp. 262-3, 274-5, 277, 287, 291.

[179] *Examen*, pp. 278-9.

well as the validity of the criticisms that have been leveled against his predestinarianism. Following the tendency of supralapsarians in general, Rutherford does as William Twisse does and orders the divine decrees according to the 'received Rules of Schooles', which differentiate between ends and means. According to these scholastic rules, 'the end must be acknowledged both first in intention, and last in execution, and contrarily the means last in intention and first in execution'.[180] When applied to salvation, this translates into a supralapsarian scheme, because 'the means by which God brings some [men and women] to salvation' must be decreed after the end or, in other words, after God decrees the fact of their salvation itself.[181] The contrary— decreeing the means to accomplish salvation before decreeing salvation itself— would make no sense. With this in mind, the *ordo decretorum* will proceed as follows in Rutherford's understanding:

1. Election and Non-Election (or Preterition).[182] As we have just seen, Rutherford places election and its corresponding antithesis, non-election, ahead of all other divine decrees. Election and non-election represent the ultimate ends that God has ordained for his creatures and, therefore, must be decreed prior to the means he will use to accomplish those ends. This is confirmed by his definition of non-election as a denying of divine favor to individuals who are 'guilty of nothing evil'. By defining it in this way, Rutherford is implying that this passing over occurs before the decree of the fall. Otherwise, these individuals would be guilty of sin in the mind of God.

2. Creation. Creation, for Rutherford, is the first means by which God works out the ends of election and non-election.[183]

3. Fall. God decrees the fall also as a means to the ends of election and non-election. The divine decree to permit the fall (by his *voluntas permittens*) is the 'intrinsic basis for punishing and pardoning'.[184]

4. 'Ad extra' Decrees. As we mentioned above, Rutherford believes that God, although just, merciful, and good in and of himself (*ad intra*), is under no compulsion to be just, merciful, and good to his creatures. But once he decrees to act *ad extra* in this way, he is bound by his decree to do so. This is just what God has done; he has decreed to be just, merciful, and good (etc.) to his creatures. This decree presupposes the creation of creatures to whom God will

---

[180] W. Twisse, *The Riches of Gods Love unto the Vessels of Mercy, Consistent with his Absolute Hatred or Reprobation of the Vessels of Wrath* (Oxford, 1653), p. 4.

[181] Unpublished manuscript, La.II.394, pp. 5-6.

[182] Rutherford presents an *ordo decretorum* of sorts in his discourse on Ephesians 1.4. But he only mentions three 'decrees', all of which appear to be part of this first decree. God will glorify himself (the first decree he mentions), Christ (the second decree), and *homo creabilis* in Christ (the third decree) by electing some and passing over others. Unpublished manuscript, La.II.394, p. 9.

[183] *Catachisme*, pp. 163-4.

[184] *Examen*, p. 283.

be just, merciful, and good, and also their fall into sin, because before God could decree 'to illustrate the glory of his punitive Justice and sparing Mercy, it was necessary, by *hypothetical necessity*, that sin should exist'.[185]

5. Salvation and Preterition$_2$. It is only at this point that the second act of reprobation, what we are calling preterition$_2$, comes into play in Rutherford's thinking. After the fall and the *ad extra* decrees, God now chooses to show mercy to the elect, applying to them the benefits of Christ's atonement, and to pass over the non-elect, leaving them to his *ad extra* justice.[186]

Rutherford's catechism further substantiates this interpretation of the decrees and, in particular, of reprobation, and it confirms his use of infralapsarian language. In his catechism, he states that there are two decrees of God concerning mankind: 'the decrees of electione and reprobatione'. The key, however, is in how he defines election and reprobation. Election is 'the Lordis free appoyntment setting some men apairt for glorie (Eph. i.5, 6; Joh. xvii.6), and making them his sones in Christ (Ephes. i.5; 2 Thess. ii.13), for the praise of his glorie (Eph. i.6)', whereas reprobation is 'Godis free appoyntment q^{r}by [whereby] he decreeth to pass by some and to leave them to the hardness of their owne heart'. In this case, reprobation at least, and, quite possibly, election as well, should be understood in a broad sense, as encompassing not just the first decree but the fifth as well. Note that election includes not just 'setting some men apairt for glorie', but also, 'making them his sones in Christ', which could presuppose the fall and the application of salvation in Christ. Regardless of how election is to be taken, however, reprobation explicitly involves the first and fifth decrees. It includes both the decree 'to pass by some' (non-election) and the decree 'to leave them to the hardness of their owne heart', which obviously presupposes the fall.[187]

What is unavoidable, both here in his catechism and in the *Examen*, is Rutherford's use of infralapsarian language.[188] He plainly refers to reprobation as a 'passing by'. If Rutherford is a supralapsarian, which he clearly seems to be, and if he believes in two decrees, which he clearly seems to do, and if he distinguishes between non-election, or preterition, and reprobation, which he

---

[185] *Examen*, p. 284.

[186] *Examen*, p. 283.

[187] *Catachisme*, p. 163. William Perkins speaks of election and reprobation as encompassing two distinct acts each. We have already mentioned the two acts of reprobation. Election's two acts, according to Perkins, are 'foreknowledge, whereby hee doth acknowledge some men for his owne, before the rest', and 'predestination, whereby he hath determined from eternitie to make them like unto Christ'. Here, too, election could be read as encompassing both the first and fifth decrees, although not necessarily, because God could have chosen to make his elect like Christ without having first to cleanse them from sin. *A Christian and Plaine Treatise*, pp. 6-8 and 24-7.

[188] Fesko also notes that 'Rutherford defines reprobation [in his catechism] in terms of preterition, which is typical nomenclature for infra- rather than supralapsarians.' *Diversity Within the Reformed Tradition*, p. 272.

also clearly seems to do, then the above schema is the only possible one. Reprobation must be a broader category in Rutherford, as it was in Perkins, involving two steps. But in a way that is different from Perkins, Rutherford speaks of both steps as 'preteritions' or as involving God's passing over of some: one preterition occurs alongside election and one occurs after the decrees of creation and the fall. This 'passing over' language is certainly uncharacteristic of supralapsarianism in general. Whereas supralapsarians typically define election and reprobation as 'positive, coordinate decrees of God by which God chooses those who will be saved and those who will be damned',[189] Rutherford, at least on the surface, appears to express his understanding much more moderately. His supralapsarianism is defined in terms of election with little or no regard for reprobation; and he consistently uses infralapsarian language to refer to reprobation as a negative decree in which God passes over some, rather than positively ordaining them to destruction. John Fesko offers this description of infralapsarianism:

> Infralapsarianism is often called *praedestinatio ad vitam*, or single-predestination, because there is only one decree of predestination: the decree of election. Those who are non-elect are simply passed by in the decree of election, or are not elect by default, and are left in their sin unto their ultimate damnation.[190]

This description of infralapsarianism is consistent with Rutherford's expression of election and preterition, except for the fact that Rutherford believes in two decrees and two preteritions. Rutherford is a supralapsarian, to be sure, but one who expresses his views in infralapsarian language.

SUMMARY

After examining Rutherford's supralapsarianism, his doctrines of election and reprobation, and the *ordo decretorum*, it should be evident that Rendell's evaluation is incorrect or, at least, unfair. Rather than making his 'stern' view of predestination 'even sterner', reprobation actually moderates it.[191] Most of the other critiques of Rutherford's supralapsarianism also fall at this point along with Rendell's. They overlook his tendency toward the use of infralapsarian language in regard to reprobation in particular. While Rutherford speaks about election in strict supralapsarian terms, he unmistakably speaks about reprobation more in line with an infralapsarian system.

A recent thesis by San-Deog Kim explains Rutherford's use of infralapsarian language by concluding that it stems from a consideration of the decrees from the perspective of the creature rather than from God's point of view. The idea, according to Kim, is that the decrees, when considered from God's perspective, will have a supralapsarian formulation in Rutherford and an infralapsarian

---

[189] Muller, *Dictionary*, p. 235.
[190] Fesko, 'The Westminster Confession and Lapsarianism', p. 481.
[191] Rendell, *Samuel Rutherford*, p. 82.

formulation, when viewed from the creature's perspective.[192] While there is truth in Kim's explanation, insofar as it is true that Rutherford's use of infralapsarian language is partially a product of the difficulty inherent in supralapsarian schemes in general, namely, that it makes God the ultimate cause of his creatures' eternal destruction, it is not true that Rutherford's supralapsarian language is reserved only for speaking of election and reprobation from God's perspective or that his infralapsarian language is relegated to speaking of election and reprobation from the perspective of the creature. Kim ignores the fact that Rutherford defines reprobation solely in infralapsarian terms. His supralapsarian terminology is reserved not for speaking of election and reprobation from God's point of view but for speaking of election without respect to reprobation.

The interpretation of Rutherford's predestinarianism that is offered in the current study is further supported by Arminius' own seventeenth-century appraisal of the contemporary theological landscape, which can be found in his *Declaration of Sentiments* (1608). According to Arminius, the version of predestinarianism that we later see in Rutherford should properly be distinguished from the more severe variety held by Theodore Beza. Whereas Beza espouses 'the very highest' form of supralapsarianism that sees election and reprobation as virtually equal and opposite decrees, Rutherford's convictions comport best with 'a second kind of Predestination', a 'modified supralapsarianism' that Arminius locates mid-way between Beza's supralapsarianism and infralapsarianism.[193] This modified position places greater emphasis on the positive decree of election and subdivides reprobation into two distinct acts, what he calls '*preterition*' and '*predamnation*'. Arminius describes these two acts as follows:

> Two means are fore-ordained for the execution of the act of Preterition: (1) *Dereliction* [or *abandoning*] in a state of nature, which by itself is incapable of every thing supernatural: And (2) *Non-communication* [or a *negation*] of supernatural grace, by which their nature (if in a state of integrity,) might be strengthened, and (if in a state of corruption,) might be restored....Predamnation is antecedent to all things, yet it does by no means exist without a fore-knowledge of the causes of damnation: It views man as a sinner, obnoxious to damnation in Adam, and as on this account perishing through the necessity of Divine Justice.[194]

The current interpretation of Rutherford's understanding of predestination also places it in substantial continuity with Reformation thought. According to Frank James, Vermigli's predestinarianism is best interpreted in a way that is

---

[192] Kim, 'Time and Eternity', pp. 176-7.
[193] Cf. *WJA*, I, pp. 613-15, with 645-7. See also, A.S. Wood, 'The Declaration of Sentiments: The Theological Testament of Arminius', *The Evangelical Quarterly* 65:2 (1993), pp. 116-20. Wood reminds us that Arminius knew Beza's doctrine of predestination well, since he was mentored by Beza in Geneva.
[194] *WJA*, I, p. 646.

strikingly similar to—and, possibly, even more severe than—Rutherford's view, as we have outlined it here. Although, as James says, some scholars have interpreted Vermigli's predestinarianism as 'extreme supralapsarian[ism]' because of its overarching emphasis on the *propositum Dei*,[195] this overlooks his infralapsarian tendencies. There is a 'distinctly infralapsarian cast' to Vermigli's thought, which, more than anything else, is due to the explicit 'christological orientation' of his theology: 'Since Christ is the first effect of predestination and is exclusively associated with saving sinners, Vermigli's primary emphasis in predestination tends to infralapsarianism.'[196] As we will see in the next section, this Christocentricity parallels Rutherford's understanding of election as well.

One wonders whether such a conception of predestination, couched as it is in infralapsarian language, could also apply to Calvin's understanding of this doctrine. While scholars have lined up on both sides, pronouncing Calvin as either supra- or infralapsarian,[197] their pronouncements tend to trivialize the fact that there are clear elements of both in his theology. As Richard Muller remarks, 'Calvin sometimes speaks as if the object of predestination is fallen humanity in need of redemption, sometimes as if the decree is radically prior, given God's predestining of the fall itself.'[198] Taking Calvin's own express Christological emphasis into account could help to explain the infralapsarian language in the Genevan reformer as well. Whether this is so or not, there are still good reasons for seeing Rutherford's view as continuous with Calvin's. First, according to Alister McGrath's lucid claims, Calvin is part of the same Augustinian tradition as is Rutherford—the *schola Augustiniana moderna*—a tradition that, from its inception, embraced a doctrine of double predestination, especially as that doctrine is understood in a Calvinian sense.[199] Second, Calvin uses language when speaking of election that is reminiscent of the language we have found in Rutherford. In defining election, for instance, Calvin begins by

---

[195] F.A. James III, *Peter Martyr Vermigli and Predestination: The Augustinian Inheritance of an Italian Reformer* (Oxford: Clarendon, 1998), p. 88. James cites Reinhold Seeberg and J.P. Donnelly as arguing for a supralapsarian understanding of Vermigli.

[196] James, *Vermigli and Predestination*, pp. 88-9.

[197] Among those who see Calvin as infralapsarian are, F. Turretin, *Institutes* 4.9.30, I, pp. 349-50; H. Blocher, 'Calvin infralapsaire', *La Revue Réformée* 31 (1980), p. 273. Among those who see him as supralapsarian are, K. Barth, *CD*, II/2, pp. 127-8; E. Dowey, *Knowledge of God*, pp. 186-7; J. McNeill, *Institutes* II.xii.5, p. 469n5; G.C. Berkouwer, *Divine Election*, p. 257; P.K. Jewett, *Election and Predestination* (Grand Rapids, MI: Eerdmans, 1985), p. 89; and, most recently, J. Fesko, *Diversity Within the Reformed Tradition*, especially pp. 81-106.

[198] *PRRD*, I, p. 127.

[199] McGrath, 'John Calvin and Late Mediaeval Thought', pp. 70-73. McGrath states: 'It will be clear that this school of thought developed opinions which, especially in relation to the doctrine of grace in general, and predestination in particular, foreshadow those of John Calvin.'

saying that it is not a universal category but one that necessarily implies reprobation, 'since election itself could not stand except as set over against reprobation'.[200] When addressing the *causa* of reprobation, moreover, Calvin, like Vermigli and Rutherford, 'expresses himself from the vantage point of eternity and the *propositum Dei aeternum*' and states that 'God's secret plan is the cause of hardening' those 'whom he pleases' to harden.[201]

Perhaps the most noticeable *difference* between Rutherford's treatment of predestination and Calvin's is the respective locations of their discussions. Whereas Calvin discusses his view of election and reprobation under soteriology in book three of the *Institutes*, Rutherford locates it under Theology proper. While this may reflect an element of discontinuity between them, we need to be careful not to read too much into this difference for the following three reasons. First, Rutherford's view should not be interpreted as being wholly, or even chiefly, speculative just because he locates it in the doctrine of God; the Christological and soteriological emphasis of his view is patent. Second, the location of predestination has little, if anything, to do with the way that Reformation and post-Reformation theologians understand election and reprobation. Calvin—who is not explicitly infralapsarian—places election and reprobation after the fall and redemption in Christ, whereas Turretin—who is unambiguously infralapsarian—places them prior to the fall.[202] Third, post-Reformation theologians do locate their discussions of predestination elsewhere besides the doctrine of God. Thus, in his *Exposition of the Creede*, William Perkins places election and reprobation after ecclesiology and prior to union with Christ.[203] What this means is that Rutherford's supralapsarian predestinarianism, especially as it is couched in infralapsarian language, is at least in significant continuity with men like Calvin and Vermigli.

OBJECTIONS TO SUPRALAPSARIANISM

In his work on the doctrine of God, Herman Bavinck mentions a common objection to supralapsarianism, which was also raised by the Arminians in the sixteenth and seventeenth centuries.[204] If the decree to create follows the decree to elect and reprobate (or pass over), then supralapsarians like Rutherford make a non-entity the object of the first divine decree. But, as Bavinck says,

> how are we to conceive of a decree respecting *possible* men, whose *actual* future existence has as yet not been determined? In the consciousness of God there is an infinite number of '*possible* men', who will never live. Hence, the decree of

---

[200] *Institutes* III.xxiii.1, p. 947.

[201] James, *Vermigli and Predestination*, p. 88; *Institutes* III.xxiii.1, pp. 948-9. Vermigli expressed his agreement with Calvin on election and reprobation in two letters written in 1557 and 1558 (James, *Vermigli and Predestination*, p. 252).

[202] *PRRD*, I, p. 127.

[203] Perkins, *Workes*, I, pp. 278-98.

[204] Cf. Bavinck, *Doctrine of God*, p. 388; with Episcopius, *Opera theologica* (1665), II, pp. 138-43; *WJA*, III, pp. 532, 536-7, 541.

election and reprobation has for its object 'non-entities', not definite persons known to God by name.[205]

Rutherford responds to this criticism in the *Examen* by denying that it presents a problem to his position. God is sovereign and, therefore, can will and do as he so pleases. What is more, he says, everyone who believes in the traditional doctrine of creation *ex nihilo* also makes a non-entity the object of the divine decree. The universe, just like the elect in Rutherford's *ordo decretorum*, is *creandum et nondum creatum* when God first makes his decree.[206] But, while Rutherford's comments may adequately respond to Bavinck and to those who hold to creation *ex nihilo*—to the extent that it casts the very same charge back upon those who level it—it is not certain that they fully exonerate his supralapsarianism from Arminius' critique. As Richard Muller has shown, it is doubtful that Arminius embraced the traditional doctrine of creation *ex nihilo*. Even though he did embrace the traditional language, he identified 'the *nihil*, the nothing, as in some sense belonging to the material causality of the universe', and, as such, 'considered [it] as first or primary matter'.[207] If this is true, then the criticism that Arminius brings against supralapsarian predestinarianism cannot be turned back upon himself. And Rutherford would fail to respond adequately to the Arminian criticism. Moreover, Rutherford's comments notwithstanding, it is difficult to understand how God could be said to 'foreknow' those he elects under the supralapsarian scheme—in the way that passages like Romans 8.29 would seem to require—if they are considered by him no differently than 'an infinite number of "*possible* men"' would be.

Several additional objections to Rutherford's view of predestination were also raised by the Arminians in the sixteenth and seventeenth centuries. First and perhaps most significant among them is the claim that Rutherford's supralapsarianism is 'diametrically opposed to the act of creation'. As we have seen, creation, for Arminius, is 'a communication of good' by the 'intrinsic property of its nature'. But creation, for a supralapsarian, cannot be a communication of good, because it is a means 'by which the reprobation that had previously been determined may obtain its object'.[208] In Arminius' thinking, therefore, it would be impossible for God to create men and women whom he had already reprobated, because, by creating them, he would not be communicating good but harm to them. This would seem to require that predestination must follow creation instead of preceding it.

Two things need to be said at this point in regard to the Arminians' view of creation as a communication of good and their critique of Rutherford. First, if the Arminians are correct about creation, then their critique is also correct. If creation really is a communication of good, then it is impossible for God to create creatures he has passed by, because in doing so he would be withholding

---

[205] Bavinck, *Doctrine of God*, p. 388.
[206] *Examen*, pp. 271-2.
[207] Muller, *God, Creation, and Providence*, 215-16.
[208] *WJA*, I, p. 626. Cf. Muller, 'Patterns in Arminius's Theology', p. 437.

good rather than communicating it. Second, the Arminian understanding of creation affects the nature of predestination as well as its place in the *ordo decretorum*. Since creation, as defined by Arminius, produces human beings 'capable of God and of His life and blessedness', predestination must be such that this capability and the creature's good are preserved.[209] In short, it must be conditional and subsequent to other more basic decrees. Predestination cannot be an absolute decree, because then it would override the created capabilities of humans and prevent the divine communication of good. It must be conditional upon the creature's own free decision to believe or not to believe. But more than this, predestination must follow other decrees that establish a universal environment of 'goodness' in the created world. God is obliged first to decree to make salvation in Christ possible for all creatures, then to receive those who repent and believe, and then to grant the means whereby this salvation can be achieved. Only then, in the Arminian scheme, can God decree to elect those who will exercise faith by way of their own capabilities and to pass over those who will not.[210] Here too, if the Arminians are correct about creation, they are also correct about the nature of predestination and about every other decree as well, and, by consequence, not only is Rutherford wrong but infralapsarians, Amyraldians, and the majority of the church at that time are also.

The important thing for our discussion, however, is not to determine whether or not the Arminians are correct about creation—something that goes beyond the scope of this thesis—but to demonstrate its principial status in Arminian theology and to establish the extent of the opposition between Rutherford and the Arminians. The dispute between Rutherford and the Arminians cannot be limited to a difference of opinion over a single doctrine. It is a clash between the whole of two competing systems, at the heart of which is a disagreement over the doctrine of God and his relationship to creation. As Arminius himself recognized, the two systems are indeed 'diametrically opposed' to one another.

Secondly, the Arminians criticize Rutherford for not making enough of the biblical teaching that God, in the words of Ephesians 1.4, predestined 'us *in Christ* before the foundation of the world' (NRSV, emphasis added). The supralapsarian position, they say, contradicts this verse by eliminating the need for election to be in Christ, because sin would not exist in the mind of God when he makes his decree. But, more than anything else, this criticism calls attention to a profound difference that exists between the Arminians and Rutherford, a difference that hearkens back to their disagreement over the doctrine of the Trinity and points ahead to soteriological variances that will be explored in the next chapter.

Rutherford and many Reformed orthodox theologians of his day understand Ephesians 1.4 as referring to the 'action of election' rather than to the 'object about which it is exercised'. The idea is not that 'in Christ we are made holy' but that the 'blessing of election [is ours] in Christ'. For Rutherford, election is

---

[209] *WJA*, III, p. 579; Muller, 'Patterns in Arminius's Theology', p. 436.

[210] For the order of the divine decrees in Arminius, see *WJA*, I, p. 653-4.

thoroughly Christocentric, as we will see in more detail in the next chapter.[211] Christ—to borrow the language of Karl Barth—is the 'electing and elected' God.[212] He *elects*, because the 'action of election' is 'in Christ' just as much as it is in the Father and in the Spirit. All the 'proper *operations* of God', Ames reminds us, 'are attributed not only to the Father, but also to the Sonne, and the holy spirit'.[213] Each divine person is consubstantial with the others and, thus, shares equally in all the divine operations. As a result, the blessing of election is ours in Christ partially because Christ elects. But, more than this, Christ is also *elected*. He is the chief elect, appointed by the Father and the Spirit, and voluntarily appointed by himself, on behalf of the elect to be 'the first born of the house, and of the many brethren'.[214] The blessing of election is, therefore, ours in Christ, because it is initiated in him and carried out by him.

Arminius' understanding of Ephesians 1.4, however, differs significantly from the typical Reformed orthodox explanation, as revealed in Rutherford. Reflecting his own view of the Trinity, Arminius sees Christ not as 'electing and elected' but, exactly the opposite, as 'elected and electing'. Just as the Son is generated by and receives his deity from the Father, so Christ is elected or appointed by the Father to be the *fundamentum electionis*, in the first decree, but he does not elect until the fourth decree.[215] The inherent subordinationism in Arminius' doctrine of the Trinity appears to provide the grounds for the Father's appointment of the Son to his work as mediator, whereas, as we saw in the Reformed orthodox, the consubstantiality of the persons of the Godhead translates not just into the Son being appointed to his work but also into the Son's appointing himself. What is more, the separation of Christ's election in the first decree from the action of election in Christ in the fourth decree also reflects a different view of the objects of election in Arminius' thinking. Not only is sin in view within the individual before election is carried out but faith and final perseverance are as well. This understanding of the relationship between Christ and election has deep soteriological significance for the respective theologies of Rutherford and the Arminians, as we will see in the next chapter in connection with the covenant of redemption.

Thirdly, the Arminians criticize Rutherford's predestinarianism by arguing that it 'fights against' the universal free offer of the gospel. If God has decreed absolutely, irrevocably, and immutably both who will and who will not be saved, then this seems to suggest that those and those only will necessarily be saved and not-saved, no matter what. It appears disingenuous, then, for God to offer the gospel to those whom he knows will never respond to it. Rutherford's

---

[211] Unpublished manuscript, La.II.394, p. 1. For more on the Christological and soteriological emphasis of election, see the section below entitled 'The Covenant of Redemption and the Decrees of God'.

[212] *CD*, II/2, pp. 94ff. Cf. the discussion in Richard A. Muller, 'The Christological Problem in the Thought of Jacobus Arminius', *NAvK* 68:1 (1988), pp. 158-60.

[213] Ames, *Marrow*, p. 19.

[214] *COL*, p. 303.

[215] *WJA*, I, pp. 653-4. See also Muller, 'Christological Problem', pp. 158-60.

answer to this objection is noteworthy, because it draws attention to the influence of the *potentia absoluta et ordinata* on his thinking and illustrates the difference between him and the Arminians in the use of it.

The underlying reason that Rutherford gives as to why the Arminian criticism is misplaced is that it ignores the distinction between the 'intention of the Evangel', and the 'intention of him who proposeth the Evangel to men'.[216] Put more simply, there is a difference between the purposes of the gospel and the purposes of the one who gave us that gospel. God's purposes to elect or to reprobate in general belong to the realm of the *potentia ordinata*. But his purposes to elect or to reprobate John or Jane or Peter, in particular, belong to the realm of the *potentia absoluta*. The gospel, or God's *voluntas signi*, reveals his general decrees to us and the provisions for and stipulations of our salvation. It nowhere reveals who is elect and who is reprobate. That knowledge is reserved for God's hidden will, his *voluntas beneplaciti*. Within the realm of the *potentia ordinata*, we know that God offers salvation to all people and that he commands those who hear his offer to turn from their unbelief to faith in Christ. We also know that he uses that offer as a means to two different ends: it renders some 'inexcusable' for their not responding to it and it brings the elect to faith, because faith comes by hearing the gospel.[217] While God's offer of salvation and his command to believe falls within the sphere of the *potentia ordinata*, his application or his withholding of efficacious grace belongs to the sphere of the *potentia absoluta*. Some people, known by God's *voluntas beneplaciti*, are given efficacious grace, thereby enabling and ensuring that they will respond to the free offer of the gospel. Others are passed by and denied efficacious grace, thereby guaranteeing that they will remain in their sins, because of the hardness of their own hearts.[218]

The Arminians, on the other hand, because they limit the current world order to the realm of the *potentia ordinata*, understandably agree with everything that Rutherford says in connection with that sphere but reject the notion of a hidden will, which is associated with God's *potentia absoluta*. There is no hidden will of God to choose this or that individual. There is only God's offer and command. God cannot intervene in this world order either to save or to not-save.

Before turning to look at the atonement of Christ, we need to point out that Rutherford's strict predestinarianism (although it is perhaps not as strict as some have assumed) was taken to an extreme in succeeding generations and, as a result, produced several serious soteriological problems within the church. This extreme position has been aptly portrayed in James Hogg's *Confessions of a Justified Sinner*. Hogg's treatise, which takes place in the early eighteenth century, presents a main character, Robert Wringhim Colwan, who engages in pronouncing individuals either elect or reprobate and then uses this pronouncement as justification for taking action against the reprobate, even

---

[216] *Tryal*, pp. 92-3.
[217] *Examen*, p. 291.
[218] *Examen*, pp. 139-41, 182, 289.

such radical action as murder. The main character's behavior, though, does not originate with himself but finds precedence in the actions of his adopted father—a minister within the Calvinist tradition—who immutably and definitively pronounces Robert to be 'elect' but declares others to be 'reprobate'. As a result of his definitive pronouncement, the reprobate are immediately and irreparably consigned to the fate of eternal condemnation and, because they are beyond all hope of salvation, they are to be cut off from every association with the elect.[219]

Such an extreme position, while it may ultimately have been engendered by Rutherford's views, would, nonetheless, have been roundly condemned by Rutherford himself. It is not our place, he says, nor do we have the ability even if it were, to discern who is and who is not elect. Our place is to offer salvation in Christ to all people without exception, freely and repeatedly. No person is ever to be written off as reprobate, and 'no one is to consider himself or herself reprobate from eternity, until he or she finally rejects *Christ* in this lifetime [*in tempore*]'.[220] Moreover, predestination, according to Rutherford, is not to be the basis for spiritual pride, as it would seem to be for Hogg's main character. Predestination should, instead, produce a genuine humility and deep-seated piety within the individual. If it does not, Rutherford says, then he or she is probably not presently among the elect: 'no one knows himself or herself to be absolutely elect unto glory, who does not approach [God] in fear and pious care'. Rather than leading to arrogance and to a disregard for others and for preaching, predestination should lead to humility, piety, and reverence before God, and a concern for all people without exception.[221]

The Atonement of Christ

As previously indicated in this chapter, Rutherford's doctrine of God and, in particular, his view of God's will, affects his understanding of the atonement of Christ. This can be seen primarily in regard to two controversial areas: limited atonement and the necessity of the atonement. While our intention here is not to discuss these two topics comprehensively, we will seek to examine the impact of the *voluntas Dei* upon them in Rutherford's thinking and, then, to assess relevant contemporary and modern-day criticisms.

LIMITED ATONEMENT

One of the most controversial topics in Rutherford's own day, as well as in all times since, is the doctrine of limited atonement. It was a main area of contention between Rutherford and the Arminians in the seventeenth century and has been the focus of intense criticism among a number of scholars in

---

[219] J. Hogg, *Confessions of a Justified Sinner* (London: Random House, 1992), especially pp. 85, 102.
[220] *Examen*, p. 296.
[221] *Examen*, p. 273.

recent times. These modern scholars have claimed that supralapsarian predestinarianism and limited atonement, as evidenced in Rutherford and others of the late-sixteenth and seventeenth centuries, represents, in the words of Brian Armstrong, 'a radical change of emphasis' when compared to the theology of John Calvin.[222] T.F. Torrance and Charles Bell have specifically vilified Rutherford by referring to him as an 'extreme hyper-Calvinist' for his belief in limited atonement, a doctrine that they say is 'derived...logically' from his double predestinarianism and, for that reason, represents a 'further step' away from the teaching of Calvin.[223] Such evaluations, however, are misleading and unfair and, as we will attempt to demonstrate below, entirely unjustified.

Although it can be—and has been—argued that both Scripture and Calvin are somewhat unclear as to the extent of the atonement,[224] this does not mean that they have nothing at all to say about the matter. According to Rutherford, Scripture teaches that the *nature* of the atonement is such that Christ does not merely make people *redeemable*, as the Arminians suggest, but one in which he *actually redeems* them: 'The fruits and effects of God's curse, the punishment due to sinners, even that satisfactory, and penall curse and punishment, which infinite Justice requireth, was laid upon Christ, while as he died upon the crosse, and suffered the effects of Gods wrath upon his soul for our sins.'[225] And the nature of the atonement, being one in which divine justice is completely satisfied, such that no punishment remains for sin, in turn, has a direct bearing upon the extent of the atonement in Rutherford's thinking. If the extent is universal, then all people without exception will necessarily be saved to the utmost, because Christ has fully paid the price for their sins upon the cross. Rutherford understands both Scripture and experience to rule this option

---

[222] Armstrong, *Calvinism and the Amyraut Heresy*, p. xvii. Cf., Hall, 'Calvin Against the Calvinists', pp. 25-7; H. Rolston III, 'Responsible Man in Reformed Theology: Calvin versus the Westminster Confession', *SJT* 23 (1970), p. 137; Kendall, *Calvin and English Calvinism*, pp. 29-30; idem, 'The Puritan Modification of Calvin's Theology', pp. 199-214; A.C. Clifford, *Atonement and Justification: English Evangelical Theology 1640-1790, An Evaluation* (Oxford: Clarendon, 1990), pp. 69-111; J.B. Torrance, 'The Incarnation and "Limited Atonement"', *The Evangelical Quarterly* 55 (1983), pp. 82-94; idem, 'The Concept of Federal Theology—Was Calvin a Federal Theologian?', in *Calvinus Sacrae Scripturae Professor: Calvin as Confessor of Holy Scripture*, ed. W. Neuser (Grand Rapids, MI: Eerdmans, 1994), p. 20; M.C. Bell, 'Calvin and the Extent of the Atonement', *The Evangelical Quarterly* 55 (1983), pp. 115-23.

[223] Torrance, *Scottish Theology*, pp. 109-10; Bell, *Calvin and Scottish Theology*, p. 83.

[224] For comprehensive examinations of Calvin's view of the extent of the atonement that arrive at different conclusions, see R. Nicole, 'John Calvin's View of the Extent of the Atonement', *WTJ* 47:2 (Fall 1985), pp. 197-225; and C. Daniel, 'Hyper-Calvinism and John Gill' (unpublished Ph.D. dissertation, University of Edinburgh, 1983), pp. 777-828. Cf. W.R. Godfrey, 'Tensions Within International Calvinism: The Debate on the Atonement and the Synod of Dort, 1618-1619' (unpublished Ph.D. dissertation, Stanford University, 1974), especially chapter 2.

[225] *Tryal*, p. 187; cf. *Catachisme*, pp. 179, 188; *Christ Dying*, pp. 153-4.

out. Because universalism is eliminated as a viable option by the nature of the atonement, the extent of the atonement, for Rutherford, must be definite or particular. Otherwise people perishing in hell who had their sins forgiven by Christ's atonement would, in Rutherford's words, 'happilie suffer for their sinne in hell, [and] God shall be unjust in punishing Christ for their sinnes and in punishing those same sinnes in hell'.[226] This, in itself, is evidence that Rutherford does not believe in limited atonement simply because it derives logically from predestination. He sees Scripture as teaching that the nature of the atonement is such that the extent must be limited.

It is, nevertheless, true, as Torrance and Bell claim, that limited or particular atonement does flow logically from double predestination. But it should also be pointed out that Rutherford's understanding of predestination is grounded in the eternal intratrinitarian 'Covenant of Suretyship or Redemption', which plainly anchors the decree within the context of soteriology.[227] Moreover, just because limited or definite atonement follows logically from Rutherford's conception of predestination does not mean that it is fair to accuse him of 'hyper-Calvinism', as Torrance and Bell have done, because, as Karl Barth has remarked, limited atonement 'logically follow[s] from *Calvin's* conception of predestination' as well.[228] Rutherford, furthermore, wholly embraces the traditional scholastic language that we find first in Peter Lombard and then later in Calvin and other post-Reformation theologians, which says that Christ's atonement is 'sufficient for all but efficacious for the elect'.[229] Christ's death can rightly be considered sufficient for all 'because of the infinitnesse of the person [of Christ], before and without [respect to] the decree of God' to apply it only to the elect.[230] Therefore, however much one may disagree or dislike the doctrine of limited atonement, it does seem unjustified to claim that it represents hyper-Calvinism.

THE ABSOLUTE NECESSITY OF THE ATONEMENT

One final critique of Rutherford's doctrine of the divine will remains for us to discuss. It involves the seventeenth-century debate over the necessity of punitive justice in God and the resulting soteriological and christological implications of it. John Owen, in his *Dissertation on Divine Justice*, published in 1653, attacks both Rutherford and William Twisse for their views on divine vindicatory justice and their denial of the absolute necessity of the atonement of

---

[226] *Catachisme*, p. 188; *Examen*, pp. 535-6.

[227] *COL*, p. 290. The covenant and its relation to the divine decrees will be discussed in the next chapter.

[228] *CD*, IV/1, p. 57, emphasis added. It should be noted that the debate over the extent of the atonement is one that Calvin never faced in his day. It did not really surface until the Synod of Dort addressed the problem in the *Remonstrances* in 1618-19.

[229] For more on the use of this phrase in medieval, Reformation, and post-Reformation thought up to the Synod of Dort, see W.R. Godfrey, 'Reformed Thought on the Extent of the Atonement to 1618', *WTJ* 37:2 (Winter 1975), pp. 136-70.

[230] *COL*, p. 239.

Christ.[231] Following Twisse, Rutherford argues that, although justice is a divine attribute *ad intra*, God is in no way required to exercise that justice *ad extra*, towards his creatures.[232] Because 'God's own free will', Rutherford continues, 'was above, beyond, and before' his 'set and decreed law of justice',[233] God is not required by any necessity of his nature to punish sin. He freely decrees to be just and to punish sin, but no essential necessity—i.e., no necessity resulting from his essence—forces the decree upon him.

'Mercy', likewise, 'floweth not from *God* essentially, especially the mercy of Conversion, Remission of sins, [and] Eternal life, but of meer Grace; for then *God* could not be *God*, and deny these favours to Reprobats.'[234] If God was required by necessity of his own nature to be merciful *ad extra*, he would be required to act mercifully to all people, both elect and reprobate, and, thus, to remove the hardness of every heart. But, Rutherford says, this runs counter to the justice of God, in the first place, because 'the Attribute of Justice is as essential as Mercy, *Exod*. 34.6-7'. One attribute cannot take precedence over the other. If one is essential, they both must be essential. The intellectualist position, thus, wrongly places divine justice above divine mercy by suggesting that God must punish sin by necessity of nature but does not have to show mercy until and unless he decides to do so. In the second place, necessary mercy or justice in God runs counter to Scripture, which Rutherford understands as teaching that God chooses to be merciful and just *ad extra*. Passages like Romans 9.18, Exodus 34.6-7, and Ephesians 1.11, are interpreted by Rutherford as proving that God is free to show justice to those whom he will

---

[231] Owen, *Works of John Owen*, X, pp. 481-624.

[232] Owen is uncertain as to whether Rutherford sides with Twisse or with the Socinians in his exposition of divine justice. He says: 'Twisse, indeed, maintains that the exercise of that justice is free to God, but grants that justice itself is a natural attribute of God; the Socinians, that it is only a free act of the divine will. Which party this learned author [Rutherford] favours appears not from his words. If by justice he mean the habit, he sides with the Socinians; if the act and exercise, he is of the same opinion with Twisse, although he expresses his sentiments rather unhappily' (*Works of John Owen*, X, p. 608). Owen's confusion is due to the fact that Rutherford really is less than clear. He says things like this: 'At vero justitia punitiva, per haec quae dicta sunt, nullo modo Deo inest ex necessitate naturae, sed libere.' But, as we have already seen, Rutherford means, even with this unhappy language, that punitive justice is not required *ad extra* by necessity of nature. He plainly sides with Twisse in this debate. All Owen had to do was turn back a few pages in Rutherford's treatise and he would have read this: 'Quia enim Deus est Creator infinite bonus, sapientissimus, justissimus, &c. Ideo ei, qua Deus, debita est omnis subjectio tum naturalis tum moralis, & omnis obedientia.' And this: 'Deus est essentialiter justus & bonus.' *Disputatio*, pp. 342, 345. Cf. *Examen*, pp. 174-5; *Exercitationes*, pp. 348-9, 356; and Trueman, *Claims of Truth*, p. 108n21.

[233] *Communion*, p. 28. Later in the same sermon, Rutherford further explains this idea: 'Justice (as manifested to us) is a voluntary decree of God to punish sinners.' *Communion*, p. 30.

[234] *Tryal*, p. 17.

and to show mercy to those whom he will and that no necessity of nature forces his hand in either direction.[235] But even though there is no absolute necessity for God to punish sin or to show mercy, there is a *relative* necessity for him to do so. Once God decrees to be just and merciful *ad extra*, he must of necessity do so; 'yet this is but necessity conditionall, and at the second hand'.[236]

Coordinate with Rutherford's denial of the necessity of vindicatory justice and saving mercy in God is his denial of the absolute necessity of the atonement of Christ. Not only can God choose either to be just or not-just and merciful or not-merciful *ad extra*, he can also choose to forgive by way of Christ's atonement or some other way: '*God*, if wee speake of his absolute power, without respect to his free decree, could have pardoned sinne without a ransom, and gifted all *Mankind* and fallen *Angels* with heaven, without any satisfaction of either the sinner, or his Surety; for he neither punisheth sin, nor tenders heaven to *Men* or *Angels* by necessity of nature...but freely.'[237] What is important to notice here is the distinction Rutherford makes between the 'absolute power' and the 'free decree' of God. By making this distinction, he shows that he is speaking in terms of the *potentia Dei absoluta et ordinata*. According to his *potentia absoluta*, God is free to forgive sin or not to forgive sin and, if the former, to do so by way of the cross or some other way. There is, therefore, no absolute necessity that Christ should die upon the cross. Once God decrees to permit the fall and to be just and merciful to his creatures, however, the cross becomes necessary, 'because God did never forgive debtis for nothing at all'.[238] God's decree to be just towards his creatures requires that he punish sin; likewise his decree to be merciful requires that sin be atoned for. The result: Christ's atonement is necessary, but only consequently so. It is necessary only because God has decreed to be just and merciful *ad extra* to his creatures. As we saw above, this necessity is not absolute but 'conditionall, and at the second hand'.[239]

For Owen, however, as Carl Trueman remarks, it is only 'a small step' from denying the necessity of divine punitive justice and the absolute necessity of the atonement 'to denying the punitive, substitutionary character of Christ's sacrifice', as the Socinians do.[240] Far better, according to Owen, is his

---

[235] *Examen*, pp. 174-5.
[236] *Christ Dying*, pp. 8-9.
[237] *Christ Dying*, pp. 7-8.
[238] *Catachisme*, p. 187.
[239] Although the conditional necessity of the atonement is largely a product of the medieval voluntarist tradition, even thoroughgoing intellectualists like Aquinas believed that it was hypothetically possible for God to forgive sin without satisfaction (by way of his *potentia absoluta*). See Aquinas, *Summa theologiae* IIIa.46.2.
[240] C. Trueman, 'John Owen's *Dissertation on Divine Justice*: An Exercise in Christocentric Scholasticism', *CTJ* 33 (1998), p. 88. Trueman states: 'The classic Socinian statement of Christology is Faustus Socinus's 1578 treatise, *De Jesu Christo servatore*. This work was a sustained attack on the doctrine of satisfaction and does contain some indications that emphasis on God's absolute power, an element held in

alternative, which sees divine justice as essential *ad extra*. '[T]he justice of God, *absolutely* considered', says Owen, 'is the universal *rectitude and perfection* of the divine nature', which is 'antecedent to all acts of his will and suppositions of objects towards which it might operate.'[241] In other words, Owen is teaching that divine justice is the totality of the divine perfections, that these perfections must logically precede every act of the will of God, and that every act must be wholly consistent with them. Thus, while God is never free to be not-just towards his creatures in an absolute sense, because this would mean that he would be acting contrary to who he is, he is free to be not-just specifically towards sin but only prior to the fall. Once sin is taken into account, God must of necessity 'legislate' and act in accord with his justice.[242] This means that the atonement is absolutely necessary given God's decree to permit the fall and to save sinful men and women. In proving his claims, Owen raises a damaging critique of Rutherford's denial of the absolute necessity of Christ's atonement: why would God send his Son into the world to die unless it was absolutely necessary for him to do so? Rutherford's position seems to make the atonement of Christ an arbitrary product of the divine will. But, why would God arbitrarily opt for the cross, instead of some other way, if there was an equally viable alternative?[243]

While this critique has real teeth only for those who, like Rutherford, believe in substitutionary atonement,[244] it is not at all apparent that its bite is as damaging as Owen may have first assumed. A closer look at Rutherford's position with respect to the *ad extra* decrees reveals that it may not be as arbitrary as would appear from his dispute with Owen. As we saw earlier in our discussion of the essence and attributes of God, divine simplicity requires that God's essential attributes must be the same as the divine will *ad intra*. This means that when the will of God acts *ad intra*, it harmonizes each of the essential attributes in its action. And the same can be said of God's will *ad extra*. When the divine will acts *ad extra*, it harmonizes the 'relative' attributes of God.[245] In other words, the divine will first determines how the essential attributes of God will operate relative to humankind and then harmonizes those attributes in its actions *ad extra*. This is perhaps best seen, according to

---

common with men such as Twisse and Rutherford, was a contributing factor in this rejection of the orthodox position' (see 'John Owen's *Dissertation*', p. 88n2). Cf. A.W. Gomes, '*De Jesu Christo Servatore*: Faustus Socinus on the Satisfaction of Christ', *WTJ* 55:2 (Fall 1993), pp. 209-31.

[241] Owen, *Works of John Owen*, X, p. 498.
[242] Owen, *Works of John Owen*, X, p. 499; and, Trueman, 'John Owen's *Dissertation*', pp. 92-3.
[243] Owen, *Works of John Owen*, X, p. 548.
[244] Others, like the Socinians, for instance, who do not believe in a substitutionary atonement, sidestep the barb of Owen's critique by positing that the cross was simply an expression of God's love and an example of the way that salvation can be gained. See, e.g., Gomes, '*De Jesu Christo Servatore*', pp. 210ff.
[245] *COL*, pp. 33, 304.

Rutherford, in the covenant of redemption, a covenant in which 'the harmony of the Attributes of God in the [*ad extra*] declaration of mercy, truth, &c. is sweetly made out'.[246]

For the purposes of our discussion here, the relationships of two particular attributes to the divine will require separate attention. The first of these attributes is love. Rutherford's understanding of the relationship between the love of God and the divine will, while complex, appears to be largely dependent upon the thinking of Duns Scotus. According to Duns Scotus, 'love resides in the will', and so God's *ad extra* decrees are, therefore, expressions of his love.[247] In a similar way to this, Rutherford believes that God's love for his people is inextricably linked with his decree to save them. Since God's decree to save his people is eternal, immutable, and irrevocable, so is his love for them. The divine will *ad extra* is God's love expressed to his creatures freely in his *ad extra* works, which is why Rutherford could say that 'Love is the Cause of Christ's death.'[248] This relationship of the will and love, borrowed largely from Duns Scotus, may help us to explain why Rutherford chooses to adopt infralapsarian language in expressing his supralapsarianism. The reprobate, rather than being willed by God unto damnation, are actually non-willed or simply passed over, because, as Duns Scotus says, 'the will cannot hate...nor will misery'.[249] It also explains how it is that God can permit sin and suffering in the world. These things are willed, not as ends in themselves, but as means to conveying the depth of divine love, both *ad intra*—as an expression of eternal intratrinitarian love culminating in the covenant of redemption, as we will see—and *ad extra*—as a manifestation of God's love for his people culminating in the covenant of grace.

More important than the relationship of love to the will of God is the relationship of wisdom to the divine will. Wisdom or *sapientia*, for Rutherford and for scholastic theologians in general, is understood in the Aristotelian sense of knowledge directed towards divine purposes or goals. It differs from the divine knowledge (*scientia*), which is a more theoretical knowledge of causes and their effects, even though both belong to the intellect of God.[250] As Herman Bavinck explains, 'knowledge [*scientia*] is a matter of the mind apart from the will; wisdom [*sapientia*] is a matter of the mind made subservient to the will.'[251] Given the will's determination of the divine purposes, therefore, it is the wisdom of God that ensures that God knows the best ways to accomplish those purposes. Even though God could have chosen some other way to save

---

[246] *COL*, p. 304.

[247] Copleston, *History of Philosophy*, II, p. 540, citing Duns Scotus, *Opus Oxoniense*, 4.49, *quaestio ex latere*, no. 21.

[248] *Christ Dying*, pp. 409-10.

[249] J. Duns Scotus, *Duns Scotus on the Will and Morality*, ed. and trans. with introduction by A.B. Wolter (Washington, DC: Catholic University of America, 1986), pp. 194-5.

[250] See, e.g., Muller, *God, Creation, and Providence*, p. 144.

[251] Bavinck, *Doctrine of God*, p. 195.

his people—i.e., he could have opted not to punish sin or to forgive sin by some other way than the death of Jesus—or, reflecting a typical scholastic emphasis from the time of Peter Lombard, 'he could have made a more perfect world' than the current one, divine wisdom ensures that God knows and, as a result, chooses the best world to create and the best way to save his people.[252] There are, according to Rutherford, certain 'connections' between the wisdom of God and his *ad extra* works, and these connections 'precede every act of the will of God' *ad extra*.[253] This means that while it is true that there is no absolute necessity that God punish sin or that he pardon sin by the atoning sacrifice of Christ, it is also true that these *ad extra* decrees are not wholly arbitrary in God. Divine love and divine wisdom work together with the divine will under the auspices of God's sovereignty to bring about the *ad extra* decrees and a harmonization of his relative attributes. In spite of this, however, Owen's critique does still seem to be warranted in some measure. It is difficult to understand why, in Rutherford's theological system, God would have sent his Son into the world to die—wisdom and love notwithstanding—unless it was necessary to accomplish his purposes in reconciling the world to himself.

---

[252] *Influences*, p. 52. Cf. Oakley, 'The Absolute and Ordained Power of God', p. 438.
[253] *Examen*, p. 164.

CHAPTER 4

Soteriology

Karl Barth has described soteriology as 'the very heart and centre of the Christian message' and, in doing so, has reminded us that there are certain questions that we cannot escape once the doctrine of God is presupposed: 'How can I lay hold of a gracious God? and, How can I live in accordance with the fact that I have a gracious God?'[1] The answers that we give to such questions, according to Barth, reveal the 'heart and centre' of our understanding of the Christian gospel. And differences over the answers to these questions are, therefore, differences over issues that are fundamental to Christianity.

If Barth is right, then for the present study of Rutherford's opposition to Arminian theology to ignore the soteriological differences that exist between them would be for it to neglect 'the very heart and centre' of their respective theologies and to overlook the ways in which the deep truths of their doctrines of God actually work themselves out in the lives of individuals. For this reason, the current chapter will take up the issue of soteriology, with the goal that we will be able better to understand how fundamental the opposition is between Rutherford and the Arminians and how influential their views of God are in shaping their ideas about salvation. We will once again follow the same basic outline that Rutherford does in the *Examen*, concentrating on the subjects of covenant theology, conversion, living by faith, and assurance.[2]

Covenant Theology

It is impossible to describe adequately Rutherford's doctrine of soteriology without taking up the study of covenant theology, at least to some degree. This is because of the close association that exists in his thinking between these two concepts. Covenant theology is the vehicle that transitions between his doctrine of God and his doctrine of salvation. It answers Barth's aforementioned questions, because, at its most basic level, covenant theology is the expression of God's relationship with his creatures. And, for this reason, the covenant idea functions—in the words of Donald Macleod—as 'an architectonic principle for

---

[1] *CD*, IV/1, p. 108.
[2] *Examen*, chapters 10-14.

the systematizing of Christian truth',[3] or—to use words more determinative of Rutherford's own views—'all the worde of God appertaines to some covenant: for God speaks nothing to man without the covenant'.[4] Every aspect of theology having reference to God's relationship with his creatures—which is all theology, if we remember Rutherford's emphasis on *praxis*—must necessarily be organized around the principle of covenant, if covenant is indeed the way of expressing the divine-human relationship. This necessity is not missed by David Weir, who acknowledges that, because the 'covenant idea is a common inheritance of the Judaeo-Christian tradition found in the Bible' and is used to refer to God's dealings with humankind, '[a]lmost all Christian theologians ultimately practice some form of covenant theology' and, thus, employ a 'system in which the covenant forms the basic framework and acts as the controlling idea'.[5] In this section, we will seek to demonstrate how covenant theology is an 'architectonic principle' in Rutherford's theology and how it is not. But before we do so, we must, first, seek to understand what Rutherford believes in regard to the covenants. What is a covenant? And, how many are there? After answering these questions, we can turn our attention to establishing how Rutherford uses the covenant idea.

In his *Tryal and Triumph of Faith*, Rutherford defines a covenant as 'a joynt and mutual bargain between two; according to which they promise freely such and such things each to [the] other'.[6] In other words, a covenant is by nature a bilateral agreement between two persons in which promises are made and commitments given. According to J.B. Torrance, such a definition of covenant

---

[3] D. Macleod, 'Covenant Theology', in *DSCH&T*, p. 214. Recently, San-Deog Kim has argued against seeing the covenant as an organizing principle in Rutherford's theology and has suggested, instead, that covenant should be interpreted in a 'practical' or 'relational way', as expressing 'God's relationship with man in history' (Kim, 'Time and Eternity', p. 287). But Kim's evaluation overlooks the fact that covenant theology is a systematizing principle in Rutherford precisely because it is an expression of God's relationship with his creatures. There is no reason to deny the one in favor of the other. Rutherford, his post-Reformation peers, and later generations of federal theologians all held these two ideas together in tension.

[4] R. Rollock, *A Treatise of Gods Effectual Calling* (1597; London, 1603), p. 6. As the first principal of the University of Edinburgh, Rollock carried great influence with students well into the seventeenth century, as can be seen from two factors. First, Rollock's successor Henry Charteris was hand-selected because he was a faithful disciple who could be 'trusted to keep things as they were' (Grant, *University of Edinburgh*, II, p. 242). Second, Rollock's curriculum remained in place unchanged until after Rutherford had left for Anwoth in 1627 (A. Morgan, ed., *University of Edinburgh Charters, Statutes, and Acts of the Town Council and the Senatus: 1583-1858* [Edinburgh: Oliver and Boyd, 1937], pp. 110-25).

[5] D.A. Weir, *The Origins of the Federal Theology in Sixteenth-Century Reformation Thought* (Oxford: Clarendon, 1990), p. 3.

[6] *Tryal*, p. 45.

is too narrow, because it overlooks another more important type—the unilateral covenant, which, he says, is not 'open-ended and contingent upon the mutual response of both parties', as is the bilateral covenant. Torrance offers a helpful example from the Bible of what he means by a unilateral covenant:

> [Such occurs] when in old Israel at the time of his coronation a king made a covenant for (rather than 'with') his people, saying, 'This is the kind of king I am going to be, and this is the kind of people you are going to be!' The classical example again is Rehoboam, where the people either said, 'Amen' to it, or, 'To your tents O Israel, we shall not have this man to reign over us!'[7]

For Rutherford, this simply begs the question. The ability of the people to respond either in accepting the terms of the king or in rejecting and rebelling against them proves that it is *de facto* a bilateral covenant. Rutherford does not deny the presence of a unilateral covenant in the Bible. But he does deny that such a covenant is wholly and exclusively unilateral, because it would then be universalist and would allow no room for human choice. In continuity with such reformers as Wolfgang Musculus, Rutherford believes that the unilateral covenant is—as Torrance's example proves—actually both unilateral and bilateral at the same time. It is unilateral in its 'origin' or 'initiation' by God *for* humankind and bilateral in its 'fulfillment' or 'administration' by God *with* them.[8]

Thus, by defining covenant as a bilateral agreement, Rutherford is not denying the presence of a unilateral covenant but is seeking the lowest common denominator in order to encapsulate every biblical covenant under one heading. Every covenant in the Bible, no matter who are the parties involved, is bilateral to some degree and, so, can fall within the bounds of his all-encompassing definition. With this definition of covenant in place, we can move on to examine the question of how many covenants there are for Rutherford. His answer: three—the covenant of redemption, the covenant of works, and the covenant of grace. We will explore each in turn.

The Covenant of Redemption

While Rutherford does not devote any space to discussing the existence of a covenant of redemption in the *Examen*, it is clear from others of his works— most particularly *The Covenant of Life Opened* (1655)—that he does believe in

---

[7] J.B. Torrance, 'Covenant or Contract? A Study of the Theological Background of Worship in Seventeenth-Century Scotland', *SJT* 23 (1970), pp. 54-5.
[8] A.A. Hoekema, 'The Covenant of Grace in Calvin's Teaching', *CTJ* 2 (1967), p. 140; A.A. Woolsey, 'Unity and Continuity in Covenant Thought: A Study in the Reformed Tradition to the Westminster Assembly', 2 vols. (unpublished Ph.D. dissertation, University of Glasgow, 1998), I, pp. 87-8. For Musculus' views on the dual nature of the covenant, see his *Common Places*, pp. 285-6.

such. The covenant of redemption or, as Rutherford also refers to it, the 'Covenant of Suretyship', is to be considered in two ways: '1. As transacted in time between *Jehovah* and *Christ*, in his actuall discharge of his office of King, Priest and Prophet'; and '2. As it is an eternall transaction and compact between *Jehovah* and the second Person the *Son of God*, who gave personall consent that he should be the Undertaker [of our salvation], and no other.'[9] The second of these is foundational. The first flows from the second and is necessary only because Christ's relationship with God while he was on earth cannot rightly be explained by the covenant of grace, as ours can be. Christ, unlike us, is sinless and, thus, has no need for a gracious covenant to restore a relationship that was broken by sin. What is more, the second of these—the eternal, pre-temporal, intratrinitarian covenant of redemption—is also foundational for God's covenant of grace with humankind: 'the Covenant of Suretyship is the cause of the stability and firmnesse of the Covenant of Grace'. The first two persons of the Trinity, who are consubstantial with one another, freely and willingly enter into an eternal, irrevocable, and immutable covenant (of redemption) in order to save select ones of their creatures by entering into a covenant (of grace) with them in time. This relationship ensures Rutherford will say that although these two covenants must be distinguished, they should never be separated.[10]

Rutherford's justification for believing in a pre-temporal covenant of redemption between God the Father and God the Son is derived exclusively from Scripture. Passages like Isaiah 49.6-12 are understood by Rutherford, as they are by others like John Owen,[11] to refer directly to such a covenant. Other passages that refer to the temporal relationship of the incarnate Christ with God are indirectly and rather intricately woven together to show that they must have their foundation in an eternal and pre-temporal covenant.[12] Still other passages of Scripture, which speak of God's temporal covenant with humankind, are shown by Rutherford to imply that standing behind this temporal covenant is an eternal and pre-temporal pact between God and Christ. Among such passages is Psalm 89, in regard to which Rutherford says that the reason why '*David* and his seed stand sure in an everlasting Covenant of Reconciliation [i.e., of Grace]' is because an eternal pact between God and Christ undergirds it and ensures it (vv. 28-9, 34).[13] In order to add weight to this argument, Rutherford appeals to Calvin's acknowledgment that the covenant in Psalm 89 ultimately finds its true eternity (*vera aeternitas*) only in Christ.[14] And while it is true that Calvin

---

[9] *COL*, p. 302.
[10] *COL*, pp. 290-302, 309.
[11] Owen, *Works of John Owen*, X, p. 170. Cf. *COL*, p. 282.
[12] *COL*, pp. 290-302.
[13] *COL*, p. 309.
[14] Cf. J. Calvin, *Commentary on the Book of Psalms*, trans. J. Anderson, 5 vols. (Edinburgh: CTS, 1845-1849), III, p. 437; with *COL*, p. 337.

never explicitly speaks of a pre-temporal covenant between the first and second persons of the Trinity in any of his writings, he does make statements like these in which such an idea is implicit: 'We call predestination God's eternal decree, by which he *compacted with himself* what he willed to become of each man'; and, 'Now it is useful to know this, for we are taught that God is ever so consistent with himself, that his covenant, *which he has made with Christ* and with all his members, never fails'; and, 'the *covenant of God* is nothing else than his *secret* or *counsel*'.[15] These statements, although clearly not definitive, do seem to suggest, as Peter Lillback indicates, that 'Calvin may have provided the impetus for the later development of the covenant of redemption'.[16] Regardless of whether or not this is the case, it must be acknowledged that the belief in such a covenant can hardly be taken as a substantial departure from Calvin. In seeing a pre-temporal covenant of redemption in Scripture, Rutherford positions himself squarely within the neo-Augustinian tradition, a tradition which undeniably includes such men as Caspar Olevianus (1536-1587)—who was himself a disciple of Calvin and whose thinking mirrors Calvin's own at several points[17]—David Dickson (c.1583-1663), Johannes Cocceius (1603-1669), John Owen, and Patrick Gillespie (1617-1675).[18]

While the existence of such an eternal pre-temporal covenant, which forms the basis for God's covenant of grace with humankind, does appear neat and tidy on the surface, or, as Barth playfully suggests, 'sublime and uplifting',[19] its necessity, upon further reflection, seems rather perplexing. If God is one God with one divine will, why must there be a covenant or contract between the

---

[15] *Institutes* III.xxi.5, p. 926, emphasis added; idem, *Commentaries on the Book of the Prophet Jeremiah and the Lamentations*, trans. J. Owen, 5 vols. (Edinburgh: CTS, 1850-1855), III, p. 127, emphasis added; and idem, *Commentary on Psalms*, I, p. 430, emphasis original. Cf. P.A. Lillback, *The Binding of God: Calvin's Role in the Development of Covenant Theology* (Grand Rapids, MI: Baker Academic; Carlisle, Cumbria: Paternoster, 2001), p. 213.

[16] Lillback, *The Binding of God*, p. 213.

[17] L.D. Bierma, *German Calvinism in the Confessional Age: The Covenant Theology of Caspar Olevianus* (Grand Rapids, MI: Baker, 1996), pp. 107-112, 149-50. Bierma argues—because of the great influence of Calvin upon Olevianus—that 'it is very well possible that a number of themes in Olevianus' covenant theology can be attributed to Calvin's direct influence' and goes on to describe extensive parallels in their thinking.

[18] D. Dickson, *Therapeutica sacra, Shewing Briefly the Method of Healing the Diseases of the Conscience Concerning Regeneration* (1656; Edinburgh, 1664); Dickson and J. Durham, *The Sum of Saving Knowledge* (Edinburgh, 1650), II.1-3, in *WCF*, p. 324; J. Cocceius, *Summa doctrinae de foedere et testamento Dei* (1648; Amsterdam, 1683), chapter 5; Trueman, *Claims of Truth*, pp. 133-40; and the most extensive of these, P. Gillespie, *The Ark of the Covenant Opened: or, A Treatise of the Covenant of Redemption between God and Christ, as the Foundation of the Covenant of Grace* (London, 1677). Cf. *RD*, pp. 374-9.

[19] *CD*, IV/1, p. 66.

persons of the Godhead? Certainly there would be no need to ensure agreement or to maintain accountability among the persons of the Trinity, as there would be among human persons.[20] It is hard to escape the conclusion that Rutherford and his Reformed contemporaries were perhaps more influenced by the socio-political and economic climates of their day than they were by the teaching of Scripture in their formulation of this doctrine.[21] Even the Arminians, who were on the fringe of Reformed orthodoxy, still retained in their theology the notion of an eternal, pre-temporal covenant between God and Christ.[22] No doubt, this is partly because 'the people of the 17th century understood the language of bands, pacts, covenants, [and] contracts', and, so, it made sense to speak accordingly.[23] But it should also be noted that the divine decrees, whether one understands them according to the Arminian or the Calvinist systems, do assume that decisions are being made within the Trinity that will then be executed by God within the temporal economy of salvation. These eternal and pre-temporal decisions are what Rutherford, and the Arminians, are seeking to identify and to explain in language that is both biblically founded and culturally sensitive.

The increased emphasis on covenant theology and, in particular, on the covenant of redemption in the sixteenth and seventeenth centuries is due to more than simply the socio-political and economic climates of this period; it is also strongly influenced by new theological and polemical challenges which arise from within Reformed orthodoxy during this time. Perry Miller, in his work on New England Puritanism, has helpfully identified the encroaching threat of Arminianism as a key to understanding the increased emphasis of the Reformed orthodox on covenant theology.[24] While Miller's claims are over simplified, as George Marsden has demonstrated,[25] they are, nonetheless, valid and helpful to some extent. One of the main reasons why Rutherford and his Reformed orthodox contemporaries emphasize covenant theology and, in particular, the covenant of redemption, to the degree that they do is because they perceive that the soteriological discrepancies between their system and the Arminian alternative are founded upon key differences in regard to the eternal, pre-temporal relationship between the Father and the Son and the divine decrees.

---

[20] Barth offers a similar criticism to this in *CD*, IV/1, p. 65.

[21] This is a criticism that has been raised by J.B. Torrance in several of his articles: e.g., 'Covenant or Contract?', pp. 52-4; and, 'The Covenant Concept in Scottish Theology and Politics and its Legacy', *SJT* 34 (1981), pp. 225-8. Cf. S.A. Burrell, 'The Covenant Idea as a Revolutionary Symbol: Scotland, 1596-1637', *CH* 27 (1958), pp. 338-50.

[22] See *WJA*, I, p. 416.

[23] Torrance, 'The Covenant Concept', p. 227.

[24] P. Miller, *The New England Mind* (New York: Macmillan, 1939), pp. 366-7.

[25] G.M. Marsden, 'Perry Miller's Rehabilitation of the Puritans: A Critique', *CH* 39 (1970), pp. 91-105, especially 99-100.

The Covenant of Redemption and the Decrees of God

Though the Arminians speak of a covenant of redemption between God and Christ, they define it, according to Rutherford, in such a way that 'it is a far other thing then such as we hold'.[26] For the Arminians, the covenant of redemption is summarized in the first of the divine decrees: the appointment of Christ as Mediator and High Priest for the whole world. In this covenant, God '*demand*[s]...an action to be performed' by Christ and '*promise*[s]...an immense remuneration' in return.[27] But it is not certain that this is a promise that God can rightly make. As we saw in our discussion of the *potentia absoluta et ordinata* in the previous chapter, the Arminian God cannot impose his will upon the free wills of his creatures, given his decree to create them. Thus, there can be no promised remuneration in this covenant but only a promised *potential* remuneration. This is further illustrated by the fact that the Arminians separate the covenant of redemption from the decree of predestination, which, as we saw in the previous chapter, is made possible by the subordinationism in their doctrine of the Trinity. Christ is not the electing and elected God, as he is for the Reformed orthodox, but the elected and electing God instead; he is appointed by the Father in the first decree—the covenant of redemption—but does not elect until the fourth decree.[28] God cannot rightly promise Christ an immense remuneration in the covenant of redemption, the first decree, if he does not elect until the fourth decree. The result of separating the covenant of redemption from election is that the Arminians propose a pre-temporal covenant in which Christ takes on the task of salvation for nobody in particular.

In contrast to the Arminians, Rutherford sees the covenant of redemption as encapsulating all the divine decrees together. This is clear from his comments that the covenant of redemption is 'a mutuall agreement between Jehovah and the Son...to have us saved'; it is one in which Christ undertakes to be our Mediator and 'our Surety, Saviour, and Redeemer' as well.[29] In speaking of the covenant in this way, Rutherford demonstrates that it includes the decree to allow the fall, the *ad extra* decrees, and the decree to apply salvation in Christ. In other words, for Rutherford, the covenant of redemption is the intratrinitarian structure within which all the divine decrees are presented and planned out by God. Not only does it include the appointment or election of Christ as Mediator, but it also includes the decree of predestination, as well as the decree to apply the salvation obtained by Christ to those so elected. There is, therefore, a unity of Christ's priestly and mediatorial works within the covenant of redemption. Christ's role in the covenant is 'not simply' to die, as the

---

[26] *COL*, p. 327.
[27] *WJA*, I, p. 416.
[28] See *WJA*, I, pp. 653-4; II, pp. 29-32; and Muller's discussion in 'The Christological Problem', pp. 158-60.
[29] *COL*, p. 293.

Arminians suggest, but to elect, then to offer himself as a sacrifice 'for, and in the name of' the elect, and then to intercede for them and to ensure that what he has offered for them will be applied to them.[30]

Because the covenant of redemption includes all the divine decrees, it cannot be maintained, as David Weir has argued, that the covenant is merely 'an explanation of the working out of the decrees of God'.[31] Rather, the covenant is the relational context in which the decrees are given and committed to. But, more than this, because the covenant of redemption comprises the unity of Christ's priestly and mediatorial works, and because it forms the pre-temporal basis for Christ's actual work in time and space, it, and not the decrees themselves, functions as the 'causal foundation of the whole economy of salvation' for Rutherford and for the Reformed orthodox in general.[32] The covenant of redemption, and not the decrees *per se*, guarantees the salvation of the elect and provides an absolute and objective 'anchor' to support faith with assurance of salvation.[33] Such is not the case for the Arminians, however. By separating the covenant of redemption from Christ's decree of predestination and from his intercession—moves that are made possible by the fact that the Son is subordinate to the Father, not only in terms of his office but also in terms of his divinity—the Arminians reduce the eternal, pre-temporal covenant from being the causal foundation of all of salvation to being the causal foundation of a universal, common grace after the fall, which makes salvation possible for all people but does not guarantee it for any. Not only so, but in separating the covenant of redemption from Christ's predestination and intercession, the Arminians institute a sharp divide between the wills of the Son and the Father in the economy of salvation. In order to maintain the harmony of the divine will in salvation, Arminius appeals to the 'authority' of the Father, once again reflecting a subordinationism in his doctrine of the Trinity and calling the consubstantiality of the Son into question.[34]

It should be no surprise, therefore, that Reformed orthodox theologians like Rutherford choose to place greater emphasis on covenant theology and on the covenant of redemption in particular than previous generations do. They are reacting against what they perceive to be harmful soteriological implications arising from the Arminian doctrine of the Trinity and its relationship to the

---

[30] *COL*, p. 360. Cf. *WJA*, I, p. 416; with *COL*, pp. 327-33.

[31] Weir, *Origins of the Federal Theology*, p. 157.

[32] Trueman, *Claims of Truth*, p. 137.

[33] *COL*, pp. 331, 360. Rutherford says that this covenant should not be the 'object of faith', nor will the believer always derive assurance from it; but the believer's 'faith often is, and ought, and may be supported thereby'. See the section on faith and assurance below.

[34] *WJA*, I, p. 416. Arminius does suggest that Christ entered into the covenant of redemption willingly and with 'a voluntary engagement to perform' the required duty. But had Christ not done so, the Father could have forced his engagement 'by a display of his authority'.

divine decrees. Arminianism is not just presenting a theological system that is different in one or two points but a system that is opposed to Reformed orthodoxy from the outset. What is surprising is that Rutherford makes no mention of this profound difference in the *Examen*. One would expect in a treatise devoted wholly to refuting Arminianism that there would be extensive reference made to such a profound and fundamental difference of opinion. The omission is a glaring one. It probably reflects an immaturity in Rutherford's thinking on the covenant in the *Examen*. Even though he clearly falls within the pale of federal theology at this early juncture in his career by believing in a covenant of works and a covenant of grace, Rutherford appears to add this third covenant—the covenant of redemption—only later, in *The Covenant of Life Opened* (1655), most likely as a result of the influence of David Dickson and James Durham (1622-1658).[35] In spite of this *lacuna* in the *Examen*, however, Rutherford's later work on federal theology demonstrates that he is aware of the radical discrepancy that exists between his theology and that of the Arminians. Although he may not have seen it as early or as clearly as Owen did in his *A Display of Arminianism* (1642),[36] he did see it, nonetheless, and he reacted against it by emphasizing the covenant of redemption and the close, practical relationship that it has with the divine decrees.

The Covenant of Works

Whereas the covenant of redemption is a pre-temporal pact enacted between God and Christ, the covenant of works is the first of two temporal covenants that God enters into with humankind. In the covenant of works, 'God promiseth to us lif everlasting, and wee ar oblished to keep the law by the strength of our nature.'[37] This statement should not be taken to imply that Rutherford would disagree with the Westminster Confession's statement that 'life was promised to Adam, and in him to his posterity, *upon condition of perfect and personal obedience*'.[38] There can be no doubt but that Rutherford sees obedience to the law as the condition of satisfying this covenant.[39] No significance should be attached to his omission of the word 'condition' in his catechism. He is simply speaking with covenantal (i.e., bi-lateral) language. Rutherford would wholeheartedly agree with Robert Rollock that God 'promised [Adam] eternall

---

[35] Dickson and Durham published their *Sum of Saving Knowledge* in 1650, five years before Rutherford's work. For their statements on the covenant of redemption, see sections II.1-3 in *WCF*, p. 324.

[36] On Owen's use of the covenant against the Arminians, see Trueman, *Claims of Truth*, pp. 133-9.

[37] *Catachisme*, p. 175.

[38] *WCF*, § 7.2, p. 42, emphasis added. Unfortunately, San-Deog Kim has recently and incorrectly asserted this in 'Time and Eternity', p. 299.

[39] See, e.g., *Tryal*, pp. 55-6.

life, under the condition of holy and good works, which should be answerable to the holinesse and goodnesse of their creation, and conformable to his law'.[40]

But in saying that God promises life to Adam upon condition of his obedience, Rutherford does not mean to imply that God intended to save Adam by his law-keeping: '*Adam* in his first state was not predestinate to a law glory.' God decreed, by his *voluntas permittens*, that Adam, as 'a publick person representing all his sons' and daughters, should fall from 'the state of Law-life both *totally* and *finally*'. But, as an individual, Adam did not fall from 'the state of Gospel election to glory'. As a private person, Adam is saved by faith in Christ, just as we are today. The Edenic, pre-lapsarian dispensation, according to Rutherford, was never intended by God to be an end in itself but merely a temporary means, 'an earthly condition', to show his love and grace in Christ:

> For the Lord had in the Law-dispensation a love designe, to set up a Theatre and stage of free grace; And that the way of works should be a time dispensation, like a summer-house to be demolished again: As if the Lord had an aime that works and nature should be a transient, but no standing Court for righteousnesse: Hence it is now the reliques of an old standing Court, and the Law, is a day of assyse, for condemning of malefactors, who will acknowledge no Tribunall of grace, but only of works: And it is a just Court to terrifie robbers, to awe borderers and loose men, but to beleevers it is now a Court for a far other end.[41]

The point that Rutherford is trying to emphasize here is the graciousness of the covenant of works, a theme that is consistently taken up by such Reformation and post-Reformation theologians as Musculus, Zanchi, Du Moulin, and Turretin.[42] The Lord had a 'love designe' for Adam when he entered into this covenant with him. 'Law-obedience' was never intended to be 'the effectuall means leading to' Adam's eternal glory. This does not imply that life is not promised upon condition of obedience. The condition remains, but it is not Adam, the 'publick person', who fulfills it. Rather, Christ fulfills the condition on Adam's behalf, insofar as Adam is considered a private and individual person and not the federal representative of his posterity. But more than this, the graciousness of the covenant of works is also seen in the fact that it is the means by which individuals recognize their need of God's mercy and grace in Christ and receive eternal life. Thus, even though law-breakers and 'malefactors' will be 'terrifie[d]' and ultimately condemned by it, believers will be comforted and encouraged to give praise to God for his 'Theatre and stage of free grace'.[43]

---

[40] Rollock, *Treatise of Gods Effectual Calling*, p. 7.
[41] *COL*, pp. 2-3.
[42] W. Musculus, *Loci communes sacrae theologiae* (Basel, 31573), pp. 620-21; J. Zanchi, *Opera theologicorum D. Hieronymi Zanchii*, 9 vols. (Geneva, 1617-19), III, p. 697; Du Moulin, *Anatomy of Arminianisme*, pp. 42-3; Turretin, *Institutes*, I, pp. 574-8.
[43] *COL*, pp. 2-3, 14, 225.

Soteriology 149

Such an understanding of the covenant of works is not uncommon among seventeenth-century theologians. Although the specific terminology used to describe the pre-lapsarian relationship between God and Adam is not completely uniform among the Reformed orthodox,[44] the notion that this relationship itself, as well as God's intention in entering into it, is gracious is generally agreed upon. Thomas Blake (c.1597-1657) represents the typical post-Reformation attitude to the pre-lapsarian covenant when he states that,

> the fountain, and first rise [of both the covenant of works and the covenant of grace]...was the free grace, and favour of God. For howsoever the first covenant was on condition of obedience, and engaged to the reward of Works, yet it was of Grace, that God made any such promise, of reward to any work of man, when man had done all (even in that estate) which was commanded, he was still an unprofitable servant, he had done no more then duty, and no emolument did thence accrew to his Maker.[45]

Even those whose theology is at odds with the post-Reformation orthodox—men like Arminius, for example—still embrace the idea of a gracious pre-lapsarian covenant between God and Adam. For Arminius, this covenant is one in which 'God require[s] obedience, and...promise[s] a [gracious] reward...[or, bestows a deserved] punishment'.[46] For his later followers, however—men like Episcopius and Van Limborch—there is no such thing as a pre-lapsarian covenant in which Adam is deemed the 'Representative of his Posterity, so that whatsoever he might do should be imputed likewise to them'.[47]

Although it is true that the definitive expressions of Episcopius' and Van Limborch's thoughts in regard to the covenant of works are not published until 1650 and 1686 respectively,[48] it is, nonetheless, quite significant that Rutherford nowhere finds fault with them, or with any others of the Arminians

---

[44] See the examples provided in E.F. Kevan, *The Grace of Law: A Study in Puritan Theology* (London: Carey Kingsgate, 1964), p. 111.

[45] T. Blake, *Vindiciae foederis; or, A Treatise of the Covenant of God Entered with Man-kinde* (London, ²1658), p. 9. Cf. also the similar statements in other post-Reformation theologians: e.g., Goodwin, *Works of Thomas Goodwin*, V, p. 82; VII, p. 25; Owen, *Works of John Owen*, V, p. 277; J. Ball, *A Treatise of the Covenant of Grace* (London, 1645), pp. 7, 9; A. Burgess, *Vindiciae legis* (London, 1646), pp. 123, 129; J. Graile, *A Modest Vindication of the Doctrine of Conditions in the Covenant of Grace* (London, 1655), p. 26; and F. Roberts, *Of God's Covenants* (London, 1657), p. 17.

[46] *WJA*, II, pp. 369-73.

[47] *ACS*, I, p. 197; Episcopius, *Opera theologica* (1665), II, pp. 149-55. Cf. J. Corvinus, *Petri Molinaei novi anatomici mala encheiresis: seu Censura anatomes Arminianismi* (Francofurti ad Moenum, 1622), 8.7, 9.5; R.A. Muller, 'The Federal Motif in Seventeenth Century Arminian Theology', *NAvK* 62:1 (1982), pp. 102-22.

[48] S. Episcopius, *Institutiones theologicae*, first published in *Opera theologica*, vol. 1, ed. E. de Courcelles (Amsterdam, 1650); Van Limborch, *Theologia Christiana* (originally published in 1686 as *Institutiones theologiae Christianae*).

for that matter, for their refusing to embrace the terminology, 'covenant of works', or even for their refusing to endorse a pre-lapsarian covenant at all. The most likely explanation for this is that the existence of a pre-lapsarian covenant is not explicitly mentioned in Scripture, and Rutherford appears to be willing to allow for some leeway in light of this fact. Where he does find fault with the Arminians is in connection with the theological or, better, the soteriological, implications that flow from their understanding of the disobedience of Adam—or, as he sees it, from their understanding of Adam's breaking of the covenant of works—and the resulting propagation of his sin.[49]

While maintaining, on the whole, a fairly traditional view of original sin,[50] the Arminians teach that 'the most bountiful God' immediately and universally removes its stain by providing Christ as a 'free Remedy for al against that Evil or Malady, which was derived unto us from Adam'.[51] As a result of this universal 'Remedy' or atonement, the Arminians reduce the effects of Adam's disobedience—or, as Rutherford would see it, the effects of Adam's failure to keep the covenant of works—upon his progeny to a simple 'Misfortune', which not only includes death and the physical corruption of the world (i.e., disease, pain in childbirth, and labor in producing food), but also—and more importantly from a soteriological perspective—an 'Inclination to sin'. This means that no person is born sinful—i.e., dead in sins and trespasses, as Rutherford and the Calvinists believe—but with only, at the very most, an inherited predisposition to sin.[52]

Although the underlying issue between Rutherford and the Arminians is really the extent and nature of the covenant of grace and the atonement of Christ, the differences highlighted thus far are significant because they once again show the profound and systematic influence of their respective perceptions of God upon their theologies. The reason why the Remonstrants believe that the effects of Adam's disobedience cannot apply to his posterity is because that would violate the free wills of Adam's descendents. God 'could not carry out' such a covenant of works, as the federalists suggest; he cannot hold his free creatures liable for a sin which is not actually theirs but is so only 'by imputation'. The problem is especially poignant in regard to infants. How can God 'cast infants in[to] hell' for a sin that is not their own? To do so is to act against human freedom and, thus, to contradict the decree of creation, which, as we saw in the last chapter, is wholly a communication of good.[53] As far as Rutherford is concerned, however, this kind of thinking puts God in the dock and evaluates his ways by human conventions. 'God is not unjust and

---

[49] *Examen*, pp. 449-52.
[50] See, e.g., *Confession*, pp. 117-20.
[51] *Confession*, p. 120.
[52] *ACS*, I, pp. 191-2; Muller, 'Federal Motif', pp. 107-8, 111, 116-17.
[53] *Examen*, pp. 449-50; *COL*, p. 56. Cf. *ACS*, I, pp. 193-4; Corvinus, *Molinaei novi anatomici mala encheiresis*, 8.7, 9.5.

cruel'; who are we to suggest that he is? Even if God would never have provided a savior to redeem humankind and 'Adam and all his posterity', including infants as well, 'would have paid the penalty of death, both temporal [*temporaria*] and eternal' in themselves, God would still not be unjust for his actions or the lack thereof. He wills and acts according to his own standard of justice and always for his own glory.[54]

The question of whether God holds people accountable for a sin they did not commit may be a difficult one to answer—especially so in the case of infants. But there is one thing that is not so difficult to say: both Rutherford and the Arminians are expressing a theology that is influenced by their respective views of God and his corresponding relationship with the created order. Rutherford's opinion exalts the position of God by preserving his sovereignty and freedom but, at the same time, creates problems for human liberty and responsibility. The Arminian option, on the other hand, solves the human conundrum but does so with a radically smaller view of the sovereignty of God. The two systems arrive at different conclusions because they begin with different premises.

The Covenant of Works—Continuity or Discontinuity?

Since the seventeenth century, the idea of a covenant of works has largely fallen into disuse. In many cases—especially in the twentieth century—it has been openly criticized and cited as primary evidence that the post-Reformation orthodox drifted from the theology of Calvin and the reformers.[55] A big part of the problem for those twentieth-century scholars who are critical of the covenant of works is the fact that a pre-lapsarian covenant is not explicitly present within Reformed theology until at least the late sixteenth century, at the close of the Reformation and the onset of the post-Reformation period. Even though Zacharias Ursinus (1534-1583) first overtly describes Adam's pre-fall condition by way of a covenant in 1562,[56] two years before Calvin's death, it is

---

[54] *Examen*, pp. 450-51.

[55] Among scholars who endorse this viewpoint are M. McGiffert, 'Grace and Work: The Rise and Division of Covenant Divinity in Elizabethan Puritanism', *Harvard Theological Review* 75:4 (1982), pp. 463-502; idem, 'The Perkinsian Moment of Federal Theology', *CTJ* 29 (1994), pp. 117-48; J.B. Torrance, 'Strengths and Weaknesses of the Westminster Theology', in *The Westminster Confession*, ed. A.I.C. Heron (Edinburgh: St. Andrews, 1982), pp. 40-53; idem, 'Calvin and Puritanism in England and Scotland— Some Basic Concepts in the Development of "Federal Theology"', in *Calvinus Reformator* (Potchefstroom: Potchefstroom University for Christian Higher Education, 1982), pp. 264-77; H. Rolston III, *John Calvin versus the Westminster Confession* (Richmond, VA: John Knox, 1972); idem, 'Responsible Man in Reformed Theology', pp. 129-56.

[56] R. Letham, 'The *Foedus Operum*: Some Factors Accounting For Its Development', *SCJ* 14:4 (1983), p. 459; P.A. Lillback, 'Ursinus' Development of the Covenant of Creation: A Debt to Melanchthon or Calvin?', *WTJ* 43:2 (Spring 1981), pp. 247-88.

not until the 1580s and 90s that this idea becomes more commonplace.[57] The phrase *foedus operum* does not even appear in print until 1585, when the Puritan Dudley Fenner (c.1558-1587) uses it in his *Sacra theologia* to help distinguish the pre-lapsarian and post-lapsarian covenants.[58] After Fenner, however, the phrase does gain a rapid acceptance. Amandus Polanus, William Perkins, Franciscus Junius, and Robert Rollock—the first in Scotland—all use the phrase *foedus operum* in the 1590s to describe Adam's pre-fall situation,[59] a trend that continues well into the seventeenth, eighteenth, and nineteenth centuries.[60]

Among those twentieth-century scholars who see the covenant of works as a *locus* of discontinuity between the Reformation and post-Reformation periods, some, like Michael McGiffert, have argued for discontinuity not only between the Puritans and Calvin but also amongst the Puritans themselves. McGiffert specifically sees three strands within Puritan covenant theology: the first, following men like William Ames, perceived the covenant of works as 'partially embedded in the covenant of grace'; the second, following Robert Rollock and John Cameron (c.1579-1625), believed grace to be the overriding feature of the pre-lapsarian covenant; and the third—representing 'the majority of federalists', who sided more completely with William Perkins—equated the covenant of works with the moral law, thus opposing law to grace and establishing the Adamic covenant as merely an 'agent of reprobation'.[61] The implication of McGiffert's analysis seems to be that, of the three strands, the second comes the closest to Calvin's position. Interestingly, he sees Arminius' views as being more in line with this strand than the mainstream of Puritan thought. Other scholars, like Karl Barth, Paul Althaus, and August Lang, for instance, see the covenant of works as stemming more from the influence of Melanchthonian views of natural law and the law-gospel contrast than from the

---

[57] E.g., C. Olevianus writes of a 'primus foedus' between Adam and God in 1585 (*De substantia foederis gratuiti inter Deum et electos, item de mediis, quibus ea ipsa substantia nobis communicavit* [Geneva, 1585], p. 9). Johannes Piscator speaks of a 'foedus legale' in 1589 (*Aphorismi doctrinae Christianae* [1589; Oxford, 1630], p. 50). And Franciscus Gomarus refers to the pre-lapsarian arrangement between God and Adam as a 'foedus naturale' in 1594 (*Opera theologica omnia* [Amsterdam, 1664], p. 2).

[58] D. Fenner, *Sacra theologia, sive veritas quae est secundum pietatem* (Geneva, 1585), p. 88.

[59] Polanus, *Partitiones*, p. 53; Perkins, *Workes*, I, p. 70; F. Junius, *Opuscula theologica selecta*, ed. A. Kuyper (Amsterdam: Miller and Kruyt, 1882), p. 184; and R. Rollock, *Quaestiones et responsiones aliquot de foedere Dei* (Edinburgh, 1596), pp. A3-A5c.

[60] E.g., S. Crooke, *The Guide unto True Blessedness* (London, 1613), p. 30; Ames, *Marrow*, p. 55; Ussher, *Body of Divinitie*, pp. 124-5. Herman Witsius' classic work on federal theology, *De oeconomia foederum Dei cum hominibus*, was originally published in 1677, and was kept in print well into the nineteenth century.

[61] McGiffert, 'The Perkinsian Moment', pp. 119, 121, 123, 146-8.

thinking of Calvin.⁶² Still others, like David Bruggink, have claimed that a pre-lapsarian covenant of works represents a 'perversion of great seriousness', both theologically and exegetically, when compared with Calvin's theology of grace. And others, like David Weir, have similarly argued that the whole 'doctrine of a *foedus* with Adam' develops as a result of 'the seemingly harsh decretal doctrines of Theodore Beza', in order to soften the extremes of the Bezan form of Calvinism.⁶³

Without minimizing the helpfulness of these twentieth-century studies, three points bear mentioning in connection with their evaluations of the idea of a pre-lapsarian covenant and of the question of substantial discontinuity not only within the Reformed community of the seventeenth-century but also between the post-Reformation period and that of Calvin and his Reformation peers. First, although the phrase 'the covenant of works' does not appear in Calvin's writings, there is ample evidence to suggest that both Calvin and the Augustinian tradition before him recognized the existence of a pre-lapsarian covenant with Adam. In the *Institutes*, Calvin refers to the tree of life as a sacrament, which 'proves' and 'seals' God's covenant with Adam. Not only so, but he also makes repeated reference to the biblical parallel that exists between Adam and Christ. Because the new covenant is initiated with the latter, it is appropriate in light of this parallel to conclude that the old covenant must be initiated with the former.⁶⁴ Augustine, moreover, whose thinking probably represents the greatest influence upon Calvin, also specifically points both to a pre-lapsarian covenant between God and Adam and to the Adam-Christ parallel in the economy of salvation.⁶⁵

Second, the Melanchthonian influence that is said to result in the covenant of works in Ursinus and in the post-Reformation orthodox could just as easily be traced to Calvin as to Melanchthon. For one thing, there is little, if any, difference between the way Philip Melanchthon (1497-1560) articulates his view of natural law and the way Calvin writes on the same subject. Melanchthon states, in words that could easily pass for Rutherford's own, or for those of any other Calvinist as well, for that matter:

---

⁶² Barth, *CD*, IV/1, pp. 54ff; Althaus, *Die Prinzipien*, pp. 148-52; A. Lang, *Der Heidelberger Katechismus und vier verwandte Katechismen* (Leipzig: Deichert, 1907), pp. lxiv-lxvii.

⁶³ D.J. Bruggink, 'Calvin and Federal Theology', *The Reformed Review* 13 (1959-60), pp. 15-22, cited in Lillback, *The Binding of God*, p. 18; and Weir, *Origins of the Federal Theology*, p. 63.

⁶⁴ See *Institutes* IV.xiv.18, p. 1294; II.i.6, pp. 248-9; II.vi.1, pp. 340-42; II.xii.3, pp. 466-7; II.xvii.3, pp. 530-31; IV.xvi.17, pp. 1339-41.

⁶⁵ Augustine, *The City of God*, trans. M. Dods (Edinburgh: T&T Clark, 1878), 16.27, II, pp. 142-3. According to Leonard J. Trinterud, Athanasius follows in this vein as well, making reference to both a pre-lapsarian covenant and the Adam-Christ parallel. See L. Trinterud, 'The Origins of Puritanism', *CH* 20 (March 1951), pp. 42, 56n17.

> Est ergo vera definitio legis naturae, legem naturae esse notitiam legis divinae, naturae hominis insitam. Ideo enim dicitur homo ad imaginem Dei conditus esse, quia in eo lucebat imago, hoc est, notitia Dei et similitudo quaedam mentis divinae, id est, discrimen honestorum et turpium, et cum his notitiis congruebant vires hominis.

And Calvin, likewise, says:

> The very things contained in the two tablets (of the law) are in a way dictated to us by that internal law...written and stamped on every heart....The law of God, which we call moral, is nothing other than the testimony of the natural law and of that conscience which God has engraved on the minds of men....The gifts which God hath left to us since the fall, if they are judged by themselves, are indeed worthy of praise; but as the contagion of wickedness is spread through every part, there will be found in us nothing that is pure and free from every defilement. That we naturally possess some knowledge of God, that some distinction between good and evil is engraven on our conscience, that our faculties are sufficient for the maintenance of the present life, that—in short—we are in so many ways superior to the brute beasts, that is excellent in itself so far as it proceeds from God; but in us all these things are completely polluted.[66]

Lest we think that the Calvinian emphasis on the effects of sin upon the usefulness of natural law is missed by Melanchthon, the great disciple of Luther comments:

> Now, one might ask, since an understanding of the Ten Commandments is implanted in all men at their creation, why then did God proclaim the Ten Commandments [at Sinai] with so many great miracles before so many hundreds of thousands of men? Answer: There are many important reasons for this open magistral proclamation, but two are especially important. In the wake of sin, the light in human reason was not as clear and bright as before. Men became ever more shameless and savage, and incurred more blindness. The heathen invented and invoked many eternal beings and repugnant gods. They permitted all sorts of immorality, and did not record it as vice. Against such blindness God not only proclaimed his law on Mt. Sinai, but has sustained and upheld it since the time of Adam in his Church.[67]

For another thing, Ursinus' understanding of the distinction between the law and the gospel—and, thus, the post-Reformation understanding of the same—may be more similar to Calvin than to Melanchthon. Peter Lillback has cogently argued that '[i]f one reads Ursinus' *Summa Theologiae* in...light [of the difference between Calvin and Luther on the law-gospel contrast], it

---

[66] Lillback, 'Ursinus' Covenant of Creation', pp. 260-61; idem, *The Binding of God*, pp. 279-80.
[67] P. Melanchthon, *Melanchthon on Christian Doctrine: Loci communes, 1555*, trans. and ed. C.L. Manschreck (New York: Oxford University, 1965), pp. 128-9.

becomes apparent that he was working with Calvin's letter-spirit distinction rather than Luther's law/gospel distinction.'[68] Moreover, if, as at least one scholar has claimed, Melanchthon's views later in life actually became more Calvinistic than Lutheran, then the dissimilarity between these two reformers would virtually disappear.[69] And, as a result, Lillback's conclusions would seem justified:

> if Calvin's conception of the law/gospel distinction prohibited a development of the covenant of works, then Melanchthon's expression could not have been contributory either. If Melanchthon's view was a positive stimulus for Ursinus, then Calvin's presentation could have equally served as a prime mover.[70]

Third, to contrast federal theology—with its emphasis on the covenant of works—with Calvin's theology of grace is to overlook Calvin's own view of the law, in the first place, and, in the second, the fact that post-Reformation theologians followed Robert Rollock by employing the covenant of works for the express purpose of emphasizing the grace of God. The covenant of works was, as we have already seen, intended to highlight the graciousness of God in sending his Son into the world to redeem his creatures by pointing to their need for this redemption. Contrary to Michael McGiffert, there is no substantial discontinuity either among the post-Reformation orthodox or between them and Calvin. Rutherford's own position is enough to demonstrate this. He, like William Perkins and, before him, Calvin and Melanchthon, writes that the law of nature is written on people's hearts at creation and is equivalent to the moral law, which was later revealed at Sinai.[71] But Rutherford does not set this natural law in opposition to grace, nor do other post-Reformation theologians. The covenant of works is, to be sure, an 'agent of reprobation'. But it is an agent of election as well. Thus its end is the revelation of the grace of God unto either salvation or merited damnation. What is more, as we have already seen in connection with Rutherford's dispute with the Arminians, neither the terminology 'covenant of works' nor the existence of a pre-lapsarian covenant between God and Adam is of primary importance to him. Rutherford's main concern is to protect the theology of the fall that stands behind this covenant. And this theology falls squarely within the tradition of Calvin.[72]

Thus, regardless of what one may think of the doctrine of the covenant of works, three things must be acknowledged in reference to the question of its

---

[68] Lillback, *The Binding of God*, p. 281. Cf. idem, 'Ursinus' Covenant of Creation', pp. 264-7.

[69] C.E. Maxcey, *A Study in the Development of Bona Opera: The Doctrine in Philip Melanchthon* (Nieuwkoop: B. De Graaf, 1980).

[70] Lillback, 'Ursinus' Covenant of Creation', p. 267.

[71] See the section on the *duplex cognitio Dei* above.

[72] See *Institutes* II.i.7, pp. 249-50; and the helpful discussion in Lillback, *The Binding of God*, pp. 282-6.

discontinuity with Calvin: (1) the theological seedbed of what would later become this covenant can plainly be seen in Calvin and at least as far back as Augustine; (2) the association of the pre-lapsarian covenant of works with Melanchthon rather than with Calvin overlooks the clear theological affinities that exist between Melanchthon and Calvin; and (3) the Calvinistic emphasis upon a theology of grace remains front and center throughout the post-Reformation period, occurring alongside their emphasis on the covenant of works. Far from inaugurating a theological shift away from Reformation thought, this covenant actually worked to preserve it.

The Covenant of Grace

According to both Rutherford and the Arminians, God enters into a covenant of grace with his creatures beginning with post-lapsarian Adam. After Adam's fall into sin, God provides the gracious solution to the problem of humankind—he enters into covenant in order to bestow grace in Christ. Such an idea does not begin with the seventeenth century. Rutherford and the Arminians are following closely upon the heels of sixteenth-century theologians like Bullinger and Calvin, both of whom traced the beginning of God's covenant to Adam.[73] But this is about as far as the similarities between Rutherford and the Arminians extend. While they agree in regard to when the covenant of grace is enacted in time and why it is so enacted, they differ over its purpose, extent, nature, and unity. We will conclude our discussion of covenant theology by examining each of these areas of disagreement, beginning with the last.

Rutherford understands the covenant of grace to be one covenant that unifies the Old and New Testaments and binds together the people of God into one people who are saved by their faith in either a coming or an already come Christ. In proving this, he appeals wholly to Scripture, beginning with Genesis 3.15, which he interprets as the gospel 'proclaimed to Adam'.[74] His remaining arguments break down into three categories. First, Jesus and salvation through him are prophesied in the Old Testament, such that, Old Testament saints would have, and should have, been aware of them (Isaiah 7.14; 9.6; 53.1-12; and Acts 3.24). Second, Scripture teaches that the saints of the Old Testament actually did look ahead to Christ by faith for an eternal salvation (Job 19.25-7;

---

[73] H. Bullinger, *De testamento seu foedere Dei unico et aeterno* (Tiguri, 1534), as translated by and published in McCoy and Baker, *Fountainhead of Federalism*, p. 120; *Institutes* II.x.7, p. 434; II.x.20, p. 446; IV.i.17, p. 985; IV.xiv.12, p. 1287; IV.xiv.18, p. 1294. See also the discussion in Lillback, *The Binding of God*, pp. 142-6.

[74] The *Examen* reads 'Gen. 3.14', but Rutherford's reference to the 'blessed seed' and its being 'proclaimed to Adam' proves he is speaking about verse 15 (*Examen*, p. 430). Rutherford shows that he sees in Genesis 3.15 what some scholars have referred to as the 'protevangelium, the first utterance of the gospel after the Fall into sin'. See C. Van Dam, 'שׁוּף', in *New International Dictionary of Old Testament Theology and Exegesis*, ed. W. VanGemeren (Carlisle, Cumbria: Paternoster, 1997), IV, p. 67.

Psalm 16.9-11; 17.14-15; 39.6-8; 73.24-6; John 8.56; Acts 15.11; and 1 Cor. 10.1-4). Third, the Bible teaches that the Old Testament covenant is not primarily a physical covenant but a spiritual one with spiritual blessings (Gen. 17.7; Deut. 30.6; Isaiah 59.21; Jer. 31.31-5; and Ezek. 36.26).[75] Christ is revealed in both the Old and New Testaments—although he is 'vailed' in the former—and grace and forgiveness of sins in Christ are held forth for all to see—albeit 'darkly' and 'sparingly' in the former.[76] It is for this reason that Christ is said to be the unifying agent who binds together not only the covenant of grace but also the whole of the Bible and redemptive history. Such an idea is not original to Rutherford, however. Others, who preceded him—most notably, Bullinger, Calvin, Musculus, Ursinus, and Zanchi—explicitly embrace the same view of the unity of the covenant of grace in the person of Jesus Christ.[77]

Having said this, there are at least two things that stand out in connection with Rutherford's treatment of the unity of the covenant and the Arminian understanding of it. First, Rutherford relies solely upon Scripture proof-texts in order to justify his contention that there is only one covenant. Granted, part of the reason for this could be that the prior work of men like Bullinger eliminates the necessity of his dealing with this issue in greater detail than he does. Be that as it may, it is surprising that Rutherford does not go into more detailed exegesis when the very argument raised by the Arminians is that Rutherford's adversaries are using the same Bible verses that he does in order to disprove his findings. To respond conclusively to the Arminians, one would expect him to validate his interpretation of Scripture as over against that of his adversaries. Second, and more important as far as this thesis is concerned, Rutherford's response to the Arminians reveals his total disregard for their system of beliefs. Instead of solidifying his exegesis, he rather disingenuously strikes out at the Arminians by accusing them of believing that 'the faith of the people of the Old Testament did not consider spiritual things at all' but only physical things, when it is not at all evident that this is actually the case.[78] In his *Apology*, Arminius explicitly states that he is 'not...denying that the opinion of the brethren on this matter is true [that Old Testament believers understood the ceremonies instituted by God to be types pointing ahead to Christ]'. His concern is that there should be a degree of tolerance 'to bear with the weakness of that man who dares not act the part of the dogmatist on this subject'.[79] More than anything else, the response that Rutherford makes to Arminius substantiates this concern. Rutherford makes no attempt to answer Arminius; he simply dismisses him, not giving him the time of day and conveying the very

---

[75] *Examen*, pp. 430-32.
[76] *COL*, p. 63.
[77] Muller, *Christ and the Decree*, pp. 41, 50, 69, 118; Lillback, *The Binding of God*, chapter 7.
[78] *Examen*, p. 430.
[79] *WJA*, II, pp. 6-9.

intolerance that Arminius decries.

A second area of disagreement between Rutherford and the Arminians relates to the extent of the covenant of grace. Is the extent of this covenant universal or particular? Has God entered into covenant with all of humankind? or, with only the elect? For Rutherford, the covenant of grace is enacted with the elect alone; but, for the Arminians, it is enacted with all of humankind without exception. The reasons for this difference lie in their respective views of the nature of the covenant of grace and of the atonement of Christ, views which are, in turn, affected by the ways in which they see the relationship between God and the created world order and which reflect their respective soteriologies. According to Rutherford, the nature of the covenant is such that '[f]orgivenes of our sinnes, renovatione of our natur, and lif eternall' are actually and, thus, eternally promised.[80] These promises are grounded in the atonement of Christ, which, as we saw in the previous chapter, provides full and absolute remission of sin for all to whom it is applied. As Rutherford says in the *Examen*, the 'promises of the Covenant are not universal. *Therefore*, neither is the Covenant itself'.[81] If the promises were, in fact, universal, then the nature of the atonement would force us to believe in a universal salvation. The particular nature of the covenant promises, and of the atonement of Christ standing behind it, requires that the extent of the covenant itself be particular as well.

The Arminians, on the other hand, regard the nature of the covenant to be such that the forgiveness of sins and eternal life is made possible for all people without exception but guaranteed for none. The atonement of Christ does not actually provide remission of sin for anyone in and of itself in the Arminian system; it simply makes remission of sin possible for the one who, as we will see, believes and perseveres in faith to the end.[82] In justifying this position scripturally, the Arminians rely on universalist passages like 1 John 2.2; John 1.19; 6.51; Romans 14.15; and 2 Peter 2. 1, 3; which state that Christ's death made atonement in some way for the whole world.[83] In justifying it theologically, the Arminians draw attention to the 'antecedent love of God', by which he is inclined to the good, i.e., the freedom, of all his creatures after their

---

[80] *Catachisme*, p. 176.

[81] *Examen*, p. 433.

[82] This is only the case according to the original intent of God not in the way that things are executed in time. In the first of the divine decrees, God establishes the salvation of humankind generally and universally by way of the sin-destroying death of his Son. But it is not until the fourth decree that he decides to predestine those who will believe in Christ and persevere in their faith to the end. In time, however, God predestines those who will believe and, then, Christ dies to obtain their redemption. According to the temporal outworking of God's decrees, therefore, Arminius could rightly say that Christ dies to provide redemption for the elect. But such cannot be said in regard to God's original intent. Cf. *WJA*, II, pp. 9-10 with I, pp. 653-4.

[83] *WJA*, II, pp. 9-10.

Soteriology

creation. Rutherford rightly perceives that this is the theological 'foundation' (*fundamentum*) of the Arminian doctrine of universal atonement and, thus, of the universal extent of the covenant.[84] For God to provide actual salvation for his creatures would be to violate their free wills, something he cannot do after creating them. But, to Rutherford's way of thinking, there is no such theological prohibition or limitation. God is sovereign. He reigns on high, even over the free wills of his creatures. Thus, while it is the nature of the covenant that establishes its extent for both Rutherford and the Arminians, it is the relationship of God with the created world order that determines their respective views on the nature of the covenant.

A third area of disagreement between Rutherford and the Arminians involves the purpose of the covenant of grace. And here, too, we see the pervasive influence of their doctrines of God. In Rutherford's estimation, the purpose of God's entering into the covenant of grace is the glory of God in the redemption of sinful creatures. There is no necessity for God to make this covenant with his creatures. He enters into it wholly 'of his own free good pleasure [*beneplacitum*]' and, by doing so, chooses to manifest his own glory by freely making his grace and mercy known to pitiful sinners.[85] But, as Rutherford perceptively indicates, the same cannot be said for the Arminians. Even though they 'teach with their words that this covenant has been made freely', they 'deny it in truth'.[86] The Arminians—or at least those earlier Arminians who follow Arminius in holding to the traditional view of the fall and the imputation of Adam's sin—end up forcing God into making the covenant of grace with all humankind.[87] This necessity arises in their theology by implication of the relationship between God and his created order. If God is bound to communicate good to his creatures, such that he cannot act against their free wills, then he cannot impose upon them the effects of someone else's, namely Adam's, sin. But if God cannot impose the effects of the fall upon his creatures without violating their free wills, then he has no choice but to enter into the covenant of grace with every one of them. This would make the purpose of the covenant of grace the preservation of the autonomy of the created world order rather than the glory of God. Such a move is, in

---

[84] *Examen*, p. 429.

[85] See *Examen*, pp. 427-8. Rutherford uses the imagery of Ezekiel 16.1-8 to convey the condition of sinful creatures and God's merciful and sovereign initiation of the covenant.

[86] *Examen*, pp. 427-8.

[87] It does not appear that Episcopius in his later life and others, like Van Limborch, embraced the traditional view of Adam's fall and the federal imputation of his sin to all humankind. Assuming that is the case, Rutherford's criticism would not necessarily apply to them. On Episcopius' and Van Limborch's understandings of the fall, see Muller, 'Federal Motif', pp. 109-21. For Arminian statements of the traditional view of Adam's fall, see *WJA*, II, pp. 156-7, and *Confession*, pp. 119-20, both of which are cited by Rutherford in *Examen*, p. 428.

Rutherford's opinion, paramount to dethroning God and placing men and women there in his place. As a result, it cannot be tolerated.

After surveying Rutherford's thinking in regard to federal theology, it should be evident that the covenant idea does in fact function as an architectonic principle. It forms the structure for the biblical story of redemption by providing the context into which the decrees are given, establishing the parameters for the temporal work of the triune God in salvation, and expressing the nature of the relationship between God and his creatures. It should also be evident that while there does seem to be clear progression in the development of the covenant beyond what is found in the reformers, there is also clear continuity in the theology the covenant idea was intended to convey. It will soon be obvious, if it is not already, that federal theology is crucial to understanding the soteriological differences between Rutherford and the Arminians. The ideas we have sketched out set the stage for the profound variations that will soon arise in regard to conversion, justification, sanctification, perseverance, and assurance. The remainder of this chapter is devoted to evaluating these variations in more detail. But, before we turn our attention to this task, two statements need to be made in connection with Rutherford's covenant theology and our examination of it here. While there has been some evaluation and interaction with modern day criticisms of covenant theology in general, and of Rutherford's version of it in particular, throughout the course of the preceding section, this should not imply that there is nothing else to be said on the matter. Certain modern day criticisms of federal theology will be revisited in the course of this chapter, especially those pertaining to conditions in the covenant and the relationship of the covenant to assurance of salvation. Furthermore, a general criticism of Rutherford's covenant theology would seem to be in order. In this vein, it must be acknowledged that any system that claims to be the architectonic principle of all of Scripture must not be held so stridently that it prevents dialoguing with other viewpoints. Scripture's teaching on salvation is so multi-faceted, it is hard to see how one principle can do justice to it all. That in itself should be enough to ensure that we are more charitable towards the differing views of others, even if it was not so in Rutherford's own case.

Conversion

The doctrine of conversion represents a climax in the clash between Rutherford and the Arminians over soteriological issues. It draws upon everything that we have discussed thus far in connection with the doctrine of God and his relation to the created world order and raises several issues that will resurface later when we explore the Arminian doctrines of justification, perseverance, and assurance. For these reasons, it forms a central part of the *Examen* and of our discussion here.

Rutherford follows William Perkins in thinking of conversion more comprehensively than do others among the Puritans.[88] He, like Perkins, believes that conversion consists in two distinct acts: the divine act of regeneration and the human response of faith and repentance.[89] This should not be overlooked, and we will return to this feature of Rutherford's theology later. But, for now, it is worth noting that Rutherford, because of his dispute with the Arminians, consistently emphasizes in the *Examen* that the essence of conversion is to be found in the divine act rather than in the human response. He says:

> We establish that conversion [consists], essentially and primarily [*actu primo*], not in the free act of believing [as the Arminians suggest]—although Conversion is active, and the consummation [*actus secundus*] of our Conversion to God, which is commanded to us as our duty, is essentially [found] in such an act [of believing]—but in the infusion of new life.[90]

His contention is that the Arminians, following the Jesuits, place their emphasis in conversion on human effort not on divine initiative, and, by doing so, they 'divide the glory of Conversion between God and the wretched creature'. Such a position is untenable, for Rutherford, because 'the glory [in converting men and women to Christ] should be wholly and entirely ascribed to God'.[91] In order to explain further how and why Rutherford locates the essence of conversion in God's act rather than in our response and to evaluate his perception of and response to the Arminian view of conversion, we will treat its component parts in more detail. What follows is a discussion of regeneration and the role of human ability, grace and free will, calling, and the nature and object of faith.

God's Work of Regeneration

In his catechism, Rutherford affirms that regeneration is a 'work of Godis Spirit', involving no human effort.[92] In the *Examen*, he states this more explicitly: 'the creature [*homo*] who is dead in sins contributes *nothing* to his or her own regeneration' (an assertion he is keen to prove from Scripture: John 3.3, 5.25, and Eph. 2.5).[93] Such a view is not peculiar to Rutherford. Even Arminius and his early disciples wholeheartedly embrace the fact that

---

[88] Edward Leigh, for example, defines conversion narrowly as 'our act' in his *Body of Divinity*, p. 491. See also J. Von Rohr, *The Covenant of Grace in Puritan Thought* (Atlanta, GA: Scholars Press, 1986), pp. 88-90.
[89] Cf. *Examen*, pp. 459, 461, 463, 472, and, especially, 481; with Perkins, *Workes*, I, pp. 613-14, 627.
[90] *Examen*, p. 481.
[91] *Examen*, p. 471.
[92] *Catachisme*, p. 199.
[93] *Examen*, p. 460, emphasis added.

regeneration is 'the act of God' alone.[94] The difference between Rutherford and the Arminians on the doctrine of regeneration lies not in its author but in its nature. According to Rutherford, the nature of regeneration is such that it is an 'inward sanctificatione', whereby God 'put[s] in us the lif of Christ and renew[s] all the powers of our soul'.[95] By defining the nature of regeneration in this manner, Rutherford distinguishes himself from the Arminians and, at the same time, demonstrates his continuity with Calvin and the Reformers. And he does so primarily in two ways.

First, in continuity with Calvin and the Reformation, Rutherford and his post-Reformation contemporaries ascribe a fundamental place in soteriology to union with Christ. This union is initiated at regeneration and maintained throughout the *ordo salutis* by the Holy Spirit. It consists in Christ's being joined together with us and in his life being implanted within us.[96] By speaking of the life of Christ being implanted within us, Rutherford and Calvin do not mean that the resulting union is an essential one; it is not the divine essence that is infused within us.[97] Nor is it a personal union like that between the humanity and divinity of Christ, as the New England Antinomians wrongly believe. Rather, it is a spiritual union, a union in which 'Godis Spirit mak[es] us one with Christ' both by imputation—which applies to our justification—and by participation—i.e., that vital union in which '*Christ* (by His Spirit) *lives in me*' and his life becomes ours in and through the work of the Holy Spirit.[98] This vital union, according to Reformation and post-Reformation thinking, begins at regeneration and continues through faith, repentance, justification,

---

[94] See *WJA*, II, p. 237. Some later disciples like Vorstius appear to have believed that a special work of regenerating grace was not necessary for conversion. See Du Moulin, *Anatomy of Arminianisme*, pp. 299-300.

[95] *Catachisme*, p. 199.

[96] See W. Kolfhaus, *Christusgemeinschaft bei Johannes Calvin, Beiträge zur Geschichte und Lehre der Reformierten Kirche*, vol. 3 (Neukirchen: Buchhandlung des Erziehungsvereins, 1939), p. 80. On union with Christ in Calvin, see M.A. Garcia, 'Life in Christ: The Function of Union with Christ in the *Unio-Duplex Gratia* Structure of Calvin's Soteriology with Special Reference to the Relationship of Justification and Sanctification in Sixteenth-Century Context' (unpublished Ph.D. dissertation, University of Edinburgh, 2004). On union in Rutherford, see Strickland, 'Union with Christ.'

[97] This is one of the problems that Calvin has with Osiander. According to Calvin, Osiander has introduced the 'strange monster of 'essential' righteousness', in which he claims that 'we are substantially righteous in God by the infusion both of his [Christ's] essence and of his quality'. Whereas Calvin agrees that 'we are one with Christ', he denies 'that Christ's essence is mixed with our own'. *Institutes* III.xi.5, pp. 729-31. Cf. Garcia, 'Life in Christ', chapter five.

[98] *Catachisme*, p. 199; *SA*, p. 179; *Influences*, p. 178. See also Strickland, 'Union with Christ', p. 68. Dennis Tamburello understands Calvin's doctrine of union with Christ in this same way. See his *Union with Christ: John Calvin and the Mysticism of St. Bernard* (Louisville, KY: Westminster John Knox, 1994), pp. 86-7.

sanctification, and glorification, undergirding and ensuring each step along the way.[99] It is, as James Ussher says, 'the soule of spirituall life, and [the] fountaine of supernaturall grace' and, as William Perkins remarks, 'the ground of the conveyances of al grace'.[100] Those who have Christ within them, says Rutherford, 'have all things—[they] have "the Father and the Spirit, the word, life, and death"'.[101] Those who do not have Christ within them do not have all things, because, as Calvin explains:

> as long as Christ remains outside of us, and we are separated from him, all that he has suffered and done for the salvation of the human race remains useless and of no value for us. Therefore, to share with us what he has received from the Father, he had to become ours and to dwell within us.[102]

The centrality of this doctrine to Reformed soteriology has led one scholar to argue that union with Christ, rather than predestination, should be considered the 'normative dogma...of the theology of the Reformation'.[103] This is one reason why it is so surprising that Rutherford devotes no space at all to discussing union with Christ in the *Examen*. While this may be because there is little in the Arminian doctrine to offend Rutherford's sensibilities directly, one cannot help but think that Rutherford's oversight has more to do with his failure to think through the implications of the language that Arminius is using to describe his view of union with Christ. Simply put, Rutherford is not known for his leniency and tolerance, especially towards the Arminians. When presented with an opportunity to lash out at them, especially one that reveals the fundamental differences between his system and theirs, it is uncharacteristic of him to pass it over in silence. And Arminius' definition of union with Christ quite obviously reveals those fundamental differences, not only those that pertain to regeneration and conversion but those that pertain to the whole of soteriology as well.

By defining union with Christ as 'being ingrafted into [Christ] by a conformity to his life', Arminius shows that he is emphasizing human activity and obedience. Our conformity to the life of Christ is what unites us to him and, thus, makes us 'partakers of the whole [*vim*] power of his life, and of all the benefits which flow from it'.[104] But, based upon what we have outlined above, Rutherford would argue that our union with Christ depends not on our

---

[99] Such is the case in *Institutes* III.i.1, pp. 537-8; III.ii.24-5, pp. 569-72; III.iii.9, pp. 600-601; III.xi.5, pp. 729ff; Ames, *Marrow*, pp. 123ff; Ussher, *Body of Divinitie*, pp. 192-3; Leigh, *Body of Divinity*, pp. 486-7; Perkins, *Workes*, I, pp. 299-300.
[100] Ussher, *Body of Divinitie*, p. 192; Perkins, *Workes*, I, p. 300.
[101] *Communion*, p. 247. Cf. *Institutes* III.xi.5, pp. 730-31.
[102] *Institutes* III.i.1, p. 537.
[103] J.C. McClelland, 'The Reformed Doctrine of Predestination According to Peter Martyr', *SJT* 8:1 (March 1955), p. 255.
[104] *WJA*, II, p. 404.

obedience but on the Holy Spirit's gracious infusion within us. In other words, according to Rutherford, it is not that we are engrafted into Christ by our obedience to his life but that, just the opposite, we live in obedience to Christ's life *because* we are engrafted into him. Arminius' definition shows his propensity to emphasize the response of the individual over God's initiative, which propensity ultimately arises from the world order that he believes God has put in place—the limited world order of the *potentia ordinata*. The Arminian notion of creation goodness prevents God from infringing upon human free will in any way and from acting immediately by the Holy Spirit in uniting individuals to Christ. The covenant of grace institutes a world order of grace, in which it is now possible for all people to unite themselves to Christ.[105] It is, therefore, surprising, to say the least, that Rutherford would make no mention of this doctrine in the *Examen*. Union with Christ not only reveals Rutherford's continuity with Calvin and the Reformers, but it also epitomizes his soteriological dispute with the Arminians, who, as we will see next, deny the infusion of grace into every faculty of the soul in regeneration and defend staunchly the ability of the individual to resist God's actions in salvation.

The second way in which Rutherford demonstrates his continuity with Reformed thinking and differentiates himself from the Arminians is by applying the renewal of the Holy Spirit in a once-for-all-time manner to 'all the powers of our soul'.[106] Two things present themselves for our consideration here as well. First, Rutherford extends the activity of God in the renewal our souls in regeneration to every faculty within the human psychology. The mind, will, and affections are all immediately corrupted with sin and in need of immediate restoration.[107] And while the Arminians *prima facie* do seem to follow suit by claiming to extend regeneration to 'the human mind and will' and, thus, to 'the whole man', it is not at all clear that they do so in their actual practice.[108] Rutherford and others of his contemporaries, like Pierre Du Moulin for example, accuse the Arminians of leaving the will unaffected by sin after the fall and free from the need for regeneration. Rutherford notes that the Arminians speak accurately about each person's need for the 'Illumination of the mind' and the 'Vivification of the affections' in regeneration but remarks that they leave the will free to 'assent and dissent' as it pleases.[109] Du Moulin also has a similar assessment: 'I finde that they [the Arminians] determine, that

---

[105] The Arminians, to be sure, do not believe that men and women save themselves. Divine grace is necessary—both prevenient grace and co-operating grace. But, as we will see later in this chapter, especially in the section on calling and preparation below, there is a real sense in which the Arminians believe men and women must *faciunt quod in se est* in order to gain salvation.

[106] *Catachisme*, p. 199.

[107] *Examen*, pp. 324-5, 331-2.

[108] *WJA*, II, p. 194.

[109] *Examen*, pp. 333ff, 457.

by the corruption of nature, mans understanding is darkened, and his affections are depraved; but I no where finde in their writings, that his will is of its owne nature depraved and prone to sinne.'[110]

The sentiments of Rutherford and Du Moulin, while ultimately grounded in the truth, are, nonetheless, exaggerated slightly for their polemical purposes. Both men exploit, rather unfairly, what they perceive to be an erroneous philosophy of anthropology among the Arminians. Lying behind the Arminian claims in regard to the human will is a soteriological intellectualism that Rutherford and Du Moulin perceive and eschew.[111] According to this intellectualism, the mind or intellect has causal priority over the will, to the degree that 'the will follows the dictate of the intellect as it proposes the good'.[112] What this means for Arminius is that the will is not immediately affected by the fall in and of itself or, as Du Moulin says, 'of its owne nature', but mediately through the intellect. Because the intellect directs the will even after the fall,[113] and because the intellect is itself darkened by sin, the will too carries the stain of sin and has a corresponding need to be renewed, but only indirectly. That this is actually the case for Arminius is confirmed by the fact that he locates choice within the intellect and then 'transfers' it to the will, because of the close relation between the two:

> The word, *arbitrium*, 'Choice', or 'Free Will', properly signifies both *the faculty of the mind or understanding*, by which the mind is enabled to judge about any thing proposed to it,—and *the judgment itself* which the mind forms according to that faculty. But it is transferred from the Mind to the Will, on account of the very close [*unionem*] connection which subsists between them.[114]

Thus, while Arminius does maintain that the will is corrupted by sin after the fall, the claims of Rutherford and Du Moulin do appear justified to the degree that sin affects the will only indirectly through the intellect. Regeneration, then, need only concern itself with the intellect in order to free the will from its corruption.

This is in contrast to the mainstream of Reformation and post-Reformation anthropology, which, from at least Calvin onwards, has tended to view pre-

---

[110] Du Moulin, *Anatomy of Arminianisme*, pp. 291-2.
[111] See, e.g., *Examen*, pp. 333ff, 456. R.T. Kendall has asserted that Arminius is a voluntarist in regard to his view of faith and salvation (*Calvin and English Calvinism*, pp. 147-9). This claim, however, has been convincingly, if not conclusively, refuted by R.A. Muller in his article, 'The Priority of the Intellect in the Soteriology of Jacob Arminius', *WTJ* 55:1 (Spring 1993), pp. 55-72.
[112] Muller, 'Priority of the Intellect', p. 58.
[113] On this see *WJA*, II, pp. 189, 191-4; and the discussion in Muller, 'Priority of the Intellect', pp. 64-6.
[114] *WJA*, II, p. 189. This takes on further significance when we understand that Arminius defines saving faith as assent. See the discussion in the section on faith below.

lapsarian human nature from an intellectualist perspective but post-lapsarian human nature from a voluntarist perspective.[115] The idea is that whereas before the fall the mind has hegemony over the will to direct it according to a knowledge of the good, after the fall not only has the mind lost its capability of discerning good from evil and directing the will accordingly, but the will itself 'resist[s] truth in the minde...[and] imprison[s it] and cast[s it] in fetters'.[116] Arminius' post-lapsarian intellectualism precludes precisely this hamartiological effect of the will upon the mind. The intellect, although fallen and darkened by sin and needing illumination, remains free to operate 'within the normal [and pre-lapsarian] realm of intellective function'.[117] But, for Rutherford, the intellect cannot and does not function in the same capacity before and after the fall; the rebellion inherent in the post-lapsarian will suppresses the normal function of the intellect. Therefore, as William Ames notes, the 'enlightning of the mind [alone] is not sufficient to produce [conversion]...because it doth not take away that corruption which is in the will'.[118] Every faculty of the human psychology—mind, will, and affections—must, therefore, be directly renewed by God in regeneration, in order to overcome the effects of sin.

Second, when Rutherford states in his catechism that regeneration is a 'renewing [of] all the powers of our soul', he means something different than the Arminians do in regard to the way this is accomplished. According to Rutherford, regeneration involves an infusing of 'habitual grace'—a term that is used widely in Britain from about the 1630s and that traces its roots, with certain adaptations, back to Thomas Bradwardine in the fourteenth century rather than to Aquinas.[119] In the act of regeneration, a *'supernatural habit is infused by God supernaturally'*.[120] Rutherford variously refers to this infused habit (*habitus*) as a 'habit of faith', a 'habit of sanctifying grace', a 'habit of the life of God', a 'habit of grace', a 'habit of supernatural grace',[121] and a 'habit of

---

[115] Cf. *Institutes* I.xv.8, p. 195; and *RD*, pp. 240-43; with *Institutes* II.ii.26-3.14, pp. 286-309. Kendall has also claimed that Calvin's theology should be understood from an intellectualist rather than a voluntarist perspective (*Calvin and English Calvinism*, p. 19). Richard Muller has again convincingly argued against this claim in '*Fides* and *Cognitio* in Relation to the Problem of Intellect and Will in the Theology of John Calvin', *CTJ* 25 (November 1990), pp. 207-24.

[116] *HOC*, p. 16.

[117] Muller, 'Priority of the Intellect', p. 70.

[118] Ames, *Marrow*, p. 127.

[119] See Bradwardine, *De causa Dei contra Pelagium* (London, 1618); Owen, *Works of John Owen*, III, pp. 472ff; and J. Davenant, *A Treatise on Justification, or the Disputatio de justitia habituali et actuali*, trans. J. Allport, 2 vols. (London, 1844-6), chapter 3. Cf. Aquinas, *Summa theologiae*, II.1.109-14.

[120] *Examen*, p. 482.

[121] *Examen*, pp. 436, 455, 473, 485, 489.

sanctification'.[122] Like John Owen, he defines it as 'a fixed disposition infused into the soul by the Lord, purchased by Christs merit of his death', enabling and ensuring our 'perform[ance of] supernatural duties'.[123] Rutherford contrasts this supernatural habit with the 'habit of corruption', which is natural to humankind after the fall of Adam.[124] In regeneration, God removes the habit of corruption—what Rutherford expresses in biblical language as the 'stony heart' (Ezek. 36.26) or sinful nature (Eph. 2.3)—and replaces it with an infused habit of grace, or a 'new heart' and a new nature. All human actions in the economy of salvation flow from this infused habit of grace. Were this not the case, then, to Rutherford's way of thinking, faith, repentance, and all our acts of human obedience would flow from human merit and free will rather than from grace. The only way faith can truly be considered 'the gift of God' and humans can truly be free in receiving this gift is for the habit of faith to be infused within the individual at regeneration, thus enabling and ensuring that he or she will in fact respond in faith.

Such a conception of regeneration is anathema to the Arminians, however. If those who believe do so because they are first infused with the habit of faith, 'then Free Will would be overturned [*everteretur*]'.[125] Regeneration cannot consist in an infusion of habitual grace because that would make human obedience necessary and would eliminate true freedom. It would require God acting in a way that is contrary to the good of his creatures, which is impossible for him after creation. The issue at hand between Rutherford and the Arminians is not whether regeneration is an act of God, nor whether it involves an infusion of grace, nor, even, whether this grace is necessary for faith, but whether regeneration involves an infusion of *habitual* grace.[126] According to the Arminians, it cannot. This would completely rule out human freedom by forcing the individual to live and choose according to this habit. Grace would then become permanent and effectual, and thus irresistible, necessitating the compliance of the human will to the will of God. But how can this be true and significant freedom? Whether one agrees with them or not, it has to be

---

[122] *Christ Dying*, p. 271; *SA*, II, p. 112. Although Rutherford nowhere speaks explicitly of a definitive sanctification, the idea lying behind such a doctrine is roughly analogous to his understanding of habitual grace infused at regeneration. But this appears to be out of step with the doctrine as it is elucidated by John Murray. As Murray explains, definitive sanctification is a fruit of union with Christ, which is itself initiated at regeneration, and, so, it must be distinguished from regeneration and should not be 'subsume[d]' under it (J. Murray, 'Definitive Sanctification', *CTJ* 2 [April 1967], p. 12). For Rutherford, however, definitive sanctification, so called, clearly falls under the auspices of regeneration.

[123] *Influences*, p. 218. For similar post-Reformation conceptions of habitual grace, see, e.g., Ames, *Marrow*, pp. 126-7; and Leigh, *Body of Divinity*, p. 486.

[124] *Examen*, p. 454.

[125] *Examen*, p. 485.

[126] See *WJA*, I, pp. 659-64.

acknowledged that they raise a point that cannot be easily ignored. How can Rutherford and the Reformed maintain that God regenerates by infusing a habit of grace and, at the same time, that we humans truly have free will?

GRACE AND FREE WILL

Rutherford and the Reformed in general plainly assert the reality of human free will. But they mean something different by freedom than do the Arminians. For Rutherford, human freedom consists primarily in two things: a freedom from external compulsion (*immunitatem a coactio*) and a freedom from natural necessity.[127] In regard to the former, there is very little, if any, difference of opinion among church fathers, Pelagians, scholastics, reformers, papists, post-reformers, and Arminians; they are all in agreement with Edward Leigh, that 'no external principle can compel [an individual] to work' without violating his or her free will.[128] In regard to the latter, there is also very little disagreement, at least insofar as Rutherford is defining it. Common sense (*communis sententia*), Rutherford says, tells us that human freedom can only act in one of two ways. Either it acts necessarily (*necessario*), that is, 'naturaliter, ex interno principio'—as fire does when it naturally and necessarily consumes everything in its path—or it acts freely, which means that 'potest vel operari, vel non'.[129] As Rutherford sees it, human freedom falls into the second category. The will 'naturally' has the freedom of choosing and refusing; it can either act or refuse to act. It is not like fire, which is forced into acting by its own 'internal principle'. And when it does act, the resulting choice will be, in the words of Zacharias Ursinus, 'in accordance with...its nature, and to enjoy the good things suited to it'.[130]

For Calvin, a freedom from internal necessity is part and parcel of what it means to be free from compulsion. Unlike Rutherford, Calvin does not distinguish between external compulsion and internal necessity, and thankfully so, too.[131] Rutherford's view of free will is rather difficult to grasp precisely because he uses terms like compulsion and necessity interchangeably.

---

[127] *Exercitationes*, pp. 1, 6-7.

[128] Leigh, *Body of Divinity*, p. 496. See the entire discussions in Leigh, *Body of Divinity*, pp. 495-9; Vermigli, *Common Places*, II.ii, pp. 252-80; Perkins, *Workes*, I, pp. 558-61, 717-46; and *WJA*, II, pp. 189-96.

[129] *Exercitationes*, p. 1.

[130] *RD*, p. 244.

[131] In an article aimed at replying to Vincent Brümmer's views of free will in Calvin (i.e., V. Brümmer, 'Calvin, Bernard and the Freedom of the Will', *Religious Studies* 30 [1994], pp. 437-55), Paul Helm has helpfully shown that '[t]o be free from compulsion is not, for Calvin, to be indeterministically free, but to be psychologically free, to be acting in accordance with one's particular preferences'. See Helm, 'Calvin and Bernard on Freedom and Necessity: A Reply to Brümmer', *Religious Studies* 30 (1994), p. 461. Psychological freedom, so called, would, thus, appear to take into consideration both elements of Rutherford's freedom, external compulsion and internal necessity.

Sometimes he uses the term *coactio* to refer to external compulsion and at other times he uses it to refer to necessity, in an Augustinian and Calvinian sense (of which more will be said in a few moments). At times he speaks of natural necessity in terms of an internal principle (i.e., the example of fire) and at other times he uses the same phrase to refer to a necessity that arises as a result of our nature or of God's nature.[132] In spite of this difficulty, however, it does appear that Rutherford is following the lead of 'Theologi nostri', among whom he includes men like Calvin, Augustine, Bonaventure, Lombard, and Aquinas—especially insofar as the last four are read through the interpretive lens of the Reformation.[133] In order to show his continuity with Reformation thought and to develop Rutherford's own views in more detail, we must examine human freedom in each of the following four states of human nature—pre-lapsarian, post-lapsarian, post-regeneration, and post-mortem.[134]

In the post-creation, pre-lapsarian state, Rutherford, like Edward Leigh, identifies free will as consisting of two parts: (1) a natural freedom to choose, apart from external compulsion and internal necessity, and (2) an inclination (*inclinatio*) towards using that freedom to choose the good, or, what Leigh calls a 'Sanctified freedom'.[135] The point that Rutherford, Leigh, and the Reformed are seeking to overturn, in speaking this way, is the Lutheran and Arminian assertion that the will is indifferent in its choosing.[136] To the post-Reformation

---

[132] E.g., Rutherford states that the nature of freedom exists in 'immunitatem a coactione' and then adds that it 'naturali etiam necessitate ortam'. But he has just overtly stated that freedom is both a freedom from compulsion (*coactio*) and a freedom from natural necessity (e.g., fire). Cf. *Exercitationes*, pp. 1, with 6-7.

[133] During the Reformation, there was (and has been for centuries since then) disagreement over how Augustine, in particular, and later scholastics, in general, were to be understood on the issue of free will. Calvin devoted a specific treatise to answering the Dutch Roman Catholic Albert Pighius (*The Bondage and Liberation of the Will: A Defence of the Orthodox Doctrine of Human Choice against Pighius*, ed. A.N.S. Lane, trans. G.I. Davies [Grand Rapids, MI: Baker, 1996]), in which he attempted to demonstrate conclusively that his—and the Reformation's—interpretation of Augustine, and those who followed him, was the correct one. The current thesis is, therefore, more interested in knowing where Rutherford's view of free will stands in relation to Augustine, and to later Augustinians, as it is understood by reformers like Calvin, than in knowing where it stands in relation to Augustine, and later Augustinians, *per se*, even though the editor of Calvin's treatise, A.N.S. Lane, has stated that 'it is very widely conceded today that the main thrust [of Calvin's interpretation of Augustine] is accurate' (*Bondage and Liberation of the Will*, p. xxiv). For a sample of the views of the above-mentioned men on free will, see, e.g., Calvin, *Bondage and Liberation of the Will*, especially, pp. xix-xxi, 67-9; Aquinas, *Summa theologiae* Ia.82.1, Ia.83.1-3; Lombard, *Sententiae* II.xxv.1-9, I, pp. 461-9; and Augustine, *City of God* 22.30, II, p. 542.

[134] *Exercitationes*, pp. 6-7.

[135] Leigh, *Body of Divinity*, p. 495.

[136] On the Lutherans, see Muller, *Dictionary*, p. 177. On the Arminians, see the above examination of intellectualism in Arminius and its effects upon the will (in the section

mind, the essence of freedom cannot consist in indifference to good and evil. For, if such indifference is the determining feature of free will, then, according to Leigh, 'so God and the good Angels should not be free, seeing they cannot will anything but that which is good'.[137]

It is at this juncture that a slight difference arises between Rutherford and Calvin. Whereas free will, or *liberum arbitrium*, is, for Rutherford, the ability of choosing or refusing the greatest good according to the individual's nature, for Calvin, it is more than that; it is the ability actually to choose the good.[138] The only real consequence that comes from this difference is that Rutherford can rightly say that the post-lapsarian individual still has *liberum arbitrium*, whereas Calvin cannot. For Calvin, the individual no longer has *liberum arbitrium* after Adam's fall but only *arbitrium*.[139] The bottom line, however, is that no real discrepancy exists between these two men. Calvin would agree with Rutherford, in the way that the latter is defining *liberum arbitrium*, and the same can be said for Rutherford. The slight difference that there is all but disappears when it is applied to the pre-lapsarian state. For both Rutherford and Calvin, the pre-lapsarian will is not indifferent to good and evil, nor is it inclined to sin, but wholly 'inclinabatur ad Dei legem praestandam'.[140] And Adam's original freedom consists, for both, not in the freedom either to obey or disobey with equal propensity, but in the freedom to obey God perfectly.

This should not suggest, however, that Adam's will, like God's, cannot choose anything except that which is good. Adam was created with a mutable will, one that was dependent upon God's gracious support in order for him to continue willing the good. In other words, while Adam does not have an inclination to evil (*inclinatio ad malum*) in his pre-lapsarian state, he does have the natural power (*potentia naturalis*) to resist and reject God's gracious support. To borrow Augustinian categories, Adam is *posse peccare et posse non peccare*, despite his being inclined to the good. Following the general trend among the Reformed—including such men as Calvin, Polanus, Leigh, Cocceius, and Perkins—Rutherford could, therefore, say that Adam's fall into sin is the result of the mutability of the powers of his will rather than of the nature of the *liberum arbitrium*. Adam sins not because his will, which is indifferent to good and evil, somehow selects the latter over the former, but because the powers of his will change from consenting with to rejecting both God and his gracious support.[141] Perkins helpfully explains this by saying that,

---

on regeneration) and the remainder of what follows below. Cf. *Exercitationes*, p. 4; *Christ Dying*, p. 326.

[137] Leigh, *Body of Divinity*, p. 498.

[138] Helm, 'Calvin and Bernard on Freedom', p. 459.

[139] Calvin, *Bondage and Liberation of the Will*, pp. 67-9.

[140] *Exercitationes*, p. 4.

[141] *Exercitationes*, pp. 2-7. Cf. *RD*, pp. 242-8; Calvin, *Bondage and Liberation of the Will*, pp. 67-9; *Institutes* I.xv.8, pp. 195-6; and Perkins, *Workes*, I, pp. 727-8.

in addition to 'the goodnes of his will', Adam also 'received of God a power constantly to persevere in goodnes, if he would'. But, God himself did not actually preserve Adam in his original state. Rather, 'the act of perseverance was left to the choice and liberty of his [Adam's] own [mutable] will'.[142] And, as a result, Adam fell, and he and all those he represents in the covenant of works lost the inclination to good and, along with it, the natural power of obeying God.

In turning to look at the post-lapsarian individual, we are confronted once again with the above-mentioned difference between Rutherford and Calvin. For Rutherford, the post-lapsarian will is free, in that it is not forced to act by external compulsion or by internal necessity. Although Calvin would agree with this definition as it is given, it is not the way he chooses to speak. For Calvin, the post-lapsarian will is no longer free, in the sense that it cannot, as a result of the fall, freely choose the good—i.e., it cannot please God. It remains 'self-determined' and free from coercion, but it is now 'bound' by 'man's innate wickedness'.[143] And while Rutherford would agree that the post-lapsarian will cannot please God, he would attribute this not to a loss of free will *per se*, but to a loss of Adam's original inclination to good and to the acquisition of a new and sinful nature.

Even taking this difference into account, there is still a sense in which the post-lapsarian individual is both free and not free for Rutherford and Calvin. He or she is free, insofar as each retains the natural freedom to choose or to refuse according to the greatest good without any external compulsion or internal necessity forcing the decision (*arbitrium*, for Calvin, and *liberum arbitrium*, for Rutherford). But he or she is not free, insofar as each has lost what Leigh referred to as 'Sanctified freedom'. This means, in both Calvin and Rutherford, that the post-lapsarian individual has lost the ability to use natural freedom in the way that he or she ought, i.e., in the way that God commands. Although the individual can still choose the greatest good—that is, the best option which is contained in the mind—he or she cannot choose God's good. In addition to this, the 'Sanctified freedom' of Adam's pre-lapsarian nature has now, as a result of the fall, been replaced with a sin nature, such that Rutherford can say in language that is reminiscent of Calvin and Luther, 'servitus quidem & vitiosa ad peccandum inclinatio inest homini', and he or she is powerless to do anything about it.[144]

Thus, according to Rutherford, and this is where the complexity comes in, the post-lapsarian person is free from external compulsion and from internal natural necessity but is not free from the necessity of his or her sinful nature. The will is 'self-determined', insofar as it 'voluntarily' wills of its own accord,

---

[142] Perkins, *Workes*, I, p. 728.

[143] Calvin, *Bondage and Liberation of the Will*, p. 69.

[144] *Exercitationes*, p. 5. Cf. *Institutes* II.iii.5, pp. 294-6; idem, *Bondage and Liberation of the Will*, p. xx; and Luther, *De servo arbitrio*, in *WA*, XVIII, pp. 600-787.

but it wills necessarily as it is in bondage to sin and death.[145] This necessity, for reformers like Calvin, Luther, and Vermigli, and for post-Reformation theologians like Perkins, Leigh, and Rutherford, all of whom are consciously following in the way of Augustine, does not preclude the idea of human freedom, because, as we have already seen, God himself wills freely and, yet, necessarily for good and not for evil.[146] Human freedom after the fall consists in the absence of compulsion, for Calvin, and in the absence of both external compulsion and internal natural necessity, for Rutherford and for Leigh, but not in the absence of the necessity of our sinful nature. To use biblical language, the post-lapsarian individual is dead in sins and trespasses and wholly incapable of any spiritual good. To use Augustinian language, he or she is *non posse non peccare*. Even the best deeds that he or she may perform are now simply '*splendid sins*',[147] because they either spring from sinful motivations (rather than a love for Christ) or are done for sinful purposes (rather than to give all glory and praise to God). Our only hope is *Deus in nobis*, granting us a new power (*nova potentia*)—but not, in Rutherford's thinking anyway, a new freedom (*nova libertas*)—by implanting within us a sanctified inclination (a habit of grace) and removing from us the inclination to sin (the habit of corruption), so that we can once again live in conscious dependence upon God.

Although the post-regeneration individual has received the sanctified inclination, as Rutherford would refer to it, or the restored *liberum arbitrium*, as Calvin would, this does not mean that he or she is thrust back into the very same condition as pre-lapsarian Adam. For one thing, the new inclination, or freedom, is not perfect, as it was in Adam. It exists in seed form only and will grow in a process of sanctification that lasts the entire course of the believer's life.[148] For another thing, while it is true that the root of sin has been destroyed in the removal of the inclination to sin, the branches still remain and are alive and well in every faculty of the human psychology. Here too, the process of dealing with branch-sin is part and parcel of progressive sanctification. The infused habit of grace is effectual unto salvation; it ensures that the individual will freely but necessarily embrace Christ by faith and freely but necessarily persevere in that faith. It also ensures that the believer is capable of obeying God. Even though sin and, thus, disobedience, remains, the new inclination ensures that the Christian is, in the words of Augustine, *posse non peccare*. Once the process of sanctification is complete, however, the individual will enjoy perfection in the final state—post-mortem—in which it will be impossible to sin (*non posse peccare*), not only because he or she is fully

---

[145] *Exercitationes*, pp. 4-5; Calvin, *Bondage and Liberation of the Will*, p. 69.
[146] See, e.g., the discussions in Calvin, *Bondage and Liberation of the Will*, pp. xix-xx, 69; Vermigli, *Common Places*, II.ii.6, p. 256; Perkins, *Workes*, I, p. 558; Leigh, *Body of Divinity*, p. 496.
[147] *Examen*, p. 347.
[148] Sanctification will be discussed in more detail below.

sanctified (as was Adam) but also because the individual's will is no longer mutable.[149] Free will exists in these two final states, for Rutherford and for Calvin, insofar as it free from compulsion but not from necessity.

As far as the Arminians are concerned, such a conception of freedom wholly misses the mark. Freedom, they say, cannot consist in necessity of any kind, 'whether...from an external cause compelling, or from a nature inwardly determining absolutely to one thing'.[150] In either case, the will would not be free to choose but would simply be operating according to predetermined criteria. The Arminians see any kind of necessity as undermining 'man's proper dignity' by making him 'a puppet' and not free.[151] Freedom from necessity, Arminius claims, 'is by nature situated in the will, as its proper attribute, so that there cannot be any will if it be not free'.[152] The will must, therefore, be equally able to choose either the good or the evil presented to it by the mind, both before and after the fall.

These statements, more than anything else, are products of Arminius' desire to reconcile human freedom with the grace and justice of God. Contrary to what Rutherford might think, Arminius is not trying to detract from the glory of God's grace. He explicitly states that he in no way wishes to do 'the least injury to Divine Grace, by taking from it any thing that belongs to it'. And, so, he peppers his writings with phrases that exalt divine grace by teaching the utter impossibility of salvation apart from it. But, at the same time, Arminius is wrestling, and quite commendably so, with how it is that God could be just and yet create individuals who have no chance at all of being saved, as Rutherford's system would seem to require.[153] How could God justly require certain things of all people if he knows that it is impossible for them to fulfill those things? How could God do this all the while holding the sole efficacious means of anyone's fulfilling them? The only thing that makes sense of these issues, according to the Arminians, is for human beings to be free from all necessity and, thus, for grace to be resistible.

> For in vain and without cause doth he [God] command this Obedience, and require it of another, and promise to reward the Obedience, who himself both ought and will work the very act of Obedience by such a force as cannot be resisted; and ineptly & against reason is he rewarded, as one truly and really

---

[149] *Exercitationes*, pp. 4-5. The post-mortem will is immutable, because God himself provides the ingredient that was missing from the Garden of Eden, i.e., perseverance. See Perkins, *Workes*, I, p. 728.

[150] *WJA*, II, p. 190.

[151] Sell, *The Great Debate*, p. 17.

[152] *WJA*, II, p. 190.

[153] *WJA*, II, pp. 52, 189-96, 700-701; I, pp. 659-60. Arminius is desirous to protect God's right to will what he pleases to will, but not at the cost of his justice, because, for Arminius, God's will is 'circumscribed within the bounds of justice' (Sell, *The Great Debate*, p. 13).

Obedient, in whom this very Obedience is effected by such a kind of force of another's. Lastly, punishment, especially eternal, is unjustly and cruelly inflicted on him, by whom this Obedience is not performed through the sole and alone defect of that irresistible Grace.[154]

In Rutherford's opinion, however, grace does not have to be resistible in order for humans to be genuinely free. Grace does not compel the will to act against its desires. It changes its desires so that it will necessarily but freely and always choose for God. The key, for Rutherford, lies in the will's desires or inclination. Once the Holy Spirit gives a new inclination, infuses a new power into the will, and illumines the mind to understand the greatest good (not just subjectively speaking, as before regeneration, but objectively speaking as well, i.e., God himself), the will freely and assuredly chooses that greatest good. But, having said this, it should be obvious that what lies at the heart of Rutherford's expression of free will and the irresistibility of grace is the premotionism that we discussed in chapter three. God's grace is irresistible because it 'moves [*movet*] free will [*liberam voluntatem*] in such a way that it [i.e., the will] would move itself most freely to that same [end] to which it is pre-moved [*praemovetur*] by God'. Note that Rutherford does not say that grace moves *liberum arbitrium*; that would be compulsion. Grace moves the *voluntas*, or the faculty of the will. The *voluntas* then chooses freely (*liberum arbitrium*), but necessarily, according to its new inclination and power.[155]

In his treatise against Albert Pighius (c.1490-1542), John Calvin expresses an identical opinion concerning the relationship between human freedom and divine grace:

> We acknowledge that the human mind sees, but when it has been enlightened. [We acknowledge that] human judgment decides and chooses, but under the control of the Spirit's guidance. [We acknowledge that] the human heart is willing, but after it has been remade by the hand of God. [We acknowledge that] man himself endeavours and acts and applies his powers to obedience to God, but in accordance with the measure of the grace which he has received.[156]

When we contrast this kind of thinking with the Arminian cooperationism, we see the theological basis upon which the differences between Rutherford and the Arminians are founded. God's grace is not needed to pre-move the individual in the Arminian system. God creates humankind with the necessary freedom and ability to will and move in cooperation with him. The Arminian cooperationism is no less gracious than the premotionism of the Reformed, but it is more resistible, in fact, altogether so.

Rutherford believes that the Arminian understanding of grace and free will

---

[154] *Confession*, p. 206.
[155] *Examen*, pp. 486-7.
[156] Calvin, *Bondage and Liberation of the Will*, p. 200.

contradicts the teaching of Scripture and right reason. He demonstrates this by offering no less than nineteen proofs that establish—to his way of thinking anyway—the irresistibility of grace. His arguments can be condensed into three overarching categories. First, the Bible teaches that God's grace always operates according to divine omnipotency, which cannot be resisted. Thus, God is said to bring about (*efficit*) 'faith in us by his own *strength and power*, [the same strength and power] *by which he raised Christ from the dead*, Eph. 1.18, 19'; to obtain the salvation of many 'by [his own] will and power' (Matt. 19.16; John 10.29; Rom. 1.16; 11.23; 15.13; 16.25; Jude 24; 1 Pet. 1.5); and to work out unfailingly his own 'decrees of election', 'his plans', and 'his intentions' (Psal. 33.10; Isa. 14.26-7; 46.10-11). Secondly, God's salvific grace is irresistible by definition. When God regenerates, he necessarily 'takes away both resistance and resistibility', by removing '*the stony heart*'—which is 'the habitual principle [*principium*] of resisting the calling of God'—and replacing it with a 'new heart', thereby ensuring (*efficit*) that his creatures will respond in obedience to his call. Because regeneration, by definition, involves an infused habit, all who are thus regenerated are invariably justified and glorified.[157] Thirdly, Rutherford argues that the doctrine of resistible grace creates two pastoral problems: it renders prayer for conversion meaningless, and it ultimately detracts from the glory of God by ascribing it to the individual instead. While all of these arguments are slightly exaggerated, especially the claims in regard to the pastoral problems caused by Arminianism, it is still fair to say with Rutherford that the Arminian understanding of grace and free will is 'diametrically opposed' to his own.[158]

More than anything else, the aforementioned arguments in support of the resistibility of grace only confirm to Rutherford that the Arminians are indeed 'New *Pelagians*'.[159] In the *Examen*, Rutherford repeatedly accuses the Arminians of Pelagianism and even enters into a five-page diatribe in which he associates the doctrines of Arminianism with those of the Pelagians and Semi-Pelagians, raising eleven points of similarity.[160] Rather than entering here into an exhaustive examination of each of these points to determine its validity—a digression that would take us well beyond what we can do in the space that we have—we will instead concentrate on three factors that should help us to evaluate Rutherford's claims and, in addition, his relationship to Calvin and the Reformation. First, it must be said that Arminius goes to great lengths to differentiate his views from those of the Pelagians. In regard to free will, for example, he says that it 'is unable to begin or to perfect any true and spiritual

---

[157] In order to prove this point, Rutherford cites the following biblical texts: Ezek. 11.19-20; 36.26-7; Deut. 30.6; Jer. 24.7; 31.33-4; John 6.44-5; 14.16; Phil. 2.13; and Rom. 8.29-30.

[158] *Examen*, pp. 458-64.

[159] *Christ Dying*, p. 326; *Examen*, p. 504.

[160] *Examen*, pp. 357-62.

good, without Grace'. And then he adds: 'That I may not be said, like Pelagius, to practise delusion with regard to the word "Grace", I mean by it that which is the Grace of Christ and which belongs to regeneration.'[161] Although there are areas of similarity between Arminius and the Pelagians, which Arminius himself acknowledges, there are also areas of similarity between the Calvinists and the Manicheans and Stoics. Both Rutherford and the Arminians are painstaking in distinguishing themselves from Manicheism or Stoicism, on the one hand, and Pelagianism, on the other. Second, Arminius' professed intention in crafting his doctrine of free will is to get at Christian truth by charting a *via media* between the Scylla of Pelagianism and the Charybdis of Manicheism, the very thing that Augustine himself was attempting to do as well.[162] Third, Rutherford's association of the Arminian doctrines of free will and grace with the heresy of Pelagianism is itself enough to stand him in close approximation to the Reformation. If, as Susan Schreiner argues, the Reformation is basically 'a continuation of late medieval attacks on the resurgence of semi-Pelagianism' and if, as Schreiner says, its theology is chiefly a reaction to the Pelagian doctrines of human nature and justification, then it follows that, in directing his life's efforts to refuting the Arminians—who were self-professed semi-Pelagians—and to overturning the Pelagian doctrines of human nature and justification that he perceived in their theology, Rutherford is demonstrating a clear affinity with men like Luther and Zwingli, and even Calvin himself.[163]

In light of these three facts, it would appear that Rutherford perceives that he is taking up the mantle of the reformers by fighting a similar battle over similar views regarding grace and free will. He sees himself as representing the theological seed of the Reformation and as taking up arms against the progeny of Erasmus and Pighius. But he also reveals a deep-seated intolerance towards Arminian theology. Rutherford is not interested in engaging in a meaningful dialogue with the Arminians. Dialoguing with them would only give them a measure of credibility, something he apparently is not willing to have happen. By employing the epithet 'Pelagian' in describing Arminian theology, Rutherford is placing himself in league with the pious and the orthodox of the Reformation and the Arminians in league with the devil and untruth. The significance of this will be more apparent in chapter five, after we examine the grounds for Rutherford's systematic opposition to Arminianism.

---

[161] *WJA*, II, p. 700. Later Arminians effectively embraced the Pelagian heresy by denying that 'the effective operation of inward grace is necessary for conversion'. Vorstius is to be numbered among this group. See W. Ames, *De conscientia* IV.iv.10 (Oxford, 1659), p. 172; Du Moulin, *Anatomy of Arminianisme*, pp. 299-300.
[162] *WJA*, II, pp. 56-7.
[163] S.E. Schreiner, 'Pelagianism', in *The Oxford Encyclopedia of the Reformation*, ed. H.J. Hilderbrand, 4 vols. (New York: Oxford University, 1996), III, pp. 238-9. See Calvin, *Bondage and Liberation of the Will*, e.g., pp. 189-91; and Luther, *De servo arbitrio*.

Rutherford's intolerance of the Arminian view of grace and free will aside, it must be said in defense of their view that it is just as biblically-derived and just as biblically-defended as is Rutherford's view. Both parties in this dispute are wrestling with the relationship of God's sovereignty to human freedom without diminishing either, and all within the bounds of biblical Christianity. But the answers they give in order to resolve this relationship are diametrically opposed to one another. Whereas Arminius' theistic intellectualism requires that he perceive human free will as significant and divine grace as resistible, Rutherford's voluntarism ensures that he will see both from the opposite perspective. Because God is good and just, the Arminians believe, he cannot impose upon human free will in any way after creation. To do so, by requiring free will to act necessarily, is unjust for God and a contradiction of creation goodness. On the other hand, Rutherford's theistic voluntarism understands the divine will to be a rule unto itself. God can do whatever he pleases, and because he pleases to do it, it is, therefore, right and just. This means that, for Rutherford, it is no violation of divine justice or goodness for God to decree an individual's end absolutely, without regard to his or her free choice. The Arminian system emphasizes the justice and goodness of God towards humankind more than the justice and goodness of God towards himself. Rutherford perceives that the Arminian system places too much weight on the human side of the continuum, and so he consciously sets up his camp on the opposite side. He would 'rather contend for the Lord and grace, than for the creature and free will'.[164]

CALLING AND PREPARATION

Many contemporary theologians, who embrace the idea of an *ordo salutis*, place calling before regeneration in logical order.[165] But Rutherford, following Calvin, places it under the umbrella of regeneration, broadly speaking.[166] A similar tendency is also reflected in Perkins' *A Golden Chaine*, in Ames' *Marrow of Sacred Divinity*, and in the Westminster Confession of Faith, which has no separate chapter on regeneration but speaks of calling as being synonymous with it.[167] According to Rutherford, 'Godis proper work' in

---

[164] *Christ Dying*, p. 330.
[165] Among the theologians who do this are, H. Bavinck, *Gereformeerde Dogmatiek* (Kampen: Bos, 21906-11), IV; J. Murray, *Redemption Accomplished and Applied* (Grand Rapids, MI: Eerdmans, 1955), p. 87; and C. Hodge, *Systematic Theology*, 3 vols. (London and Edinburgh: Thomas Nelson and Sons, 1883), II, p. 639; and III, p. 3.
[166] Calvin refers to regeneration as the beginning of salvation and defines it in terms that are virtually identical with Rutherford. See *Institutes* II.iii.6, p. 297; and R.S. Wallace, *Calvin's Doctrine of the Christian Life* (Edinburgh and London: Oliver and Boyd, 1959), p. 88.
[167] Perkins, *Workes*, I, pp. 9-116; Ames, *Marrow*, p. 126; WCF chapter 10, specifically cf. § 1 with § 3. Ames actually speaks of calling, conversion, and regeneration interchangeably. It is not until later in the seventeenth century that regeneration becomes

regeneration is one in which he calls his people to himself in two ways: 'He calleth us by the Word outwardlie'—what the reformers and reformed orthodox both referred to as a *vocatio externa*—and he 'infuseth in us grace to obey the calling, q^{lk} [quhilk = which] is his inward calling'—or *vocatio interna*.[168] In other words, God accomplishes the regeneration of an individual by first calling him or her externally, through the preaching of the Word and, thereby, preparing him or her to receive his internal call, which is the infusion of habitual and effectual grace into every faculty of the soul. Whereas the external call is inefficacious—although it is preparative—the internal call is wholly effectual in producing the faith and obedience that God requires.[169]

Recently, Charles Bell has argued that Rutherford's emphasis on preparation going before effectual calling is proof positive that J.B. Torrance is correct in his claim that federalists, like Rutherford, reversed Calvin's emphasis on grace coming before law in God's saving economy.[170] Bell cites from Rutherford's catechism and sundry others of his works as evidence that Rutherford places 'preparation for faith [as a step before effectual calling] in his *ordo salutis*, thereby subordinating grace and gospel to law'.[171] And, *prima facie*, from the statements Bell cites, it does seem as though he is correct. For instance, in response to the question of whether preparation goes before God's effectual calling, Rutherford says: 'Yes, God casteth us downe with the terrours of the law, making us see our miserable estait.'[172] In *Christ Dying*, Rutherford also affirms that certain preparations must precede faith, even going so far as to use absolute language to express their necessity in this process:

> [It is] unpossible, that any can beleeve, but some preparation fore-going there must be; and because *all sinners as sinners* have not such preparation, *all sinners as sinners* are not at the first clap, to beleeve in the soule Physitian *Christ*, but onely such as in *Christs* order are plowed, ere *Christ* sow on them, and selfe-condemned ere they beleeve in *Christ*.[173]

When these statements are reflected upon more deeply, however, and especially

---

distinguished from calling. See, e.g., the work of Owen in this regard (*Works of John Owen*, III, pp. 188-366).

[168] *Catachisme*, p. 199.

[169] *Examen*, pp. 476-7.

[170] Torrance's claims appear in a series of articles, including: 'Covenant or Contract?', pp. 51-76; 'The Covenant Concept', pp. 225-43; 'Strengths and Weaknesses of Westminster Theology', pp. 40-53; 'Incarnation and "Limited Atonement"', pp. 83-94; and 'Interpreting the Word by the Light of Christ or the Light of Nature? Calvin, Calvinism and Barth', in *Calviniana: Ideas and Influence of Jean Calvin*, ed. R.V. Schnucker (Kirksville, MO: Sixteenth Century Journal, 1988), pp. 256-67.

[171] Bell, *Calvin and Scottish Theology*, p. 77.

[172] *Catachisme*, p. 201.

[173] *Christ Dying*, p. 103.

when they are juxtaposed with other statements from his writings, and particularly from the *Examen*, Bell's conclusions (and those of Torrance as well) are shown to be suspect. The following three arguments will not only demonstrate this but will also provide a necessary jumping-off point for us to examine some of the differences between Rutherford and the Arminians in more detail.

First, Rutherford's comments regarding preparation must be interpreted in light of his conviction that God is in no way required to avail himself of external preparations in calling an individual inwardly and effectually to himself. This is simply the norm that he chooses to employ to do so. God ordinarily (*ordinarie*) uses external means, 'such as *to read* and *to hear* the word', in preparing an individual to receive his grace.[174] But, in keeping with his theistic voluntarism, Rutherford believes that God retains the freedom to work without regard to such external devices, according to his good pleasure: 'I dare not peremptorily say, that God useth no prerogative Royall, or no priveledges of Soveraignty, in the conversion of some.'[175]

Secondly, the suggestion that Rutherford places law before grace is one that completely overlooks the overt comments that he makes in regard to the gracious nature and intention of the law. As we saw above in regard to Rutherford's view of the covenant of works,[176] and as E.F. Kevan has conclusively demonstrated in the theology of the Puritans, the law was not so much intended as an end in itself but as a means of grace and of pointing ahead to Christ.[177] Rutherford has no trouble at all in attributing the preparations of the law to divine 'Grace', although they can neither merit nor ensure salvation in any way. Those men and women who are called externally by the gospel are led physically and materially (*conducentiam Physicam & materialem*) 'by the grace of God'. But Rutherford is clear that this grace is of a different kind than 'saving grace'.[178] Preparations, while gracious, do not guarantee that saving and effectual grace will be applied to us, because they 'have no effective influence to produce our conversion'; nor do they have 'any promise of Christ annexed to them'.[179]

This is actually a key question for Rutherford in the *Examen* in his dispute with the Arminians. As he understands it, the Arminians believe that

---

[174] *Examen*, p. 337.

[175] *Christ Dying*, p. 244.

[176] Bell correctly recognizes the gracious nature of the covenant of works by pointing out that Rutherford disregards Robert Rollock's terminology, 'natural covenant'. But he incorrectly claims that Rutherford undoes this gracious emphasis and reverts back to a legalist interpretation. Bell, 'Saving Faith and Assurance of Salvation in the Teaching of John Calvin and Scottish Theology' (unpublished Ph.D. dissertation, Aberdeen University, 1982), p. 105.

[177] Kevan, *The Grace of Law*, especially pp. 119-26. Cf. *COL*, pp. 2-3.

[178] *Examen*, p. 338; *Tryal*, p. 225.

[179] *Christ Dying*, pp. 240-41.

'preparations have, of themselves, necessary connections [*nexum*] with the grace of Conversion'. Because of this, Rutherford associates the Arminian doctrine of preparation with the Jesuit view of *facere quod in se est*, as it is classically set forth by Luis de Molina in his *Concordia liberi arbitrii cum gratiae donis, divina praescientia, providentia, praedestinatione et reprobatione*.[180] And while Rutherford makes no effort to substantiate his claim or to be charitable to the Arminians in the least, his contention does appear to be justified in the main. The similarities between the Jesuit Molina and Arminius extend beyond their common acceptance of cooperationism and *scientia media*. Both Molina and Arminius disregard 'Luther's insight into the nature of grace as the unmerited favor of God', and prefer instead to think of grace 'as a sort of divine assistance or power given to men to enable them to perform certain [preparatory] acts, which they in their corrupted natural state could not do' in and of themselves. Such grace is prevenient and universally available to all people without exception. It assists them *facere quod in se est* in such a creative way that grace can seemingly remain the cause of human good and, yet, significant human freedom can be maintained. God's 'particular concurrence' in prevenient grace differs slightly from his 'general concurrence', which we outlined in the previous chapter. In the particular divine action of prevenient grace, God acts *on* the will rather than *with* it, as he does in his general concurrence. In effect, then, God pre-moves—to borrow the language of the premotionist—once and for all time in a universal way to grant all people the ability to respond to (or to reject) his divine initiative in salvation.[181] The individual who freely responds, *faciendo quod in se est*, and, thus, shows a '[s]erious sorrow on account of sin', can be assured that God, 'according to the multitude of his mercies', will be 'moved to bestow [efficacious, secondary, subsequent, and saving] grace' upon him or her.[182] The genius of this position is lost on Rutherford, who sees it as ascribing a status to post-lapsarian human ability that is far too grandiose and entirely unwarranted.

Rutherford's contention is that such a view exalts human ability to the status of being a co-operator with God in salvation. True it does not exalt human activity above divine grace, because all human action unto salvation is founded upon God's grace, whether that 'grace [*praevenit*] goes before, accompanies, [or] follows' after human action.[183] But it does make God's efficacious grace,

---

[180] *Examen*, p. 335, cf. pp. 334-42. Heiko Oberman has traced the origins of the phrase *facere quod in se est* to the Ambrosiaster, 'which interprets the justice of God as the merciful acceptance of those who seek their refuge with him'. The phrase appears to have exerted tremendous influence within scholasticism generally, beginning with Alexander of Hales and the old Franciscan school, but with slight nuances. See Oberman, *Harvest of Medieval Theology*, pp. 132-45.

[181] Craig, *The Problem of Divine Foreknowledge*, pp. 204-5.

[182] *WJA*, II, p. 18.

[183] *WJA*, II, p. 700.

Soteriology

and, thus, his salvific will (his *voluntas beneplaciti*), to be dependent upon human *liberum arbitrium*. God is not able to show mercy on whom he will and to harden whom he will; he is required to show mercy to those who 'do what is in them' with the help of prevenient grace, and he is prohibited from showing mercy to those who do not 'do what is in them'.[184] And while there is truth in this, the Arminian would counter by saying that God chooses those upon whom he will and will not show his saving mercy, by choosing those whom he will and will not create, having foreknown their free decisions ahead of time by his divine *scientia media*. As we will see, it is when this emphasis on *facere quod in se est* is wedded to an Arminian understanding of faith and justification that the real problem of Arminian theology is laid bare.

Rutherford believes that God extends his external call to all people without exception. All who hear the gospel preached or who read Scripture for themselves are thereby called externally to respond to the Lord in faith. But since God only intends to save his elect, he calls them alone with an effectual and inward infusion of grace, thereby ensuring that they will respond in faith.[185] This, Rutherford says, is the only thing that makes sense of Scripture, which teaches that many people are externally called by the Word who have no ability to come to him in faith until and unless God calls them internally by his regenerating grace. Thus, God is said to have 'called the *Jews* externally by *word*, *signs*, and *trials*; and yet *he has not given them a heart to know, nor ears to hear, nor eyes to see, even to this day, Deut.* 29.3, 4.' They are unable to respond to God's *vocatio externa*, because 'he has not called them with an internal calling'.[186] Post-lapsarian individuals are portrayed in Scripture as having no ability in things pertaining to salvation. While God calls all externally, he only calls the elect internally by the infused and effectual grace of regeneration. The universal extent of the *vocatio externa* means that preparation is not limited to the elect alone. All who are externally called could theoretically undergo preparation under the preaching of the gospel. Such preparation, however, will only be efficacious for the conversion of the elect.[187]

Thirdly, by way of expounding on the inefficacious nature of preparations, Rutherford argues that they merely represent a step in the typical order that the Lord follows in the application of salvation: 'The Lord's order is to cast downe, and then to convert; first he draweth away some of the ill bloud and rancke

---

[184] *Examen*, pp. 336, 337.

[185] *Examen*, p. 477.

[186] *Examen*, p. 476. Rutherford also cites other biblical texts: John 12.37, 39; 1 Cor. 2.14; Matt. 11.25, 26, 27; 1 Cor. 1.23, 24; Jer. 5.8; Isa. 28.9; 2 Cor. 4.4; Matt. 13.15; Acts 17.32; 26.24; 2 Pet. 3.1, 2; and 2 Cor. 3.14, 15, 16.

[187] William Ames even allows for an 'inward offer' of Christ to be granted 'sometime, and in a certaine manner' to the non-elect under the rubric of preparation. This inward offer, he says, is a 'spirituall enlightning, whereby [the] promises [of the gospel] are propounded to the hearts of men'. *Marrow*, pp. 125-6.

humours, and pricketh the heart; and then bringeth the sicke to the Physician, the trembling Publicane to his Saviour.'[188] Here Rutherford is saying, in a way similar to Perkins before him,[189] that preparation is not a step within conversion (*gradus in re*), nor its formal beginning (*initium formale*), but a step towards it (*gradus ad rem*), materially (*initium materiale*). It is how God generally works. He does not generally 'convert people in an instant, the way water is changed into wine; and [he does not typically convert them] without [any] knowledge' of him and his gospel; 'and [he does] not [convert] unwilling and reluctant' people; 'but he converts people who are prepared, humbled, and downcast and broken by an awareness [*conscientia*] of sin and the terrors of the Law'.[190]

By speaking in this way, Rutherford shows that he is keen to adopt the Lutheran emphasis on the second use of the law, the *usus pedagogus*, also embraced by Calvin and post-Reformation theology in general.[191] Part of the reason for this is to be found in Rutherford's own conversion experience. If we follow John Coffey in seeing his conversion as the result of his being charged with fornication and removed from office as regent in Edinburgh's town college—which certainly appears to be the case—then there can be no doubt but that Rutherford would have had profound experiences of humiliation and law-consciousness and that this would have heavily influenced his own understanding of divine grace and conversion.[192] Perhaps it is because Rutherford's conversion is of a more dramatic nature—more like Luther's than Calvin's—that Rutherford's emphasis seems to gravitate towards the former and the *usus pedagogus* more than is true for the Genevan reformer.[193]

---

[188] *SA*, II, p. 3.

[189] Perkins differentiates between the beginning of preparation and the beginning of conversion, saying: 'Beginnings of preparation are such, as bring under, tame, and subdue the stubburnnesse of mans nature, without making any chaunge at all.' These things, 'though they go before to prepare a sinner to his conversion following, yet are they no graces of God', i.e., they are not necessarily works of God's Spirit unto conversion. In contrast to this, he says: 'Beginnings of composition, I tearme all those inward motions and inclinations of Gods spirit...out of which motions the conversion of a sinner ariseth.' Perkins, *Workes*, I, p. 638; cf. II, p. 13. See also Ames, *Marrow*, p. 125.

[190] *Examen*, pp. 337-8, 344. Cf. *Christ Dying*, p. 241.

[191] Post-Reformation theology tended to speak of three uses for the law of God: *usus politicus*, as a means of restraining sin in society; *usus pedagogus*, as a tool in leading the individual to Christ; and *usus normativus*, as a rule guiding the believer in living the Christian life (see Kevan, *The Grace of Law*, p. 38). On Calvin's use of the law, see *Institutes* II.viii.10, pp. 358-9.

[192] Coffey, *Politics, Religion and the British Revolutions*, pp. 84-5.

[193] On Calvin's conversion, see Wendel, *Calvin*, pp. 37-45, where he argues that although Calvin's conversion was 'an awakening to the consciousness of sin', it was 'far less dramatic' than Luther's experience. The current author is, thus, not saying that Calvin had no place for the second use of the law. As we have already stated, he clearly did, and his experience would have ensured this. What the current author is saying is

Soteriology

Rutherford unmistakably follows Calvin in ascribing a normative role to the law in the life of the Christian. In his catechism, he explicitly records his approval of Calvin's *tertius usus legis* and subsequently launches into a detailed exposition of the ten commandments to prove it. But, perhaps because of Rutherford's own experience, he seems to side with Luther in emphasizing the second use of the law more extensively than did Calvin. Rather than citing from Calvin in order to defend his position against the Antinomians in his *Survey of the Spirituall AntiChrist*, Rutherford chooses instead to rely almost exclusively upon Luther in a diatribe that lasts nearly one hundred pages.[194] If Rutherford were keen on emphasizing the third use of the law as the 'principal one', as Calvin does, then one wonders why he would cite Luther throughout his dispute with the Antinomians, when Luther gives very little, if any, attention to the third use of the law in his writings.[195] And it is Luther, rather than Calvin, that Rutherford turns to in order to substantiate external preparations: 'Yea though *Luther* be against all preparations of merits, yet is he cleare for preparations of order against the *Antinomians*.'[196]

Not only is Rutherford's experience different than Calvin's, but the context into which he is writing is different as well. And this also explains why Rutherford and British theologians in general at this time, place great emphasis on the doctrine of preparation. Whereas Zwingli had believed that baptized covenant children were not necessarily elect, Reformed theologians after Zwingli began insisting that they were with increasing levels of conviction. Heinrich Bullinger, for example, opted for the view that covenant children were probably elect.[197] Calvin's own view appears to be even more at odds with Zwingli:

> The offspring of believers are born holy, because their children while yet in the womb, before they breathe the vital air, have been adopted into the covenant of eternal life. Nor are they brought into the church by baptism on any other ground than that they belonged to the body of the Church before they were born.[198]

While neither Bullinger nor Calvin argued that every single covenant child

---

that Rutherford's experience seems to parallel Luther's more than Calvin's, and, as a result, his theological emphasis does as well.

[194] *SA*, pp. 68-163.

[195] There is uncertainty among scholars as to whether or not Luther accepted the *tertius usus legis* (see the discussions in Kevan, *The Grace of Law*, pp. 38-9; and H.H. Kramm, *The Theology of Martin Luther* [London: James Clarke, 1947], pp. 61-6). Calvin's priority on the third use can be seen in his *Institutes* II.vii.12, pp. 360-61.

[196] *SA*, p. 114.

[197] N. Petit, *The Heart Prepared: Grace and Conversion in Puritan Spiritual Life* (New Haven and London: Yale University, 1966), p. 36.

[198] *Corpus Reformatorum*, XXXV, p. 619, cited in L.B. Schenck, *The Presbyterian Doctrine of Children in the Covenant* (New Haven: Yale University, 1940), p. 13.

would necessarily be saved, it was, nonetheless, the case that 'a large portion of the Reformed community gradually came to believe that a covenant child should be considered regenerate until "the contrary became plainly evident"'.[199] According to John and Jonathan Gerstner, the result was that the Zwinglian 'distinction between regenerate and unregenerate covenant children was almost totally obscured', which in turn 'frequently led to a state of dead orthodoxy because the children (along with their parents) tended to assume their salvation, though many never had experienced God's regenerating grace'.[200] It was into this context that Rutherford began his own ministry in 1627 in Anwoth, where he found the people so apathetic towards spiritual things that he complained of it 'being spiritually *winter* in Anwoth'. The cure? His parishioners needed an experience of conversion in which they were first prepared by law-work and deep humiliation; they needed to be 'downcast and broken by an awareness of sin and the terrors of the Law'.[201]

After reviewing the doctrine of calling in Rutherford, we can at least say in regard to Bell's and Torrance's assertions, that although Rutherford unambiguously calls preparation a step towards (*gradus ad rem*) conversion, this should not be taken to mean that he sees it as a separate step in the *ordo salutis*. Preparation is part of God's *vocatio externa*, which is itself subsumed under regeneration in Rutherford's *ordo*. It cannot be considered a separate step, because all who are prepared are not necessarily converted, and all who are converted are not necessarily prepared. But, more significantly, Bell and Torrance overlook the gracious character and intention of the law in Rutherford's thinking. And one can readily understand how they do so. It is quite easy to interpret Rutherford's doctrine of preparation in a legalistic manner. During the early eighteenth-century Marrow Controversy, the legalistic opponents of the 'Antinomian' Marrowmen interpreted Rutherford in the same way as have Bell and Torrance, appealing to his perceived legalism in order to support their assertion that forsaking sin was necessary 'in order to our coming to Christ'.[202] But David Lachman has argued in his definitive study of this controversy that it is the Marrowmen who were most likely right in claiming Rutherford for their side. Rutherford takes great pains to protect himself against incipient legalism by teaching that preparations are only typical means to conversion. They are never meritorious.[203] There is no theological

---

[199] J.H. Gerstner and J.N. Gerstner, 'Edwardsean Preparation for Salvation', *WTJ* 42:1 (Fall 1979), p. 7, citing P.Y. Dejong, *The Covenant in New England Theology, 1620-1847* (Grand Rapids, MI: Eerdmans, 1945), p. 56.

[200] Gerstner and Gerstner, 'Edwardsean Preparation', p. 7.

[201] *Letters*, p. 6; *Examen*, p. 338.

[202] *Memoirs of the Life, Time, and Writings of the Reverend and Learned Thomas Boston, A.M.*, ed. G.H. Morrison (Edinburgh and London: Oliphant Anderson & Ferrier, 1899), p. 317.

[203] D.C. Lachman, *The Marrow Controversy, 1718-23* (Edinburgh: Rutherford House, 1988), p. 14.

shift here between Rutherford and Calvin, though there does seem to be a slight change in emphasis. Because of Rutherford's own dramatic conversion experience and the context in which he lives and writes, he tends to stress the second use of the law more so than Calvin does.

It is probably his tendency to emphasize the second use of the law and a deeply experiential view of conversion that led Rutherford to the extreme position of questioning whether or not the Arminians were themselves genuinely converted. To his way of thinking, no one who has genuinely experienced the converting grace of God could exalt human freedom and human nature and diminish the sovereignty of divine grace to the extent that the Arminians did. Divine preparations would ensure that all Christians would have a proper view both of themselves and of divine grace and that they would 'fall in love with' God's grace and be 'loath to say anything against it'. But because, as Rutherford believed, the whole Arminian system ran counter to this, he could only conclude that the Arminians knew 'nothing of the grace of God themselves'.[204]

Our Response of Faith

In order to bring our discussion of conversion to a close, we need to examine the doctrine of faith. Rutherford does not devote a separate chapter to treating this doctrine in the *Examen*.[205] But he does take it up in connection with the central tenet of Protestantism—justification. The likely reasons for this are twofold. On the one hand, the differences between Rutherford's view of faith and that of the Arminians are relatively inconsequential, as we will soon see. The real issue is not faith *per se* but faith as it relates to justification. On the other hand, the fact that Rutherford does not include a separate chapter on faith to refute the Arminians regarding the nature and object of faith but discusses it under the auspices of justification instead is significant in light of the polemical thrust of the *Examen* and the grounds of his opposition to Arminianism. After all, justification is, according to Reformation thinking, the 'chief article...which preserves and governs every doctrine of the church'.[206] By casting aspersion on the Arminian doctrine of justification, Rutherford is suggesting that their whole system is corrupt and worthy of being rejected together with Roman Catholicism. While this is not entirely true, it is, as we will see in the next chapter, quite instructive for determining the grounds of

---

[204] Rutherford, *Quaint Sermons*, p. 332.
[205] This is in contrast to the WCF, which devotes chapter fourteen to 'Of Saving Faith'.
[206] B.A. Gerrish, *The Old Protestantism and the New: Essays on the Reformation Heritage* (Edinburgh: T&T Clark, 1982), p. 303n2, citing Luther, whose precise comment is: 'Articulus iustificationis est magister et princeps, dominus, rector, et iudex super omnia genera doctrinarum, qui conservat et gubernat omnem doctrinam ecclesiasticam et erigit conscientiam nostram coram Deo.' *WA* XXXIX, I, p. 205.

Rutherford's opposition to Arminianism.

We have opted to examine Rutherford's doctrine of faith under the heading of conversion in this chapter rather than under justification. The primary reason for our doing so is that Rutherford himself regards faith as part of conversion. There are two acts in conversion, for Rutherford: God's initiatory act in regeneration—which includes internal and external calling—and our responsive act in faith. In his conflict with the Arminians, his emphasis clearly falls upon the former, since the Arminians place their emphasis on the latter. But, citing Calvin, Rutherford also acknowledges that we are '*co-laborers* [*consortes laboris*] *with God*' in our conversion, to the extent that 'we and we alone are the ones who will and believe' to be saved.[207] Not only is the 'act of believing' ours, but there is 'some moral property [*proprietas*]' that is ours as well when we respond in faith. This is apparent, he says, because '*Christ* praises the faith of the *Canaanite* woman, the *Centurion*, *Abraham*, and others, and rewards it'. The 'principal causality' of our conversion, however, resides not in ourselves but in 'the power of God'. God infuses us with the habit of faith, which 'dominates, determines, and effects the *will*' so that it will respond freely, but necessarily, in faith.[208] Thus Rutherford can say that although the 'consummation [*actus secundus*] of our Conversion to God, which is commanded to us as our duty', is 'the free act of believing', the essence of our conversion is to be found *actu primo* 'in the infusion of new life'. The Arminians, as he sees it, take the opposite tack. They locate (*locant*) the essence of conversion 'in the free act of believing alone'.[209] Rutherford makes this assertion, despite explicit statements to the contrary on the part of the Arminians,[210] because they deny that regeneration is an infusion of habitual grace and because they believe that grace can be resisted by human free will. If grace can be resisted in conversion, then the decision to believe or not to believe, as well as the power to accomplish either, ultimately resides in the will of the individual rather than in the will of God. This, for Rutherford, is wholly unacceptable.

Undergirding and empowering Rutherford's disagreement with the Arminians over the essence of conversion is a distinctive view of the nature and object of faith. Ultimately the differences between them are inconsequential, as far as the doctrine of faith itself is concerned. But they set the stage for more profound differences that will arise in regard to justification. In order to demonstrate this, we will briefly turn our attention to the nature and object of faith in both Rutherford and the Arminians and then to the implications they

---

[207] *Examen*, p. 472. Perkins also speaks of us as God's 'co-worker' in this step (*Workes*, I, p. 558).

[208] *Examen*, p. 472.

[209] *Examen*, p. 481.

[210] Even the later Arminians explicitly state that a person is not 'born again or converted by the power of his own free will' (*Confession*, 203).

have for justification.

THE NATURE OF FAITH

Rutherford defines faith in his catechism as 'ane assurance of knowledge that Christ cam into the world to die for sinners...and a resting and a hanging upon Christ with all the heart for salvation'.[211] By defining it in this way, Rutherford shows that he, like Calvin, stands within a tradition extending at least as far back as Aquinas, which teaches that faith has both an intellectual and a voluntaristic aspect.[212] But whereas Aquinas emphasizes the intellectual over the voluntaristic, Rutherford and Calvin, following Duns Scotus (or at least the later Scotists), assign predominance to the will. Like Luther and Zwingli, they understand that faith includes both information (*notitia*) and assent (*assensus*). Thus, Rutherford explains the reason why faith is an 'assurance of knowledge' by saying that it is merely 'a blind gessing', and not faith at all, 'to beleeve as the kirk beleeveth quhen [when] we know not quhat [what] we beleeve'. Faith necessarily and in the first instance involves the intellect. Certain facts must be known and believed to be true.

But saving faith is more than that, because 'it is not enough to salvation [simply] to beleeve that God is true in his Word'.[213] Saving faith also contains the voluntaristic element of trust or *fiducia*. And, in continuity with Calvin, specifically, and Reformation and post-Reformation thinking generally—including such men as Musculus, Ursinus, Ames, Leigh, Ussher, and Maccovius—Rutherford places *fiducia* at the very center of his definition of faith:[214]

---

[211] *Catachisme*, p. 203.

[212] Aquinas, *Summa theologiae* Ia.82.2. While Thomas believes that 'faith is lodged in the intellect', he admits that the intellect 'receive[s] its specification and motivation from the will'. See R. Garrigou-Lagrange, *The Theological Virtues*, 2 vols., trans. T. à Kempis Reilly (St. Louis, MO: Herder, 1965), I, pp. 273-4.

[213] *Catachisme*, p. 203.

[214] Calvin says that faith is more than *cognitio* and *assensus* and ascribes the 'chief part of faith' to *fiducia* (see *Institutes* III.ii.1-2, pp. 542-5; III.ii.6-7, pp. 548-51; III.ii.33, p. 581; and J.R. Beeke, *Assurance of Faith: Calvin, English Puritanism, and the Dutch Second Reformation* [New York: Peter Lang, 1991], pp. 47-9). For a more complete look at Calvin's doctrine of faith, see W.E. Stuermann, 'A Critical Study of Calvin's Concept of Faith' (unpublished Ph.D. dissertation, University of Tulsa, 1952); and V. Shepherd, *The Nature and Function of Faith in the Theology of John Calvin* (Macon, GA: Mercer University Press, 1983). Although there are slight differences between Reformation and post-Reformation theologians in regard to how they define faith—i.e., Calvin speaks of faith as knowledge, but one that includes *cognitio*, *assensus*, and *fiducia*, with the chief emphasis on the latter, and Beza speaks of faith in terms of *assensus*, but includes a fiducial component within it—many, but not all, still locate the 'essence' of saving faith in its fiducial aspect. The above-mentioned men are among those who do (Musculus, *Common Places*, pp. 474-5; Ames, *Marrow*, pp. 5-6; Leigh,

> True *Faith* in the Scriptures is not merely a firm assent [*assensus*] to the way of worshiping God, which is prescribed by *Christ*; this is the *Historical* and *dogmatic* faith of the *Papists*; but more than an assent [*assensus*] of the mind, true faith is determined by the heart's trusting [*fiduciam*] in God through the Mediator, and by a fiducial [*fiducialis*] leaning upon him.

To prove this, Rutherford launches into a detailed and protracted exegetical survey of biblical texts, citing from the Hebrew and Greek originals, even down to the tenses of the verbs. His conclusion: to believe is to 'lean upon God in *Christ*, as though we were a weary pilgrim [*viator*] with a staff or a rod', and to roll (*convolvit*) and turn (*contorquet*) ourselves and our burdens upon him.[215]

The Arminians disagree with this understanding of faith. Rather than seeing faith as containing both an intellectual and a voluntaristic character, with the emphasis being on the latter, they define faith in almost exclusively intellectualist terms. This is not to suggest that the Arminians remove volitional aspects from faith entirely; they do not. But they do confine faith to knowledge (*notitia*) and assent (*assensus*) alone, relegating *fiducia* to a 'necessary consequence or effect' of faith.[216] Richard Muller has cogently argued that the reason why Arminius 'wants to set the final, purely volitional/affective confidence or trust [*fiducia*] outside of the definition of faith properly so called', is that he is seeking to remove the 'lower affections [or, in the words of Arminius, the 'irascible' affections] from the definition, leaving faith a matter of both intellect and will, [but] with the primary emphasis on the intellect'.[217] It is important to note, however, that although Arminius defines saving faith only in terms of *notitia* and *assensus*, he does include an affective and volitional aspect by placing initial movements of the will and affections 'together with the intellect in the act of assent'.[218] The result is a definition of faith that is very similar to that of Rutherford and the Reformed, perhaps even more so than is

---

Body of Divinity, p. 500; Ussher, *Body of Divinitie*, pp. 199-200; Maccovius, *Loci communes*, chapter 71; and *RD*, pp. 532-5). William Perkins, however, is an example of one who does not. He defines saving faith in intellectual terms—it is 'a supernaturall gift of God in the minde, apprehending the saving promise with all the promises that depend on it'—and locates the essence of it in 'apprehension', which he defines as a 'particular perswasion, whereby a man is resolved that the promise of salvation belongs unto him, which perswasion is wrought in the minde by the holy Ghost'. *Workes*, I, pp. 123-4.

[215] *Examen*, pp. 544-5. In proving his claims, Rutherford cites these biblical texts: Prov. 3.5; Isa. 3.1; 10.20; 31.1; 48.2; 50.10; Psal. 22.8; 37.5; 71.6; 112.8; 125.1; 2 Sam. 1.6; 22.19; Jer. 34.4; Gen. 29.10; John 1.12; 6.37, 46; 14.1; Matt. 11.28-9; and Rom. 10.11.

[216] *WJA*, I, p. 176 note.

[217] Muller, 'Priority of the Intellect', pp. 61-2. Muller explains that irascible affections, in scholastic terminology, 'have to do with aversion or repulsion and their opposites, expectation and attraction, and are placed, together with the concupiscible affections (i.e., desire, joy in attainment and their negative, lust) below the will in its operation'. See 'Priority of the Intellect', p. 62n23.

[218] Muller, 'Priority of the Intellect', pp. 62-3. Cf. *WJA*, I, p. 177.

the view of William Perkins:[219]

> Evangelical faith is an assent of the mind, produced by the Holy Spirit, through the Gospel, in sinners, who through the law know and acknowledge their sins, and are penitent on account of them: By which they are not only fully persuaded within themselves, that Jesus Christ has been constituted by God the author of salvation to those who obey Him, and that He is their own Saviour if they have believed in Him; and by which they also believe in Him as such, and through Him on God as the Benevolent Father in Him, to the salvation of believers and to the glory of Christ and God.[220]

In spite of the fact that Arminius' definition of faith contains both intellectual and volitional elements, the emphasis is overwhelmingly on the intellectual. This can be seen from the fact that he defines faith as 'an assent of the mind' or, perhaps better, of the 'rational soul' (the word he uses is *animus*).[221] But it can also be seen from the fact that he portrays the ground of faith in terms that are wholly intellectual:

> The foundation on which...faith rests, is two-fold,—the one external and...the other internal....(1.) The external foundation of faith is the truth itself as spoken [*enunciantis*] of God, who can declare nothing that is false. (2.) The internal foundation of faith is two-fold,—both the common conception [*communis notio*] by which we recognize that God is true,—and the knowledge [*notitia*] by which we recognize that this word is from God.[222]

And while he does acknowledge that the Holy Spirit is the 'Author of faith', he articulates the work of the Spirit in establishing faith within the individual as one in 'which the Spirit proposes' the sense (*sensum*) of the gospel 'concerning God and Christ...to the intellect' and then persuades (*persuadet*) the intellect.[223]

It is precisely this intellectualist approach to faith that gets Arminius into trouble with Rutherford and the Reformed orthodox, not *per se*, because Perkins defines faith in strikingly similar terms, but because he combines this intellectualist view of faith with an anthropological or soteriological intellectualism. Whereas Perkins acknowledges that the post-lapsarian will suppresses intellective function, Arminius admits of no such negative influence of the will upon the intellect. And, as we have already seen, it is precisely because the post-lapsarian will exerts no such negative influence that both the intellect and the will are left free *facere quod in se est* in accepting the divine grace of regeneration, or in rejecting it. 'In other words', for Arminius, as

---

[219] See note 214 above.
[220] *WJA*, II, p. 400.
[221] See Arminius, *Opera theologica* (Leiden, 1629), *Disp. priv.* 44.3.
[222] *WJA*, II, p. 400, as modified according to the original Latin, *Disp. priv.* 44.2. Cf. Muller, 'Priority of the Intellect', p. 64.
[223] *WJA*, II, p. 401; again, see the Latin, *Disp. priv.* 44.6.

Muller has again pointed out, 'in its fallenness, the intellect does not know the truths of the gospel, but it is not the case that the will prevents their appropriation. The gospel must simply be heard, understood, and approved, all within the normal realm of intellective function.' As a result, the causal antecedent to faith, for Arminius, is the knowledge that is 'instrumentally communicated by the gospel to the mind'.[224] Rutherford himself criticizes the later Arminians in this same way by pointing out a twofold antecedent causality that is wholly intellectual: 'they require only two things for faith to be generated [in us], 1) *Plausible arguments*, 2) *Docility*', which is, in Episcopius' own words, an 'honesty of Mind' or 'teachableness'.[225]

For Rutherford, however, and for Perkins as well, the causal antecedent to faith can only be the work of the Holy Spirit in regeneration, giving the individual the ability to believe. The Spirit must quicken (*animans*) 'the mind, will, and affections', granting each faculty a 'new power' to function.[226] Prior to the quickening work of the Spirit, the faculties of the soul were able *facere quod in se est*; but since what is in them was a 'habit of corruption' and an 'inclination to sin', this only and always meant that they chose to sin.[227] In Rutherford's opinion, the will and affections not only suppress the natural knowledge of God that is contained in the intellect—the *semen religionis* or *sensus divinitatis* that we saw in chapter two—but they also work to prevent the intellect from appropriating future truths about God and the way of salvation.[228] The Spirit's regeneration must first breathe new life into the 'powers of the soul'—by removing the old habit and infusing a new one, a habit of grace and faith, and inclining the will towards the things of salvation—before these powers are able to appropriate and understand the gospel and then to choose to embrace Christ by faith.[229] It is, therefore, primarily Arminius' intellectualist definition of faith that Rutherford is reacting against here. Such an approach to faith affects its nature by overemphasizing assent and relegating *fiducia* to a mere consequence of true faith. But it also affects the object of faith, because the two are integrally related.

THE OBJECT OF FAITH

In the course of Rutherford's dispute with the Arminians over the nature of faith, which is in itself relatively minor, at least one thing stands out: there is more at stake here than a mere difference of opinion over the way faith is to be defined. By denying that *fiducia* is of the essence of saving faith, the Arminians

---

[224] Muller, 'Priority of the Intellect', p. 70. Cf. *WJA*, II, pp. 192-3, 400-401; III, p. 459.
[225] *Examen*, p. 473; *Confession*, p. 148.
[226] *Examen*, pp. 476, 478-9. See Perkins' comments in *Workes*, I, p. 124.
[227] *Examen*, p. 454; *Exercitationes*, p. 5.
[228] *Examen*, pp. 326-7. Also, see the section on the *duplex cognitio Dei* in chapter two above.
[229] *Examen*, pp. 478-9.

are, as Rutherford sees it, placing their emphasis on the rational rather than on the experiential. This is not necessary with an intellectualist view of faith—as we have seen in the example of Perkins, whose view of faith is clearly intellectualist and, yet, whose theology is profoundly experiential. But, as we have also seen previously, the Arminians go the extra step beyond Perkins and wed their intellectualist view of faith to a post-lapsarian anthropological intellectualism. As a result, the Christian life becomes primarily a rational pursuit rather than an intimate relationship with the God of this universe involving every faculty within the individual. That this is the case with Arminian theology is confirmed, to Rutherford's way of thinking, by the fact that they reduce the object of faith merely to factual information that must be personally understood, believed, and trusted in. Such a view, according to Rutherford, is wholly 'misleading' and 'futile',

> [b]ecause the object of *Faith*, in this way of thinking, is not *Christ*...but the History of the Gospel, by which I firmly believe that I avoid hell and obtain eternal life only through *Christ* and his reasoning [*rationem*], as prescribed in the Gospel...[and because] to believe in *Christ* in this way is merely to believe in *Christ* recounting [*narranti*] that people obtain eternal life by repentance and faith: But this is an *Historical* faith, which is in the Demons and many of the reprobate.[230]

Rutherford is not completely justified in calling the Arminian conception of faith 'an Historical faith'. As we have just seen, Arminius quite explicitly includes actions of both the will and the affections within his understanding of assent.[231] But, in spite of this, Rutherford does seem to be justified in arguing that because the Arminians define the nature of faith in intellectualist terms, they, as a result, characterize the object of faith in more intellectualist terms as well. Although this is not always the case in actuality, as is apparent from the example of Perkins, who in spite of defining faith in intellectualist terms, goes on to speak of the object of faith in terms that are identical to Rutherford, it is, nevertheless, true in theory that an intellectualist definition of faith best coincides with an intellectualist view of the object of faith.

In continuity with Calvin, Rutherford acknowledges that there is unequivocally a rational or intellectual component to faith, which must always rest on God's Word. For both of them, faith is essentially knowledge, with the

---

[230] *Examen*, pp. 542, 544.

[231] Arminius differentiates between three kinds of *assensus*: 'Intellectual Assent is that which assents to a true proposition, without any consideration whether that proposition also contains any good'; an 'Assent of the Affections occurs, when the proposition is both true, and has something good joined with it which we are desirous or inclined to obtain'; and, lastly, a 'Practical Assent occurs, when the proposition is true, and when it also proposes a good which must be performed by us.' According to Arminius, faith belongs to the assent of the affections. *WJA*, I, p. 177.

overarching emphasis on the fiducial.[232] In the language of the Westminster Shorter Catechism, faith receives Christ 'as he is offered to us in the gospel'.[233] There is in Rutherford's theology, then, an intellectual component to the object of faith. Scripture, or, more accurately, the promises of Scripture, is the *objectum quo fidei*, the object *in which* we believe. But this can never be separated from Christ himself, the *objectum quod fidei*, the object *that* (or, on whom) we believe, because all of Scripture's promises find their ultimate fulfillment in him. Christ is the living Word, the sum total of the written Word, all of which is 'yea and amen' in him.[234] To concentrate wholly on the intellectual element of faith when defining the nature of faith is, as Rutherford sees it, to concentrate wholly on the written Word—rather than on the living Word—when distinguishing the proper object of faith. Saving faith not only involves receiving and trusting Christ's promises in the Word; it also, and more importantly to Rutherford and Calvin, among others, involves receiving and trusting Christ himself.

As we mentioned in chapter two, Rutherford, in keeping with the overall trend among the Puritans, is much more concerned with the experiential side of faith (with *praxis* rather than *contemplatio*). Although theology is partly a speculative discipline for him, it is not merely nor even primarily so. All theology is directed towards the practical end of pious living, in order that the individual might 'glorify God, and…enjoy him for ever'.[235] This experiential emphasis in faith is reflective of the Augustinian tradition in general and English Ramists, like Perkins and Ames, in particular.[236] That is what makes it all the more surprising that Perkins would define faith intellectually. From Rutherford's point of view, such a conception of faith would seem to run counter to the deeply personal, even intimate, relationship between Christ and the believer that lies at the very heart of the Christian life.[237] Granted, Perkins minimizes the differences between himself and Calvin and Rutherford by confessing that he has defined faith in intellectual terms only because he cannot understand how it is that 'one particuler and single grace should be seated in divers parts or faculties of the soule' (i.e., the mind and the will together, as in Rutherford and Calvin) and by explicitly stating that the person of Christ is the

---

[232] Rutherford's embrace of Calvin's *duplex cognitio Dei* ensures this link. Cf. Calvin with *Catachisme*, pp. 161, 174; and *SA*, p. 310.

[233] *WCF*, p. 310. Cf. J. Calvin, *The Gospel according to St. John 1-10*, trans. T.H.L. Parker, *Calvin's Commentaries*, eds. D.W. Torrance and T.F. Torrance (Edinburgh and London: Oliver and Boyd, 1959), pp. 83-4; idem, *Commentary on Psalms*, II, pp. 145-7.

[234] *Examen*, pp. 499, 541, 544. Cf. J. Calvin, *Commentaries on the First Book of Moses called Genesis*, trans. J. King (Edinburgh: CTS, 1847), I, pp. 404-10; idem, *Commentary on a Harmony of the Evangelists*, I, pp. 125-6; and J. Beeke's discussion in *Assurance of Faith*, pp. 47-8.

[235] *WCF*, p. 287.

[236] See *PRRD*, I, pp. 343-7.

[237] See the section on sanctification below.

proper object of faith, as he is revealed in his written Word.[238] The Arminians, however, do not take these protective measures. In fact, they run in the opposite direction by linking an intellectual view of faith with an intellectual view of post-lapsarian anthropology. The upshot is that they deemphasize the experiential element of faith in favor of the rational. Here again is reason why Rutherford could brashly maintain that the Arminians were unconverted. Their emphasis on the intellectual aspect of faith completely overlooks the fiducial and experiential nature of saving faith. The Christian is not the one whose head is fully stocked with all the right doctrines but the one who is full of love for Christ, to such an extent that 'nothing is fixedly sought after, but God, he onely [sic] feared and served...[he] only desired...[he] only loved...[whose] soul [is] sick of love [i.e., lovesick] for only only Christ...he only trusted in'.[239] To be fair to the Arminians, however, it should be noted that they do emphasize the fiducial aspect of faith, and, thereby, the person of Christ as a proper object of faith, but this appears in their theology only as a necessary consequence of true and saving faith, which is itself intellectual. And it is just this fact that gets them into trouble with Rutherford and the Reformed in regard to justification.

Living by Faith

We will look at Rutherford's understanding of justification and the related topic of sanctification under the common heading of 'living by faith'. Following Calvin, Rutherford 'defines what we receive from Jesus Christ by faith as a "double grace", or a twofold benefit [*duplicem gratiam*], the whole of which can be summed up for the purpose of theological discussion under two headings: Justification and Sanctification'. The former explains how it is that we live or are made alive by faith, whereas the latter relates to how we go on living by faith. Again following Calvin's lead, Rutherford believes that '[j]ustification and sanctification together comprise a "twofold cleansing (*double lavement*)"', giving us, respectively, an imputed purity and an actual purity (*pureté actuelle*).[240] These doctrines form two sides of the same coin, so to speak, and will, therefore, be treated under the same heading.

While Rutherford devotes a chapter of the *Examen* to discussing justification in some detail, he, like Calvin, does not formally address the issue of sanctification at all. When Rutherford does mention it, he does so only in passing. This is not unexpected, however, as the Arminians' view of progressive sanctification closely mirrors that of Rutherford. Both parties view it as a joint venture between God and the individual. The only real difference between them is that the Arminians place their emphasis on the human side of the equation, whereas Rutherford places it on the divine. This will be seen more

---

[238] Perkins, *Workes*, I, p. 124.
[239] *COL*, p. 152.
[240] Wallace, *Calvin's Doctrine of the Christian Life*, p. 23.

fully in our discussion of unconditional perseverance, which follows below in the section on assurance. For now, we will limit our examination to presenting Rutherford's understanding of justification and sanctification and to exploring the differences between him and the Arminians in regard to the former of these.

Justification

In his catechism, Rutherford defines justification in a way that is typical of the Reformation and post-Reformation periods. His definition reads almost word for word with those of Ames and Ussher. It is, as Rutherford says, 'the gracious sentence of the judge of the world esteeming beleeving sinners to be pardoned and righteous for the satisfaction of Christ their cautioner, quho died for them'.[241] Two main things need to be mentioned here in connection with this definition. First, justification is, for Rutherford and for Reformation theology in general, a forensic declaration; it is the 'gracious sentence of the judge of the world'.[242] In justification,

> [our] sins are removed...*Legally*...[in a way that is] plainly *judicial* and *forensic*, not [in such a way] *that they might not exist, but that they might not be imputed*, as *Augustine* says. And for this reason, justification causes no Physical change in the justified person; but only a moral or legal change, in which the individual is released from the obligation to punishment.[243]

The forensic nature of justification demonstrates how an individual can be said to remain, in the well-known words of Luther, *simul justus et peccator*, after his or her justification; it is because justification does not effect a physical change within him or her but only a change in legal status.[244] The individual is now once and for all pronounced to be sinless and in right standing before the tribunal of God. But the physical or ontological presence of sin is not dealt with by this doctrine. That happens only in sanctification.

---

[241] *Catachisme*, p. 205. See also *SA*, II, p. 105. Rutherford speaks of justification in two ways: 1) a 'universall' justification, which is not tied to the individual's act of faith in time but takes place once for all the elect when Christ makes atonement for their sins upon the cross; and 2) a 'partiall' or 'formal' justification, which occurs in order of time when each individual actually believes in Christ for himself or herself. The latter idea is what Rutherford generally means by justification, because, as he says, this is the sense of the Apostle Paul in Scripture (*Tryal*, pp. 161-2). Cf. Ames, *Marrow*, p. 130; Ussher, *Body of Divinitie*, p. 193.

[242] *RD*, pp. 543ff.

[243] *Examen*, p. 539.

[244] On Luther and justification, see C.R. Trueman, '*Simul peccator et iustus*: Some Reflections upon Martin Luther and Justification', paper delivered to the 10th Edinburgh Dogmatics Conference, Rutherford House, 25-28 August 2003; and B. Lohse, *Martin Luther's Theology: Its Historical and Systematic Development*, trans. and ed. R.A. Harrisville (Minneapolis, MN: Fortress, 1999), pp. 74-8, 258-66.

Before moving on to look at the second feature of Rutherford's view of justification, one criticism needs to be raised at this juncture. Because he perceives justification as a wholly forensic declaration concerning an individual's legal status without regard for what is really or ontologically the case, Rutherford opens himself up to the charge that he makes it purely a legal fiction. Rutherford protects himself against this charge to some degree by making both justification and sanctification to be products of our initial vital union with Christ. Both are 'act[s] of the life of Christ', which is first infused within us at regeneration.[245] As far as justification is concerned, this means:

> before we be *actually in Christ*, by justification, and branches in him, by order of nature; first, wee so farre find favour in the Lords eyes, or please him, or rather he is of free grace pleased with us, that he giveth his holy Spirit to us, and upon the same ground may we, being yet not justified; and so, in that sense, not in Christ, by order of nature, first beleeve, before we be justified; nor is it justification that formally united us in this *actuall union*, as branches to the Vine tree, but *union is a fruit of life*, as is the joyning of soule and body together, and so a fruit of the infused life of God, or of the habit of sanctification, and thus it followeth not, that we beleeve before we be united to Christ; as branches to the Vine tree, but onely that we beleeve, by order of nature, before we be justified, which the Scripture saith.[246]

In spite of this, however, it remains true that Rutherford safeguards himself only implicitly from the charge that he makes justification to be a legal fiction. Modern-day theologians like John Murray have taken an extra step beyond Rutherford and have further protected themselves against such an indictment by explicitly establishing a special category of sanctification that is coordinate with justification—definitive sanctification. According to this extra step, a definitive righteousness is said to be infused within the individual at the same time that he or she is justified but in an act that is distinct from justification.[247]

The second characteristic of Rutherford's view of justification is again a hallmark of Reformation teaching, and that is double imputation. There are, he says, two 'pairts of our justification...first the not reckoning or counting our sinnes to be ours...and [second] the counting of Christ's righteousness [to be] ours'.[248] In other words, in justification our sins are first of all imputed to Christ, and he is treated as we deserve to be for our sins. He is punished in our

---

[245] *Christ Dying*, p. 271; *SA*, II, p. 112.

[246] *SA*, II, p. 113, emphasis added.

[247] See Murray's article, 'Definitive Sanctification.' Rutherford's concept of a 'habit of sanctification' fulfills a similar purpose in his theology as definitive sanctification does in Murray's. But Rutherford does not develop this idea anywhere near to the extent that Murray does. It remains only an implicit part of his thinking.

[248] *Catachisme*, p. 206. Cf. *Institutes* III.xi.2-4, pp. 726-9; Musculus, *Common Places*, p. 541; Ames, *Marrow*, p. 130; Perkins, *Workes*, I, p. 567; Ussher, *Body of Divinitie*, pp. 193-6.

stead and in our place (*vice et loco nostri*). And, second of all, Christ's perfect obedience, his 'Surety-righteousness [*justitia Fidejussoria*]' or 'active and passive righteousness', is imputed to us, and we are treated as he deserves to be for his record of sinless perfection.[249] In strongly Calvinian language, Rutherford says that as a result of our justification, we stand before God with our 'debtis...payed' and as those who are 'maid rich and clothed in fair apparel'.[250]

For the Arminians, however, such a view of imputation is contrary to right reason, because it insists that the 'righteousness of Christ is imputed to us for righteousness'. But whatever is imputed *for* righteousness cannot be righteousness itself. Since 'the righteousness of Christ, which He hath performed in obeying the Father, is righteousness itself strictly and rigidly taken: Therefore it is not imputed for righteousness.' Rather, according to Arminius, the fourth chapter of Romans teaches that *faith* is imputed for righteousness.[251] This does not mean that Arminius denies that Christ's righteousness is imputed in justification. He holds both statements to be true: '*The righteousness of Christ* is imputed to us' and our '*Faith* is imputed for righteousness.' In order to illustrate how this can be, he gives the following example: 'if [a] man owe[s] a hundred florins and pay[s] only ten, then the creditor, forgiving him the remainder, may justly say, "I impute this to you for full payment; I will require nothing more from you"'.[252] From this example, it would seem that Arminius believes Christ's righteousness to be imputed *negatively* in justification, insofar as it eliminates the remainder of the ninety-florin debt, and the individual's faith to be imputed *positively* for righteousness, just as the ten-florin payment is imputed for the full one-hundred. Christ's righteousness cannot be imputed positively in any way. If it were, righteousness would be imputed for righteousness, which right reason eschews.

To sum up, then, while the Arminians do appear to favor a double imputation in their doctrine of justification, it is not a double imputation in the way that doctrine had typically been understood. The Arminians limit the imputation of Christ's righteousness only to his passive obedience and replace

---

[249] *Examen*, pp. 506-7. Rutherford helpfully calls active and passive obedience 'Surety-righteousness', thereby clarifying what he means by the former terms. Theologians like Rutherford and Perkins understood that there was overlap between the terms active and passive obedience. Christ's active obedience was at times passive, and his passive obedience was active. See Perkins, *Workes*, I, p. 567.

[250] *Catachisme*, p. 206. Cf. *Institutes* III.xi.2, pp. 726-7.

[251] The Arminians are not alone in this; even Reformed theologians like Richard Baxter understood justification to be an imputation of our faith for righteousness. See J.I. Packer, *The Redemption & Restoration of Man in the Thought of Richard Baxter: A Study in Puritan Theology* (Vancouver, BC: Regent College, 2003), p. 251.

[252] *WJA*, II, pp. 44-5. Cf. *Confession*, chapter 10. Arminius' example would seem to suggest that he, like Socinus, thinks of sin more as a pecuniary debt than a break in relationship.

the imputation of his active obedience with the imputation of the individual's faith.[253] In his customary polemical manner, Rutherford condemns this idea in the Arminians as justification by works, lumping them together with 'Papists' and 'Socinians' and dismissing them all with a wave of his hand.[254] To his way of thinking, when the Arminians say that faith, which is by definition our act of believing, is imputed as our righteousness in justification, it is the same thing as saying that something we do becomes our righteousness before the divine tribunal. And, what is this but a justification by works?

In keeping with the Westminster Confession, Rutherford denounces the notion that faith is imputed to us in justification as our righteousness.[255] We are not justified because of our faith or on account of it but by it or through it.[256] Faith is not considered as our righteousness; rather, as Calvin says, it is the 'vessel' or 'the instrument' by which we lay hold of Luther's *justitia aliena*, i.e., the righteousness of Christ.[257] The fourth chapter of Romans should not, Rutherford insists, be understood in a wooden sense but according to the pattern of 'metonymical and figurative speech'. Just as when 'someone says, my hand has made me rich' and means by it, 'my acquired riches have grown by the diligence [*industria*] and labor of my hands', so when the Apostle Paul says 'that Abraham believed God and it was imputed to him for righteousness', he means 'that which [Abraham] apprehends [i.e., Christ and his active and

---

[253] Recently, advocates of a so-called New Perspective on Paul have argued, quite persuasively, for a new understanding of justification that in some ways parallels the Arminian doctrine. Among the most prolific of these advocates is N.T. Wright, who asserts that justification, while it is a forensic declaration, only entails a single imputation—our sins are imputed to Christ—and who then claims that justification is a present declaration in anticipation of the future verdict that will be pronounced on the basis of our own righteous works, thereby incorporating in a loose sense both aspects of the Arminian 'double imputation'. See N.T. Wright, 'New Perspectives on Paul', paper delivered to the 10th Edinburgh Dogmatics Conference, Rutherford House, 25-28 August 2003. For more on Wright's views of justification, see his 'Romans and the Theology of Paul', in *Pauline Theology*, eds. D.M. Hay and E.E. Johnson (Minneapolis, MN: Fortress, 1995), pp. 30-67; and idem, *The Letter to the Romans: Introduction, Commentary, and Reflections*, in *The New Interpreter's Bible*, vol. 10 (Nashville, TN: Abingdon Press, 2002), pp. 393-770. For responses to Wright's claims, see S.J. Gathercole, *Where is Boasting? Early Jewish Soteriology and Paul's Response in Romans 1-5* (Grand Rapids, MI: Eerdmans, 2002); and D. Macleod, 'How Right are the Justified? or, What is a Dikaios?', *Scottish Bulletin of Evangelical Theology* 22:2 (Autumn 2004), pp. 173-95.

[254] *Examen*, pp. 500-501.

[255] *WCF*, § 11.1, p. 57.

[256] Here again the Arminians have an ally among the Reformed in Richard Baxter, who unabashedly speaks of faith as the *causa sine qua non* of justification. See Packer's discussion in *Redemption & Restoration of Man*, pp. 254-7. Cf. *Catachisme*, p. 206.

[257] *Institutes* III.xi.7, pp. 733-4; Lohse, *Martin Luther's Theology*, p. 69.

passive obedience] is imputed...for righteousness'.[258]

Whether or not this interpretation of Romans 4 is to be preferred over the one offered by Arminius is beyond the scope of this study. What matters here is determining whether or not Rutherford is warranted in denouncing Arminius' view that the act of believing is imputed for righteousness. In other words, what matters is determining whether or not Rutherford is justified in calling this idea a justification by works. While it is true that Rutherford is rather uncharitable in his dealings with the Arminians (i.e., he overlooks the fact that Arminius explicitly states that divine grace is necessary in order for us to believe and in order for our faith to be accepted by God as righteousness, as well as the fact that Arminius says that 'God is the primary Cause of justification'),[259] it is, nonetheless, also true that, as Richard Muller has acknowledged, there is 'the smallest possible opening for human initiative in the work of salvation' in Arminius' teaching on justification.[260] This opening is the result principally of Arminius' intellectualist understanding of faith.

Because, as we saw previously, the Arminians believe that the post-lapsarian will does not affect the operation of the intellect, both the fallen intellect and the fallen will are able *facere quod in se est* in receiving God's special grace of illumination and regeneration. 'In other words', as Muller has summarized, 'in its fallenness, the intellect does not know the truths of the gospel, but it is not the case that the will prevents their appropriation. The gospel must simply be heard, understood, and approved, all within the normal realm of intellective function.'[261] When this intellectualist view of faith is then combined with the idea that our faith is imputed for righteousness, we are left with a human activity in which the fallen faculties of the understanding and will *faciunt quod in se est* in appropriating the divine grace to believe, and, as a result, the individual is counted as righteous in God's sight. While it may not be fair to call this a synergistic salvation, it does grant the smallest of openings for the charge to be made.

In opposition to the Arminians, Rutherford staunchly defends the Reformation doctrine of justification by grace alone through faith alone in Christ alone, to the extent that everything is of grace. We do not offer a payment of ten florins towards a hundred-florin debt, as Arminius has suggested. Rather, Christ pays the full one hundred on behalf of all 'those for whom he has offered bail and surety'.[262] And then, to continue the analogy, Christ gives the elect his personally acquired bank balance, which gift can only be received by faith. This is not because there is an 'innate power, merit, excellence, or dignity' in faith, but because 'faith apprehends...*Christ*, who is

---

[258] *Examen*, p. 510.
[259] *WJA*, II, p. 49.
[260] Muller, 'Priority of the Intellect', p. 69.
[261] Muller, 'Priority of the Intellect', p. 70.
[262] *Examen*, pp. 508-9.

our righteousness *by imputation [imputativè]*.²⁶³ It is faith, apart from any work, that receives the justification that is merited by Christ.

But it is not a faith without works that receives this justification. Saving faith necessarily produces the fruit of good works. It is not the fruit that justifies, but only the faith. The fruit is the proof of the genuineness of the faith. Because of this, Rutherford, in continuity with Calvin and others of the Reformers, could argue that works are necessary for salvation, not in the sense that they are meritorious causes of it but insofar as saving faith will never be lacking good works. Citing 'our Calvin', Rutherford calls 'good works the inferior cause of the actual possession of eternal life'. This is because good works ordinarily precede the possession of eternal life in the divine 'order of dispensation', not because they merit eternal life in and of themselves. In this sense, good works are 'means' of 'gaining the crown' of eternal life, but only ordinarily.²⁶⁴ Someone may believe 'at the nick of the extremity of his twelfth and last houre' and not have the opportunity to perform good works before his death. Following Luther, Rutherford therefore argues that the presence of good works is necessary to salvation *necessitate praecepti* alone not *necessitate medii*.²⁶⁵

At the heart of Arminius' intellectualist understanding of faith and his belief that faith is imputed for righteousness in justification is his theistic intellectualism. The divine justice that prevents God from acting contrary to an individual's free will also prevents him from imputing Christ's righteousness to another. For, this would impose a guaranteed salvation on people without regard to their ultimate perseverance in the faith.²⁶⁶ It would remove all possibility of their freely choosing not to persevere and, thus, of their rejecting God's justification. Since free will cannot be compelled by any necessity and must remain free, Arminius concludes that the Reformed conception of justification must be in error. Rutherford's voluntarism, on the other hand, makes no such demands upon the doctrine of justification. Instead, it places its emphasis on God's freedom to work where and when he pleases for his own glory and to be the sole cause of human justification. Because the Arminians emphasize human freedom over the divine in justification, Rutherford accuses

---

²⁶³ *Examen*, p. 500. Faith, according to Rutherford, is 'a palsie hand under Christ to receive him...as an almes' (*Tryal*, p. 59). It does not offer anything but receives everything.

²⁶⁴ *Examen*, p. 531; *Institutes* III.xiv.21, p. 787. Calvin borrows Aristotelian causal categories to explain that 'the efficient cause of our salvation consists in God the Father's love; the material cause in God the Son's obedience; the instrumental cause in the Spirit's illumination, that is, faith; the final cause, in the glory of God's great generosity.' And to these he adds good works as 'inferior causes'. In addition to Calvin, Rutherford also cites Bernard of Clairvaux, Martin Bucer, Jerome Zanchi, and Gisbertus Voetius in support of the inferior causality of works (*Examen*, pp. 531-2). See also *Institutes* III.xvi.1, p. 798.

²⁶⁵ *SA*, II, p. 62; Strickland, 'Union with Christ', p. 77n4.

²⁶⁶ *Examen*, p. 506, citing from Arminius' *Letter to Hippolytus*, in *WJA*, II, pp. 685-705.

them of 'detract[ing] from the glory of the merits and death of Christ and from mercy and [divine] grace' by substituting the glory of free choice in its place.[267]

Sanctification

Rutherford's doctrine of sanctification is again quite typical for Reformation and post-Reformation thinking. He is very much in line with Calvin and with his contemporaries Perkins, Ames, Leigh, and Ussher. Although they use several different terms to refer to this doctrine—among them, glorification (Ussher), repentance (Calvin, at times, and Perkins), and regeneration (Calvin and Rutherford)—there appears to be unanimity as to what sanctification means, where it comes from, what its parts are, and how it differs from justification.[268] Whereas in justification our sins are removed legally and by imputation, Rutherford says, in sanctification our '[s]ins are removed really and Physically...[but] only by parts and successively; just as the early morning light or the first light of dawn expels the darkness of night only successively and by degrees'. Justification is a once and for all act. Sanctification is a continuous work that remains 'imperfect...in this life'.[269] According to Ames, 'it admits of divers degrees, of beginning, progresse, and perfection'.[270] As we have seen earlier in this chapter, Rutherford and Calvin and Reformation soteriology in general locate the foundation of sanctification in union with Christ. 'By partaking of him', Calvin says, 'we principally receive a double grace', the second of which, sanctification, begins, broadly speaking, at regeneration with the removal of the habit of corruption and the infusion of a new sanctified habit.[271] No longer does the regenerated person have a sinful nature. He or she is now a new creation, once dead in sins and trespasses but now made alive together with Christ. Yet, in spite of this, sin still remains in the new creature, tainting every faculty of the person. Even though some righteousness has been infused at regeneration and, with it, a new inclination for spiritual things, sin, or, in the words of the Apostle Paul, the sinful flesh, remains. Progressive sanctification is essentially, then, in Reformation and post-Reformation thinking, the life-long struggle to purge the new creature of his or her remaining sin. Almost without exception it involves a twofold process: mortification and, its positive counterpart, vivification.

Perhaps it is because of his own conversion experience and the humiliation he endures for his public sin of fornication that Rutherford places his

---

[267] *Examen*, pp. 502, 459.
[268] Ussher, *Body of Divinitie*, p. 202; *Institutes* III.iii.3, p. 595; III.xi.1, p. 725; Perkins, *Workes*, I, pp. 455-7; *Catachisme*, pp. 199, 201. Cf. Ames, *Marrow*, pp. 140-44; Leigh, *Body of Divinity*, pp. 535-49.
[269] *Examen*, pp. 539-40.
[270] Ames, *Marrow*, p. 140.
[271] *Institutes* III.xi.1, p. 725; *Catachisme*, p. 199.

overwhelming emphasis on the first of these—mortification.[272] Whatever the reason, he remains consciously aware throughout his lifetime of the extent of his own sinfulness and of his need to put sin to death for the sake of Christ. In *The Covenant of Life Opened*, he devotes twenty pages to the issue of mortification, beginning with a definition:

> [Mortification] is a deadning of the whole powers and inclinations of the soul in their bentnesse and operations, in order to things forbidden by the Law of God, or in things indifferent and commanded. Hence, not the affections only, but the understanding and mind must be deadned. And therefore this is no mortification until sin original be subdued in its damnation by Christs death, and in its dominion by the Spirit of Sanctification.[273]

In other words, according to Rutherford, mortification does not begin until a person is justified before God and the legal condemnation for his or her sin is removed, and it does not end until sanctification is complete. This should not imply, however, that sanctification flows from justification in Rutherford's thinking, but only that it follows after justification in the ordinary dispensation of God's temporal order. As we have already indicated, both justification and sanctification flow from union with Christ. And because sanctification flows from union with Christ, so does mortification:

> Hence, from our being crucified with Christ crucified, something is to be said in a practicall way of our mortification; for mortification flows originally from Christs death, we being crucified in him and with him....*Christ* dying doth merit by blood the Spirit, and infused grace, which deadens the whole life of sin. [Nothing else accomplishes mortification.] But in the infusing of the life of God, Christ applyes the reall principle of mortification.[274]

Rutherford's emphasis on mortification and vivification in the Christian life extends to anything and everything that may distract one from the experiential love of Christ. Above all else, God's chief aim 'in all His dealings with His children' is for their love of 'the world' and 'earthly delights' to be mortified, so that their love of Christ can be vivified.[275] In continuity with medieval mystics like Bernard of Clairvaux, Rutherford believes that the ultimate goal of

---

[272] Rutherford rarely, if ever, speaks of vivification as such. He does, however, use the synonym 'quickening' and, at times, speaks of mortification in a positive way, as when he says: 'Yet acts of sanctified reason and Industery [sic] spiritualized with the infused life of Christ, and informed with the pure light of faith beholding Christ crucified, doe work mortification.' See *Catachisme*, pp. 201-2; and *SA*, p. 341.

[273] *COL*, p. 261. Rutherford then lists no fewer than twenty-seven ways for us to engage in mortifying the sin that remains in us (*COL*, pp. 268-81).

[274] *COL*, pp. 261-2.

[275] *Letters*, p. 70.

the Christian life is union with God.[276] Thus, the purpose of sanctification is to wean the Christian from other loves and to fix his or her love on Christ alone.[277] Again following Bernard, and, before him, Origen, Rutherford ascribes a central place in this process to the affections.[278] Although he virtually equates the affections with the emotions, he is careful to stipulate that they are not wholly 'irrationall...fit[s] of madnesse, that hath no reason, but its owne fire'. In other words, the affections are not animal passions, but, prefiguring Jonathan Edwards' (1703-1758) momentous *Treatise concerning Religious Affections* (1746), he says that they are informed by the intellect and closely allied to the will.[279] The affections are central to the Christian life, because 'God detesteth lukewarmnes, and coldnes in his matters' and demands '*all the heart, all the soul,* [and] *all the strength*' of his people.[280] The Christian life is the life-long process of fixing the affections on Christ alone and keeping them there, so that, as we said earlier, 'the soul [is] sick of love for only only Christ'.[281] Such a process requires sustained mortification and vivification.

Rutherford's emphasis on the importance of the affections in sanctification is also reflected in his preaching and in his letters to friends and parishioners. Echoing another characteristic of Cistercians like Bernard, Rutherford embraces the frankly sexual language of the Song of Songs in order to communicate the essence of salvation, union with Christ, to the affections of his hearers and readers.[282] Granted, part of the reason for his use of the Song of

---

[276] The term mystic is quite slippery. As Martin Thornton comments, it is 'usually undefined and often misunderstood'. At times in history, any show of affection in a prayer or sermon has been enough to earn one the label 'mystic' (*English Spirituality: An Outline of Ascetical Theology according to the English Pastoral Tradition* [London: SPCK, 1963], pp. 12-13). See also R.C. Petry, ed., *Late Medieval Mysticism* (London: SCM Press, 1957), pp. 17-22; and D. Knowles, *The English Mystical Tradition* (London: Burns & Oates, 1961), pp. 1-3. In this thesis, the term will be used to refer to elements of Cistercian mysticism in general and to Bernard of Clairvaux in particular.

[277] Rutherford's fear of idolatry extends even to benefits or gifts of Christ, lest anyone should fall in love with these instead of with Christ himself.

[278] See A.E. Matter, *The Voice of My Beloved: The Song of Songs in Western Medieval Christianity* (Philadelphia: University of Pennsylvania, 1990), p. 128.

[279] *Christ Dying*, p. 363. Edwards too links the affections to the will and the mind and speaks of 'holy affections' as being central to the Christian life. See G.M. Marsden, *Jonathan Edwards: A Life* (New Haven and London: Yale University, 2003), pp. 284-90. The Yale edition of his works explicitly credits Rutherford as influencing Edwards to some degree on the issue of the 'importance of affections and "heart religion"'. See the editor's introduction to *The Works of Jonathan Edwards*, vol. 2, ed. J.E. Smith (New Haven, CT: Yale University, 1959), p. 72.

[280] *HOC*, pp. 17, 23.

[281] *COL*, p. 152.

[282] According to Ann Matter, the entire history of the tropological interpretation of the Song of Songs is one of 'passion and union' and of 'conscious eroticism'. *Voice of My Beloved*, pp. 138, 140.

Songs in his preaching could be linked to the vast illiteracy rate in rural Scotland in the seventeenth century. Margo Todd has estimated that only ten to twenty percent of the rural population at that time could read. Because of this fact, sermons became the primary means of conveying biblical truth to the illiterate. The more effective the preaching, the longer the people would listen, and the more biblical truth could be conveyed. And, as Todd has remarked, the 'sign of an effective preacher [at this time] was his ability to transfer his own emotional intensity to the auditory'; and the sign of effective preaching, 'in the absence of icons in the kirk', was the use of 'language to draw pictures in the imagination'.[283] Rutherford's use of the Song of Songs would have fulfilled both requirements. It allowed him to preach affectively and pictorially.

But, more than this, there are theological reasons as well for his homiletical use of the Song—which should not surprise us in the least given Rutherford's emphasis on *praxis* in theology rather than on *contemplatio*. As we demonstrated earlier in the chapter, Rutherford believes that post-lapsarian free will is the ability to choose the greatest good according to the inclination of the will. While this is relatively straightforward both before and after the fall, it takes on a new twist after regeneration. The new convert has a spiritual nature or inclination but two competing desires—to live according to the spiritual nature or to live according to the sin that remains in him or her. These competing desires vie for supremacy within the individual in the lifelong process of sanctification. What determines which one he or she will follow? Quite simply, it is the 'disposition' of the affections.

> The affections are like the needle, the rest of the soul like the thread; and as the needle makes way and draws the thread, so holy affections pull forward and draw all to Jesus. The affections are the ground and lower part of the soul, and when they are filled they set all the soul on work; when there is any love in the affections, it sets all the rest of the faculties of the soul on work to duty, and when there is any corruption in the affections, it stagnates the soul, will, mind, and conscience. Affections are the feet of the soul, and the wheels whereupon the conscience runs. When a man is off his feet he cannot run or walk; so when the affections are lame, the soul moves on crutches.[284]

Rutherford, therefore, believes that every minister should preach in such a way as to appeal to and excite all the faculties of the soul, but especially the affections. A sermon that concentrates only on the presentation of information to the mind fails to excite the affections and, thus, leaves its hearers no better off in their pursuit of sanctification. Truth must be crafted and presented in such a way so as to encourage love in the affections for Christ. What better way to do this than by adopting the vivid and strongly affective language of the

---

[283] M. Todd, *The Culture of Protestantism in Early Modern Scotland* (New Haven and London: Yale University, 2002), pp. 25, 48, 53-4.

[284] *Communion*, p. 316.

Song of Songs? After all, the Song was read tropologically by Rutherford, and by others in the Cistercian tradition, as representing the relationship between Christ and the individual Christian. Adopting the highly affective language of the Song of Songs enabled the preacher to put, in the words of Richard Sibbes (1577-1635), 'lively colours upon common truths' and, by doing so, to present the truth in such a way that it 'hath oft a strong working both upon the fancy and our will and affections'.[285]

It is vital to note here that what is important in sanctification, for Rutherford, is not the affections *per se* but the 'disposition' or state of those affections. By dispositions, Rutherford means 'moveable qualities of the soul', which can be either sinful or gracious. When the affections are hot with love for Christ, they are operating according to a gracious or 'heavenly' disposition. When they are cold or dead towards Christ, they are operating according to a sinful or 'ill' disposition. While it is possible that 'under such [ill] dispositions there may be some stirring of the habit of grace, and of the new creation', the soul will, nonetheless, to use Rutherford's words cited above, 'move on crutches'. The key to the Christian life, therefore, is keeping 'heavenly' dispositions in the affections of the soul. And Rutherford lists five ways of doing this:

> Now the way to get heavenly dispositions is 1. to be much in perusing the word and promises: Davids meditating 2. Learning. 3. Observing, loving the testimonies of God, prove that David was a heavenly disposed man, Psal. 119.
>
> 2. Keep communion with God in praying, hearing, reading, conferring. He who is much and daily among the oyntments of the Apothecaries, smels shall cleave to him whether he will or not, Luke 24.34. John 7.45, 46. Cant. 2.4, 5, 6, 7.
>
> 3. Mind much, seek much the things that are above, Col. 3.1, 2, 3.
>
> 4. Cherish the Spirit, obey him, grieve him not, work with him, be instrumental under his breathings, follow sweetly and willingly his drawings. See Ephes. 4.29, 30. I Thess. 5.19, 20. Cant. 5.8, 9, 10, 11, 12, &c.
>
> 5. Beware of frequent smoaring [smothering] divine light; deal tenderly with the light of the natural conscience, and tenderly with convictions and warnings; if so, you can hardly want divine dispositions and suitable influences, I Sam. 24.4, 5, 6.[286]

---

[285] R. Sibbes, 'The Soul's Conflict with Itself', in *The Complete Works of Richard Sibbes, D.D.*, 7 vols., ed. A. Grosart (Edinburgh: James Nichol, 1862-4), I, p. 184. The relationship between preaching and sanctification in Rutherford reflects his belief that there is no ordinary salvation apart from the church. Mirroring the Augustinian emphasis also found in Calvin, Rutherford states that when we are united to Christ in salvation, we become members of his 'mystical body' and are, therefore, united to others who are themselves united to Christ. The church is 'a fragment and a piece of mysticall Christ', albeit an earthly piece rather than a heavenly one. Just as the head of the body (Christ) cannot forget the rest of his body, so the members cannot forget one another. See *Christ Dying*, p. 529; *PP*, p. 31; *Letters*, pp. 43, 336.

[286] *Influences*, pp. 240-50, 301-2.

Seen in this light, it is not hard to understand why Rutherford would believe in preaching that extends to the affections. Such preaching would encourage and motivate the individual to pattern his or her life according to these five ways and, thereby, to get and keep heavenly dispositions. And it is principally the disposition of our affections that determines whether we will choose and act according to the new spiritual inclination or the old remnant of sin.

Rutherford's doctrine of sanctification balances on the tightrope between two extremes: Antinomianism, on the one hand, and Arminianism, on the other. Whereas the Antinomians wrongly define sanctification in terms of the imputed righteousness of justification and, as a result, deny the necessity of on-going human activity and obedience in salvation,[287] the Arminians go to the opposite extreme by attributing the deciding role in sanctification to human effort. In contrast to the former group, Rutherford maintains the necessity of human activity in sanctification. Just as a 'bow cannot bend itself, [but] a man's arm must do it; [and just as] it cannot shoot itself, [but] a hand must put the arrow on the string, and draw and loose it'; so also 'ye must learn the gate [i.e., the way] to heaven'.[288] The Christian life is anything but sedentary. It involves actively working out our salvation in fear and trembling. In contrast to the Arminians, Rutherford, reflecting his Calvinian roots, emphasizes that sanctification is founded upon union with Christ and the infused habit of grace. We work in our sanctification, to be sure, but we do so because God is active within us enabling us to work according to his will and ensuring that we do.

Any problems that Rutherford may have had with the Arminian doctrine of sanctification are completely overlooked in the *Examen*. He has no substantive examination of progressive sanctification anywhere on its pages. Instead, he is content to confine his invective to regeneration and to the Arminians' denial of infused habitual grace, both of which we have discussed above. For the related issues of perseverance and assurance, however, the story is altogether different. Rutherford dedicates a substantial chapter of the *Examen* to defending the unconditional promise of the perseverance of the saints and, then, follows that with a chapter devoted to the assurance of salvation. Because these two topics are related, we will present them both together under the heading of assurance. The differences that will arise between Rutherford and the Arminians here will summarize much of what has already been said thus far.

Assurance

The issue of the assurance of salvation represents a major area of contention not

---

[287] For a thorough and helpful treatment of Antinomianism in the Puritan era, especially as it developed in the years leading up to the civil war in England, see D.R. Como, *Blown by the Spirit: Puritanism and the Emergence of an Antinomian Underground in Pre-Civil-War England* (Stanford, CA: Stanford University, 2004).
[288] *Communion*, p. 183.

only for Rutherford and the Arminians during the seventeenth century but also for many scholars in our own day who see this as a prime example of how the post-Reformation orthodox like Rutherford distorted the theology of Calvin and the early Reformers. Among these modern-day scholars, Basil Hall and R.T. Kendall, along with others like Charles Bell, have argued that Beza and Perkins initiated an avalanche in regard to the doctrine of assurance that plunged away from Calvin with greater violence and speed until it culminated in Rutherford's and the Westminster Confession's ultimate betrayal of Calvin's own beliefs.[289] While Calvin believes that assurance is of the essence of faith,[290] they say, Rutherford 'separates assurance of salvation from faith, and teaches that certainty is achieved only as a result of self-examination and syllogistic deduction'.[291] The Westminster Confession sanctions this 'distinction between faith and assurance' with 'apparently unquestioned acceptance', because "Faith" was one heading in the Confession, and "Certainty of Salvation" another'.[292] Recently, however, such claims have been roundly criticized by Joel Beeke, in particular, who has argued that the 'discrepancy between Calvin and Calvinism on faith and assurance was largely *quantitative* and *methodological*, i.e., a matter of emphasis and method, rather than *qualitative* or *substantial*'.[293] In drawing this chapter to a close, we will use Rutherford to support Beeke's thesis in the main. In doing so, we will interact with the Arminian understanding of assurance at the same time by first exploring the relationship of assurance to faith and then the grounds of assurance. And we

---

[289] Hall, 'Calvin against the Calvinists', pp. 19-37; R.T. Kendall, 'Living the Christian Life in the Teaching of William Perkins and His Followers', in *Living the Christian Life* (London: The Westminster Conference, 1974), pp. 45-60; idem, *Calvin and English Calvinism*; idem, 'The Puritan Modification of Calvin's Theology', pp. 199-214; Bell, *Calvin and Scottish Theology*, especially chapter 3; idem, 'Saving Faith and Assurance of Salvation in the Teaching of John Calvin and Scottish Theology.' Other scholars who agree with Hall, Kendall, and Bell to some degree include: Brian Armstrong, Karl Barth, John Beardslee, Ernst Bizer, James Daane, Johannes Dantine, Edward Dowey, Otto Gründler, Philip Holtrop, Walter Kickel, Donald McKim, Philip McNair, Jurgen Moltmann, Charles Munson, Wilhelm Niesel, Norman Pettit, Pontien Polman, Jack Rogers, Holmes Rolston III, and Hans Emil Weber. For more, see J.R. Beeke, *Assurance of Faith*, p. 5n3.

[290] For more on Calvin's view of assurance as the essence of faith, see *Institutes* III.ii.7, p. 551; III.ii.16, pp. 561-2; III.ii.42, pp. 590-91; Kendall, *Calvin and English Calvinism*, p. 19; Beeke, *Assurance of Faith*, pp. 49-51.

[291] Bell, *Calvin and Scottish Theology*, pp. 83-4.

[292] Kendall, 'The Puritan Modification of Calvin's Theology', p. 214.

[293] Beeke, *Assurance of Faith*, p. 21. See also idem, 'Personal Assurance of Faith: The Puritans and Chapter 18.2 of the Westminster Confession', *WTJ* 55:1 (Spring 1993), pp. 1-30. And, cf. Wallace, *Calvin's Doctrine of the Christian Life*, pp. 299-306; P. Helm, *Calvin and the Calvinists* (Edinburgh: Banner of Truth, 1982), pp. 23-31; and R.M. Hawkes, 'The Logic of Assurance in English Puritan Theology', *WTJ* 52:2 (Fall 1990), pp. 247-61.

will conclude by examining some of the differences between Rutherford and the Arminians.

Assurance and Faith

In *Christ Dying and Drawing Sinners to Himselfe*, Rutherford remarks: 'that faith is essentially a perswasion and assurance of the *love of God* to me in *Christ*, its more then I could ever learne to bee the nature of Faith, a consequent separable I beleeve it is'.[294] When we contrast such a statement with one from Calvin, in which he says that faith is 'a firm and certain knowledge of God's benevolence toward us...in Christ',[295] it certainly appears, *prima facie*, that Kendall and Bell are correct in finding Rutherford and Calvin on opposite sides of the issue. Whereas Calvin sees assurance as essential to faith, Rutherford, in agreement with Puritan thought in general, argues that it is a fruit of faith instead.[296] But if we look more deeply into both Rutherford and Calvin, we will see that the differences between them are a matter of emphasis and method rather than of substance.

It bears repeating at this point that both Rutherford and Calvin describe faith in terms of intellectualism and voluntarism, as we saw in our discussion of the nature of faith above. Not only so, but Rutherford's definition of faith, as both 'ane assurance of knowledge that Christ cam into the world to die for sinners' and a 'resting and hanging upon Christ with all the heart for salvation', demonstrates that he believes assurance to be essential to saving faith, at least intellectually. It is at least necessary that the Christian be assured of the object and content of his or her faith, because saving faith is never simply a 'blind gessing'.[297] There are at least certain basic facts that the Christian must not only know but also be assured of in his or her own experience.

But more than this, when removed from the context of his dispute with the Antinomians, Rutherford comes even closer to Calvin's understanding of assurance and faith. In the *Examen*, for instance, he first differentiates between an objective or ontological (*entitativa*) certainty, 'by which the things [*res*] of the faith are most certain in themselves', and a subjective certainty, 'by which a thing [*res*] is certain to me and in my apprehension'. Then, he subdivides subjective certainty into two components: intellectual, 'by which *I am certain* about all the truths in the Word of God'; and fiducial, 'by which we [are certain that we] recline and hope in God'. Both components, according to Rutherford, are essential to saving faith to some degree. An intellectual certainty is necessary, as can be seen from the way that he defines faith; but a fiducial certainty is also necessary in principle. This does not mean that saving faith

---

[294] *Christ Dying*, p. 85.
[295] *Institutes* III.ii.7, p. 551.
[296] Beeke, *Assurance of Faith*, p. 142.
[297] *Catachisme*, p. 203.

will necessarily have a fiducial certainty that 'always and at all times exclude[s] every fear [*formidinem*]', but it does mean that an 'habitual certainty [will] always remain' within the believer, which is itself essential to a true and saving faith.[298] In other words, for Rutherford, there is a difference between fiducial certainty in *principle* and in *experience*. All Christians will necessarily have fiducial certainty in principle, because this is of the essence of saving faith, but not all will actually experience this certainty in the normal course of their lives.

Paul Helm and Joel Beeke have argued that this distinction between fiducial certainty in habit and in experience is a key for unlocking the relationship between faith and assurance in Calvin. They maintain that Calvin cannot be accurately understood on this issue unless we distinguish between 'the definition of faith' and 'the reality of the believer's experience' or between faith 'in principle' and faith 'in practice'.[299] Whereas Calvin defines faith in terms that bind it together with assurance, he clearly admits that the believer's experience of faith is 'something far different'. In principle, faith is tied to assurance, but, in practice, it 'is tossed about by various doubts, so that the minds of the godly are *rarely* at peace'.[300] To borrow the language of the *Examen*, then, this means that Calvin believes that there is an habitual fiducial certainty, which is essential to a true and saving faith, but which is not always experienced by the Christian in this life. Calvin's point, thus, appears to be the same as that emphasized by Rutherford and others of the post-Reformation period, namely, that the principle of faith is always directed towards full assurance, even if it may not actually achieve it in practice.[301] Echoing Calvin, Rutherford denounces 'the Papists' for teaching that the Christian 'could, [and] indeed ought to, ordinarily fear and doubt whether he or she would be in grace'.[302] Such a position runs counter to the habitual principle of assurance within the believer. Although faith might ever be 'tinged with doubt, or...assailed by some anxiety', ideally, for both Rutherford and for Calvin, it 'ought to be certain and assured'.[303]

---

[298] *Examen*, pp. 625-7.

[299] Beeke, *Assurance of Faith*, pp. 54-5; Helm, *Calvin and the Calvinists*, pp. 25-6.

[300] *Institutes* III.ii.17, p. 562; Beeke, *Assurance of Faith*, p. 55.

[301] Cf. *Institutes* III.ii.17, p. 562; with *Examen*, p. 627. William Perkins says that 'to bee certaine, and to give assurance, is *of the nature of faith*' (emphasis added) but then acknowledges that the believer will not always experience this: 'We hold that with assurance of salvation in our hearts is joined doubting; & there is no man so assured of his salvation, but he at sometime doubteth thereof, especially in the time of temptation' (*Workes*, I, pp. 563-4). These revealing statements teach us that, if Bell is right about the relationship of faith and assurance in Rutherford (which he does not appear to be), then rather than a Calvin-Calvinist divide, we should perhaps look for a Perkins-Perkinsist divide instead, because Perkins—a 'Calvinist'—explicitly employs the language of Calvin.

[302] *Examen*, p. 627.

[303] *Institutes* III.ii.17, p. 562.

But if it is true that Rutherford and Calvin speak of faith in the same way in principle and in practice, then how are we to explain the differences between them? How do we explain Rutherford's unambiguous comment that assurance is not of the essence of faith but a consequent of it instead? Before we attempt a reply to these questions, we need first to examine the grounds of assurance in both Calvin and Rutherford. After doing so, we will be in a better position to formulate an answer.

The Grounds of Assurance

Rutherford, in continuity with Calvin and the Puritans, distinguishes between the objective and subjective grounds of assurance but ascribes a primary role to the objective grounds.[304] Contrary to the Arminians, who 'teach that the whole certainty of Perseverance [in salvation] is ultimately resolved in the steadfastness [*constantia*] of Free Will [*Liberum Arbitrium*], which [of itself] has the power to persevere or not to persevere', Rutherford argues 'the opposite, namely, that every such certainty is established in the Veracity, Immutability, and Steadfastness [*Constantia*] of God; in the Intercession of the *Mediator*; and in the sealing of the *Holy Spirit*'.[305] At least two things are apparent from this. The first is the explicitly trinitarian framework in which Rutherford expresses his thoughts as to the proper grounds of assurance. As certain as are the promises of God the Father, the redemptive work of God the Son, and the application of redemption by God the Holy Spirit, so certain is the believer's final perseverance and, thus, his or her assurance that faith will in fact gain the victory in its struggle against unbelief. The second thing to note in what Rutherford says about the grounds of assurance is their unconditional nature. This is especially clear in the *Examen*, where Rutherford takes particular aim at the conditionality in the Arminian doctrine of assurance. Because the Arminians are keen to protect human freedom, they acknowledge only a temporary 'hypothetical' assurance that is possible so long as the individual is persevering in the Christian life. But such an idea is anathema to Rutherford, because, as we will see, it cuts across the heart of his doctrine of God and of his understanding of soteriology.

The Arminian notion of conditional certainty, i.e., an assurance conditioned upon the individual's perseverance, is, in the first place, a *reductio ad absurdum*, according to Rutherford, because it makes no distinction between the elect and the reprobate. Under the Arminian schema, assurance of salvation would apply equally to Christian and non-Christian alike. But surely it is problematic, says Rutherford, if one's definition of *Christian* assurance applies to both Christians and non-Christians equally. In the second place, and more notably, a conditional certainty based upon a conditional perseverance detracts

---

[304] See *Catachisme*, p. 213.
[305] *Examen*, p. 640.

from the glory of God. It 'is in conflict with God's immutability and veracity', since it subjects his promises to preserve us to the condition of our perseverance. God's promises to elect, to enter into and remain in covenant, and to atone for sin are not absolute promises, for the Arminians, but are conditioned upon human free will. Such an idea has two important consequences. First, it removes God from his rightful place at the center of the universe by denying his sovereign power to work according to his own will in salvation:

> *Not even Christ, by his own intercession and prayers, nor God the Father, by his own gracious keeping [custodia] and protection, nor the Holy Spirit, by his own superlatively powerful grace, can procure my Perseverance and, thus, my eternal glory; if I have discarded the grace of God and faith.*

Secondly, it removes all possibility of comfort for Christians in this life. If the Arminians are right, then 'this suggests that true believers [will experience] terror, fear of hell, wretched desperation, and the melancholy [*tristitia*] of the Devil, and [will be] without every consolation'.[306] The chief end of humankind envisioned by the Westminster Shorter Catechism, 'to glorify God, and to enjoy him for ever', would become altogether impossible.

In opposition to the Arminians, Rutherford argues for an unconditional certainty based upon an unconditional salvation:

> Indeed, the certainty of salvation, according to the word of God, is as *absolute* and *certain*...as is the promise of God that he would not cover the earth again with the waters of *Noah, Isa.* 54.9-10, and as is the faithful Covenant of God with respect to the succession of the nights and the days, and the movements of the Sun and the Moon, *Jer.* 31.35-6.[307]

The salvation of the Christian is certain, because 'the eternal predestination of God', the 'intercession of the *Son*', and the 'sealing of the *Holy Spirit* for the day of redemption', are as absolute, unconditional, and certain as are all the other promises of God, as certain as the sun rising in the morning and setting in the evening.[308] In his chapter on perseverance in the *Examen*, Rutherford enters into a lengthy dialogue with the Arminians in order to demonstrate that God's promise of final perseverance is unconditional.[309] Although Rutherford does believe that Christians are free and active agents and, as such, are responsible for actively working out their salvation in fear and trembling, he explicitly maintains that they will ultimately continue to do so only because God promises that they will persevere to the end in the Christian life (re: the earlier

---

[306] *Examen*, pp. 635-8.
[307] *Examen*, p. 636.
[308] *Examen*, p. 631.
[309] *Examen*, pp. 549-624.

discussion on the mutability of the human will and the preservation of God).[310] The primary grounds of assurance, for Rutherford, contra the Arminians, are the objective, absolute, and unconditional promises of God, which are themselves founded upon the character of God.

In light of this, it is rather perplexing that R.T. Kendall can argue that the Westminster Confession's doctrines of faith and assurance are 'crypto-Arminian' instead of Calvinistic.[311] Rutherford's clear denunciation of Arminian conditionality should be enough to overturn any such claim. While it is true, as men like Charles Bell and J.B. Torrance have reminded us,[312] that Rutherford speaks of faith as a condition of the covenant, it is also true that he uses the word condition in a different sense than does Arminianism or, even, Baxter's neo-nomianism.[313] As Rutherford sees it, a condition is not something that is required of us which must then be fulfilled by us. Rather, a condition is something that is required of us but that is fulfilled *in us* by God: 'God hes promised to call us by his grace to doe our pairt...and so [he] fulfilleth both his pairt of the covenant and ouris.' This is not to say that we can 'sleepe and fold our handis and commit all the cair to God of our salvatione'. God fulfills our part of the covenant, but he does so by regenerating us so that we will necessarily exercise faith in Christ and then by working *in us* so that we are 'carefull to work out our salvatione in fear and trimbling'.[314] Torrance's apparent concern to protect the Christian message from a conditional gospel, i.e., one that says that repentance or forsaking of sin is a necessary pre-condition to salvation, is both legitimate and honorable. But he is incorrect to find such a conditional gospel in federal theology. Although Rutherford, the so-called 'prince of the federal theologians',[315] speaks of conditions in the covenant—as do others like William Ames—he explicitly states that God himself fulfills those conditions by working in us. John Von Rohr reminds us, in regard to the Puritans, that the covenant had,

---

[310] E.g., Rutherford says things like this against the Arminians: 'There is, therefore, no condition in Perseverance: For [if there were] then God would promise that Saints will unfailingly persevere provided that they would persevere.' *Examen*, pp. 554-5.

[311] Kendall, *Calvin and English Calvinism*, p. 209.

[312] Torrance, 'The Covenant Concept', pp. 225-43; idem, 'Covenant or Contract?', pp. 51-76; Bell, *Calvin and Scottish Theology*, p. 76.

[313] J.I. Packer states: 'Whereas orthodox Calvinism taught that Christ satisfied the law in the sinner's place, Baxter held that Christ satisfied the Lawgiver and so procured a change in the law.' This law-change meant, for Baxter, that the condition for justification under the new covenant is faith, which, he says, is 'all out of Christ in ourselves'. Later in his life, Baxter even called faith and the life of faith, merit. See Packer, *Redemption & Restoration of Man*, pp. 254-62; and R. Baxter, *Aphorismes of Justification* (London, 1649), pp. 121ff, 137ff.

[314] *Catachisme*, p. 213.

[315] Bell, *Calvin and Scottish Theology*, p. 70.

a twofold nature, that is, it was conditional and it was absolute. The conditional character of the Covenant is, of course, expressed in the idea of compact and mutual obligation. The Covenant is of grace because God's gifts within it are those of mercy to the undeserving, but it is conditional because the promises are to those who present a faith, a sincerity, a 'pitching on Christ'. Grace is given if conditions are fulfilled. But to leave the covenant idea at that point [is] to commit grievous error and to be guilty of serious absurdity in Puritan understanding....Faith is required as a condition within [the covenant] antecedent to salvation, but that faith is already granted by [the covenant] as a gift consequent of election.[316]

It is the Arminians, not Puritans like Rutherford, who endorse a conditional covenant and a conditional gospel. Rutherford's thinking in the *Examen* is the polar opposite of Arminian theology. Its unconditionality allows us no room for calling Westminster theology 'crypto-Arminian'.

It is precisely because the covenant is unconditional that it can function as an absolute and objective 'anchor' for the Christian's assurance in Rutherford's understanding. Christians ultimately rest assured because their salvation is not founded upon anything that they do but wholly upon what God has promised to do in and through them. Since, as we previously mentioned, all of soteriology finds its causal foundation in the covenant of redemption, the believer's assurance is bound up together with intratrinitarian promises and commitments made between the Father and the Son.[317] The salvation of the elect is as absolute, certain, and incontrovertible as is the Godhead itself. Such an emphasis on absolute election, however, naturally raises a question: how are we to know the elect from the non-elect? It should be no surprise that this was the question that haunted people in the wake of the Reformation. In order to answer it, Rutherford and many of his post-Reformation peers pointed towards certain subjective grounds whereby the Christian might gain an assured answer to his or her query into divine election.

This tendency of the post-Reformation orthodox to implement subjective grounds for conveying assurance, especially the use of the practical syllogism,[318] is perhaps the principal reason why scholars like Kendall argue for

---

[316] J. Von Rohr, 'Covenant and Assurance in Early English Puritanism', *CH* 34 (1965), pp. 200-201. William Ames expresses this fact as follows: 'the condition of the Covenant is also promised in the Covenant'. And, for this reason, he could also say that the covenant is wholly God's act. Ames' words are cited in *The Covenant of Grace, not Absolute, but Conditional, Modestly Asserted, and the Preachers thereof Vindicated from the unjust Aspersions of Arminianism and Popery* (London, 1692), p. 63. See also Ames, *Marrow*, pp. 90-91, 97-9.

[317] *COL*, pp. 283-301, 331.

[318] Practical syllogisms should be differentiated from mystical syllogisms. The former bases assurance on logical deductions made from external criteria, i.e., the fruit of faith, whereas the latter bases it on deductions made from internal criteria. On this, see Barth, *CD*, II/2, pp. 333-40; and Weber, *Foundations of Dogmatics*, II, pp. 358-62.

discontinuity between Calvin and his successors. Following this characteristic Puritan methodology, Rutherford remarks:

> But we contend against them [the Arminians] that people ought to be certain about their own eternal Election, not, to be sure, with an *a priori* certainty *(for who has known the mind of God?)* but with an *a posteriori* certainty....Because all who are elected unto glory are also predestined to Conversion and Adoption as Sons of God, *Eph.* 1.5-6. But God has given us many τεκμήρια, *proofs,* by which we should know that we are converted; Therefore, also by which we should know that we are elected unto glory.[319]

The practical syllogism is designed to enable the individual to draw a conclusion about the reality of his or her faith from certain τεκμήρια, or proofs, by using logic as follows: '*The one who overcomes the world and observes the commands of God, believes (as in 1 John 5.4-5 and James 2.18); But I have overcome the world and observed the commands of God; Therefore, I believe.*'[320] The purpose of such syllogisms is to help those who are struggling with assurance by pointing to evidence for the reality of their conversion and, thus, of their election.

According to Wilhelm Niesel, the use of practical syllogisms like this to grant personal assurance is an altogether foreign concept in Calvin.[321] But, as Karl Barth has pointed out, Niesel's conclusions are overstated. Although the use of the practical syllogism may not have appeared in Calvin formally, it is not 'possible to deny...that...the *syllogismus practicus* did constitute one element in the theology of Calvin'.[322] Indeed, Calvin, at least on occasion, speaks in much the same way as does Rutherford:

> Therefore, as it is wrong to make the force of election contingent upon faith in the gospel, by which we feel that it appertains to us, so we shall be following the best order if, in seeking the certainty of our election, we cling to those latter signs which are sure attestations of it.[323]

Luther, too, according to Bernhard Lohse, speaks on occasion of our works as 'signs of faith' from which we can 'ascertain and recognize...true faith' and,

---

[319] *Examen*, pp. 638-9. For examples of the practical syllogism in the post-Reformation orthodox, see Perkins, *Workes*, I, pp. 87, 510, 529, 547; Dickson, *Therapeutica sacra*, pp. 4, 216, 407; D. Pareus, *Theological Miscellanies of Dr. David Pareus* (London, 1645), p. 808.

[320] *Examen*, p. 21.

[321] Niesel, *The Theology of Calvin*, pp. 170-81; idem, 'Syllogismus practicus?' in *Aus Theologie und Geschichte der reformierten Kirche* (Neukirchen: K. Moers, 1933), pp. 158-79.

[322] *CD*, II/2, p. 335.

[323] *Institutes* III.xxiv.4, p. 968. See Wallace's discussion in *Calvin's Doctrine of the Christian Life*, pp. 301-3.

thus, be assured of our salvation.[324]

That being said, there can be no hiding the fact that Rutherford and the Puritans place greater weight on the use of subjective signs or proofs than Calvin and Luther. But this is due in large part to the contextual differences between the eras of the Reformation and post-Reformation. It should be no surprise that their emphases and methodologies differ somewhat if the questions that they are seeking to answer are themselves different. For Calvin, speaking primarily against the Roman Church's denial of full assurance, the accent is understandably on the objectivity of God's benevolence in Christ or what we have called the principle of faith.[325] Whereas the Christian's *experience* of faith oftentimes confirms the Roman Church's position on assurance, it is the *definition* of faith that effectively counters it. But, for Rutherford and the Puritans, the stress is upon the individual's experience of faith. Later in *Christ Dying*, Rutherford seems to make just this point when he says: 'The assurance of *Christ's* righteousnesse is a direct act of faith, apprehending imputed righteousnesse: the evidence of our justification *we now speak of*, is the reflect light [sic], not by which wee are justified, but by which we know that we are justified.'[326] William Ames is even more to the point:

> This justifying Faith of it[s] own nature doth produce, and so hath joyned with it a speciall and certaine perswasion of the grace and mercy of God in Christ: *whence also justifying Faith is oftentimes not amisse described by the orthodox [i.e., Calvin et al.] by this perswasion, especially when they doe oppose that generall Faith to which the Papists ascribe all things:* but 1. This perswasion as touching the sense of it, is not always present. For it may and often doth come to passe, either through weaknesse of judgement, or through divers tentations and troubles of mind, that he, who truly believeth, and is by Faith justified before God, yet for a time may thinke according to that which hee feeles, that he neither believeth, nor is reconciled to God. 2. There be divers degrees, of this perswasion, so that neither all believers have altogether the same assurance of the grace and favour of God, nor the same believers at all times.[327]

This explains how it is that Rutherford can define faith in the same basic terms as Calvin, especially when speaking against the Roman Church, and then explicitly state that assurance is not of the essence of faith, in the context of his dispute with the Antinomians. He is talking primarily about the individual's

---

[324] Lohse, *Martin Luther's Theology*, pp. 265-6.
[325] See Beeke's discussion of assurance in the Roman Church up to the Council of Trent (*Assurance of Faith*, chapter 2). There were, of course, differences of opinion within the Roman Church both at Trent and after it. For more on these intra ecclesial variances, see William Cunningham's discussion of Catharinus and Bellarmine in 'The Reformers and the Doctrine of Assurance', in *The Reformers and the Theology of the Reformation*, pp. 143-5.
[326] *Christ Dying*, p. 111, emphasis added.
[327] Ames, *Marrow*, pp. 132-3, emphasis added.

experience of faith, or the reflex act of faith, while Calvin is concentrating on faith's direct act. Whereas Rutherford's context demands that faith and assurance be articulated in such a way as to avoid certain errors of Christian living, or of sanctification, Calvin's warrants an expression of faith aimed against wrong conceptions of justification.[328] As we previously mentioned, the Reformed emphasis on absolute predestination probably also played a role in bringing about this contextual change. It increasingly brought to the fore questions of whether or not individuals were themselves elect. Subjective aspects became more prominent in Rutherford than they did in Calvin, because they were needed to cope with the exigencies of the time in which he lived and ministered.

In developing the subjective characteristics of faith and assurance, however, Rutherford accentuates three important features that draw his thinking closer to the priorities of Calvin. First, Rutherford substantiates the use of practical syllogisms by appealing to the example of Scripture:

> *1 John 2.3, By this we know that we know [God], if we keep his commands; and 3.14, We know that we have passed from death to life, because we love the brothers; 1 John 5.2, By this we know that we love the sons of God, since we love God and keep his commands; 1 John 4.16, And we know and believe the love that God has toward us....*[W]e know that we are called and justified [by God] by our peace of conscience, by our παρρησία, *boldness*, by our sense of the love of God poured out in our hearts, by our hope, which is not ashamed, and by our boasting in our afflictions, *Rom.* 5.1-4; and 8.15-17.[329]

Scripture delineates certain proofs whereby we may know that we possess saving faith. And Scripture also substantiates the application of the rules of logic in drawing conclusions from its premises. In Matthew 21.31-2, Jesus himself argues 'from an Antecedent to a consequent by naturall logick' and

---

[328] It is primarily the Antinomian denial of sanctification as a basis for providing assurance that drives Rutherford and his contemporaries to place their emphasis where they do. In *The Tryal & Triumph of Faith*, Rutherford complains of Tobias Crisp (1600-1643) in much the same way that John Winthrop (1588-1649), during the American Antinomian controversy, complains of Ann Hutchinson's (1591-1643) 'two dangerous errors: (1) That the person of the Holy Ghost dwells in a justified person. (2) That no sanctification can help to evidence to us our justification' (P. Miller, ed., *The American Puritans: Their Prose and Poetry* [New York: Anchor Books, 1956], p. 50). Winthrop's and Rutherford's positions are in direct opposition to such views. See, e.g., *Tryal*, p. 132. On the American Antinomian controversy, see D.D. Hall, ed., *The Antinomian Controversy 1636-1638* (Middletown, CT: Wesleyan University, 1968); J.W. Jones, *The Shattered Synthesis: New England Puritanism before the Great Awakening* (New Haven and London: Yale University, 1973); and M.P. Winship, *Making Heretics: Militant Protestantism and Free Grace in Massachusetts, 1636-1641* (Princeton: Princeton University, 2002).

[329] *Examen*, p. 639.

critcizes the religious leaders of the day for not having done the same thing themselves.[330]

Second, Rutherford links the use of practical syllogisms to the objective grounds of assurance by way of the ministry of the Holy Spirit. The Spirit testifies with our spirits that we possess the signs or proofs given by God in Scripture and, thus, that the objective promises of salvation apply to us personally. This reflex knowledge is not discernable by the human mind or free will alone but is as much a work of the Spirit as faith itself is:

> As Faith which is the direct act of knowing and relying on *Christ* for pardon, is a worke of the Spirit, above the reach of reason; so also the reflect act of my knowing and feeling, that I beleeve and am in *Christ*...is a supernaturall work, above the compasse and reach of our Free-wil, and is dispensed according to the spirations and stirrings of the free grace of *God*.[331]

But the Spirit does more than simply testify to the *presence* of the signs or proofs of faith within us. He enables the entire syllogistic process: 'while the *Holy Spirit* brings it about [*efficit*] that we would know and perceive by a reflex act that we believe, repent, and hope, he also brings it about [*efficit*] that from this we would conclude that we are the Sons of God'.[332]

Third, Rutherford seems to attach greater significance to the direct testimony of the Spirit than to the reflex testimony just described. Joel Beeke has rightly noted that Rutherford falls into the category of divines who, along with William Twisse and Thomas Goodwin, distinguish the Spirit's 'witnessing *to* the believer's spirit by direct applications of the Word' from the Spirit's 'witnessing *with* the believer's spirit by syllogism'. But he then claims, rather perplexingly, that Rutherford 'stresses that the reflex act of faith is as a rule 'more spiritual and helpful' than are direct acts'.[333] It is true that Rutherford tends to emphasize the reflex testimony of the Spirit more so than the direct testimony. In light of his context, this ought not to surprise anyone. But it is not at all evident that Rutherford sees the reflex testimony as, therefore, somehow more important or 'more spiritual and helpful' than the direct testimony, as others of the Puritans do.[334] The phrase 'more spiritual and helpful' does not, as far as the current author has been able to tell, occur in any of the writings of Rutherford, at least not in those cited by Beeke. Not only so, but when Rutherford is presented with the opportunity to declare which testimony is most important to assurance, he stresses the direct over the reflex. In answer to the question, 'How ar wee assured of our continuance in grace in our owne

---

[330] *SA*, pp. 49-50.

[331] *Christ Dying*, p. 86.

[332] *Examen*, p. 23.

[333] Beeke, *Assurance of Faith*, pp. 170-71.

[334] Beeke cites Anthony Burgess and Thomas Brooks as warning against relying upon the direct testimony of the Spirit. *Assurance of Faith*, p. 203n149.

conscience?', Rutherford responds by saying 'Godis Spirit witnesseth with our spirit that we ar Godis sonnes and heiris.' But then he defines this 'witnes of Godis Spirit' as the direct testimony: 'the voyce of Godis Spirit accompanying the Word, so speaking to the heart and making all the promises of God to be myne as if the new covenant wer ritten and spokin to me by name'. And he clearly distinguishes it from the reflex act of faith.[335] Why would Rutherford answer this specific catechism question about how we subjectively gain assurance by referring to the Spirit's direct testimony if he truly believes that the reflex witness is 'more spiritual and helpful', as Beeke has claimed? It must be because he believes that the direct witness is more significant to the Christian's assurance, even though his methodology is to emphasize the reflex witness when addressing the needs of his culture.

All this is to say that Rutherford's understanding of faith and assurance, while differing from Calvin's understanding in emphasis and method, is substantially the same, perhaps even more so than is the case for others of his contemporaries. He defines faith, principially, as assurance, both intellectually and fiducially. And, even though he emphasizes the subjective grounds of assurance more than Calvin does, he places great stress on the testimony of the Holy Spirit. The Spirit directly testifies to the believer's spirit, applying the absolute and unconditional promises of God to him or her directly. And the Holy Spirit also testifies with the spirit of the Christian, allowing him or her to discern certain subjective signs or proofs and then to draw the appropriate conclusions from them. Although Rutherford's methodology favors the latter, the reflex testimony, his theory favors the former, the direct testimony. This strongly pneumatological emphasis in Rutherford certainly seems to parallel Calvin's own perspective, which can be seen in the following quote:

> the Spirit of God affords us such a testimony that our spirit is assured of the adoption of God, when He is our Guide and Teacher. Our mind would not of its own accord convey this assurance to us, unless the testimony of the Spirit preceded it.[336]

It does, therefore, seem best to conclude with Beeke that there is no substantial difference between Rutherford and Calvin on the doctrine of assurance.

The criticisms of Bell and Torrance—although offering conclusions that are questionable—do, nonetheless, contain well-founded warnings. Despite Rutherford's good intentions and his care to link the practical syllogism to the work of the Holy Spirit, there can be no doubt but that such a subjective emphasis actually served in succeeding generations to exacerbate the believer's struggles over assurance and to push him or her to look *intra se* rather than *ad Christum*. This, when later coupled with a harmful sacramental theology,

---

[335] *Catachisme*, pp. 213-14.
[336] Calvin, *Romans and Thessalonians*, p. 170.

resulted in a profoundly paralyzing introspection within the Scottish kirk, the effects of which can still be seen in some regions of the Highlands today. Rutherford himself, however, clearly warned against putting too much stock in these subjective external signs as over against the objective promises of God, even going so far as to say that 'it is Adultery to seek a signe, because we cannot rest on our Husbands word'.[337] Others of Rutherford's contemporaries, like George Gillespie for instance, were even more patent in their warnings against relying upon subjective and external signs: 'Beware that marks of grace do not lead us from Christ, or make us look upon ourselves as anything at all out of Christ.'[338] The Puritans were aware of the problems associated with guiding believers to look within themselves for landmarks of saving faith, and they warned against such problems. But they persisted in using such τεκμήρια because they could not stand seeing their parishioners excessively burdened with unnecessary anxiety and fear and because they—like Calvin—believed that assurance was principially of the essence of faith.

The significant thing to note in Rutherford's treatment of faith and assurance, as far as this thesis is concerned, is that it summarizes many of the central differences that exist between him and the Arminians. The Arminians teach a conditional or hypothetical assurance which is based decisively upon human free choice, and they fit their view of divine sovereignty in around that. God's sovereign promise that the Christian will persevere is, according to them, conditional upon the individual's free perseverance in the faith. Having begun in the faith, a person can freely choose to reject the faith and, thus, render the promises of God that were initially given to him or her null and void. But Rutherford teaches an unconditional assurance based upon the sovereign promises of God, and he fits his view of human freedom in around that. Evidence for this can be found in the God-centeredness of Rutherford's grounds for assurance. Every grounds for assurance given by Rutherford ultimately finds its end in God. The primary objective grounds are presented within a framework that is wholly trinitarian, and the secondary subjective grounds are inextricably tied to the ministry of the Holy Spirit, so much so that it is 'above the compasse and reach of our Free-wil'.[339] Rutherford and the Arminians are diametrically opposed to one another. The Arminians offer a theology that defends human freedom, while Rutherford tenders one that exalts God in every conceivable way.

---

[337] *Tryal*, p. 10.
[338] G. Gillespie, *A Treatise of Miscellany Questions*, in *The Works of George Gillespie*, 2 vols. (Edinburgh: Robert Ogle and Oliver and Boyd, 1846), II, p. 104.
[339] *Christ Dying*, p. 86.

CHAPTER 5

Rutherford's Theology and the Grounds for his Opposition to Arminianism

Margo Todd has helpfully pointed out that a common error among historians is their tendency to read history through their own 'interpretive structures' and, in doing so, to lose 'the thread of the story' that a certain era in history is trying to tell.[1] What is true for historians, however, can also be said about theologians who try to read theology without regard for the historical context in which it is written: they lose sight of the story that a particular individual or era is telling. In the case of Rutherford and his tirade against Arminian theology in the *Examen*, there is indeed a story that needs to be told, and we miss it if we concentrate purely on the theological elements of the debate. But the theological elements are themselves a vital part of the process, because the particular story comes to light only through questions that are raised by Rutherford's theology and his reaction to the Arminians.

By examining Rutherford's theology systematically beginning with his understanding of revelation and the distinction between *theologia archetypa et ectypa*—the *terminus a quo* for our study—and ending with his view of assurance as grounded in the unconditional and absolute promises of God—our *terminus ad quem*—we have painted a picture of a God that is radically transcendent, even breathtakingly so. Rutherford's voluntarism, which considers the will of God to be a rule unto itself, limited only by divine immutability or the law of non-contradiction, is so austere that it can leave one wondering how he actually escapes accusations of divine caprice, as he insists he does. Rutherford's supralapsarian predestinarianism, although not as strict as it perhaps could be nor as some have assumed it to be, is still quite severe, insofar as it teaches that God creates some people unto destruction without regard to their sin, having already decreed to pass them over. Such an exalted view of the will of God seems to call into question the New Testament picture of Jesus as one who is full of love and compassion and concern for the justice of all. Rutherford's understanding of salvation, likewise, exalts the freedom of God's will over human freedom. The divine will, rather than the human will, is the final arbiter in matters of salvation. Although humankind is said to have

---

[1] M. Todd, '"All One with Tom Thumbe": Arminianism, Popery, and the Story of the Reformation in Early Stuart Cambridge', *CH* 64 (1995), p. 563.

true freedom, this freedom can never be such that it encroaches upon divine freedom in any way.

The significant thing to notice here is that these doctrines in Rutherford are diametrically opposed to Arminian theology. Rutherford's voluntarism directly contradicts Arminian intellectualism, and his overwhelming emphasis on divine freedom runs counter to the prominence the Arminians give to human freedom. While Rutherford's God reigns and rules on high in the current world order, the Arminian God voluntarily places himself in subjection to his creatures. The two systems lie on opposite ends of the continuum. This is true not simply *theologically*, however; it is also true *attitudinally*. The *Examen* does not contain a friendly disagreement between two brothers trying to work out their petty differences but an outright frontal attack, an internecine feud. Rutherford has no tolerance whatsoever for Arminian theology.[2] He is not interested in dialoguing with the Arminians but in annihilating their views. And in his bid to do this, he associates their theology with the beliefs of practically every known group that has espoused heretical or, at least, anti-Reformational ideals, including: Anabaptists, Antitrinitarians, Arians, Atheists, Dominicans, Epicureans, Jesuits, Libertines, Papists, Pelagians, Pseudo-Lutherans, Separatists, Socinians, and Tritheists.[3]

This immediately raises several questions. Why is Rutherford opposed to Arminianism to such an extent that he is altogether intolerant of it? Why does he spend most of his lifetime writing against it? And, why does he devote his classroom lectures to refuting its doctrines? These questions become further intensified if David Mullan is correct in his claim that there was a Calvinist consensus in Scotland in the seventeenth century.[4] If Mullan is right that very

---

[2] Rutherford is not a man known for his tolerance. He is overtly dogmatic and uncompromising, even in matters that may seem trivial to us today. During the Protester-Resolutioner controversy, for instance, Rutherford absented himself in protest from the General Assembly of the church and never attended again for the last ten or so years of his life; he dissolved intimate friendships with fellow-Calvinists David Dickson and Robert Blair, because they disagreed with him over what stance should be taken towards Charles II and the Scots army; he printed a scathing denunciation of his opponents in the preface to his *Survey of the Survey of that Summe of Church Discipline*; and he persisted in verbally accosting James Wood, a colleague at St. Mary's College, until Wood became 'wearie of his place exceedingly' and moved to St. Salvators College in 1657 (Coffey, *Politics, Religion and the British Revolutions*, pp. 56-60).

[3] See, e.g., *Examen*, pp. 5-9, 15-16, 46, 87-8, 94-7, 162, 166, 196-7, 200, 210, 212, 221, 223-5, 230-31, 234-5, 265, 305, 307-8, 310-11, 313-14, 316, 319, 321-3, 325, 327, 337-8, 353, 356-63, 369, 371, 375, 386, 398, 400, 431, 436, 453, 457, 488, 492, 496-8, 500, 501, 503-5, 507, 511, 517-18, 520, 527, 530, 541, 543, 545-6, 550, 553, 591, 596, 622, 625, 628, 630, 643-6, 662, 664-5, 675, 677, 679, 691-2, 709-10, 716-17, 721-6, 728-30, 753, 759.

[4] D.G. Mullan, 'Theology in the Church of Scotland 1618-c.1640: A Calvinist Consensus?', *SCJ* 26:3 (1995), p. 595; idem, *Scottish Puritanism*, pp. 1-2. In seeing a

little actual Arminianism existed in Scotland at this time and that the term 'Arminian' was simply an epithet used by *jus divinum* Presbyterians like Rutherford 'to denounce the other [Episcopalian] faction', then one is left wondering why Rutherford could be so completely preoccupied by a system of thought that posed no threat whatsoever in itself.[5] Was Rutherford deceived? Or, was he simply being disingenuous? Part of the answer to our questions lies in the fact that Rutherford is not to be understood merely from a Scottish perspective. He lived, was educated, and wrote in a continental context, one that transcended the bounds of his native Scotland. But to confine our answer to this is to miss the primary grounds for Rutherford's opposition to Arminianism and, thus, to overlook our story. In this final chapter, we will survey those grounds and tell that story and then conclude by drawing out relevant implications not only for the Calvin-Calvinist debate but, more practically, for the church in the twenty-first century as well.

The Grounds for Rutherford's Opposition to Arminianism

The Two Strands of Arminianism

In November 1638, the first 'true' General Assembly in thirty-six years convened in Glasgow.[6] The moderator for this momentous Assembly, Alexander Henderson (1583-1646), initiated its proceedings by pointing to two strands of Arminianism, each of which he believed ran to a different end:

> One is that which hes troubled the Low Countries, and hath spred itself so farr, and that is nothing but the way to Socinianisme, and *Socinianismus inchoatus* is *Arminianismus consociatus*. Certainlie no man that will consider aright of the

---

Calvinist consensus in Scotland, Mullan is following those who argue for the same thing in England: e.g., P.G. Lake, 'Calvinism and the English Church 1570-1635', *Past and Present* 114 (1987), pp. 32-76; Tyacke, *Anti-Calvinists*; D.R. Como, 'Puritans, Predestination and the Construction of Orthodoxy in Early Seventeenth-Century England', in *Conformity and Orthodoxy in the English Church, c.1560-1660*, eds. P. Lake and M. Questier (Woodbridge, Suffolk: Boydell Press, 2000), pp. 64-87; D.D. Wallace, *Puritans and Predestination: Grace in English Protestant Theology, 1525-1695* (Chapel Hill, NC: University of North Carolina, 1982); P. Collinson, *The Religion of Protestants: The Church in English Society, 1559-1625* (Oxford: Clarendon Press, 1982).
[5] Mullan, 'Theology in the Church of Scotland', p. 595.
[6] Each of the six Assemblies held during this thirty-six year interval (1606, 1608, 1610, 1616, 1617, 1618) were condemned as 'illegal', because they were 'so overborne with by royal interference'. Among the first acts of the 1638 Assembly was to declare these 'pretended' Assemblies 'null and void forever'. See A. Peterkin, ed., *Records of the Kirk of Scotland* (Edinburgh: John Sutherland, 1838), pp. 14, 24-6.

poyntes of Arminianisme, but he will see more nor [than] the seids and grossnesse of Socinianisme. There is ane uther Arminianisme mentioned by some in England, and uthers in Scotland, and that runs in ane uther way—it runs to Papistrie, and is *inchoatus Papismus*.[7]

David Mullan cites these words by Henderson as proof that what existed in Scotland in the early seventeenth century was not in fact true Arminianism.[8] He argues that these words suggest that Scottish 'Arminianism' had no clear association with the errors of the Remonstrants and was, instead, a polemical ploy to denounce William Laud and his prelatic party for their ecclesial convictions. While it is beyond question that Mullan's work on the whole represents a significant contribution to our understanding of the church in early modern Scotland, his claims about Arminianism are, nonetheless, rather unsatisfactory for at least the following three reasons.

First, according to Henderson, what existed in England and Scotland at this time is at least similar enough to the theology of the Remonstrants to be classified under the genus of Arminianism. The mere fact that Henderson refers to two strands of Arminianism by the same name is indicative of doctrinal similarities between the two groups. This should be enough in itself to overturn the idea that Arminianism in Scotland was somehow not actual Arminianism. But Robert Baillie goes even further than Henderson and explicitly connects the Scottish variety of Arminianism with the Dutch strain by characterizing the errors of the former in terms of the five articles of the Remonstrants.[9]

Second, although modern scholarship is divided as to whether William Laud was himself an Arminian,[10] it is clear that he was perceived as such by his Reformed contemporaries in Scotland on theological grounds, not simply because of his ecclesial innovations. The reason that Laud was perceived as an Arminian by men like Rutherford is because his theology was distinguished by

---

[7] Peterkin, *Records of the Kirk of Scotland*, p. 155. Robert Baillie makes a similar statement in his *Antidote against Arminianism*, p. 18.

[8] Mullan, *Scottish Puritanism*, p. 227.

[9] Baillie, *Antidote against Arminianism*, pp. 22-3; idem, *Ladensium autokatakrisis*, pp. 8-32.

[10] Nicholas Tyacke has offered solid evidence in favor of understanding Laud as an Arminian (*Anti-Calvinists*, pp. 266-70; and idem, 'Archbishop Laud', in *The Early Stuart Church, 1603-1642*, ed. K. Fincham [London: MacMillan, 1993], pp. 51-70). Tyacke's view has been challenged by several scholars, e.g., K. Sharpe (*The Personal Rule of Charles I* [New Haven: Yale University, 1992], pp. 286-92), J. Davis (*The Caroline Captivity of the Church* [Oxford: Clarendon, 1992], pp. 95-103), and P. White (*Predestination, Policy and Polemic* [Cambridge: Cambridge University, 1992], pp. 276-86). The scholarly divide over Laud is largely the result of Laud's ambiguity in expressing his own position in regard to the doctrines of grace, which, according to Peter Lake, is itself typical of English Arminians. See Lake, 'Calvinism and the English Church', p. 72.

an unambiguous embrace of conditional predestinarianism.[11] In speaking out against the Puritan view of predestination, Laud demonstrates this conviction: 'almost all of them say that God from all eternity reprobates by far the greater part of mankind to eternal fire, *without any eye at all to their sin.* Which opinion my very soul abominates.'[12] According to Robert Baillie, this is all that is necessary to label an individual an Arminian. He or she does not have to embrace overtly all five articles of the Remonstrants in order to be guilty of Arminianism, because all five articles are connected logically as 'a chaine, any one link whereof, but speciallie the first, will draw all the rest'.[13] It is only necessary, therefore, that someone embrace the conditional predestinarianism of the first article for the charge of Arminianism to apply. Even if not explicitly sanctioned, the other four articles are implicit within the first, such that the only thing that could prevent an individual from accepting the entire Arminian system, according to Baillie, was logical inconsistency.[14] Because Laud unambiguously endorsed the conditional predestinarianism of the first article, he would have been perceived as believing in all five and, thus, as being an Arminian, irrespective of his claims—or the lack thereof—or of his ecclesial beliefs. When we couple this fact with Laud's Arminian-like emphasis on reason in matters of faith—as we saw in chapter two—we have good cause for concluding, with Nicholas Tyacke, that Laud was, in fact, an Arminian or, at least if not an Arminian, then one who clearly embraced several characteristic elements of that system.[15]

Third, it is clear from the proceedings of the Glasgow Assembly of 1638 that Arminianism was in fact present in Scotland. Many of the bishops who were brought before this Assembly for trial were closely allied with Laud and the 'Canterburians'.[16] Even so, the most common charge leveled against men at the

---

[11] The same can be said for the Aberdeen Doctors. See note 43 below.

[12] *The Works of the Most Reverend Father in God, William Laud*, ed. J. Bliss, 7 vols. (Oxford: John Henry Parker, 1847-60), VI, p. 133, emphasis added.

[13] Baillie, *Ladensium autokatakrisis*, p. 18.

[14] Richard Muller's research confirms this. He notes: 'By the beginning of the seventeenth century, early Reformed orthodoxy had produced a fairly comprehensive summation of doctrine, an enclosed system of theology...in which no major *locus* of doctrine could be altered without effecting a modification of the entire system' (see Muller, 'Federal Motif', p. 102; and 'The Christological Problem', p. 146). To apply this to the Arminians: one cannot deny limited atonement without also making significant modifications to total depravity, the irresistibility of grace, and the perseverance of the saints. Alterations at one point would necessarily affect other points as well.

[15] See the discussion on the role of reason in Laud and the Arminians near the end of the section entitled, 'The Role of Reason and the Necessity of Supernatural Knowledge' in chapter 2 above.

[16] Such was the case with Thomas Sydserff, John Crighton, John Spottisswood, John Maxwell, Walter Whiteford, and James Wedderburn. See Peterkin, *Records of the Kirk of Scotland*, pp. 163-73; G. Donaldson, *The Making of the Scottish Prayer Book of 1637*

Assembly was that of Arminianism. David Mullan admits that over two-dozen men were so charged.[17] In many of the cases in which men were accused of Arminianism, the charges were further explained by particular reference to the errors of the Remonstrants in regard to the doctrines of grace. David Mitchell (d.1663), for example, a minister in Edinburgh, was thus accused 'that his doctrine is the doctrine of the remonstrances that they avowed at the Counsell of Dort...for he defends universall grace, resistabilitie of Grace—efficacie of Christs death—[and] apostacie of the Saints'.[18] Although many men were charged with Arminianism in Glasgow, others were not. At least eight other bishops and ministers were not charged with Arminianism. They were charged instead with episcopacy, popery, or immorality, and sometimes with all three.[19]

For these three reasons, it would seem best to conclude that Arminianism—or at least certain aspects of it—was recognizable in Scotland in the early seventeenth century, that it was not uncommon, that it was integrally related to the errors of the Remonstrants in regard to the doctrines of grace, and that it was not simply a polemical tool used to discredit those who held to episcopacy. David Mullan is probably correct in his analysis that a Calvinist consensus prevailed in early modern Scotland. Very few men, relatively speaking, explicitly embraced the full Arminian system.[20] But his thesis too quickly dismisses the fact that Arminianism was a common charge leveled against men for their erroneous views in regard to the doctrines of grace.[21] Mullan trivializes

---

(Edinburgh: University of Edinburgh, 1954), pp. 41-59; MacMillan, *The Aberdeen Doctors*, pp. 109-10.

[17] D.G. Mullan, 'Arminianism in the Lord's Assembly: Glasgow, 1638', *RSCHS* 26 (1996), p. 22. See also Peterkin, *Records of the Kirk of Scotland*, pp. 154-83.

[18] Peterkin, *Records of the Kirk of Scotland*, p. 160. John Crighton and James Fleck are two among others who were likewise accused of Arminianism and charged with teaching universal grace and the free will of mankind. *Records of the Kirk of Scotland*, pp. 163, 165; R. Baillie, *The Letters and Journals of Robert Baillie*, ed. D. Lang, 3 vols. (Edinburgh: Robert Ogle, 1841), I, p. 149; MacMillan, *Aberdeen Doctors*, pp. 110-11.

[19] Peterkin, *Records of the Kirk of Scotland*, pp. 165-6, 170-73. 'Hary Scrymsoure' is one interesting example. He was accused of, in addition to other things, 'venting of sundrie tenets of false doctrine'. He was never accused of Arminianism, however, and were it not for some sort of personal dispute, he probably would have continued on in his pastoral charge (*Records of the Kirk of Scotland*, p. 182; Mullan, 'Arminianism in the Lord's Assembly', p. 13).

[20] Mullan reports: 'Even if our listed ministers were all guilty as charged, and we were to extend the list by a few names, one is not struck by a massive, "systemic", infection' (Mullan, 'Arminianism in the Lord's Assembly', pp. 22-3). It must be said, however, that we are not looking for a 'massive, "systemic", infection' of Arminianism in Scotland. All we are looking for is the presence of a controversy over its doctrines to show that Arminianism did in fact exist and that it was not uncommon.

[21] Margo Todd notes that 'Mullan...finds little outright Arminianism in Scotland and he is probably right, but the complaints brought in the 1630s against ceremonialists like Maxwell, Sibbald, and Forbes do include their theological positions on free will' (Todd,

the presence of Arminian doctrines in Scotland in order to preserve the existence of Calvinist hegemony. But, as Peter Lake has reminded us, 'hegemony is not monopoly', and, thus, a Calvinist consensus can perfectly coexist with the presence of anti-Calvinist sentiment.[22] There is no reason to discount the charges of Arminianism in Scotland by sweeping them under the proverbial rug. We need instead to determine why the presence of Arminianism provoked such an intense reaction.

One part of the explanation for the reaction against Arminianism is the close theological association that was perceived to exist between it and Roman Catholicism. The association between 'Arminianism and popery' is so frequent in the literature of the seventeenth century that Mullan insists it 'acquired the tone of a liturgical formula'.[23] The 'formula' appears regularly in the sermons and writings of many of the leading men of the day.[24] And Rutherford is no exception to this. In the *Examen*, Rutherford links the Arminians theologically with the Roman Church no fewer than seventy-five times in connection with the following core doctrines: the authority of Scripture, grace and free will, justification, and *scientia media*.

As we saw in chapter two, Rutherford perceives that the Arminian doctrine of the liberty of prophesying undercut the Reformation's emphasis on *sola Scriptura* by denying, along with Roman Catholicism, the objective authority of Scripture. Both Arminianism and Roman Catholicism denied the Reformation's three-fold approach to biblical interpretation, which was designed to preserve the objective authority of Scripture to judge in matters of controversy. Although Arminianism was reputed to be part of 'Tradition I' (Heiko Oberman's category to describe those who believed in a single-source theory of doctrine), it actually rejected 'Tradition I', according to Rutherford, and adopted the Roman Catholic 'Tradition II' (or two-sources theory) by introducing a second source of authority—to which they ascribed the status of ultimate authority in matters of controversy—the interpreting individual.[25] For

---

The Culture of Protestantism, p. 411n25). Moreover, Rutherford, in a couple of letters written from Aberdeen, made clear distinctions between Arminianism and episcopacy when describing his disputes with several of the Aberdeen Doctors (*Letters*, pp. 239, 275).

[22] Lake, 'Calvinism and the English Church', p. 34.

[23] Mullan, *Scottish Puritanism*, p. 227. Mullan tends to overlook the theological justification for the link between the Arminians and the Papists and concentrates on the polemical.

[24] See, e.g., D. Calderwood, *A Re-examination of the Five Articles Enacted at Perth, anno 1618* (n.p., 1636), p. A2r; Baillie, *Ladensium autokatakrisis*, passim; idem, *Antidote against Arminianism*, passim; G. Gillespie, *A Dispute against the English-Popish Ceremonies*, p. A4r; Peterkin, *Records of the Kirk of Scotland*, pp. 155-159; and A. Ramsay, *A Warning to Come out of Babylon* (Edinburgh, 1638), passim.

[25] See Oberman, *Harvest of Medieval Theology*, p. 371; and the above discussions in the sections on the nature, authority, and interpretation of Scripture in chapter 2.

Rutherford, the Arminian denial of *sola Scriptura* was far more troubling than that of the Roman Church, because the Arminian denial occurred from within the bounds of 'Tradition I'. Unlike the Roman Church, the Arminians claimed the same presuppositional starting point as did Calvinists like Rutherford but reached conclusions that were, at times, far different.

In regard to grace and free will, Rutherford links the Arminians with Roman Catholic theology by showing that their understanding of the relationship between preparation and grace is drawn directly from the Jesuit view of *facere quod in se est*. Both Luis de Molina and Arminius reject 'Luther's insight into the nature of grace as the unmerited favor of God' and opt instead to think of it 'as a sort of divine assistance or power given to men to enable them to perform certain acts, which they in their corrupted natural state could not do'.[26] This 'divine assistance' is granted to men and women generally and universally, and it enables them *facere quod in se est* and, thereby, to gain for themselves the gift of eternal life.[27]

The Arminian emphasis on *faciendo quod in se est* becomes even more problematic for Rutherford, and even more like Roman Catholic theology, when it is seen in the light of their doctrine of justification. As we saw in chapter four, the Arminians believe that the post-lapsarian will does not exert any negative influence upon the function of the intellect. This means that both the fallen will and the fallen intellect are able *facere quod in se est* in receiving the divine grace of regeneration. When this is combined with the Arminian belief that our faith is imputed for our righteousness, we come face to face with a doctrine that teaches that we are righteous in the sight of God as a result of a human action (faith), which is accomplished by the will and intellect 'doing what is in them' in their appropriating of divine grace.[28] Theoretically speaking, there is not much that separates this understanding of justification from the Roman Catholic understanding of it.

But when it is placed alongside a view of conditional predestination that is derived from divine *scientia media*, the link with Roman theology becomes unavoidable. In the first place, this is because the Arminians' embrace of *scientia media* itself, according to Karl Barth, places them squarely within a tradition that was consciously in direct opposition to Luther and Calvin and the Reformation.[29] Arminius' contemporaries, both friends and foes, evidently perceived this and pointed to his reliance upon *scientia media* as that aspect of

---

[26] Craig, *The Problem of Divine Foreknowledge*, pp. 204-5.

[27] 'Doing what is in them' does not directly gain salvation for men and women, in Arminius' understanding. As we saw in chapter four, it gains God's co-operating or saving grace. But, since there are 'necessary connections' between *faciendo quod in se est* and the 'grace of Conversion', it can be said that by 'doing what is in them' individuals can and will receive eternal life. See calling and preparation in ch. 4 above.

[28] See the section on justification in ch. 4 above.

[29] See the section on the *scientia Dei* in ch. 3 above.

his theology which demonstrated 'catholic influences' most clearly.[30]

In the second place, and more significantly, this is because the Arminian view of predestination unambiguously introduces an element of conditionality into the economy of salvation, one in which God bases his decision to predestine and then to justify in time upon the condition of faith in the individual. If we take into account the Arminian view of justification and their intellectualist understanding of faith, then this can only mean that the deciding factor that determines whether or not an individual believes—and, thus, is predestined by God and then justified in time and space—given the fact of his or her creation, is ultimately whether or not that individual chooses to believe. It is for this reason that Robert Baillie could say that Arminius, like the papists, makes 'Election and Justification to depend on Faith, not as it is an instrument applying Christ, but as…a saving quality of it selfe…a true worke'.[31] And it is what induces Rutherford to pronounce:

> The *Arminians* answer right downe, the one [person] is converted [and, thus, predestined by God and justified in time], because he wills, and consents; whereas he might, if it pleased him, dissent and refuse the calling of God; and the other [person] is not converted [and, thus, not predestined and justified], because he will not be converted but refuses.[32]

The concern among the Reformed orthodox in regard to the Arminian doctrine of conditional predestination is not, therefore, first and foremost a concern about predestination itself. It is first and foremost a concern about how that doctrine affects the cardinal doctrine of Protestantism, justification by faith alone. This was the case even before the Synod of Dort in the *Collatio Hagiensis* of 1611, as Louis Praamsma has shown.[33] And it was the case in England for William Twisse, when he took his fellow Puritan John Cotton

---

[30] Dekker, 'Was Arminius a Molinist?', p. 350n60. Caspar Sibelius, a student of Arminius from 1608-1609, and Franciscus Gomarus, a fellow professor in Leiden, both indicated this feature of Arminius' theology (Dekker, 'Was Arminius a Molinist?', p. 350n60; and H.W. Tijdeman, 'Caspar Sibelius, in leven Predikant te *Deventer*; volgens zijne onuitgegeven eigen-levensbeschrijving', *Godgeleerde Bijdragen* 23 [1849], p. 522). In 1612, André Rivet alerted Robert Boyd to the fact that 'Arminius is a firm disciple of the Jesuites Molina, and De Fonseca; and that he hath learned all his slights, cunning, and termes, from them' (R. Wodrow, *Life of Robert Boyd*, p. 346, cited in Mullan, *Scottish Puritanism*, p. 214).
[31] Baillie, *Antidote against Arminianism*, pp. 35-6, 65.
[32] *Christ Dying*, p. 311. Cf. *Tryal*, p. 152; *Christ Dying*, p. 78.
[33] L. Praamsma, 'The Background of the Arminian Controversy (1586-1618)', in *Crisis in the Reformed Churches: Essays in Commemoration of the Great Synod of Dort, 1618-1619*, ed. P.Y. DeJong (Grand Rapids, MI: Reformed Fellowship, 1968), pp. 35-6. Praamsma notes that the Contra-Remonstrants were generally very subdued in their discussions about absolute predestination and much more concerned about what a denial of this doctrine would do to justification by faith alone.

(c.1585-1652) to task for what he perceived to be an Arminian view of predestination. David Como, who has examined Twisse's treatise against Cotton, traces the crux of the issue between them to Cotton's doctrine of conditional reprobation. Como explains:

> By suggesting an *intrinsic* quality in man that caused God's decree of reprobation, Cotton was in Twisse's opinion slipping unwittingly into an argument that [ultimately] compromised the concept of justification by faith alone. To put the argument more simply: no absolute predestination, no justification by faith; no justification by faith, no Protestantism.[34]

Anyone who questioned the doctrine of absolute predestination—whether an Arminian or a Puritan—attracted the wrath of post-Reformation theologians like Rutherford and Twisse, because, by questioning it, they were calling into question the very underpinnings of Protestantism. By denying *sola Scriptura* and by embracing the Jesuit ideas of *facere quod in se est* and *scientia media*, Arminianism consciously took up a position that was in direct opposition to Reformation thinking and that threatened the very heart of Reformation theology. Arminianism logically endangered everything that the Reformation stood for. It was seen as a step onto the slippery slope that would plunge the kirk towards popery and, as such, had to be resisted with all the strength one could muster.

A second part of the explanation for the intense reaction to Arminianism in Scotland—besides the theological similarities that existed between it and Roman Catholicism—is the fact that this movement entered the Scots nation largely as a result of the 'south-winds' that proceeded from William Laud and his Canterburians.[35] It is possible that the relatively little Arminianism that was present in Scotland would never have provoked the response that it did from men like Rutherford were it not for the fact that it was coupled together with an imposed episcopacy and an imposed liturgy. The Scottish kirk had dealt with the issue of episcopacy once before in 1576, which had resulted in the publication of the *Second Book of Discipline* two years later.[36] It was a relatively simple matter then: all other forms of church government besides Presbyterianism were decried as lacking the divine imprimatur. After sixty years, however, the issue had become more complex. It was not just episcopacy but liturgy that was being imposed on Scotland. 'Laud's Liturgy', which was introduced in 1637 in an effort to bring about religious uniformity,[37] was seen

---

[34] Como, 'Puritans, Predestination and the Construction of Orthodoxy', p. 84.
[35] See Baillie, *Ladensium autokatakrisis*, pp. 11-12, 21; idem, *Antidote against Arminianism*, pp. 17-18; and the discussion on polemical context in chapter 1.
[36] See J. Kirk, ed., *The Second Book of Discipline* (Edinburgh: St. Andrews Press, 1980).
[37] John Morrill argues that the 'best term' to describe the policy of James VI (and I) and Charles I in regard to the church in Scotland is 'congruity'. Rather than seeking to 'anglicanize' the church in Scotland, he says, Charles sought to gain 'uniformity of

by many in Scotland to mark a return to popery. Andrew Cant (1590-1663), speaking at the 1638 General Assembly, summarized the sentiments of the Presbyterian party in regard to Laud's Liturgy by saying: 'I think the Booke of Canons full of Popishe and Pop-lyke tyrannie ...[and] the Service Booke full of superstition and massing Poperie.'[38] This reaction to the liturgy was typical for many Scottish Calvinists, who, as John Morrill argues, perceived that it was part of a 'Popish Plot to subvert the Protestant identity of the Church of England as a prelude to the reclamation of [all of] Britain for Catholicism'. By imposing this liturgy on Scotland, Charles I and William Laud were seen as mere puppets in the hands of a 'Catholic conspiracy'.[39] In Rutherford's own words, the 'Episcopacie, and humane Ceremonies' exemplified in Laud's Liturgy were 'the gold ring' and 'love tokens' left behind by 'the Whore of Babylon' when she 'was cast out of the Church' at the beginning of the Reformation. It was part of the Roman Church's 'policy' to 'leave a token behinde her, that she might finde an errand in the house againe'.[40] Rutherford's fear was that it was just a matter of time before this policy would be carried out and the Scottish kirk would fall prey to Rome's counter-Reformation. Episcopacy with its loathsome liturgy thus represented the final step on the slippery slope leading towards popery.

The Two Ends of Arminianism

When the ceremonies and traditions of Laud's episcopacy were joined together with Arminianism in Scotland, the resulting union was, in Alexander Henderson's words, 'inchoatus Papismus'. The perception was that if the doctrine of the kirk (i.e., the Arminianism that was present within the church) reflected Roman Catholic theology, and the practice of the kirk (i.e., the liturgical episcopacy of Laud and his party) reflected Roman Catholic practice, then there was nothing left to differentiate the Scottish church from Rome except the pope himself. This was Alexander Henderson's precise warning to the Glasgow Assembly in 1638:

> if ye consider this, how our doctrine, and the particulars of our Confession of Faith, taught by the Ministers of the Kirk of Scotland since the Reformation, how thir pointes began to be depraved by Arminianisme, and poyntes of Poperie, joyned with their poyntes of Arminianisme, and next consider how that the

---

practice' (*The Nature of the English Revolution* [New York: Longman, 1993], p. 101). There can be no doubt, however, that from the perspective of the Scottish kirk—especially *jus divinum* Presbyterians like Rutherford—Charles' (and thus Laud's) insistence on congruity and uniformity of practice would have been seen as an imposition of English liturgy and practice and thus as anglicanization.

[38] Peterkin, *Records of the Kirk of Scotland*, pp. 164, 287-8.
[39] Morrill, *The Nature of the English Revolution*, p. 37.
[40] *HOC*, p. 18.

externall worship of God was in changeing by the Service Booke, I see nothing deficient for the whole bodie of Poperie but the Pope himselfe—Convertion of a Sinner—universalitie of the matters of Christs death—justification by workes—falling away of the saints; and then, if we had receaved the Service Booke, what difference had beene 'twixt the Romane faith and ours, if we had subjected ourselfes to the Pope?[41]

Since, according to Peter Lake, most Protestants in the seventeenth century regarded the Roman Church as an 'anti-religion, a perfectly symmetrical negative image of true Christianity', which 'rose by stealth and deception, pretending piety and reverence while in fact inverting and perverting the values of true religion', it was, therefore, perceived to be the most serious threat to the newly-established Reformed kirk.[42] It should be no surprise, then, that the National Covenant of 1638—largely written by Henderson himself—began by recalling the Negative Confession of 1581, and that almost half of the document itself consisted of the Negative Confession and other acts of Parliament that were directed against popery. It should also be no surprise that Rutherford reacted the way he did towards Arminianism and that he devoted his labors and his lectures to refuting its doctrines. And it should be no surprise that the Aberdeen Doctors—who were probably more Calvinistic than Arminian but who embraced conditional reprobation, just like John Cotton, and favored episcopacy over Presbyterianism—were still mercilessly run out of the church, thanks in no small measure to Rutherford's testimony against them.[43]

---

[41] Peterkin, *Records of the Kirk of Scotland*, p. 155.

[42] Peter Lake, 'Anti-popery: the Structure of a Prejudice', in *Conflict in Early Stuart England: Studies in Religion and Politics 1603-1642*, eds. R. Cust and A. Hughes (London and New York: Longman, 1989), p. 73.

[43] Many have claimed that the Aberdeen Doctors were exponents of Arminianism and that Aberdeen itself was its hub. Donald MacMillan asserts that the Doctors had all 'drunk deeply of the stream' of Arminianism (*Aberdeen Doctors*, p. 58); Andrew Stevenson contends that they were 'choked' with it (*The History of the Church and State of Scotland* [Edinburgh: Thomas Nelson, 1840], p. 435); and Rutherford himself even goes so far as to claim that in Aberdeen, 'all are corrupt' (*Letters*, p. 275). David Mullan and G.D. Henderson, however, have concluded that outright Arminianism was not actually present among the Aberdeen Doctors (Mullan, *Scottish Puritanism*, pp. 224-6; Henderson, *Religious Life*, pp. 90-92; idem, *Burning Bush*, pp. 75-93). They argue that the Doctors were more Calvinist than Arminian and were charged with Arminianism primarily because of their moderate Episcopal beliefs. This is not necessarily the case, however. Quite probably their ecclesial beliefs did contribute to their demise, but it is at least suggestive that all of the Doctors appear to have believed either in conditional predestination, outright, or in conditional reprobation. And as we have seen with the example of Twisse and Cotton, conditional reprobation would have been regarded by Rutherford as Arminianism, in that it, like Arminianism, jeopardized the doctrine of justification by faith alone. On the trials of the Doctors and their convictions, see J. Gordon, *History of Scots Affairs, from 1637 to 1641* (Aberdeen: Spalding Club, 1841),

The Reformation that had started in 1560 was seen to be hanging in the balance almost eighty years later as popery crept into the Scottish church masquerading as the twin angels of light, Arminianism and episcopacy. Both had to be exorcised; neither could be ignored. No quarter could be given, and no tolerance could be shown. Arminianism, with its similarities to Roman Catholic theology, was encroaching upon the Scottish church united with Laud's liturgical episcopacy and its similarities to Roman Catholic practice. Everything Rutherford and his forebears had staked their lives and livelihoods on in reforming Scotland was at stake. This, more than anything else, is the difference between the Arminianism in Scotland and the Arminianism in the Netherlands. Whereas the latter tended towards Socinianism, the former tended towards 'Papistrie' and was 'inchoatus Papismus'.

But popery was not the only end result of Arminianism that threatened early modern Scotland, even though it was probably the most pressing. A second threat to the Calvinist worldview was spawned by Arminian teaching, viz., theological scepticism. By advocating toleration for a wide range of beliefs within the church—including those of the *'Arians, Socinians, Papists, Pelagians, Antitrinitarians*, and all Heretics who *want [postulant] to be called Christians'*—and by undercutting objective biblical authority,[44] Arminianism helped to introduce a 'seventeenth-century Pyrrhonian crisis, as to whether truth can be known and, if so, in what measure'.[45] While this crisis may have been less of an direct issue in Scotland than it was in England and on the continent, it, nevertheless, still posed a tremendous threat to covenanters like Rutherford, who believed that there was only one incontrovertible interpretation for every text of Scripture, and who saw theological certainty and objectivity as the foundation on which their vision for a unified and uniform church would be established, not only in Scotland but in England and Ireland as well.[46] The Arminian liberty of prophesying threatened to destroy this

---

III, pp. 274-82; MacMillan, *Aberdeen Doctors*, pp. 113-14, 272-6, 279-92; J. Forbes, *Instructiones historico-theologicae de doctrina Christiana* (Amsterdam, 1645), p. 405; and J. Spalding, *The History of the Troubles and Memorable Transactions in Scotland from the Year 1624 to 1645* (Aberdeen: Evans, 1792), I, p. 245.

[44] *Examen*, p. 8.

[45] Tyacke, 'Arminianism and English Culture', p. 106. Pyrrho (c. 365-c.275 BC) was a Greek sceptic who, according to Thomas Harriot, did not 'affirme or deny any knowledge to be true or false' (Tyacke, 'Arminianism and English Culture', p. 107). On scepticism in the early modern period, see R.H. Popkin, *The History of Scepticism from Erasmus to Descartes* (New York and London: Harper & Row, 1968).

[46] That the goal of the Scots was religious unity and uniformity is perhaps best seen in the intentions that were behind their involvement in the Westminster Assembly. Robert Baillie points out that when the English approached the Scots for help in 1643, the Scots seized the opportunity to gain religious uniformity. Whereas the English were only after a 'civill League', the Scots undertook to form a 'religious Covenant'. Baillie, *Letters and Journals*, II, p. 90.

foundation by introducing a '*Pyrrhonian* Vacillation and Uncertainty', a 'perpetual fluctuation', in which individuals were '*alwayes learning, and never comming to the knowledge of the truth*'.⁴⁷ By embracing this liberty of prophesying, in which the individual engaged with Scripture wholly on a personal level, and by relegating the interpretive decisions of the church to a 'Discretionary...not Authoritative' status,⁴⁸ the Arminians, along with other sectarian groups within the Erasmian tradition, individualized biblical interpretation and opened Pandora's box releasing 'millions of faiths with millions of senses [of Scripture], and so no faith at all'.⁴⁹ This put the work of the Reformation at risk by fulfilling Rome's predictions that *sola Scriptura* would foster the hermeneutical abuse of Scripture and provide no basis for differentiating between varying interpretations. But it also put the Christian faith itself at risk, because, for Rutherford as for Calvin, certainty was of the essence of faith. To undermine certainty was, therefore, at least to introduce grave pastoral problems into the church and, at most, to undermine the work of the Christian faith itself.⁵⁰ More than placing the work of the Reformation at risk, Arminianism engendered a loss of theological certainty, which also endangered the work of the Reformation, and threatened to shatter the covenanters' hopes and dreams for a religiously unified society, and offered, instead, a future in which God would be driven 'from his sovereign's throne',⁵¹ only to be replaced by the autonomous creature. No longer would God be *Deus absconditus*; no longer would he reign and rule on high. Arminianism and the theological scepticism it helped to introduce offered a God who was limited in the current world order by the freedom of each and every individual he created. It was for these reasons that Rutherford considered Arminianism 'a most serious heresy [*haeresis gravissima*]', one that was diametrically opposed at every point to the theology of the Reformation and to his own hopes and

---

⁴⁷ *Due Right*, pp. 366, 369. The pages in this treatise are terribly corrupted. They are numbered in the following sequence: 1-208; 229-68; 259-454; 451-97; 484; and 185-468. The abovementioned references are cited from the latter group of pages.

⁴⁸ *ACS*, I, p. 39.

⁴⁹ *PLC*, p. 28.

⁵⁰ This is one reason why Hugh R. Trevor-Roper has argued that the Erasmian tradition of scepticism, tolerance, and freedom—which tradition he sees continued in the Arminians—was the main source of the eighteenth-century Enlightenment. While this is not entirely accurate, insofar as other factors clearly contributed to this dynamic, it is true that the Erasmian tradition was one important factor in the development of the Enlightenment. Cf. Trevor-Roper, *Religion, the Reformation and Social Change* (London: Macmillan, ²1972), pp. 193-236; with H. Kamen, *The Rise of Toleration* (London: Weidenfeld and Nicolson, 1967), especially pp. 161-90; and W.R. Ward, 'Orthodoxy, Enlightenment and Religious Revival', in *Religion and Humanism*, ed. K. Robbins (Oxford: Blackwell, 1981), pp. 275-96. See also Coffey, *Politics, Religion and the British Revolutions*, pp. 256-7.

⁵¹ Mullan, 'Masked Popery and Pyrrhonian Uncertainty', p. 177.

dreams for a religiously unified society.[52]

This was the threat that faced the Calvinism of Rutherford's day. It was a threat that attacked everything Rutherford wanted, everything he believed, and everything for which he, and his Reformation forebears, had worked for over three generations. It was a threat that backed him and his Calvinist brethren into a corner and put them on the defensive. The Calvinism of Rutherford's day was not the vibrant Calvinism that many think it to be. It was a Calvinism in battle array, vehemently striking out and seeking to maintain its hegemony at all costs. Sadly, it was only at the end of Rutherford's lifetime, when he knew his own death was imminent and the cause for which he had been fighting so stridently all his life was hanging on the precipice of defeat, that he realized the mire in which he and many others had been wallowing and expressed regret, saying:

> Blessed is the servant whom the Master when he cometh shall finde watching, praying, believing, not tossing and raising the dust of debating and multiplied Replies and Duplies, since the *peace and joy of believing, that we may abound in hope through the power of the holy Ghost*, is of great price with those in whom the *meekness and gentleness of Christ* hath place....it would appear that there is less of *Christ* and more of *Self* in our sickness of over-loving these truths, which suffer most bruising and grinding...between the Milstones of Sides, Opinions and Contradictions of Parties, as if that were the choicest verity which the mans own engine hath taken out of an Adversaries hand...*with his bowe and his sword*....For when the head is filled with topicks, and none of the flamings of Christs love in the heart, how dry are all disputes? for too often, fervour of dispute in the head weakens love in the heart. And what can our Paper-industry adde to the spotless truth of our *Lord Jesus*? O that Opinions were down, and the *Gospel* up; and Sides and Parties might fall, and *Christ* stand; and that all Names, Sects and Ways were low, and the *Lord alone exalted*![53]

Rutherford died in 1661 with many of his ambitions unfulfilled and others of them overturned by the new Restoration government. His vision for religious uniformity ended as a failed dream. His lifetime of work against Arminianism and its logical ends, popery and theological uncertainty, ultimately came up short. This was true in his own lifetime—as he died before he could see episcopacy defeated in Scotland and Presbyterianism adopted in its place—and it has perhaps become even more so since then—as theological scepticism and a worldview of tolerance and freedom have increasingly pushed religion and the church to the periphery of society, at least in comparison to Rutherford's day anyway. For these reasons, John Coffey appears to be right in claiming that Rutherford's life 'was more of a tragedy than a romance'.[54]

---

[52] *Examen*, p. 46.
[53] Rutherford, *A Survey of the Survey of that Summe of Church Discipline*, p. A2.
[54] Coffey, *Politics, Religion and the British Revolutions*, p. 257.

Concluding Thoughts on the Calvin-Calvinists Debate

But was Rutherford's Calvinism really Calvinism at all? Or, was what he believed and espoused something altogether different from the thinking of John Calvin? In order to answer these questions, this thesis has attempted to point out areas of continuity and discontinuity between Rutherford and Calvin throughout its examination of Rutherford's theology and to devote special attention to evaluating those specific areas where significant discontinuity was suspected. All that remains for us to do now is to summarize these findings and draw the relevant conclusions.

With the possible exception of limited atonement, every doctrine that we have surveyed in Rutherford is in substantial continuity with the Genevan reformer's theology. There is not one doctrine, not even limited atonement, that is in clear discontinuity with Calvin's thinking.[55] In those areas where there has been suspected discontinuity—i.e., accommodation, the role of reason, the verbal inspiration of Scripture, the authority of Scripture, the will of God, predestination, limited atonement, the covenant of works, the use of preparations in salvation, and the assurance of salvation—we have shown that there is actually substantial theological continuity. Where there are elements of discontinuity—and there are—we have shown that the discontinuity is not so much a theological discontinuity as one of method and emphasis. When we move from Calvin to Rutherford, we see, in the first place, an evident increase in theological systematization and in the use of logical categories and deductions. We see this most clearly in Rutherford's doctrine of Scripture (though this doctrine is not yet in its fullest expression, as it will be in Princeton theologians B.B. Warfield and A.A. Hodge, it is, nonetheless, more systematized than is Calvin's view), in his formulations of the divine will and his use of scholastic phrases and categories (though this too is in Calvin, we see a further development in Rutherford), in his application of federal theology as the architectonic principle of Scripture, and in his extensive use of the practical syllogism in providing assurance of salvation. Furthermore, when we move from Calvin to Rutherford, we also see a shift in theological emphasis. Predestination, limited atonement, the second use of the law, covenant theology (especially the covenant of works), and subjective assurance all have a greater prominence in the theology of Rutherford than they did in Calvin.

But these things should not lead us to conclude that a vast chasm exists between Rutherford and Calvin, even in regard to method and emphasis. Although there is clear discontinuity here, the discontinuity itself is not the

---

[55] As we mentioned in chapter three, it is difficult to determine precisely where Calvin would come down on the issue of limited atonement. It was not a question that he faced in his own day, and scholars are divided as to what his actual response would have been had the question been put to him. But, as Karl Barth has acknowledged, the doctrine of limited atonement does flow logically from Calvin's understanding of predestination, which is itself in substantial continuity with Rutherford's own beliefs. *CD*, IV/1, p. 57.

result of a sharp break with the Reformation but, as Richard Muller has convincingly argued, 'the product of a gradual development that had roots not only in the Middle Ages but also in the Renaissance and the Reformation'.[56] What is more, we should expect to see a development in method and emphasis as we move away from the Reformation and into the succeeding generations. Leonard Trinterud has explained that because the reformers rejected the authority of the Roman Church, they were required to re-establish 'a new basis...for personal and public religious life and morals, educations, civil governments, family life, and even international relations'.[57] In other words, he says, the reformers were required not simply to expound one or two isolated doctrines but to construct a comprehensive and cohesive system of faith. Thus, we would expect to find a move towards systematization even within Calvin himself—as Muller in fact has—which would then be carried through to the post-Reformation period and into the thinking of men like Rutherford.[58] In terms of emphasis, moreover, a shift should be expected in light of the changing climate of the culture in which Rutherford lived. Because he lived in a different period, he fought different battles, which produced different emphases in his theology. But, as we have already seen, the seedbed for Rutherford's understanding of predestination, limited atonement, federal theology, and assurance of salvation, as well as other aspects of his theology, are all found in the writings of Calvin. In speaking of a discontinuity in method and emphasis, then, we must be careful not to draw too sharp a divide between Rutherford and Calvin; even the discontinuity between them is best expressed in terms of both discontinuity and continuity.

In by far the greater number of doctrines, however, there is an overwhelming continuity between Rutherford and his Genevan predecessor. Both Rutherford and Calvin stand squarely within the *schola Augustiniana moderna*; both hold consciously to *sola Scriptura*; both are more interested in *qualis sit Deus*? than *an sit Deus*? or *quid sit Deus*?; both place great emphasis on the sovereignty of the divine will and, thus, on the ultimate incomprehensibility of God; both are strikingly similar, if not indistinguishable, in their understanding of the order of the divine decrees; both have the same basic views of natural theology, the Trinity, predestination, the sinfulness of humankind, free will, regeneration, faith, justification, sanctification, and the necessity of good works; both place union with Christ at the center of their respective soteriologies; both speak of assurance in the same terms, principially and experientially; and both assign a

---

[56] Muller, 'Calvin and the "Calvinists"', p. 366.

[57] Trinterud, 'Origins of Puritanism', p. 38.

[58] Muller notes that whereas the early versions of the *Institutes* contained a 'simple and catechetical structure', the final edition of 1559 contained a 'more formal, more systematic presentation' of theology (*Christ and the Decree*, p. 17). Muller then goes on to trace the continuation of this tendency towards systematization into the succeeding generations after Calvin (in part two of *Christ and the Decree*).

place of great prominence to the work of the Holy Spirit in their theologies. Such continuity is not wholly unexpected. Rutherford consistently quotes Calvin throughout the *Examen*, citing mainly from his *Institutes* twenty times during the course of his theological diatribe against the Arminians (see the appendix). He calls Calvin one of 'our Theologians' and believes himself to be standing in continuity with '*Calvin* and the Reformed Churches'.[59] He cites from Calvin's favorite source, Augustine, more often than any other author in the *Examen*, apart from Arminius and Episcopius, against whom he is in polemic (again, see the appendix). And in the rest of his writings, the same pattern holds true. According to estimates provided by David Strickland, Rutherford refers to Calvin and Augustine at least twice as much as the next nearest individual.[60] These two theologians stand head and shoulders above every other author in the entire Rutherford *corpus*.

What can we say, then, about the claims of scholars like Brian Armstrong, T.F. Torrance, and Charles Bell? Can Rutherford's theology rightly be considered to be at odds with Calvin? Can it rightly be considered hyper-Calvinism? Several things bear mentioning at this point in answer to these questions. In the first place, one wonders why it is that Calvin, rather than, say, Vermigli, Musculus, or Luther, is the benchmark against which theology is to be evaluated. Rutherford certainly did not see himself as a 'Calvinist'. But he did see himself as standing squarely within the tradition of the Reformation, especially as it found expression in Calvin but also in men like Vermigli, Musculus, and Luther as well. Moreover, Rutherford would never have wanted his theology to be held up to the light of Calvin (neither, for that matter, would Calvin have wanted the theologies of others to be held up to his own); he wanted his theology to be evaluated in the light of Scripture. That was his ultimate authority; that was his *principium cognoscendi theologiae*.

In the second place, contrary to Armstrong's claims, Rutherford's theology appears to be balanced, biblical, humanistic, and experiential, in at least a similar way as Calvin's.[61] While there are, to be sure, severe elements in Rutherford's theology—perhaps most especially, his understanding of the sovereignty of the divine will—he balances those elements with a warm and experiential spirituality. Like the Puritans in general and, before them, Peter Ramus, Rutherford's overarching emphasis is on making a practical and experiential use of theology, rather than on engaging in a theoretical and speculative exercise of the mind. Furthermore, as we have already mentioned

---

[59] *Examen*, pp. 602, 606; see also, 310, 353.
[60] Strickland has estimated the number of times Rutherford cites Calvin to be at least 132, Augustine, 116, and Beza and Chyrsostom, 58. Even though Strickland's counts are only approximate—as is apparent from his use (or, perhaps better, non-use) of the *Examen*—they do provide a good idea of those authors Rutherford is relying upon most. See Strickland, 'Union with Christ', Appendix II; and cf. the enclosed appendix.
[61] Armstrong, *Calvinism and the Amyraut Heresy*, p. 32.

above and seen in the *Examen*, the most important thing for Rutherford was that his theology be biblical. Granted, he may have, at times, gone beyond what Scripture says in order to try to explain how two doctrines that would appear to be contradictory can, in fact, be compatible—doctrines like the sovereignty of God and human free will, for example. But oftentimes this is because the Arminians, whom he is refuting, themselves go beyond Scripture to explain the compatibility of the two doctrines in a way that Rutherford believes is unscriptural.

In the third place, Armstrong's definition of scholasticism does not appear to be broad enough to take into consideration the presence of scholasticism both in the Reformation and in those later theologians who explicitly disagreed with the content of Calvin's theology. In the course of this thesis, we have pointed out several elements of Calvin's theology that display scholastic tendencies, most notably, his formulation of the divine will, his use of the syllogism in assurance, and his own movement towards systematization in his writings over the course of his lifetime. We have also pointed out elements of scholasticism in others of Calvin's peers, most especially, Peter Martyr Vermigli and Wolfgang Musculus. It is chiefly for these reasons that Richard Muller's comments would seem to be in order: 'Neither Calvin's own theology nor the theology of various significant predecessors, like Luther, Zwingli, and Bucer, or Reformed contemporaries, like Vermigli and Musculus, can be understood apart from the positive impact of elements of the medieval scholastic background.'[62] But, more than this, there are also elements of scholasticism that are present in later theologians who vehemently disagree with the content of not only Calvin's theology but that of Luther, Zwingli, Bucer, Vermigli, and Musculus as well. Arminius himself is one such theologian. His theology clearly evidences the distinguishing marks of scholasticism in his view of the fourfold causality of Scripture, his formulations of the divine will, his use of logical syllogisms, and his consistent reliance upon scholastic distinctions, albeit oftentimes with a different meaning than we see in Rutherford and the Reformed.

In the fourth place, and finally, it is difficult to appraise precisely Torrance's and Bell's claims that Rutherford is a hyper-Calvinist, because neither offers a definition of what he means by the term hyper-Calvinist. Peter Toon's work has shown that there has historically been much confusion over the use of this term. In an effort to bring clarity to the confusion, he offers this definition for hyper-Calvinism:

> It was a system of theology, or a system of the doctrines of God, man and grace, which was framed to exalt the honour and glory of God and did so at the expense of minimising the moral and spiritual responsibility of sinners to God. It placed excessive emphasis on the immanent acts of God—eternal justification, eternal

---

[62] Muller, 'Calvin and the "Calvinists"', p. 360.

adoption, and the eternal covenant of grace. In practice, this meant that 'Christ and Him crucified', the central message of the apostles, was obscured. It also often made no distinction between the secret and the revealed will of God, and tried to deduce the duty of men from what it taught concerning the secret, eternal decrees of God. Excessive emphasis was also placed on the doctrine of irresistible grace with the tendency to state that an elect man is not only passive in regeneration but also in conversion as well. The absorbing interest in the eternal, immanent acts of God and in irresistible grace led to the notion that grace must only be offered to those for whom it was intended. Finally, a valid assurance of salvation was seen as consisting in an inner feeling and conviction of being eternally elected by God. So Hyper-Calvinism led its adherents to hold that evangelism was not necessary and to place much emphasis on introspection in order to discover whether or not one was elect.[63]

Even if we were to compare Rutherford's theology with this definition and ignore the patent continuity that we have seen between Rutherford and Calvin, it would still be evident that Rutherford is not a hyper-Calvinist. Although his theology may tend towards hyper-Calvinism, insofar as it is 'framed to exalt the honour and glory of God', it does not emphasize divine glory at the expense of human freedom and responsibility. Rutherford repeatedly underscores the responsibility of the individual to believe in Christ for his or her salvation and, having done so, to work out diligently his or her sanctification. This can be seen in his work against the Antinomians and in the priority he gives to the importance of keeping one's affections fixed upon Christ by studying the Bible and striving after communion with God. In fact, Rutherford places so much emphasis on human responsibility in salvation that scholars like J.B. Torrance have criticized him for it, claiming that, by doing so, he jettisons Calvin's emphasis on the eternality of the covenant. What is more, Rutherford's theology is thoroughly Christ-centered and is distinguished by a particular belief that the gospel of Christ ought to be freely offered to all people without exception. He, like Calvin, clearly distinguishes between the secret will of God and the revealed will of God and, also like Calvin, encourages Christians to order their lives according to the latter. Assurance of salvation, for Rutherford, should never be based upon some sort of internal feeling but upon the objective and certain promises of God, which themselves were based upon the person of God.

It would seem best to conclude that the reappraisal school is right, that there is substantial continuity between the Reformation and post-Reformation periods—and, specifically, between Rutherford and Calvin—and that 'scholasticism' should be understood as a term that refers primarily to a method of approaching or arranging the content of theology, rather than of developing or determining the content itself.

---

[63] P. Toon, *The Emergence of Hyper-Calvinism in English Nonconformity 1689-1765* (London: The Olive Tree, 1967), pp. 144-5.

The Legacy of Rutherford's Theology

In bringing this study to a close, one question remains to be answered: *so what?* After all this, where are we to go from here? After tracing out the contours of Rutherford's theology and the intricacies of his dispute with the Arminians, is there anything that we, in the twenty-first century, can learn? What kind of legacy has Rutherford left us? Without pretending to be comprehensive in our answer to this question, we will, nevertheless, suggest four areas in Rutherford's theology from which the church today can gain benefit. This is not to suggest that the church ought to agree in every way with Rutherford in these four areas but only that it can learn something from him in regard to them. The first is his emphasis on the sovereignty of God. If there is one thing that characterizes Rutherford's theology, beyond any shadow of doubt, it is an overwhelming emphasis on divine sovereignty. This is especially evident in the context of his opposition to Arminianism, where Rutherford radically exalts the freedom and sovereignty of God and reads virtually every other doctrine through that lens. While we do not pretend, by any means, to advocate every aspect of Rutherford's view of divine sovereignty, there may be, in spite of this, something here that has been overlooked by the church in our day, which has perhaps lowered the focus of our theology somewhat in a more anthropological direction. Without diminishing the importance of the anthropological dimension of theology, perhaps it is time that we recapture something of Rutherford's vision of a God who is transcendent and worthy of both our worship and our service.

Secondly, Rutherford is a Christ-centered theologian and preacher. His doctrine of God, as T.F. Torrance has approvingly observed, is 'thoroughly Christ-centred', so much so that Torrance perceives it as 'modif[ying] the federal conception of God as Law-Giver and Judge'. In Christ, 'mercy and judgment, grace and law coincide', such that Christ becomes the embodiment of divine mercy and grace.[64] In him, the love and compassion of God are graphically and, yet, compellingly portrayed for all to see. So graphic and compelling was this sight to Rutherford that he could not but preach about it. According to historian Robert Wodrow, Rutherford developed a reputation, far above his contemporaries, for preaching 'the loveliness of Christ' and for doing so with intense fervor and profound animation.[65] One of his friends even went so far as to say that it often looked like 'he would have flown out of the pulpit' when he was speaking about Christ.[66] Unfortunately, however, Rutherford's Christ-centeredness did not always find expression in his actions. One need only think of the bitter invective he unleashed on fellow-Christians who disagreed with him in theological controversy in order to see this. But, despite his inconsistency, Rutherford remains a helpful example for us to learn from

---

[64] Torrance, *Scottish Theology*, p. 94.
[65] Wodrow, *Analecta*, III, pp. 3-4.
[66] *Letters*, p. 5.

today. His emphasis on Christ as the centerpiece of both his theology and his preaching is something for us in the church to take note of and attempt to apply more consistently than he did.

Thirdly, the significance that Rutherford gives to the role of the affections in Christianity demonstrates the cohesiveness of his theology overall. In Rutherford we see a rigorous theology combined with a warm and inviting spirituality. Many have wondered how these two extremes could exist together in one person.[67] Rutherford himself even acknowledged, with some incredulity, the fact that he was 'made of extremes'.[68] In his doctrine of the affections, however, we see how it is that these extremes could come together and form a cohesive whole theologically. Perhaps this doctrine and the cohesion it reflects may also give us in the church helpful insight not only into the nature of the Christian life but also into the practice of contemporary homiletics as well.

Fourthly, Rutherford's overriding intolerance of the Arminians and of other fellow-believers who disagreed with him on even the most trivial of issues, ought to teach us—by way of a negative example at least—the importance of appreciating different points of view and of dialoguing with other traditions. In describing Rutherford as a man who was 'quite incapable of compromise, even when it might have served [his] cause better than a dogmatic insistence on first principles', Ronald Cant has succinctly captured the nature of the man we have seen on the pages of the *Examen*.[69] But, before we are too unforgiving of Rutherford's intolerance, we need to remember that he lived in a day unlike our own, a day that was rife with intolerance and religious tension. A day in which people frequently died for what they believed. As Clarence Pott has aptly reminded us, those who stand up for their convictions and are 'willing to be burned for [their] causes have frequently been willing to burn others'.[70] Maybe, rather than evaluating Rutherford's intolerance by the standards of the twenty-first century, we can, instead, learn from it for our own day and, possibly, even appreciate the strength of his convictions from which it flowed.

---

[67] E.g., A.T. Innes, *Studies in Scottish History: Chiefly Ecclesiastical* (London: Hodder & Stoughton, 1892), pp. 15-16.
[68] See Whyte, *Samuel Rutherford and Some of his Correspondents*, chapter 2.
[69] Cant, *University of St. Andrews*, p. 72.
[70] C.K. Pott, 'Erasmus and the Reformation', in *The Heritage of John Calvin*, ed. J.H. Bratt (Grand Rapids, MI: Eerdmans, 1973), pp. 201-2.

Appendix

This appendix provides an alphabetical list of the individuals cited by Rutherford in the *Examen Arminianismi* by page number, excluding biblical references. All individuals are recorded here, whether or not Rutherford cites from a specific work of theirs. The top 20 most frequently cited authors are distinguished by numerical ranking to the left of their names.

Almain, Jaques (d. 1515). 695(x2), 696, 698, 704, 705, 706

Altissiodorensis. 62

Alvarez, Diego (d. 1631). 265, 457

Ambrose (d. 397). 652

[20]Ames, William (d. 1633). 25, 26, 32, 37, 573, 575, 638

Anselm (d. 1109). 664

Aristides (d. c.2nd cent.). 605

Aristotle (d. 322 BC). 28, 54, 67, 169, 193, 329, 330, 370-71, 496, 679(x2)

[2]Arminius, James (d. 1609). 83, 146, 147(x2), 149(x2), 150, 153, 154(x5), 162, 173(x2), 181, 184, 185, 186(x2), 189, 204, 218, 219, 233, 234, 236(x2), 247, 281, 300, 302, 305, 311, 325, 349, 350, 358, 360, 363, 370, 373, 389, 406, 408, 411, 424(x2), 425, 428, 429, 430, 442, 457, 473, 480, 497, 506, 507, 509, 510, 527, 535, 550, 665, 716, 725

Arnobius (d. 320). 347

Arriaga, Rodrique de (d. 1606). 162,

Arriaga (continued). 225, 252

Arrubal, Peter (d. 1608). 162

Athanasius (d. 373). 154, 571, 704

[3]Augustine (d. 430). 55, 74, 75(x2), 76, 155, 167, 229, 256(x2), 317-18, 342, 347(x2), 353, 358(x3), 359(x2), 360(x3), 387, 463(x2), 466(x3), 466-7, 468, 470, 474, 476, 495, 516(x2), 517, 527, 539, 555, 588, 589, 635, 652, 654, 680, 721

Azor, Juan (d. 1603). 519

Bañez, Dominico (d. 1604). 62(x2), 120, 457, 626, 652

Barclay, William (d. 1606). 750

Basil (d. 379). 229, 704

Becanus, Martin (d. 1624). 36, 316, 521

[5]Bellarmine, Robert (d. 1621). 11, 16, 18, 23, 51, 66, 204, 230, 316, 317, 375(x2), 408(x2), 475, 497, 505, 510, 519, 521, 551, 632, 659, 708(x2)

Bernard of Clairvaux (d. 1153). 472, 531

Bertius, Petrus (d. 1629). 550

[11]Beza, Theodore (d. 1605). 10, 19, 32, 37, 90, 378, 575, 606, 654, 726, 736

Bonaventure (d. 1274). 131, 358

Boniface VIII, Pope (d. 1303). 705

Bradwardine, Thomas (d. 1349). 176

Bucer, Martin (d. 1551). 531-2

Bullinger, Heinrich (d. 1575). 732

Cajetan, Tommaso de vio (d. 1534). 626, 642, 652, 691

[7]Calvin, John (d. 1564). 10, 32, 35, 38, 54, 65, 72, 81, 464, 472, 530, 531, 551, 602, 606, 624, 627, 654, 726, 758

Cameron, John (d. 1625). 19, 29, 30, 742

Casaubon, Isaac (d. 1614). 7, 8

Cassander, George (d. 1566). 50

Cassian, John (d. 435). 362, 494, 495

Castellio, Sebastian (d. 1563). 527

Catharinus, Ambrosius (d. 1553). 626(x2), 627

Chemnitz, Martin (d. 1586). 311, 464

Chillingworth, William (d. 1644). 24, 25, 66

Chrysostom, John (d. 407). 635, 642, 652, 654, 680, 689

Cicero, Marcus Tullius (d. 43 BC). 167, 236, 330, 460, 474, 475,

Cicero (continued). 478, 605

Clement VII, Pope (d. 1534). 709

Complutensian Codex. 575

Complutensian Doctors of University of Acalá (c. 17th cent.). 457

Coninck, Aegid de (d. 1633). 200

Constantius of Lyon (d. c.480). 704

[4]Corvinus, Johannes (d. 1650). 175, 217, 239, 259, 272, 301-2, 307, 311, 344, 358(x2), 359, 360, 362, 363(x2), 370, 411, 415-16, 422, 424, 427, 428, 450, 451, 454, 455(x4), 464, 473(x2), 480, 550

Council of Carthage (418). 721

Curcellaeus, Stephanus (d. 1659). 46

Cyprian (d. 258). 635, 663

Cyril of Alexandria (d. 444). 229, 361, 663

Davenant, John (d. 1641). 14

Demosthenes (d. 322 BC). 330, 460, 474

Diodorus of Tarsus (d. 392). 646

Durandus of Saint-Pourcain (d. 1334) 519

Duval, Jean (d. 1669). 652

[1]Episcopius, Simon (d. 1643). 1, 5, 7(x2), 46, 83(x5), 87, 89, 92, 97, 128, 139, 141(x2), 143, 148, 150, 151(x4), 152(x2), 155, 156, 160(x2), 166, 167, 186, 236, 241, 257, 272, 276(x2), 299,

Appendix 243

Episcopius (continued). 305, 307(x2), 311, 319, 325, 327(x3), 333, 358(x2), 359, 369, 413, 417, 428(x2), 430, 450, 455(x2), 473, 479, 496, 497, 500, 502(x3), 506-7, 516, 524, 525, 535, 540, 542, 543(x2), 600, 602, 643, 644, 662, 664, 665(x3), 670, 671, 672, 674, 684(x2), 686(x2), 687, 689, 709(x2), 710(x2), 713, 714(x2), 716(x2), 718, 721, 722, 723, 724(x3), 725(x3), 726, 727, 728(x2), 729(x2), 737, 738, 739(x2), 753(x3), 758, 759(x3)

Erasmus of Rotterdam (d. 1536). 50, 527, 575

Estius, William (d. 1613). 15, 38

Euthymius, Zigabenus (d. c.12th cent.). 663

Fasolus, Jerome (d. 1639). 24, 162, 200, 225

Faustus of Riez (d. c.495). 358, 360, 362, 457

Field, Richard (d. c.1610). 51, 66

Flavian (d. 449). 646

Fonseca, Pedro de (d. 1599). 497

Forbes, William (d. 1634). 23

Franciscus of Santa Clara. 626-7, 627

Fulgentius of Ruspe (d. 533). 654

Geisteranus, Johannes (d. c.16th cent.). 93, 149, 729, 753

Gerson, John (d. 1429). 17, 136, 517, 646, 695, 696, 708

Goodwin, Thomas (d. 1680). 136

Gratian (d. c.12th cent.). 721

Gregory I, Pope (d. 604). 75, 347

Gregory of Nazianzus (d. 390). 663

Gretser, Jakob (d. 1625). 659

[15]Grevinchovius, Nikolaus (d. 1620). 200, 249, 333, 362, 375, 389, 429, 473, 638

Grotius, Hugo (d. 1645). 50

Gualther, Sebastiano. 654

Hall, Joseph (d. 1656). 66

Hilary of Poitiers (d. 367). 154, 155, 495

[17]Hooker, Richard (d. 1600). 24(x2), 108, 110(x2), 112(x2), 113

Hosius, Stanislaus (d. 1579). 659

Hugh of St. Victor (d. 1141). 467, 468

Jackson, Thomas (d. 1640). 174

[17]Jerome (d. 420). 155, 360, 472, 652, 654, 663, 680, 704

Jewel, John (d. 1571). 54, 66

John XXI, Pope (d. 1277). 705

Julian of Eclanum (d. 454). 457

Julian II, Pope (d. 1513). 708(x2)

[15]Junius, Franciscus (d. 1602). 47, 50, 51, 53, 65, 66, 72(x2), 654

Justin Martyr (d. 165). 688

The Koran. 60

[17]Laud, William (d. 1645). 16, 50, 51, 53, 58, 59, 65-66, 66

Leiden Professors (Contra-Remonstrants). 311, 643, 691, 717, 729, 759

Leo X, Pope (d. 1521). 705

Lessius, Leonard (d. 1623). 163

Liberius, Pope (d. 366). 155

Lirinensis, Vincent (d. c.434). 16, 230

Luther, Martin (d. 1546). 56, 66, 551, 705

Martinez de Ripalda (d. 1635). 342, 464, 465-6, 467, 468, 469, 470, 472

Medina, Juan (d. 1546). 59, 626

Meisnerus, Balschaser (d. c.1624). 750

Menander (d. 290 BC). 131

Meratius, Ludovicius (d. c.1633). 45, 137, 138, 225, 336

Mirandola, Giovanni Francesco Pico della (d. 1533). 704

Molina, Luis de (d. 1600). 163, 252, 334

Murcia, Franciscus (d. 1617). 193

Musculus, Wolfgang (d. 1563). 654

Mussato, Albertino (d. 1329). 704-5

Nemesius of Emesa (d. 400). 229-30

Nestorius (d. c.451). 159

Nicholas of Lyra (d. 1340). 642

Ockham, William of (d. 1347). 45, 704(x2)

Osius, Bishop of Cordova (d. c.358). 155

Ostorodius, Christopher (d. 1611). 87, 326, 327, 729

Papists & Socinians. 511

[11]Pareus, David (d. 1622). 10, 32, 39, 49, 51, 79, 378, 571, 575, 642, 654

Parisian Doctors (c. 14th & 15th cent.). 696, 705

Parisiensis, William. 62

Paul of Samosato (d. c.272). 155

[8]Pelagius (d. 418). 256, 329, 358(x2), 359(x2), 360(x2), 361, 457(x2), 469, 474, 476

Pellicanus, Conradus (d. 1556). 758

Penottus, Gabriel. 225

Pererius, Benedict (d. 1610). 521, 708

Perkins, William (d. 1602). 79

Pighius, Albert (d. 1541). 708

Pius II, Pope (d. 1464). 705

Plantinian Codex. 575

Platina, Bartolomeo (d. 1481). 705

Plato (d. 347 BC). 496

Polyander, Johannes (d. 1640). 732

Potter, Christopher (d. 1634). 15, 58(x2), 65(x2), 82

Appendix 245

[14]Prosper of Acquitaine (d. 455). 274, 359, 360(x2), 362, 386, 421, 445, 494, 495

Racovian Catechism. 323, 662, 678, 686, 725

Radderius, Andreas. 684

Raymundus Lullius (d. c.1315). 200

Rispolis, F.J.M. de (d. c.17th century) 457

Rivetus, Andreas (d. 1643). 55, 65, 72

Roman Church, *Tridentin. Sess.* 627

Rusticus of Narbonne (d. 461). 35

Ruiz de Montoya (d. 1630). 162, 200(x2), 225

Sabellius (d. 250). 149, 150

Salamancan Doctors of University of Salamana (c. 17th cent.). 457

Sanderson, Robert (d. c.1647). 113(x2), 119, 120, 121, 123

Scotus, John Duns (d. 1308). 120, 232, 626

Seneca (d. 65). 605

Sirenius, Julius. 193

Slatius, Henricus (d. 1619). 729, 753(x2), 759

[11]Smalcius, Valentinus (d. 1622). 93, 147, 152, 307, 327, 507, 546, 665, 710-11, 724, 729

Smising, Theodorus (d. 1626). 143(x2), 255, 256

[6]Socinus, Faustus (d. 1604). 144, 149, 152, 305, 307, 319, 323, 325, 334, 359, 410, 500, 507, 528, 541, 662, 665, 717, 724, 758, 759

Socinus, Lelio (d. 1562). 758

Socrates (d. 399 BC). 577

Soto, Dominico de (d. 1560). 60, 646

Stapleton, Thomas (d. 1598). 230, 316, 334

[9]Suárez, Franciscus (d. 1617). 37, 38(x2), 120, 334, 475-6, 497, 519, 551, 646, 652, 659

Suetonius (d. 140). 326

Tertullian (d. 220). 634, 680, 689, 721

Theodoret of Cyrus (d. c.460). 646

Theophilus (d. c.412). 709

Theophylactus of Achrida (d. 1108). 347, 663

[20]Thomas Aquinas (d. 1274). 38, 62, 163, 469, 470, 517, 652

Tilenus, Daniel (d. c.1611). 48, 65, 550

Trelcatius, Lucas, Jr. (d. 1607). 149(x2)

Tremellius, Joannes Immanuel (d. 1580). 311

Turrecremata, Johannes de (d. 1468). 659

Twisse, William (d. 1645). 234

[9]Valentia, Gregory de (d. 1603). 62, 203, 204, 334, 336, 375, 497,

Valentia (continued). 521, 551, 627, 652, 659

Valentinus (d. c.161). 704

Vasqucz, Gabriel (d. 1604). 35, 120, 162, 265, 646

Vatable, François (d. 1547). 575

Vega, Andreas de (d. 1549). 26, 60

Venator, Adolphus (d. 1619). 665

Vigilius of Trent (d. 405). 32

Viguerius, Joannes (d. c.16th cent.). 646

Voetius, Gisbertus (d. 1644). 7, 326, 532, 646

Vorstius, Conrad (d. 1622). 141, 144, 147, 148, 149, 151, 169, 176(x2), 178, 204, 500

Whitaker, William (d. 1595). 72, 73, 79, 692

Wicelius, George (d. 1573). 50

Wyclif, John (d. 1384). 551

Zabarella, Franciscus (d. 1417). 453(x2), 708

Zanchius, Jerome (d. 1590). 99, 532, 606

Zumel, Franciscus (d. 1607). 457

Bibliography

Primary Sources

Ames, W. *De conscientia* (Oxford, 1659).
— *Medulla ss. Theologiae* (London, 1630).
— *The Marrow of Sacred Divinity* (London, 1642).
Arminius, J. *Opera theologica* (Leiden, 1629).
— *The Works of James Arminius*, trans. J. Nichols and W. Nichols, 3 vols. (Grand Rapids, MI, 1991 reprint).
Augustine. *The City of God*, trans. M. Dods, 2 vols. (Edinburgh, 1878).
Baillie, R. *Ladensium autokatakrisis, the Canterburians Self Conviction* (London, 1641).
— *An Antidote against Arminianism* (London, 1641).
— *The Letters and Journals of Robert Baillie*, ed. D. Lang, 3 vols. (Edinburgh, 1841).
Ball, J. *A Treatise of the Covenant of Grace* (London, 1645).
Baro, P. 'Peter Baro's Summary of Three Opinions Concerning Predestination', in J. Arminius, *The Works of James Arminius*, trans. J. Nichols and W. Nichols, 3 vols. (Grand Rapids, MI, 1991, reprint), 92-100.
Basil of Caesarea. *Epistolae*, vol. 36, in J.P. Migne, *Patrologia Graeca Cursus Completus*, 161 vols. (Paris, 1857-1866).
Bavinck, H. *Gereformeerde Dogmatiek* (Kampen: Bos, ^{2}1906-1911).
Baxter, R. *Aphorisms of Justification* (London, 1649).
— *Catholick Theologie* (London, 1675).
Beza, T. *Quaestionum et responsionum Christianarum libellus* (Geneva, 1570).
— *An Evident Display of Popish Practices* (London, 1578).
Blake, T. *Vindiciae foederis; or, A Treatise of the Covenant of God Entered with Mankinde* (London, ^{2}1658).
Boethius. *The Consolation of Philosophy*, trans. P.G. Walsh (Oxford: Oxford University, 1999).
Boston, T. *Memoirs of the Life, Time, and Writings of the Reverend and Learned Thomas Boston, A.M.*, ed. G.H. Morrison (Edinburgh and London: Oliphant Anderson & Ferrier, 1899).
Bradwardine, T. *De causa Dei contra Pelagium* (London, 1618).
Bullinger, H. *The Decades of Henry Bullinger*, ed. T. Harding, 4 vols. (Cambridge: Cambridge University, 1849-52).
— *De testamento seu foedere Dei unico et aeterno* (Tiguri, 1534), in C.S. McCoy and J.W. Baker, *Fountainhead of Federalism: Heinrich Bullinger and the Covenantal Tradition* (Louisville, KY: Westminster/Knox, 1991), 99-138.
Burgess, A. *Vindiciae legis* (London, 1646).
Calderwood, D. *A Solution of Dr. Resolutus* (Amsterdam, 1619).
— *The Speach of the Kirk of Scotland to her Beloved Children* (Amsterdam, 1620).
— *A Re-examination of the Five Articles Enacted at Perth, anno 1618* (n.p., 1636).

Calvin, J. *Commentary on a Harmony of the Evangelists, Matthew, Mark, and Luke*, trans. W. Pringle (Edinburgh: CTS, 1846).
— *Commentary on the Book of Psalms*, trans. J. Anderson, 5 vols. (Edinburgh: CTS, 1845-1849).
— *Commentaries on the First Book of Moses called Genesis*, trans. J. King (Edinburgh: CTS, 1847).
— *Commentaries on the Four Last Books of Moses*, trans. C.W. Bingham, 4 vols. (Edinburgh: CTS, 1852-1855).
— *Commentaries on the Book of the Prophet Jeremiah and the Lamentations*, trans. J. Owen, 5 vols. (Edinburgh: CTS, 1850-1855).
— *Commentaries on the Epistles to Timothy, Titus, and Philemon*, trans. W. Pringle (Edinburgh: CTS, 1856).
— *Ioannis Calvini opera*, eds. G. Baum, E. Cunitz, and E. Reuss (Brunswick: Schwetschke, 1863-1900).
— *The Gospel according to St. John 1-10*, trans. T.H.L. Parker, *Calvin's Commentaries*, eds. D.W. Torrance and T.F. Torrance (Edinburgh and London: Oliver and Boyd, 1959).
— *Acts 14-28*, trans. J.W. Fraser, *Calvin's New Testament Commentaries*, eds. D.W. Torrance and T.F. Torrance (Grand Rapids, MI: Eerdmans, 1960).
— *Romans and Thessalonians*, trans. R. Mackenzie, *Calvin's New Testament Commentaries*, eds. D.W. Torrance and T.F. Torrance (Edinburgh and London: Oliver and Boyd, 1960).
— *Institutes of the Christian Religion*, ed. J.T. McNeill, trans. and indexed F.L. Battles (Philadelphia: Westminster, 1960).
— *The Bondage and Liberation of the Will: A Defence of the Orthodox Doctrine of Human Choice against Pighius*, ed. A.N.S. Lane, trans. G.I. Davies (1543; Grand Rapids, MI: Baker, 1996).
Censura in confessionem sive declarationem sententiae eorum qui in foederato Belgio Remonstrantes vocantur (Leiden, 1626).
Cocceius, J. *Summa doctrinae de foedere et testamento Dei* (1648; Amsterdam, 1683).
Corvinus, J. *Petri Molinaei novi anatomici mala encheiresis, seu censura anatomes Arminianismi* (Frankfurt, 1622).
The Covenant of Grace, not Absolute, but Conditional, Modestly Asserted, and the Preachers thereof Vindicated from the unjust Aspersions of Arminianism and Popery (London, 1692).
Crooke, S. *The Guide unto True Blessedness* (London, 1613).
Davenant, J. *A Treatise on Justification, or the Disputatio de justitia habituali et actuali*, trans. J. Allport, 2 vols. (London, 1844-1846).
Descartes, R. *A Discourse of a Method for the Well Guiding of Reason, and the Discovery of Truth in the Sciences* (London, 1649).
— and M. Schoock. *La querelle d'Utrecht*, textes établis, traduits et annotés par Theo Verbeek (Paris: Les impressions nouvelles, 1988).
Dickson, D. *Therapeutica sacra, Shewing Briefly the Method of Healing the Diseases of the Conscience Concerning Regeneration* (1656; Edinburgh, 1664).
— *Truth's Victory over Error. Or, an Abridgement of the Chief Controversies in Religion...between those of the Orthodox Faith, and all Adversaries Whatsoever* (Edinburgh, 1684).
— and J. Durham. *The Sum of Saving Knowledge* (Edinburgh, 1650).

Du Moulin, P. *The Anatomy of Arminianisme* (London, 1620).
— *De cognitione Dei tractatus* (Hagae-Comitis, 1631).
Duns Scotus, J. *Duns Scotus on the Will and Morality*, ed. and trans. with introduction by A.B. Wolter (Washington: Catholic University of America, 1986).
Episcopius, S. *Opera theologica*, vol. 1, ed. E. de Courcelles (Amsterdam, 1650).
— *Opera theologica* (Rotterdam, 1665).
— *The Confession or Declaration of the Ministers or Pastors, Which in the United Provinces are called Remonstrants, Concerning the chief Points of Christian Religion* (London, 1676).
— *Opera theologica* (Hagae-Comitis, ^{2}1678).
Fenner, D. *Sacra theologia, sive veritas quae est secundum pietatem* (Geneva, 1585).
Forbes, J. *Instructiones historico-theologicae de doctrina Christiana* (Amsterdam, 1645).
Fraser of Brea, J. *Memoirs of the Life of the Very Rev. Mr. J.F. of Brea* (Edinburgh, 1738).
The Generall Demands, of the Reverend Doctors of Divinitie, and Ministers of the Gospell in Aberdeene, Concerning the Late Covenant, in Scotland. Together with the Answers, Replyes, and Duplyes that followed thereupon, in the Year, 1638 (Aberdeen, 1663).
Gillespie, G. *A Dispute against the English-Popish Ceremonies* (Leiden?, 1637).
— *The Works of George Gillespie*, 2 vols. (Edinburgh: Robert Ogle and Oliver and Boyd, 1846).
Gillespie, P. *The Ark of the Covenant Opened: or, A Treatise of the Covenant of Redemption between God and Christ, as the Foundation of the Covenant of Grace* (London, 1677).
Gomarus, F. *Opera theologica omnia* (Amsterdam, 1664).
Goodwin, T. *The Works of Thomas Goodwin, D.D.*, 12 vols. (Edinburgh: James Nichol, 1861-1866).
Gordon, J. *History of Scots Affairs, from 1637 to 1641*, 3 vols. (Aberdeen: Spalding Club, 1841), 3:274-82.
Graile, J. *A Modest Vindication of the Doctrine of Conditions in the Covenant of Grace* (London, 1655).
Gregory of Nazianzus. *Orationes theologica*, vol. 36, *Patrologia Graeca Cursus Completus*, ed. J.P. Migne, 161 vols. (Paris: Vives, 1857-1866).
Gregory of Nyssa. *Contra Eunomium*, vol. 45, *Patrologia Graeca Cursus Completus*, ed. J.P. Migne, 161 vols. (Paris: Vives, 1857-1866).
Hogg, J. *Confessions of a Justified Sinner* (London: Random House, 1992).
Hoornbeeck, J. *Theologia practica*, 2 vols. (Utrecht, 1663-1666).
Junius, F. *Opuscula theologica selecta*, ed. A. Kuyper (Amsterdam: Miller and Kruyt, 1882).
Kirk, J., ed. *The Second Book of Discipline* (Edinburgh: St. Andrews Press, 1980).
Laud, W. *A Relation of the Conference between William Laud...and Mr. Fisher the Jesuit* (London, ^{3}1673).
— *The Works of the Most Reverend Father in God, William Laud*, ed. J. Bliss, 7 vols. (Oxford: John Henry Parker, 1847-60).
Leigh, E. *A Systeme or Body of Divinity* (London, 1654).
Locke, J. *Some Familiar Letters between Mr. Locke, and Several of his Friends* (London, 1708).

Lombard, P. *Sententiae in IV libros distinctae*, 2 vols. (Rome: Collegii S. Bonaventurae ad Claras Aquas, 1971-1981).
Luther, M. *Luthers Werke*, Kritische Gesamtausgabe, 68 vols. (Weimar: Hermann Böhlaus Nachfolger, 1883-1999).
Maccovius, J. *Loci communes theologici* (Amsterdam, 1658).
Maimonides, M. *The Guide for the Perplexed*, trans. M. Friedländer (London: George Routledge & Sons, ²1919).
Melanchthon, P. *Melanchthon on Christian Doctrine: Loci communes, 1555*, trans. and ed. C.L. Manschreck (New York: Oxford University, 1965).
Mitchell, A.F., and J. Struthers, eds. *Minutes of the Sessions of the Westminster Assembly of Divines* (Edinburgh and London: Blackwood & Sons, 1874).
Molina, L., de. *Concordia liberi arbitrii cum gratiae donis, divina praescientia, providentia, praedestinatione et reprobatione* (Antwerp, 1595).
Morgan, A., ed. *University of Edinburgh Charters, Statutes, and Acts of the Town Council and the Senatus: 1583-1858* (Edinburgh: Oliver and Boyd, 1937).
Murray, J. *Redemption Accomplished and Applied* (Grand Rapids, MI: Eerdmans, 1955).
Musculus, W. *Common Places of Christian Religion*, trans. J. Man (London, 1578).
— *Loci communes sacrae theologiae* (Basel, ³1573).
Olevianus, C. *De substantia foederis gratuiti inter Deum et electos, item de mediis, quibus ea ipsa substantia nobis communicavit* (Geneva, 1585).
Owen, J. *The Works of John Owen*, ed. W. Goold, 24 vols. (London: Johnstone & Hunter, 1850-55).
Pareus, D. *Theological Miscellanies of Dr. David Pareus* (London, 1645).
Perkins, W. *A Christian and Plaine Treatise of the Manner and Order of Predestination, and of the Largeness of Gods Grace* (London, 1606).
— *The Workes of that Famous and Worthy Minister of Christ, in the Universitie of Cambridge, Mr. William Perkins*, 3 vols. (Cambridge, 1616-1618).
Peterkin, A., ed. *Records of the Kirk of Scotland* (Edinburgh: John Sutherland, 1838).
Piscator, J. *Aphorismi doctrinae Christianae* (1589; Oxford, 1630).
Polanus von Polansdorf, A. *Partitiones theologicae* (London, 1591).
— *Syntagma theologiae Christianae* (Geneva, 1617).
The Racovian Catechism (Amsterdam, 1652).
Ramsay, A. *A Warning to Come out of Babylon* (Edinburgh, 1638).
Ramus, P. *De religione Christiana* (Frankfurt, 1576).
Roberts, F. *Of God's Covenants* (London, 1657).
Rollock, R. *Quaestiones et responsiones aliquot de foedere Dei* (Edinburgh, 1596).
— *A Treatise of Gods Effectual Calling* (1597; London, 1603).
Rutherford, S. *Exercitationes apologeticae pro divina gratia* (1636; Franeker, 1651).
— *A Peaceable and Temperate Plea for Pauls Presbyterie in Scotland* (London, 1642).
— *The Due Right of Presbyteries* (London, 1644).
— *Lex, Rex, or The Law and the Prince* (London, 1644).
— *A Sermon Preached before the Honourable House of Commons, January 31, 1644* (London, 1644).
— *A Sermon Preached before the Honourable House of Lords, June 25, 1645* (London, 1645).
— *The Tryal and Triumph of Faith* (London, 1645).
— *The Divine Right of Church Government and Excommunication* (London, 1646).

— *Christ Dying and Drawing Sinners to Himselfe* (London, 1647).
— *A Survey of the Spirituall AntiChrist* (London, 1648).
— *Disputatio scholastica de divina providentia* (Edinburgh, 1649).
— *A Free Disputation against Pretended Liberty of Conscience* (London, 1649).
— *The Last and Heavenly Speeches and Glorious Departure of John Gordoun, Viscount Kenmuir* (Edinburgh, 1649).
— *The Covenant of Life Opened* (Edinburgh, 1655).
— *A Survey of the Survey of that Summe of Church-Discipline Penned by Mr. Thomas Hooker* (London, 1658).
— *Influences of the Life of Grace* (London, 1659).
— *Examen Arminianismi* (Utrecht, 1668).
— *The Power and Prevalency of Prayer* (Edinburgh?, 1713).
— *A Testimony to the Work of Reformation in Britaine and Ireland* (Glasgow, 1719).
— *Fourteen Communion Sermons*, ed. A.A. Bonar (Glasgow: Glass & Co., 1877).
— *Quaint Sermons...Hitherto Unpublished* (London: Hodder and Stoughton, 1885).
— *Ane Catachisme conteining the Soume of Christian Religion*, in *Catechisms of the Second Reformation*, ed. A.F. Mitchell (London: James Nisbet, 1886).
— *Letters of Samuel Rutherford*, ed. A.A. Bonar (Edinburgh and London: Oliphant Anderson & Ferrier, 1891).
— Unpublished manuscript containing Latin notes of lectures on the doctrine of Scripture given by Rutherford in 1654, National Library of Scotland, Edinburgh, MSS16475.
— Unpublished manuscript containing Latin notes by W. Tullidelph of lectures on the doctrine of Scripture given by Rutherford in 1648, St. Andrews University Library, BS540.R8.
— Unpublished manuscript containing a treatise on supralapsarianism and a discourse on Ephesians 1.4, University of Edinburgh Library, La.II.394.
Sibbes, R. *The Complete Works of Richard Sibbes, D.D.*, 7 vols., ed. Alexander Grosart (Edinburgh: James Nichol, 1862-1864).
Taylor, J. *Unum necessarium: or, The Doctrine and Practice of Repentance* (London, 1655).
Thomas Aquinas. *Summa theologiae* (Blackfriars; London: Eyre & Spottiswoode; and New York: McGraw-Hill, 1963).
Tuckney, A. *Eight Letters of Dr. Anthony Tuckney, and Dr. Benjamin Whichcote*, in *Moral and Religious Aphorisms, Collected from the Manuscript Papers of the Reverend and Learned Doctor Whichcote*, ed. S. Salter (London: Pater-Noster-Row, 1753).
Turretin, F. *The Doctrine of Scripture: Locus 2 of Institutio theologiae elencticae*, ed. and trans. J.W. Beardslee III (Grand Rapids, MI: Baker, 1981).
— *Institutes of Elenctic Theology*, trans. G.M. Giger, ed. J.T. Dennison Jr., 3 vols. (Philipsburg, NJ: P&R, 1992-7).
Twisse, W. *A Discovery of D. Jacksons Vanitie* (n.p., 1631).
— *A Treatise of Mr. Cottons, Clearing certain Doubts Concerning Predestination. Together with an Examination Thereof* (London, 1646).
— *The Riches of Gods Love unto the Vessells of Mercy, Consistent with his Absolute Hatred or Reprobation of the Vessells of Wrath* (Oxford, 1653).
Ussher, J. *A Body of Divinity, or the Summe and Substance of Christian Religion* (London, 1645).

Van Limborch, P. *Theologia Christiana ad praxin pietatis ac promotionem pacis Christiana unice directa* (Amsterdam, 1735; originally published as *Institutiones theologiae Christianae*, 1686).
— *A Compleat System, or Body of Divinity*, 2 vols. (London, ²1713).
Vermigli, P.M. *In Epistolam S. Pauli Apostoli ad Romanos* (Basel, 1558).
— *The Common Places of the most famous and renowned Divine Doctor Peter Martyr*, ed. and trans. A. Marten (London, 1583).
— *Philosophical Works*, ed. and trans. J.C. McLelland, *The Peter Martyr Library*, vol. 4 (Kirksville, MO: Sixteenth Century Journal, 1996).
Voetius, G. *Selectarum disputationum pars prima* (Utrecht, 1648).
— *Ta asketika sive Exercitia pietatis in usum juventutis academicae nunc edita. Addita est, ob materiam affinitatem, Oratio de pietate cum scientia conjungenda habita anno 1634* (Gorinchem, 1664).
Vorstius, C. *Tractatus theologicus de Deo* (Steinfurt, 1606).
— *Apologetica responsio ad ea omnia* (n.p., 1618).
Westminster Confession of Faith (Glasgow: Free Presbyterian Publications, 1995).
Whitaker, W. *A Disputation on Holy Scripture*, trans. and ed. W. Fitzgerald (Cambridge: Cambridge University, 1849).
Willard, S. *A Compleat Body of Divinity* (Boston, 1726).
Zanchi, J. *Opera theologicorum D. Hieronymi Zanchii*, 9 vols. (Geneva, 1617-1619).
Zwingli, U. *Commentary on True and False Religion*, eds. S.M. Jackson and C.N. Heller (1929; Durham, NC: Labyrinth Press, 1981).

Secondary Sources

Adams, R.M. *The Virtue of Faith and Other Essays in Philosophical Theology* (New York: Oxford University, 1987).
Althaus, P. *Die Prinzipien der deutschen reformierten Dogmatik im Zeitalter er aristotelischen Scholastik* (Leipzig: Deichert, 1914).
Armstrong, B.G. *Calvinism and the Amyraut Heresy: Protestant Scholasticism and Humanism in Seventeenth Century France* (Madison, WI: University of Wisconsin, 1969).
Bagchi, D.V.N. 'Sic Et Non: Luther and Scholasticism', in *Protestant Scholasticism: Essays in Reassessment*, eds. C.R. Trueman and R.S. Clark (Carlisle, Cumbria: Paternoster, 1999), 3-15.
Bangs, C. *Arminius: A Study in the Dutch Reformation* (Nashville, TN: Abingdon Press, 1971).
— 'Arminius as a Reformed Theologian', in *The Heritage of John Calvin*, ed. J.H. Bratt (Grand Rapids, MI: Eerdmans, 1973), 209-22.
Barth, K. *Anselm: Fides Quaerens Intellectum, Anselm's Proof of the Existence of God in the Context of his Theological Scheme* (London: SCM Press, 1960).
— *Church Dogmatics*, ed. G.W. Bromiley and T.F. Torrance, 4 vols. (Edinburgh: T&T Clark, 1936-1975).
Bavinck, H. *The Doctrine of God*, trans. W. Hendriksen (Edinburgh: Banner of Truth, 1977).
Beeke, J.R. *Assurance of Faith: Calvin, English Puritanism, and the Dutch Second Reformation* (New York: Peter Lang, 1991).

— 'Personal Assurance of Faith: The Puritans and Chapter 18.2 of the Westminster Confession', *Westminster Theological Journal* 55:1 (Spring 1993), 1-30.

Bell, M.C. 'Saving Faith and Assurance of Salvation in the Teaching of John Calvin and Scottish Theology' (unpublished Ph.D. dissertation, Aberdeen University, 1982).

— 'Calvin and the Extent of the Atonement', *The Evangelical Quarterly* 55 (1983), 115-23.

— *Calvin and Scottish Theology: The Doctrine of Assurance* (Edinburgh: Handsel Press, 1985).

Berkouwer, G.C. *Divine Election*, trans. H. Bekker (Grand Rapids, MI: Eerdmans, 1960).

— *Holy Scripture*, trans. J.B. Rogers (Grand Rapids, MI: Eerdmans, 1975).

Bierma, L.D. *German Calvinism in the Confessional Age: The Covenant Theology of Caspar Olevianus* (Grand Rapids, MI: Baker, 1996).

Bizer, E. *Frühorthodoxie und Rationalismus* (Zurich: EVZ Verlag, 1963).

Blocher, H. 'Calvin infralapsaire', *La Revue Réformée* 31 (1980), 270-76.

Bonansea, B.M. 'Duns Scotus' Voluntarism', in *John Duns Scotus, 1265-1965*, eds. Bonansea and J. Ryan (Washington: Catholic University of America, 1965), 83-121.

Boyd, G. *Satan and the Problem of Evil: Constructing a Trinitarian Warfare Theodicy* (Downers Grove, IL: InterVarsity, 2001).

Brentnall, J.M. *Samuel Rutherford in Aberdeen* (Inverness: John Eccles, c.1981).

Bridges, G. *Identity and Distinction in Petrus Thomae, O.F.M.* (St. Bonaventure, NY: Franciscan Institute, 1959).

Broadie, A. *The Shadow of Scotus: Philosophy and Faith in Pre-Reformation Scotland* (Edinburgh: T&T Clark, 1995).

Bromiley, G.W. *Historical Theology: An Introduction* (Grand Rapids, MI: Eerdmans, 1978).

Brown, K.M. 'Covenanters', in *Dictionary of Scottish Church History and Theology*, ed. N.M. de S. Cameron (Downers Grove, IL: InterVarsity, 1993), 218-19.

Brümmer, V. 'Calvin, Bernard and the Freedom of the Will', *Religious Studies* 30 (1994), 437-55.

Brunner, E. *The Christian Doctrine of God*, trans. O. Wyon (London: Lutterworth, 1949).

— and Karl Barth. *Natural Theology: Comprising 'Nature and Grace' by Professor Dr. Emil Brunner and the Reply 'No!' by Dr. Karl Barth*, trans. P. Fraenkel (1946; Eugene, OR: Wipf & Stock, 2002).

Burgess, J.P. 'The Problem of Scripture and Political Affairs as Reflected in the Puritan Revolution: Samuel Rutherford, Thomas Goodwin, John Goodwin, and Gerard Winstanley' (unpublished Ph.D. dissertation, University of Chicago, 1986).

Burleigh, J.H.S. *A Church History of Scotland* (Edinburgh: Hope Trust, 1988).

Burns, J.H. 'The Political Background of the Reformation, 1513-1625', in *Essays on the Scottish Reformation 1513-1625*, ed. D. McRoberts (Glasgow: Burns, 1962), 1-38.

Burrell, S.A. 'The Covenant Idea as a Revolutionary Symbol: Scotland, 1596-1637', *Church History* 27 (1958), 338-50.

Button, C.N. 'Scottish Mysticism in the Seventeenth Century, with Special Reference to Samuel Rutherford' (unpublished Ph.D. dissertation, University of Edinburgh, 1927).

Cameron, J.K. 'The Piety of Samuel Rutherford (c. 1621-1661): A Neglected Feature of Seventeenth Century Scottish Calvinism', *Nederlands Archief voor Kerkgeschiedenis* 65 (1985), 153-9.

— 'Andrew Melville in St. Andrews', in *In Divers Manners: A St. Mary's Miscellany*, ed. D.W.D. Shaw (St. Andrews: St. Mary's College, 1990), 58-72.
Campbell, W.M. 'Samuel Rutherford, propagandist and exponent of Scottish Presbyterianism' (unpublished Ph.D. dissertation, University of Edinburgh, 1937).
— 'Lex, Rex and its Author', *Records of the Scottish Church History Society* 7 (1941), 204-28.
— *The Triumph of Presbyterianism* (Edinburgh: St. Andrew Press, 1958).
Cant, R.G. *The University of St. Andrews: A Short History* (Edinburgh and London: Scottish Academic Press, 1970).
Clifford, A.C. *Atonement and Justification: English Evangelical Theology 1640-1790, An Evaluation* (Oxford: Clarendon, 1990).
Coffey, J. *Politics, Religion and the British Revolutions: The Mind of Samuel Rutherford* (Cambridge: Cambridge University, 1997).
Collinson, P. *The Religion of Protestants: The Church in English Society, 1559-1625* (Oxford: Clarendon, 1982).
Como, D.R. 'Puritans, Predestination and the Construction of Orthodoxy in Early Seventeenth-Century England', in *Conformity and Orthodoxy in the English Church, c.1560-1660*, eds. P. Lake and M. Questier (Woodbridge, Suffolk: Boydell Press, 2000), 64-87.
— *Blown by the Spirit: Puritanism and the Emergence of an Antinomian Underground in Pre-Civil-War England* (Stanford, CA: Stanford University, 2004).
Cook, F. *Grace in Winter: Rutherford in Verse* (Edinburgh: Banner of Truth, 1989).
— *Samuel Rutherford and His Friends* (Edinburgh: Banner of Truth, 1992).
Copleston, F. *A History of Philosophy*, 9 vols. (London: Burns, Oates & Washbourne, 1946-1975).
Craig, W.L. *The Problem of Divine Foreknowledge and Future Contingents from Aristotle to Suarez* (Leiden: E.J. Brill, 1988).
Crauford, T. *History of the University of Edinburgh, from 1580 to 1646* (Edinburgh: A. Neill, 1808).
Cross, R. *Duns Scotus* (New York: Oxford University, 1999).
Cunningham, W. *Reformers and the Theology of the Reformation* (1862; Edinburgh: Banner of Truth, 1989).
Daniel, C. 'Hyper-Calvinism and John Gill' (unpublished Ph.D. dissertation, University of Edinburgh, 1983).
Davies, B. *The Thought of Thomas Aquinas* (Oxford: Clarendon, 1992).
Davis, J. *The Caroline Captivity of the Church* (Oxford: Clarendon, 1992).
Deferrari, R., and M.I. Barry, and I. McGuiness, eds. *A Lexicon of St. Thomas Aquinas based on 'The Summa Theologica' and selected passages of his other works* (Washington: Catholic University of America, 1948).
Dekker, E. *Rijker dans Midas: Vrijheid, Genade en predestinatie in de theologie van Jacobus Arminius (1559-1609)* (Zoetermeer: Boekencentrum, 1993).
— 'Was Arminius a Molinist?', *Sixteenth Century Journal* 27:2 (1996), 337-52.
Donaldson, G. *The Making of the Scottish Prayer Book of 1637* (Edinburgh: University of Edinburgh, 1954).
Donnelly, J.P. 'Italian Influences on the Development of Calvinist Scholasticism', *The Sixteenth Century Journal* 7:1 (1976), 81-101.
Douglas, J.D. 'National Covenant', in *Dictionary of Scottish Church History and Theology*, ed. N.M. de S. Cameron (Downers Grove, IL: InterVarsity, 1993), 620.

Dowey, E.A. *The Knowledge of God in Calvin's Theology* (Grand Rapids, MI: Eerdmans, 1994).
Durkan, J. 'The Cultural Background in Sixteenth-Century Scotland', in *Essays on the Scottish Reformation 1513-1625*, ed. D. McRoberts (Glasgow: Burns, 1962), 274-331.
Fergusson, D.A.S. 'Predestination: A Scottish Perspective', *Scottish Journal of Theology* 46 (1993), 457-78.
Fesko, J.V. *Diversity Within the Reformed Tradition: Supra- and Infralapsarianism in Calvin, Dort, and Westminster* (Greenville, SC: Reformed Academic Press, 2001).
— 'The Westminster Confession and Lapsarianism: Calvin and the Divines', in *The Westminster Confession into the 21st Century: Essays in Remembrance of the 350th Anniversary of the Westminster Assembly*, vol. 2, ed. J.L. Duncan III (Fearn, Ross-shire: Mentor, 2004), 477-525.
— and G.M. Richard. 'Natural Theology and the Westminster Confession', in *The Westminster Confession into the 21st Century: Essays in Remembrance of the 350th Anniversary of the Westminster Assembly*, vol. 3, ed. J.L. Duncan III (Fearn, Ross-shire: Mentor, forthcoming 2008).
Flinn, R. 'Samuel Rutherford and Puritan Political Theory', *Journal of Christian Reconstruction* 5 (1978-9), 49-74.
Ford, J. 'Lex, rex iusto posita: Samuel Rutherford on the origins of government', in *Scots and Britons: Scottish Political Thought and the Union of 1603*, ed. R. Mason (Cambridge: Cambridge University, 1994), 262-90.
Freddoso, A.J. Introduction to Luis de Molina, *On Divine Foreknowledge*, trans. A.J. Freddoso (Ithaca, NY: Cornell University, 1988).
Fretheim, T. 'Yahweh', in *The New International Dictionary of Old Testament Theology and Exegesis*, vol. 4, ed. W. VanGemeren (Carlisle, Cumbria: Paternoster, 1996).
Garcia, M.A. 'Life in Christ: The Function of Union with Christ in the *Unio-Duplex Gratia* Structure of Calvin's Soteriology with Special Reference to the Relationship of Justification and Sanctification in Sixteenth-Century Context' (unpublished Ph.D. dissertation, University of Edinburgh, 2004).
Garrigou-Lagrange, R. 'Prémotion Physique', vol. 13, *Dictionnaire de théologie catholique* (Paris: Librairie Letouzey et Ané, 1936).
— *The Theological Virtues*, 2 vols., trans. T. à Kempis Reilly (St. Louis, MO: Herder, 1965).
Gathercole, S.J. *Where is Boasting? Early Jewish Soteriology and Paul's Response in Romans 1-5* (Grand Rapids, MI: Eerdmans, 2002).
Gerrish, B.A. *The Old Protestantism and the New: Essays on the Reformation Heritage* (Edinburgh: T&T Clark, 1982).
— 'From Calvin to Schleiermacher: The Theme and the Shape of Christian Dogmatics', in *Schleiermacher-Archiv*, International Schleiermacher-Kongress, 1984, 2 vols., eds. H. Fischer, H.-J. Birkner, G. Ebeling, H. Kimmerle, and K.-V. Selge (Berlin: Walter de Gruyter, 1985).
Gerstner, J.H., and J.N. Gerstner. 'Edwardsean Preparation for Salvation', *Westminster Theological Journal* 42:1 (Fall 1979), 5-71.
Gilmour, R. *Samuel Rutherford: A Study Biographical and Somewhat Critical, in the History of the Scottish Covenants* (Edinburgh: Oliphant Anderson & Ferrier, 1904).
Gilson, E. *The Spirit of Medieval Philosophy*, trans. A.H.C. Downes (New York: Scribner, 1936).

Godfrey, W.R. 'Tensions Within International Calvinism: The Debate on the Atonement and the Synod of Dort, 1618-1619' (unpublished Ph.D. dissertation, Stanford University, 1974).

— 'Reformed Thought on the Extent of the Atonement to 1618', *Westminster Theological Journal* 37:2 (Winter 1975), 136-70.

Gomes, A.W. 'De Jesu Christo Servatore: Faustus Socinus on the Satisfaction of Christ', *Westminster Theological Journal* 55:2 (Fall 1993), 209-31.

Grant, A. *The Story of the University of Edinburgh During its First Three Hundred Years* (London: Longmans Green, 1884).

Gründler, O. *Die Gotteslehre Girolami Zanchis und ihre Bedeutung für seine Lehre von der Prädestination* (Neukirchen: Neukirchner Verlag, 1965).

Gunton, C. *A Brief Theology of Revelation* (Edinburgh: T&T Clark, 1995).

— and S. Holmes and M. Rae, eds. *The Practice of Theology: A Reader* (London: SCM Press, 2001).

Hall, B. 'Calvin Against the Calvinists', in *John Calvin*, ed. G.E. Duffield (Appleford, Berkshire: Sutton Courtenay Press, 1966), 19-37.

Hall, D.D., ed. *The Antinomian Controversy 1636-1638* (Middletown, CT: Wesleyan University, 1968).

Hall, T.D. 'Rutherford, Locke, and the Declaration: The Connection' (unpublished Th.M. dissertation, Dallas Theological Seminary, 1984).

Harrison, A.W. *The Beginnings of Arminianism to the Synod of Dort* (London: University of London, 1926).

— *Arminianism* (London: Duckworth, 1937).

Hawkes, R.M. 'The Logic of Assurance in English Puritan Theology', *Westminster Theological Journal* 52:2 (Fall 1990), 247-61.

Helm, P. *Calvin and the Calvinists* (Edinburgh: Banner of Truth, 1982).

— 'Calvin and Bernard on Freedom and Necessity: A Reply to Brümmer', *Religious Studies* 30 (1994), 457-65.

Helseth, P.K. 'The Trustworthiness of God and the Foundation of Hope', in *Beyond the Bounds: Open Theism and the Undermining of Biblical Christianity*, eds. J. Piper, J. Taylor, and Helseth (Wheaton, IL: Crossway, 2003), 275-307.

Henderson, G.D. 'Arminianism in Scotland', *London Quarterly and Holborn Review* (October 1932), 493-504.

— *Religious Life in Seventeenth-Century Scotland* (Cambridge: Cambridge University, 1937).

— *The Burning Bush: Studies in Scottish Church History* (Edinburgh: St. Andrew Press, 1957).

Heppe, H. *Reformed Dogmatics: Set Out and Illustrated from the Sources*, rev. and ed. E. Bizer, trans. G.T. Thomson (London: George Allen & Unwin, 1950).

Hill, C. *The English Bible and the Seventeenth-Century Revolution* (London: Penguin, 1993).

Hodge, C. *Systematic Theology*, 3 vols. (London and Edinburgh: Thomas Nelson and Sons, 1883).

Hoekema, A.A. 'The Covenant of Grace in Calvin's Teaching', *Calvin Theological Journal* 2 (1967), 133-61.

Hoenderdaal, G.J. 'The Debate about Arminius outside the Netherlands', in *Leiden University in the Seventeenth Century: An Exchange of Learning*, eds. Th. H.L. Scheurleer and G.H.M. Posthumus Meyjes (Leiden: E.J. Brill, 1975), 137-59.

Holtrop, P.C. *The Bolsec Controversy on Predestination, From 1551 to 1555*, 2 vols. (Lewiston, NY: Edwin Mellen, 1993-).
Innes, A.T. *Studies in Scottish History: Chiefly Ecclesiastical* (London: Hodder & Stoughton, 1892).
James, F.A., III. *Peter Martyr Vermigli and Predestination: The Augustinian Inheritance of an Italian Reformer* (Oxford: Clarendon, 1998).
Jewett, P.K. *Election and Predestination* (Grand Rapids, MI: Eerdmans, 1985).
Jones, J.W. *The Shattered Synthesis: New England Puritanism before the Great Awakening* (New Haven and London: Yale University, 1973).
Kamen, H. *The Rise of Toleration* (London: Weidenfeld and Nicolson, 1967).
Kelly, J.N.D. *Early Christian Doctrines* (London: A&C Black, ^{5}1977).
Kendall, R.T. 'Living the Christian Life in the Teaching of William Perkins and His Followers', in *Living the Christian Life* (London: The Westminster Conference, 1974).
— *Calvin and English Calvinism to 1649* (Oxford: Oxford University, 1979).
— 'The Puritan Modification of Calvin's Theology', in *John Calvin*, ed. W.S. Reid (Grand Rapids, MI: Zondervan, 1982), 199-214.
Kevan, E.F. *The Grace of Law: A Study in Puritan Theology* (London: Carey Kingsgate Press, 1964).
Kickel, W. *Vernunft und Offenbarung bei Theodor Beza* (Neukirchen: Neukirchner Verlag, 1967).
Kim, S.-D. 'Time and Eternity: A Study in Samuel Rutherford's theology, with Reference to His Use of Scholastic Method' (unpublished Ph.D. dissertation, University of Aberdeen, 2002).
Kirk, J. 'Reformation Parliament', in *Dictionary of Scottish Church History and Theology*, ed. N.M. de S. Cameron (Downers Grove, IL: InterVarsity, 1993), 693.
— 'Reformation, Scottish', in *Dictionary of Scottish Church History and Theology*, ed. N.M. de S. Cameron (Downers Grove, IL: InterVarsity, 1993), 693-8.
Klauber, M.I. 'Francis Turretin on Biblical Accommodation: Loyal Calvinist Or Reformed Scholastic?', *Westminster Theological Journal* 55:1 (Spring 1993), 73-86.
Knowles, D. *The English Mystical Tradition* (London: Burns & Oates, 1961).
Kolfhaus, W. *Christusgemeinschaft bei Johannes Calvin*, Beiträge zur Geschichte und Lehre der Reformierten Kirche, vol. 3 (Neukirchen: Buchhandlung des Erziehungsvereins, 1939).
Kramm, H.H. *The Theology of Martin Luther* (London: James Clarke, 1947).
Kristeller, P.O. 'The Validity of the Term: "Nominalism"', in *The Pursuit of Holiness in Late Medieval and Renaissance Religion*, eds. C.E. Trinkaus and H.A. Oberman (Leiden: E.J. Brill, 1974), 65-6.
Lachman, D.C. *The Marrow Controversy, 1718-23* (Edinburgh: Rutherford House, 1988).
Lake, P.G. *Moderate Puritans and the Elizabethan Church* (Cambridge: Cambridge University, 1982).
— 'Calvinism and the English Church 1570-1635', *Past and Present* 114 (1987), 32-76.
— 'Anti-popery: the Structure of a Prejudice', in *Conflict in Early Stuart England: Studies in Religion and Politics 1603-1642*, eds. R. Cust and A. Hughes (London and New York: Longman, 1989), 72-106.
Lane, A.N.S. 'Sola Scriptura? Making Sense of a Post-Reformation Slogan', in *A Pathway into the Holy Scripture*, eds. P.E. Satterthwaite and D.F. Wright (Grand

Rapids, MI: Eerdmans, 1994), 297-327.
— Introduction to John Calvin, *The Bondage and Liberation of the Will: A Defence of the Orthodox Doctrine of Human Choice against Pighius*, ed. A.N.S. Lane, trans. G.I. Davies (Grand Rapids, MI: Baker, 1996), xiii-xxxiv.
Lang, A. *Der Heidelberger Katechismus und vier verwandte Katechismen* (Leipzig: Deichert, 1907).
Letham, R. 'The *Foedus Operum*: Some Factors Accounting For Its Development', *Sixteenth Century Journal* 14 (1983), 457-67.
Lillback, P.A. 'Ursinus' Development of the Covenant of Creation: A Debt to Melanchthon or Calvin?', *Westminster Theological Journal* 43 (1981), 247-88.
— *The Binding of God: Calvin's Role in the Development of Covenant Theology* (Grand Rapids, MI: Baker; Carlise, Cumbria: Paternoster, 2001).
Lohse, B. *Martin Luther: An Introduction to His Life and Work*, trans. R. Schultz (Philadelphia: Fortress, 1986).
— *Martin Luther's Theology: Its Historical and Systematic Development*, trans. and ed. R.A. Harrisville (Minneapolis, MN: Fortress, 1999).
Louden, R.S. 'Samuel Rutherford', in *The Westminster Directory of Christian Spirituality*, ed. G.S. Wakefield (Philadelphia: Westminster, 1983), 345.
Lynch, M. *Scotland: A New History* (London: Pimlico, 2001).
McClelland, J.C. 'The Reformed Doctrine of Predestination According to Peter Martyr', *Scottish Journal of Theology* 8:1 (March 1955), 255-71.
McCoy, C.S. 'Johannes Cocceius: Federal Theologian', *Scottish Journal of Theology* 16 (1963), 352-70.
— and J.W. Baker. *Fountainhead of Federalism: Heinrich Bullinger and the Covenantal Tradition* (Louisville, KY: Westminster/Knox, 1991).
McGiffert, M. 'Grace and Work: The Rise and Division of Covenant Divinity in Elizabethan Puritanism', *Harvard Theological Review* 75:4 (1982), 463-502.
— 'The Perkinsian Moment of Federal Theology', *Calvin Theological Journal* 29 (1994), 117-48.
McGrath, A.E. 'John Calvin and Late Mediaeval Thought: A Study in Late Mediaeval Influences upon Calvin's Theological Development', *Archiv für Reformationsgeschichte* 77 (1986), 58-78.
— *The Genesis of Doctrine: A Study in the Foundations of Doctrinal Criticism* (Oxford: Basil Blackwell, 1990).
— *Reformation Thought: An Introduction* (Oxford: Blackwell, [3]1999).
Machar, A.M. 'A Scottish Mystic', *The Andover Review* 6 (1986), 379-95.
McKay, W.D.J. 'Samuel Rutherford on Civil Government' (unpublished M.Th. dissertation, Queen's University, Belfast, 1986).
Maclear, J.F. 'Samuel Rutherford: The Law and the King', in *Calvinism and the Political Order*, eds. G.L. Hunt and J.T. McNeill (Philadelphia: Westminster, 1965), 65-87.
McLennan, B. 'Presbyterianism challenged: A study of Catholicism and Episcopacy in the North-East of Scotland, 1560-1650' (unpublished Ph.D. dissertation, University of Aberdeen, 1977).
Macleod, D. 'Covenant Theology', in *Dictionary of Scottish Church History and Theology*, ed. N.M. de S. Cameron (Downers Grove, IL: InterVarsity, 1993), 214-18.
— 'How Right are the Justified? or, What is a *Dikaios*?', *Scottish Bulletin of Evangelical Theology* 22:2 (Autumn 2004), 173-95.

Macleod, J. *Scottish Theology in Relation to Church History Since the Reformation* (Edinburgh: Publications Committee of the Free Church of Scotland, 1943).
MacMillan, D. *The Aberdeen Doctors* (London: Hodder and Stoughton, 1909).
McNeill, J.T. 'The Significance of the Word of God for Calvin', *Church History* 28 (1959), 131-46.
Marsden, G.M. 'Perry Miller's Rehabilitation of the Puritans: A Critique', *Church History* 39 (1970), 91-105.
— *Jonathan Edwards: A Life* (New Haven and London: Yale University, 2003).
Marsh, C. *The Family of Love in English Society, 1550-1630* (Cambridge: Cambridge University, 1994).
Marshall, J.L. 'Natural Law and the Covenant: The Place of Natural Law in the Covenantal Framework of Samuel Rutherford's *Lex, Rex*' (unpublished Ph.D. dissertation, Westminster Theological Seminary, 1995).
Martin, H. *Great Christian Books* (London: SCM Press, 1945).
Matter, A.E. *The Voice of My Beloved: The Song of Songs in Western Medieval Christianity* (Philadelphia: University of Pennsylvania, 1990).
Maxcey, C.E. *A Study in the Development of Bona Opera: The Doctrine in Philip Melanchthon* (Nieuwkoop: B. De Graaf, 1980).
Meier, H. 'Love, Law, and Lucre: Images in Rutherfurd's Letters', in *Historical and Editorial Essays in Medieval and Early Modern English for Johan Gerritsen*, eds. M.-J. Arn and H. Wirtjes (Groningen: Wolters-Noordhoff, 1985), 77-96.
Miller, P. *The New England Mind* (New York: Macmillan, 1939).
— ed. *The American Puritans: Their Prose and Poetry* (New York: Anchor Books, 1956).
Mitchell, A.F. *The Westminster Assembly: Its History and Standards* (London: James Nisbet, 1883).
Moonan, L. *Divine Power: The Medieval Power Distinction up to its Adoption by Albert, Bonaventure, and Aquinas* (Oxford: Clarendon, 1994).
Morrill, J. *The Nature of the English Revolution* (New York: Longman, 1993).
Mullan, D.G. 'Theology in the Church of Scotland 1618-c.1640: A Calvinist Consensus?', *Sixteenth Century Journal* 26:3 (1995), 595-617.
— 'Arminianism in the Lord's Assembly: Glasgow, 1638', *Records of the Scottish Church History Society* 26 (1996), 1-30.
— 'Masked Popery and Pyrrhonian Uncertainty: The Early Scottish Covenanters on Arminianism', *The Journal of Religious History* 21:2 (June 1997), 159-77.
— *Scottish Puritanism, 1590-1638* (Oxford: Oxford University, 2000).
Muller, R.A. '*Duplex cognitio Dei* in the Theology of Early Reformed Orthodoxy', *Sixteenth Century Journal* 10:2 (1979), 51-61.
— 'The Federal Motif in Seventeenth Century Arminian Theology', *Nederlands Archief voor Kerkgeschiedenis* 62:1 (1982), 102-22.
— 'Christ—the Revelation or the Revealer? Brunner and Reformed Orthodoxy on the Doctrine of the Word of God', *Journal of the Evangelical Theological Society* 26:3 (September 1983), 307-19.
— *Dictionary of Latin and Greek Theological Terms: Drawn Principally from Protestant Scholastic Theology* (Grand Rapids, MI: Baker, 1985).
— *Christ and the Decree: Christology and Predestination in Reformed Theology from Calvin to Perkins* (Durham, NC: Labyrinth Press, 1986).
— 'The Christological Problem in the Thought of Jacobus Arminius', *Nederlands*

Archief voor Kerkgeschiedenis 68:1 (1988), 145-63.
— 'Fides and Cognitio in Relation to the Problem of Intellect and Will in the Theology of John Calvin', *Calvin Theological Journal* 25 (November 1990), 207-24.
— *God, Creation and Providence in the Thought of Jacob Arminius: Sources and Directions of Scholastic Protestantism in the Era of Early Orthodoxy* (Grand Rapids, MI: Baker, 1991).
— 'The Priority of the Intellect in the Soteriology of Jacob Arminius', *Westminster Theological Journal* 55:1 (Spring 1993), 55-72.
— 'God, Predestination, and the Integrity of the Created Order: A Note on Patterns in Arminius' Theology', in *Later Calvinism: International Perspectives*, ed. W.F. Graham (Kirksville, MO: Sixteenth Century Journal, 1994), 431-46.
— 'Scholasticism and Orthodoxy in the Reformed Tradition: An Attempt at Definition' (Inaugural Address, Grand Rapids, MI, 1995).
— 'Calvin and the "Calvinists": Assessing Continuities and Discontinuities between the Reformation and Orthodoxy', *Calvin Theological Journal* 30 (1995), 345-75 and 31 (1996), 125-60.
— 'The Problem of Protestant Scholasticism—A Review and Definition', in *Reformation and Scholasticism: An Ecumenical Enterprise*, eds. W. J. van Asselt and E. Dekker (Grand Rapids, MI: Baker, 2001), 45-64.
— *Post-Reformation Reformed Dogmatics: The Rise and Development of Reformed Orthodoxy, ca. 1520 to ca. 1725*, 4 vols. (Grand Rapids, MI: Baker Academic, 2003).
Murray, J. 'Definitive Sanctification', *Calvin Theological Journal* 2 (April 1967), 5-21.
Murray, T. *The Life of Rev. Samuel Rutherford* (Edinburgh: Oliphant, 1828).
Niesel, W. 'Syllogismus practicus?', in *Aus Theologie und Geschichte der reformierten Kirche* (Neukirchen: K. Moers, 1933), 158-79.
— *The Theology of Calvin*, trans. H. Knight (London: Lutterworth, 1956).
Nicole, R. 'John Calvin's View of the Extent of the Atonement', *Westminster Theological Journal* 47:2 (Fall 1985), 197-225.
Oakley, F. *Omnipotence, Covenant, and Order: An Excursion in the History of Ideas from Abelard to Leibniz* (Ithaca, NY: Cornell University, 1984).
— 'The Absolute and Ordained Power of God in Sixteenth- and Seventeenth-Century Theology', *Journal of the History of Ideas* 59:3 (July 1998), 437-61.
Oberman, H.A. 'Some Notes on the Theology of Nominalism: With Attention to its Relation to the Renaissance', *Harvard Theological Review* 53 (1960), 47-76.
— *The Harvest of Medieval Theology: Gabriel Biel and Late Medieval Nominalism* (1963; Durham, NC: Labyrinth Press, ^{3}1983).
— *Forerunners of the Reformation* (New York: Holt, Rinehart and Winston, 1966).
— 'The Shape of Late Medieval Thought: The Birthpangs of the Modern Era', in *The Pursuit of Holiness in Late Medieval and Renaissance Religion*, eds. C.E. Trinkaus and Oberman (Leiden: E.J. Brill, 1974), 3-25.
— *Masters of the Reformation: Emergence of a New Intellectual Climate in Europe*, trans. D. Martin (Cambridge: Cambridge University, 1981).
Ong, W.J. *Ramus, Method, and the Decay of Dialogue* (Cambridge, MA: Harvard University, 1958).
Orr, J. *The Progress of Dogma* (London: James Clarke, n.d.).
Packer, J.I. *The Redemption & Restoration of Man in the Thought of Richard Baxter: A Study in Puritan Theology* (Vancouver, BC: Regent College, 2003).
Pannenberg, W. *Systematic Theology*, trans. G.W. Bromiley, 2 vols. (Grand Rapids, MI:

Eerdmans, 1991).
Parker, T.H.L. *Calvin's Doctrine of the Knowledge of God* (Edinburgh: Oliver & Boyd, 1969).
Pernoud, M.A. 'The Theory of the *Potentia Dei* According to Aquinas, Scotus, and Ockham', *Antonianum* 47 (1972), 69-95.
Petit, N. *The Heart Prepared: Grace and Conversion in Puritan Spiritual Life* (New Haven and London: Yale University, 1966).
Petry, R.C., ed. *Late Medieval Mysticism* (London: SCM Press, 1957).
Philip, A. *The Devotional Literature of Scotland* (London: James Clarke, 1920).
Phillips, T. 'Francis Turretin's Idea of Theology and its Bearing upon his Doctrine of Scripture' (unpublished Ph.D. dissertation, Vanderbilt University, 1986).
Plantinga, A. *Does God have a Nature?* (Milwaukee, WI: Marquette University, 1980).
Platt, J.E. *Reformed Thought and Scholasticism: The Arguments for the Existence of God in Dutch Theology, 1575-1650* (Leiden: E.J. Brill, 1982).
— 'The Denial of the Innate Idea of God in Dutch Remonstrant Theology: From Episcopius to Van Limborch', in *Protestant Scholasticism: Essays in Reassessment*, eds. C.R. Trueman and R.S. Clark (Carlisle, Cumbria: Paternoster, 1999), 213-26.
Popkin, R.H. *The History of Scepticism from Erasmus to Descartes* (New York and London: Harper & Row, 1968).
Porter, H.C. *Reformation and Reaction in Tudor Cambridge* (Cambridge: Cambridge University, 1958).
— 'The Nose of Wax: Scripture and the Spirit from Erasmus to Milton', *Transactions of the Royal Historical Society* 14 (1964), 155-74.
Pott, C.K. 'Erasmus and the Reformation', in *The Heritage of John Calvin*, ed. J.H. Bratt (Grand Rapids, MI: Eerdmans, 1973), 193-208.
Praamsma, L. 'The Background of the Arminian Controversy (1586-1618)', in *Crisis in the Reformed Churches: Essays in Commemoration of the Great Synod of Dort, 1618-1619*, ed. P.Y. DeJong (Grand Rapids, MI: Reformed Fellowship, 1968), 22-38.
Rae, C.E. 'The Political Thought of Samuel Rutherford' (unpublished M.A. dissertation, University of Guelph, 1991).
Reid, J.K.S. *The Authority of Scripture: A Study of Reformation and Post-Reformation Understanding of the Bible* (London: Methuen, 1962).
Rendell, K.G. *Samuel Rutherford: A New Biography of the Man & his Ministry* (Fearn, Ross-shire: Christian Focus, 2003).
Richard, G.M. 'Samuel Rutherford's Supralapsarianism Revealed: A Key to the Lapsarian Position of the Westminster Confession of Faith?', *Scottish Journal of Theology* 59:1 (2006), 27-44.
Roberts, M. 'Samuel Rutherford: The Comings and Goings of the Heavenly Bridegroom', in *The Trials of Puritanism: Papers read at the 1993 Westminster Conference* (privately published, 1994), 119-34.
Rogers, J.B., and D.K. McKim. *The Authority and Interpretation of the Bible: An Historical Approach* (San Francisco: Harper & Row, 1979).
Rolston, H., III. 'Responsible Man in Reformed Theology: Calvin versus the Westminster Confession', *Scottish Journal of Theology* 23 (1970), 129-56.
— *John Calvin Versus the Westminster Confession* (Richmond, VA: John Knox, 1972).
Ross, J.M. 'Samuel Rutherford', *The Month* (July 1975), 207-11.
Sanders, J. *The God Who Risks: A Theology of Providence* (Downers Grove, IL:

InterVarsity, 1998).
Schenck, L.B. *The Presbyterian Doctrine of Children in the Covenant* (New Haven: Yale University, 1940).
Schreiner, S.E. 'Pelagianism', in *The Oxford Encyclopedia of the Reformation*, ed. H.J. Hilderbrand, 4 vols. (New York: Oxford University, 1996), 3:238-40.
Seeburg, R. *Text-book of the History of Doctrines*, trans. C.E. Hay, 2 vols. (Grand Rapids, MI: Baker, 1977).
Sell, A.P.F. 'Arminians, Deists, and Reason', *Faith and Freedom* 33 (Autumn 1979), 19-31.
— *The Great Debate: Calvinism, Arminianism, and Salvation* (Grand Rapids, MI: Baker Books, 1983).
Sharpe, K. *The Personal Rule of Charles I* (New Haven: Yale University, 1992).
Shepherd, V. *The Nature and Function of Faith in the Theology of John Calvin* (Macon, GA: Mercer University, 1983).
Shriver, F. 'Orthodoxy and Diplomacy: James I and the Vorstius Affair', *English Historical Review* 85 (July 1970), 449-74.
Smith, J.E. Introduction to Jonathan Edwards, *The Works of Jonathan Edwards*, vol. 2, ed. Smith (New Haven, CT: Yale University, 1959).
Spalding, J. *The History of the Troubles and Memorable Transactions in Scotland from the Year 1624 to 1645*, 2 vols. (Aberdeen: Evans, 1792).
Spear, W.R. 'William Whitaker and the Westminster Doctrine of Scripture', *Reformed Theological Journal* 7 (November 1991), 38-48.
— 'The Westminster Confession of Faith and Holy Scripture', in *To Glorify and Enjoy God: A Commemoration of the 350th Anniversary of the Westminster Assembly*, eds. J.L. Carson and D.W. Hall (Edinburgh: Banner of Truth, 1994), 85-100.
— 'Word and Spirit in the Westminster Confession', in *The Westminster Confession into the 21st Century: Essays in Remembrance of the 350th Anniversary of the Westminster Assembly*, ed. J.L. Duncan III, vol. 1 (Fearn, Ross-shire: Mentor, 2003), 39-56.
Sprunger, K.L. 'Ames, Ramus, and the Method of Puritan Theology', *Harvard Theological Review* 59:2 (April 1966), 133-51.
— *Dutch Puritanism: A History of English and Scottish Churches of the Netherlands in the Sixteenth and Seventeenth Centuries* (Leiden: E.J. Brill, 1982).
Steinmetz, D.C. *Misericordia Dei: The Theology of Johannes von Staupitz in Its Late Medieval Setting* (Leiden: E.J. Brill, 1968).
— 'Calvin and the Absolute Power of God', *Journal of Medieval and Renaissance Studies* 18:1 (Spring 1988), 65-79.
— *Calvin in Context* (New York: Oxford University, 1995).
— 'The Scholastic Calvin', in *Protestant Scholasticism: Essays in Reassessment*, eds. C.R. Trueman and R.S. Clark (Carlisle, Cumbria: Paternoster, 1999), 16-30.
Stevenson, A. *The History of the Church and State of Scotland* (Edinburgh: Thomas Nelson, 1840).
Stevenson, D. 'Restoration', in *Dictionary of Scottish Church History and Theology*, ed. N.M. de S. Cameron (Downers Grove, IL: InterVarsity, 1993), 710-11.
Strickland, D. 'Union with Christ in the Theology of Samuel Rutherford: An Examination of his Doctrine of the Holy Spirit' (unpublished Ph.D. dissertation, University of Edinburgh, 1972).
Stuermann, W.E. 'A Critical Study of Calvin's Concept of Faith' (unpublished Ph.D.

dissertation, University of Tulsa, 1952).
Talbot, M.R. 'True Freedom: The Liberty that Scripture Portrays as Worth Having', in *Beyond the Bounds: Open Theism and the Undermining of Biblical Christianity*, eds. J. Piper, J. Taylor, and P.K. Helseth (Wheaton, IL: Crossway, 2003), 77-109.
Tamburello, D. *Union with Christ: John Calvin and the Mysticism of St. Bernard* (Louisville, KY: Westminster John Knox, 1994).
Thornton, M. *English Spirituality: An Outline of Ascetical Theology according to the English Pastoral Tradition* (London: SPCK, 1963).
Tijdeman, H.W. 'Caspar Sibelius, in leven Predikant te Deventer, volgens zijne onuitgegeven eigen-levensbeschrijving', *Godgeleerde Bijdragen* 23 (1849).
Todd, M. '"All One with Tom Thumbe": Arminianism, Popery, and the Story of the Reformation in Early Stuart Cambridge', *Church History* 64 (1995), 563-79.
— *The Culture of Protestantism in Early Modern Scotland* (New Haven and London: Yale University, 2002).
Toon, P. *The Emergence of Hyper-Calvinism in English Nonconformity 1689-1765* (London: The Olive Tree, 1967).
Torrance, J.B. 'Covenant or Contract? A Study of the Theological Background of Worship in Seventeenth-Century Scotland', *Scottish Journal of Theology* 23 (1970), 51-76.
— 'The Covenant Concept in Scottish Theology and Politics and its Legacy', *Scottish Journal of Theology* 34 (1981), 225-43.
— 'Strengths and Weaknesses of the Westminster Theology', in *The Westminster Confession*, ed. A.I.C. Heron (Edinburgh: St. Andrews, 1982), 40-53.
— 'Calvin and Puritanism in England and Scotland—Some Basic Concepts in the Development of "Federal Theology"', in *Calvinus Reformator: His Contribution to Theology, Church and Society* (Potchefstroom, Republic of South Africa: Potchefstroom University for Christian Higher Education, 1982), 264-77.
— 'The Incarnation and "Limited Atonement"', *The Evangelical Quarterly* 55 (1983), 82-94.
— 'Interpreting the Word by the Light of Christ or the Light of Nature? Calvin, Calvinism and Barth', in *Calviniana: Ideas and Influence of Jean Calvin*, ed. R.V. Schnucker (Kirksville, MO: Sixteenth Century Journal, 1988), 256-67.
— 'The Concept of Federal Theology—Was Calvin a Federal Theologian?', in *Calvinus Sacrae Scripturae Professor: Calvin as Confessor of Holy Scripture*, ed. W.H. Neuser (Grand Rapids, MI: Eerdmans, 1994), 15-41.
Torrance, T.F. *The Hermeneutics of John Calvin* (Edinburgh: Scottish Academic Press, 1988).
— *Trinitarian Perspectives: Toward Doctrinal Agreement* (Edinburgh: T&T Clark, 1994).
— *The Trinitarian Faith: The Evangelical Theology of the Ancient Catholic Church* (Edinburgh: T&T Clark, 1995).
— *Scottish Theology: From John Knox to John McLeod Campbell* (Edinburgh: T&T Clark, 1996).
— 'The Distinctive Character of the Reformed Tradition', *Reformed Review* 54:1 (Autumn 2000), 5-16.
Trevor-Roper, H.R. *Religion, the Reformation and Social Change* (London: Macmillan, ²1972).
Trinterud, L.J. 'The Origins of Puritanism', *Church History* 20 (March 1951), 37-57.

Trueman, C.R. 'Faith Seeking Understanding: Some Neglected Aspects of John Owen's Understanding of Scriptural Interpretation', in *Interpreting the Bible: Historical and Theological Studies in Honour of David F. Wright*, ed. A.N.S. Lane (Leicester: Apollos, 1997), 147-62.
— *The Claims of Truth: John Owen's Trinitarian Theology* (Carlisle, Cumbria: Paternoster, 1998).
— 'John Owen's Dissertation on Divine Justice: An Exercise in Christocentric Scholasticism', *Calvin Theological Journal* 33 (1998), 87-103.
— 'A Small Step Towards Rationalism: The Impact of the Metaphysics of Tommaso Campanella on the Theology of Richard Baxter', in *Protestant Scholasticism: Essays in Reassessment*, eds. Trueman and R.S. Clark (Carlisle, Cumbria: Paternoster, 1999), 181-95.
— '*Simul peccator et iustus*: Some Reflections upon Martin Luther and Justification' (paper delivered to the 10th Edinburgh Dogmatics Conference, Rutherford House, 25-28 August 2003).
— and R.S. Clark. *Protestant Scholasticism: Essays in Reassessment* (Carlisle, Cumbria: Paternoster, 1999).
Tyacke, N. 'Arminianism and English Culture', in *Britain and the Netherlands*, vol. 7, *Church and State since the Reformation*, eds. A.C. Duke and C.A. Tamse (The Hague: Martinus Nijhoff, 1981), 94-117.
— *Anti-Calvinists: The Rise of English Arminianism c.1590-1640* (Oxford: Clarendon Press, 1987).
— 'Archbishop Laud', in *The Early Stuart Church, 1603-1642*, ed. K. Fincham (London: Macmillan, 1993), 51-70.
Van Asselt, W.J. 'The Fundamental Meaning of Theology: Archetypal and Ectypal Theology in Seventeenth-Century Reformed Thought', *Westminster Theological Journal* 64:2 (Fall 2002), 319-35.
— and E. Dekker. *Reformation and Scholasticism: An Ecumenical Enterprise* (Grand Rapids, MI: Baker, 2001).
Van Dam, C. 'שׁוֹפֵט', *New International Dictionary of Old Testament Theology and Exegesis*, ed. W. VanGemeren, vol. 4 (Carlisle, Cumbria: Paternoster, 1997).
Van den Brink, G. *Almighty God: A Study of the Doctrine of Divine Omnipotence* (Kempen: J. Kok, 1993).
Vanhoozer, K.J. *First Theology: God, Scripture & Hermeneutics* (Downer's Grove, IL: InterVarsity, 2002).
Van Ruler, J.A. 'New Philosophy to Old Standards: Voetius' Vindication of Divine Concurrence and Secondary Causality', *Nederlands Archief voor Kerkgeschiedenis* 71:1 (1991), 58-91.
Vansteenberghe, E. 'Molinisme', vol. 10, *Dictionnaire de théologie catholique* (Paris: Librairie Letouzey et Ané, 1928).
Verbeek, T. 'Descartes and the Problem of Atheism: The Utrecht Crisis', *Nederlands Archief voor Kerkgeschiedenis* 71:2 (1991), 211-23.
Von Rohr, J. 'Covenant and Assurance in Early English Puritanism', *Church History* 34 (1965), 195-203.
— *The Covenant of Grace in Puritan Thought* (Atlanta, GA: Scholars Press, 1986).
Wainwright, W.J. 'Theological determinism and the problem of evil: Are Arminians any better off?', *International Journal for Philosophy of Religion* 50 (2001), 81-96.
Walker, J. *The Theology and Theologians of Scotland 1560-1750* (Edinburgh: Knox

Press, ²1982).
Wallace, D.D. *Puritans and Predestination: Grace in English Protestant Theology, 1525-1695* (Chapel Hill, NC: University of North Carolina, 1982).
Wallace, R.S. *Calvin's Doctrine of the Christian Life* (Edinburgh and London: Oliver and Boyd, 1959).
Ward, W.R. 'Orthodoxy, Enlightenment and Religious Revival', in *Religion and Humanism*, ed. K. Robbins (Oxford: Blackwell, 1981), 275-96.
Warfield, B.B. *Calvin and Calvinism* (New York: Oxford University, 1931).
Webb, O.K. 'The Political Thought of Samuel Rutherford' (unpublished Ph.D. dissertation, Duke University, 1964).
Weber, O. *Foundations of Dogmatics*, trans. D.L. Guder, 2 vols. (Grand Rapids, MI: Eerdmans, 1983).
Webster, J. *Holy Scripture: A Dogmatic Sketch* (Cambridge: Cambridge University, 2003).
Weir, D.A. *The Origins of the Federal Theology in Sixteenth-Century Reformation Thought* (Oxford: Clarendon, 1990).
Weisheipl, J.A. 'Scholastic Method', in *The New Catholic Encyclopedia* (New York: Catholic University of America, 1967), 12:1145-6.
Wendel, F. *Calvin: The Origins and Development of his Religious Thought*, trans. P. Mairet (London: William Collins, 1963).
White, P. *Predestination, Policy and Polemic* (Cambridge: Cambridge University, 1992).
Whyte, A. *Samuel Rutherford and Some of his Correspondents* (Edinburgh: Oliphant Anderson & Ferrier, 1894).
Winship, M.P. *Making Heretics: Militant Protestantism and Free Grace in Massachusetts, 1636-1641* (Princeton: Princeton University, 2002).
Wodrow, R. *Analecta: or, Materials for a History of Remarkable Providences; Mostly Relating to Scotch Ministers and Christians*, 3 vols. (Edinburgh: Maitland Club, 1842-1843).
Wolterstorff, N. 'Divine Simplicity', in *Philosophical Perspectives*, vol. 5, *Philosophy of Religion*, ed. J. Tomberlin (Atascadero, CA: Ridgeview, 1991), 531-52.
Wood, A.S. 'The Declaration of Sentiments: The Theological Testament of Arminius', *The Evangelical Quarterly* 65:2 (1993), 111-29.
Woodbridge, J.D. *Biblical Authority: A Critique of the Rogers/McKim Proposal* (Grand Rapids, MI: Zondervan, 1982).
Woolsey, A.A. 'Unity and Continuity in Covenantal Thought: A Study in the Reformed Tradition to the Westminster Assembly', 2 vols. (unpublished Ph.D. dissertation, University of Glasgow, 1988).
Wright, N.T. 'Romans and the Theology of Paul', in *Pauline Theology*, eds. D.M. Hay and E.E. Johnson (Minneapolis, MN: Fortress, 1995), 30-67.
— *The Letter to the Romans: Introduction, Commentary, and Reflections*, vol. 10, *The New Interpreter's Bible* (Nashville, TN: Abingdon Press, 2002), 393-770.
— 'New Perspectives on Paul' (paper delivered to 10th Edinburgh Dogmatics Conference, Rutherford House, 25-28 August 2003).
Zizioulas, J.D. 'The Doctrine of the Holy Trinity: The Significance of the Cappadocian Contribution', in *Trinitarian Theology Today: Essays on Divine Being and Act*, ed. C. Schwöbel (Edinburgh: T&T Clark, 1995), 44-60.

General Index

Aberdeen Doctors 19, 230n.
Accommodation 27-8.
Affections 40, 202-5, 240.
Agricola, R. 44.
Ames, W. 29, 55, 57, 71, 84, 152, 166, 177, 181n, 187, 192, 194, 200, 211, 214.
Anselm 79
Antinomianism 52, 54, 183, 184, 205, 207, 214, 215n.
Apologetics 40-41.
Arianism 85, 87.
Arminianism 16-20, 18, 25, 26, 33, 36, 41, 44, 47, 50, 51, 61, 64-6, 68, 69, 70, 71, 72, 73, 76, 77, 82, 85-9, 100, 101, 102, 104, 106, 107, 108, 109-11, 119, 126-9, 130, 132, 144, 145, 146, 149-50, 157-59, 161-2, 162-8, 169, 173, 174, 175-6, 179-80, 181, 185, 186, 188, 190, 190-91, 193, 196, 198, 205, 206, 209, 211-12, 218, 220.
Arminianism in England 17-18.
Arminianism in Scotland 18-20, 21, 45, 221-33.
Arminius, J. 15, 16, 36, 50, 61, 85, 89, 90, 92, 100-101, 102, 106, 116, 124, 127-9, 149, 152, 157, 159, 161, 163, 165, 166, 173, 175-6, 180, 188, 189, 190-91, 196, 198, 199, 226, 227, 236, 237.
Armstrong, B. 11-13, 25, 37, 44, 50, 96, 102, 132, 236, 237.
Assurance 205-18, 232.
Augustine 86, 94, 153, 156, 169n, 172, 236.

Baillie, R. 19-20, 222, 223, 227.
Bañez, D. 91.
Baro, P. 17.
Barrett, W. 17.
Barth, K. 32, 52, 83, 94, 117, 129, 133, 139, 143, 213, 226, 234n.
Basil of Caesarea 85.

Bavinck, H. 126, 137.
Baxter, R. 211.
Blair, R. 22.
Beeke, J. 206, 208, 216-17.
Bell, M.C. 11, 132, 133, 178-9, 184, 206, 207, 211, 217, 236, 237.
Bernard of Clairvaux 201-2.
Beza, T. 61, 116, 124, 153, 206.
Biel, G. 96.
Blair, R. 22.
Blake, T. 149.
Boethius 91.
Bradwardine, T. 80, 166.
Bucer, M. 237.
Brunner, E. 32.
Bullinger, H. 84, 156, 157, 183.

Calderwood, D. 8, 9, 15-16, 19.
Calvin vs. Calvinists 11-13, 32-3, 56-60, 67-8, 73, 78-9, 113-15, 132, 151-6, 162-8, 172, 178-85, 206-18, 234-8.
Calvin, J. 11, 32, 35, 38, 48, 49, 56-9, 61, 66-7, 78, 84, 86, 87, 94, 106, 113, 114, 115, 125, 126, 133, 142-3, 151-2, 153, 154-5, 156, 157, 162, 163, 165, 168, 169n, 170, 171, 172, 174, 176, 177, 178, 182-3, 186, 187, 191, 192, 193, 199, 200, 206, 207, 208-9, 213-14, 215, 217, 218, 226, 232, 234-8.
Cameron, J. 152.
Cant, A. 229.
Charles I 8-9, 229.
Christ, atonement of 131-8, 158.
Chrysostom 112.
Circa-fundamentalia 62-3.
Cocceius, J. 143, 170.
Coffey, J. 6, 6n, 10.
Conscience 34.
Contra-Remonstrants 93.
Conversion 160-93.
Cooperationism 106, 174, 180.
Cotton, J. 227-8, 230.

Covenant of Grace 156-60.
Covenant of Redemption 141-7, 212.
Covenant of Works 147-56.
Covenant Theology 139-60.
Covenant, definition of 140.
Covenant, unilateral vs. bilateral 141.

Descartes, R. 37, 45.
Deus absconditus 26, 27, 42, 232.
Deus revelatus 26, 27, 42, 78.
Dickson, D. 143, 147.
Du Moulin, P. 35, 148, 164-5.
Duns Scotus, J. 26, 79, 81n, 95, 97, 112, 137, 187.
Duplex cognitio Dei 33-7.
Durham, J. 147.

Edwards, J. 202.
Effectual calling (internal) 178.
Effectual calling 181.
Elizabeth I 7.
Episcopius, S. 36, 44, 71, 88, 93, 149, 190, 236.
Erasmus, D. 176, 232.
External calling 178, 181, 184.

Facere quod in se est 180-81, 189, 190, 198, 226, 228.
Faith 185-93, 207-9, 232.
Fall into sin (original sin) 38n, 148, 150, 156, 167, 169-71.
Family of Love 52n.
Fenner, D. 152.
Fonseca, P., de 90.
Free will 107-9, 111-12, 113, 119, 165, 167, 168-77, 186, 199, 203, 209, 210, 218, 219-20, 237.
Fundamentals of faith 61-3, 69.

Gillespie, G. 19, 218.
Gillespie, P. 143.
God, attributes of 79-82.
God, essence of 78-9, 83-5.
God, generic identity of 86n.
God, knowledge of 89-94.
God, nature of 77-94.
God, numerical identity of 86n.
God, omnipotency of 98-9, 111.

God, sovereignty of 98-9, 107-9, 111-12, 113, 115, 159, 177, 179, 185, 218, 220, 232, 237, 239.
God, the Trinity 85-9, 129, 145, 146.
God, will of 94-115.
Gomarus, F. 116.
Goodwin, T. 35, 216.
Grace and law 179.
Grace, habit of 166-8, 190.
Grace, prevenient 42, 180.
Grace, resistibility of 174-5.
Gregory of Nazianzus 89.
Gregory of Nyssa 85, 89.
Gregory of Rimini 80, 80n.
Grotius, H. 18.

Harderwyck 16, 116.
Helm, P. 208.
Henderson, A. 221, 222, 229, 230.
Hodge, A.A. 53.
Holy Spirit 30-31, 38-9, 40, 44, 58, 66-7, 75-6, 189, 190, 216-18.
Hooker, R. 53.
Human nature, post-death 172-3.
Human nature, post-fall 171-2.
Human nature, post-regeneration 172.
Human nature, pre-fall 169-71.
Hyper-Calvinism 12, 13, 237-8.

Imago Dei 33, 39-40, 44.
Infralapsarianism 116-20, 122-6.
Intellectualism 43, 165-6, 177, 188-90, 191, 193, 198, 199, 220, 226, 227.

James VI and I 8, 15.
John of Damascus 112.
Junius, F. 152.
Justification 193-200, 226, 227.
Justitia aliena 197.

Kendall, R.T. 206, 207, 211, 212.

Laud, W. 8, 9, 20, 21, 45, 222-3, 228, 229.
Law, uses of 182n, 182-3.
Leigh, E. 84, 86, 168, 169, 170, 187, 200.
Locke, John 45.
Lombard, P. 96.
Luther, M. 26, 32, 94, 115, 154, 171, 172,

General Index 269

176, 180, 182-3, 187, 194, 197, 213-14, 226, 236, 237.

Maccovius, J. 29, 187.
MacWard, R. 20.
Marrow Controversy 184.
McKim, D. (see Rogers, J.).
Melanchthon, P. 152, 153, 154-5, 156.
Melville, A. 8, 14, 21.
Middle knowledge (*scientia media*) 90-94, 110-11, 119, 180, 181, 226, 228.
Miller, P. 144.
Molina, L., de 90, 91, 180, 226.
Mullan, D. 64, 222, 224, 225.
Musculus, W. 35, 113, 114, 115, 141, 148, 157, 187, 236, 237.

National Covenant 9, 230.
Natural theology 32-47.
Negative Confession 230.
Neonomianism 211.
Nethenus, M. 16, 20.
New Perspective on Paul 197n.
Niesel, W. 56, 67, 213.
Nominalism 80n, 96, 97, 98, 99.

Oakley, F. 97.
Oberman, H. 12, 50, 64, 68, 97, 98.
Olevianus, C. 143.
Open Theism 108-9n.
Order of Decrees 120, 145-7.
Origen 202.
Original sin 34-5, 38n, 148, 150, 156, 167, 169-71.
Owen, J. 1-2, 133, 135, 142, 143, 147, 167.

Pelagianism 36, 45, 175-6.
Perkins, W. 17, 29, 35, 58, 66, 84, 116, 120, 126, 152, 155, 160-61, 163, 170-71, 177, 182, 189, 190, 191, 192, 200, 208n.
Perseverance 210.
Pighius, A. 174, 176.
Plantinga, A. 80-81.
Polanus von Polansdorf, A. 29, 35, 58, 152, 170.
Potentia absoluta 27, 42, 97-101, 102, 109, 114, 130, 135, 145.
Potentia ordinata 27, 42, 97-101, 102, 109, 114, 130, 135, 145, 164.
Practical syllogism 212-18.
Praeter-fundamentalia (adiaphora) 62-3.
Praxis in theology 29, 40, 43, 49, 78, 96, 140, 192, 203, 236.
Predestination 116-31, 146, 212, 219, 223, 226, 227.
Premotionism 105n, 106, 174, 180.
Preparationism 178-85.
Presbyterianism 8-10, 16.
Pyrrhonianism 65, 69, 231-3.

Ramus, P. 29, 49.
Regeneration 161-85.
Reid, J.K.S. 56, 57.
Revelation 26.
Revelation, natural 30-31.
Revelation, supernatural 31.
Rogers, J. 53-5, 60, 63-4.
Rollock, R. 14, 140n, 147, 152, 155.
Roman Catholicism 7, 12, 50, 64, 68, 70, 76, 185, 197, 208, 214, 225-31.

Sabellianism 85, 87.
Sanctification 193-4, 200-205.
Sanctification, definitive 195.
Scepticism 231-3.
Schola Augustiniana moderna 80n, 98, 125, 235.
Scholasticism 4, 10-15, 25, 37, 50, 81, 96, 115, 237, 238.
Schoock, M. 37.
Scripture alone (*sola Scriptura*) 50, 65-8, 70, 71, 76, 225-6, 228, 232.
Scripture, authority of 61-70.
Scripture, divinity of 48-51.
Scripture, inerrancy of 52n.
Scripture, infallibility of 52-3.
Scripture, inspiration of 51-2, 54-9.
Scripture, interpretation of 71-6.
Scripture, perspicuity of 71-2.
Scripture, sufficiency of 63-4.
Semi-Pelagianism 17, 36, 94, 175-6.
Sibbes, R. 204.
Simul justus et peccator 194.
Socinianism 33, 42, 47, 70, 73, 92, 135,

197, 231.
Song of Songs 202-4.
Suarez, F. 91.
Sum of Saving Knowledge 147.
Supra-fundamentalia 62-3.
Supralapsarianism 116-131.
Synod of Dort 15, 16, 17, 18, 19, 21, 227.

Tertullian 5.
Theologia archetypa 26, 27, 28-9, 30, 42, 49, 101-2, 219.
Theologia ectypa 26, 27, 28-9, 30, 42, 49, 78, 101-2, 219.
Theological *principia* 25, 44, 45-7, 48.
Thomas Aquinas 80, 81n, 91-2, 94, 97, 98, 100, 105, 110, 166, 187.
Tolerance 69-70, 82, 157, 176-7, 220-21, 233, 240.
Torrance, J.B. 140-41, 178-9, 184, 211, 238.
Torrance, T.F. 11, 132, 133, 236, 237, 239.
Traill, R. 20.
Treatise concerning Religious Affections 202.
Turretin, F. 27-8, 148.
Twisse, W. 35, 41, 97-8, 116, 121, 133-4, 216, 227-8.

Union with Christ 4, 162-4.
Ursinus, Z. 151, 153, 154, 157, 168, 187.
Ussher, J. 33n, 35, 46, 55, 57, 66, 84, 163, 187, 194, 200.
Utrecht 16, 37, 116.

Van Limborch, P. 43, 65, 68, 71, 87-8, 149.
Vermigli, P.M. 35, 84, 113, 114, 115, 124-6, 172, 236, 237.
Voetius, G. 16, 29, 37, 90, 116.
Voluntarism 35, 95, 99, 114-15, 166, 177, 188-90, 199, 219, 220.
Voluntas ad extra 96-102, 115, 120, 134, 135, 136-8, 145.
Voluntas ad intra 96-102, 115, 134, 135, 136-8.
Voluntas antecedens 112, 113.

Voluntas beneplaciti 103-5, 106, 111, 112, 113, 114, 119, 120, 130, 159, 181.
Voluntas consequens 112, 113.
Voluntas efficiens 105-12.
Voluntas permittens 105-12, 120, 148.
Voluntas signi 103-5, 106, 112, 113, 130.
Vorstius, C. 15, 43-4.

Warfield, B.B. 53.
Webster, J. 28, 30, 59.
Westminster Assembly 1-2n, 20, 22, 32, 41.
Westminster Confession of Faith 55, 79, 85, 107, 147, 177, 185n, 197, 206, 211-12.
Westminster Shorter Catechism 2, 29, 192, 210.
Whitaker, W. 17, 55-6, 57, 58.
William of Ockham 96, 97.
Wolterstorff, N. 80-81.

Zanchi, J. 148, 157.
Zumel, F. 91.
Zwingli, U. 32, 84, 176, 183-4, 187, 237.

Studies in Christian History and Thought

(All titles uniform with this volume)
Dates in bold are of projected publication

David Bebbington
Holiness in Nineteenth-Century England
David Bebbington stresses the relationship of movements of spirituality to changes in their cultural setting, especially the legacies of the Enlightenment and Romanticism. He shows that these broad shifts in ideological mood had a profound effect on the ways in which piety was conceptualized and practised. Holiness was intimately bound up with the spirit of the age.
2000 / 0-85364-981-2 / viii + 98pp

J. William Black
Reformation Pastors
Richard Baxter and the Ideal of the Reformed Pastor
This work examines Richard Baxter's *Gildas Salvianus, The Reformed Pastor* (1656) and explores each aspect of his pastoral strategy in light of his own concern for 'reformation' and in the broader context of Edwardian, Elizabethan and early Stuart pastoral ideals and practice.
2003 / 1-84227-190-3 / xxii + 308pp

James Bruce
Prophecy, Miracles, Angels, *and* Heavenly Light?
The Eschatology, Pneumatology and Missiology of Adomnán's Life of Columba
This book surveys approaches to the marvellous in hagiography, providing the first critique of Plummer's hypothesis of Irish saga origin. It then analyses the uniquely systematized phenomena in the *Life of Columba* from Adomnán's seventh-century theological perspective, identifying the coming of the eschatological Kingdom as the key to understanding.
2004 / 1-84227-227-6 / xviii + 286pp

Colin J. Bulley
The Priesthood of Some Believers
Developments from the General to the Special Priesthood in the Christian Literature of the First Three Centuries
The first in-depth treatment of early Christian texts on the priesthood of all believers shows that the developing priesthood of the ordained related closely to the division between laity and clergy and had deleterious effects on the practice of the general priesthood.
2000 / 1-84227-034-6 / xii + 336pp

Anthony R. Cross (ed.)
Ecumenism and History
Studies in Honour of John H.Y. Briggs

This collection of essays examines the inter-relationships between the two fields in which Professor Briggs has contributed so much: history—particularly Baptist and Nonconformist—and the ecumenical movement. With contributions from colleagues and former research students from Britain, Europe and North America, *Ecumenism and History* provides wide-ranging studies in important aspects of Christian history, theology and ecumenical studies.

2002 / 1-84227-135-0 / xx + 362pp

Maggi Dawn
Confessions of an Inquiring Spirit
Form as Constitutive of Meaning in S.T. Coleridge's Theological Writing

This study of Coleridge's *Confessions* focuses on its confessional, epistolary and fragmentary form, suggesting that attention to these features significantly affects its interpretation. Bringing a close study of these three literary forms, the author suggests ways in which they nuance the text with particular understandings of the Trinity, and of a kenotic christology. Some parallels are drawn between Romantic and postmodern dilemmas concerning the authority of the biblical text.

2006 / 1-84227-255-1 / approx. 224 pp

Ruth Gouldbourne
The Flesh and the Feminine
Gender and Theology in the Writings of Caspar Schwenckfeld

Caspar Schwenckfeld and his movement exemplify one of the radical communities of the sixteenth century. Challenging theological and liturgical norms, they also found themselves challenging social and particularly gender assumptions. In this book, the issues of the relationship between radical theology and the understanding of gender are considered.

2005 / 1-84227-048-6 / approx. 304pp

Crawford Gribben
Puritan Millennialism
Literature and Theology, 1550–1682

Puritan Millennialism surveys the growth, impact and eventual decline of puritan millennialism throughout England, Scotland and Ireland, arguing that it was much more diverse than has frequently been suggested. This Paternoster edition is revised and extended from the original 2000 text.

2007 / 1-84227-372-8 / approx. 320pp

Galen K. Johnson
Prisoner of Conscience
John Bunyan on Self, Community and Christian Faith
This is an interdisciplinary study of John Bunyan's understanding of conscience across his autobiographical, theological and fictional writings, investigating whether conscience always deserves fidelity, and how Bunyan's view of conscience affects his relationship both to modern Western individualism and historic Christianity.
2003 / 1-84227-223-3 / xvi + 236pp

R.T. Kendall
Calvin and English Calvinism to 1649
The author's thesis is that those who formed the Westminster Confession of Faith, which is regarded as Calvinism, in fact departed from John Calvin on two points: (1) the extent of the atonement and (2) the ground of assurance of salvation.
1997 / 0-85364-827-1 / xii + 264pp

Timothy Larsen
Friends of Religious Equality
Nonconformist Politics in Mid-Victorian England
During the middle decades of the nineteenth century the English Nonconformist community developed a coherent political philosophy of its own, of which a central tenet was the principle of religious equality (in contrast to the stereotype of Evangelical Dissenters). The Dissenting community fought for the civil rights of Roman Catholics, non-Christians and even atheists on an issue of principle which had its flowering in the enthusiastic and undivided support which Nonconformity gave to the campaign for Jewish emancipation. This reissued study examines the political efforts and ideas of English Nonconformists during the period, covering the whole range of national issues raised, from state education to the Crimean War. It offers a case study of a theologically conservative group defending religious pluralism in the civic sphere, showing that the concept of religious equality was a grand vision at the centre of the political philosophy of the Dissenters.
2007 / 1-84227-402-3 / x + 300pp

Byung-Ho Moon
Christ the Mediator of the Law
Calvin's Christological Understanding of the Law as the Rule of Living and Life-Giving

This book explores the coherence between Christology and soteriology in Calvin's theology of the law, examining its intellectual origins and his position on the concept and extent of Christ's mediation of the law. A comparative study between Calvin and contemporary Reformers—Luther, Bucer, Melancthon and Bullinger—and his opponent Michael Servetus is made for the purpose of pointing out the unique feature of Calvin's Christological understanding of the law.

2005 / 1-84227-318-3 / approx. 370pp

John Eifion Morgan-Wynne
Holy Spirit and Religious Experience in Christian Writings, c.AD 90–200

This study examines how far Christians in the third to fifth generations (c.AD 90–200) attributed their sense of encounter with the divine presence, their sense of illumination in the truth or guidance in decision-making, and their sense of ethical empowerment to the activity of the Holy Spirit in their lives.

2005 / 1-84227-319-1 / approx. 350pp

James I. Packer
The Redemption and Restoration of Man in the Thought of Richard Baxter

James I. Packer provides a full and sympathetic exposition of Richard Baxter's doctrine of humanity, created and fallen; its redemption by Christ Jesus; and its restoration in the image of God through the obedience of faith by the power of the Holy Spirit.

2002 / 1-84227-147-4 / 432pp

Andrew Partington,
Church and State
The Contribution of the Church of England Bishops to the House of Lords during the Thatcher Years

In *Church and State*, Andrew Partington argues that the contribution of the Church of England bishops to the House of Lords during the Thatcher years was overwhelmingly critical of the government; failed to have a significant influence in the public realm; was inefficient, being undertaken by a minority of those eligible to sit on the Bench of Bishops; and was insufficiently moral and spiritual in its content to be distinctive. On the basis of this, and the likely reduction of the number of places available for Church of England bishops in a fully reformed Second Chamber, the author argues for an evolution in the Church of England's approach to the service of its bishops in the House of Lords. He proposes the Church of England works to overcome the genuine obstacles which hinder busy diocesan bishops from contributing to the debates of the House of Lords and to its life more informally.

2005 / 1-84227-334-5 / approx. 324pp

Michael Pasquarello III
God's Ploughman
Hugh Latimer: A 'Preaching Life' (1490–1555)

This construction of a 'preaching life' situates Hugh Latimer within the larger religious, political and intellectual world of late medieval England. Neither biography, intellectual history, nor analysis of discrete sermon texts, this book is a work of homiletic history which draws from the details of Latimer's milieu to construct an interpretive framework for the preaching performances that formed the core of his identity as a religious reformer. Its goal is to illumine the practical wisdom embodied in the content, form and style of Latimer's preaching, and to recapture a sense of its overarching purpose, movement, and transforming force during the reform of sixteenth-century England.

2006 / 1-84227-336-1 / approx. 250pp

Alan P.F. Sell
Enlightenment, Ecumenism, Evangel
Theological Themes and Thinkers 1550–2000

This book consists of papers in which such interlocking topics as the Enlightenment, the problem of authority, the development of doctrine, spirituality, ecumenism, theological method and the heart of the gospel are discussed. Issues of significance to the church at large are explored with special reference to writers from the Reformed and Dissenting traditions.

2005 / 1-84227-330-2 / xviii + 422pp

Alan P.F. Sell
Hinterland Theology
Some Reformed and Dissenting Adjustments

Many books have been written on theology's 'giants' and significant trends, but what of those lesser-known writers who adjusted to them? In this book some hinterland theologians of the British Reformed and Dissenting traditions, who followed in the wake of toleration, the Evangelical Revival, the rise of modern biblical criticism and Karl Barth, are allowed to have their say. They include Thomas Ridgley, Ralph Wardlaw, T.V. Tymms and N.H.G. Robinson.

2006 / 1-84227-331-0 / approx. 350pp

Alan P.F. Sell and Anthony R. Cross (eds)
Protestant Nonconformity in the Twentieth Century

In this collection of essays scholars representative of a number of Nonconformist traditions reflect thematically on Nonconformists' life and witness during the twentieth century. Among the subjects reviewed are biblical studies, theology, worship, evangelism and spirituality, and ecumenism. Over and above its immediate interest, this collection provides a marker to future scholars and others wishing to know how some of their forebears assessed Nonconformity's contribution to a variety of fields during the century leading up to Christianity's third millennium.

2003 / 1-84227-221-7 / x + 398pp

Mark Smith
Religion in Industrial Society
Oldham and Saddleworth 1740–1865

This book analyses the way British churches sought to meet the challenge of industrialization and urbanization during the period 1740–1865. Working from a case-study of Oldham and Saddleworth, Mark Smith challenges the received view that the Anglican Church in the eighteenth century was characterized by complacency and inertia, and reveals Anglicanism's vigorous and creative response to the new conditions. He reassesses the significance of the centrally directed church reforms of the mid-nineteenth century, and emphasizes the importance of local energy and enthusiasm. Charting the growth of denominational pluralism in Oldham and Saddleworth, Dr Smith compares the strengths and weaknesses of the various Anglican and Nonconformist approaches to promoting church growth. He also demonstrates the extent to which all the churches participated in a common culture shaped by the influence of evangelicalism, and shows that active co-operation between the churches rather than denominational conflict dominated. This revised and updated edition of Dr Smith's challenging and original study makes an important contribution both to the social history of religion and to urban studies.

2006 / 1-84227-335-3 / approx. 300pp

Martin Sutherland
Peace, Toleration and Decay
The Ecclesiology of Later Stuart Dissent

This fresh analysis brings to light the complexity and fragility of the later Stuart Nonconformist consensus. Recent findings on wider seventeenth-century thought are incorporated into a new picture of the dynamics of Dissent and the roots of evangelicalism.

2003 / 1-84227-152-0 / xxii + 216pp

G. Michael Thomas
The Extent of the Atonement
A Dilemma for Reformed Theology from Calvin to the Consensus

A study of the way Reformed theology addressed the question, 'Did Christ die for all, or for the elect only?', commencing with John Calvin, and including debates with Lutheranism, the Synod of Dort and the teaching of Moïse Amyraut.

1997 / 0-85364-828-X / x + 278pp

David M. Thompson
Baptism, Church and Society in Britain from the Evangelical Revival to *Baptism, Eucharist and Ministry*

The theology and practice of baptism have not received the attention they deserve. How important is faith? What does baptismal regeneration mean? Is baptism a bond of unity between Christians? This book discusses the theology of baptism and popular belief and practice in England and Wales from the Evangelical Revival to the publication of the World Council of Churches' consensus statement on *Baptism, Eucharist and Ministry* (1982).

2005 / 1-84227-393-0 / approx. 224pp

Mark D. Thompson
A Sure Ground on Which to Stand
The Relation of Authority and Interpretive Method of Luther's Approach to Scripture

The best interpreter of Luther is Luther himself. Unfortunately many modern studies have superimposed contemporary agendas upon this sixteenth-century Reformer's writings. This fresh study examines Luther's own words to find an explanation for his robust confidence in the Scriptures, a confidence that generated the famous 'stand' at Worms in 1521.

2004 / 1-84227-145-8 / xvi + 322pp

July 2005

Carl R. Trueman and R.S. Clark (eds)
Protestant Scholasticism
Essays in Reassessment

Traditionally Protestant theology, between Luther's early reforming career and the dawn of the Enlightenment, has been seen in terms of decline and fall into the wastelands of rationalism and scholastic speculation. In this volume a number of scholars question such an interpretation. The editors argue that the development of post-Reformation Protestantism can only be understood when a proper historical model of doctrinal change is adopted. This historical concern underlies the subsequent studies of theologians such as Calvin, Beza, Olevian, Baxter, and the two Turrentini. The result is a significantly different reading of the development of Protestant Orthodoxy, one which both challenges the older scholarly interpretations and clichés about the relationship of Protestantism to, among other things, scholasticism and rationalism, and which demonstrates the fruitfulness of the new, historical approach.

1999 / 0-85364-853-0 / xx + 344pp

Shawn D. Wright
Our Sovereign Refuge
The Pastoral Theology of Theodore Beza

Our Sovereign Refuge is a study of the pastoral theology of the Protestant reformer who inherited the mantle of leadership in the Reformed church from John Calvin. Countering a common view of Beza as supremely a 'scholastic' theologian who deviated from Calvin's biblical focus, Wright uncovers a new portrait. He was not a cold and rigid academic theologian obsessed with probing the eternal decrees of God. Rather, by placing him in his pastoral context and by noting his concerns in his pastoral and biblical treatises, Wright shows that Beza was fundamentally a committed Christian who was troubled by the vicissitudes of life in the second half of the sixteenth century. He believed that the biblical truth of the supreme sovereignty of God alone could support Christians on their earthly pilgrimage to heaven. This pastoral and personal portrait forms the heart of Wright's argument.

2004 / 1-84227-252-7 / xviii + 308pp

www.ingramcontent.com/pod-product-compliance
Lightning Source LLC
Chambersburg PA
CBHW070235230426
43664CB00014B/2314